STARGAZERS

ALLAN CHAPMAN

Stargazers

COPERNICUS, GALILEO, the TELESCOPE and the CHURCH

The Astronomical Renaissance 1500-1700

LION

Published by Lion Books
an imprint of
Lion Hudson plc
Wilkinson House, Jordan Hill Road,
Oxford OX2 8DR, England
www.lionhudson.com/lion

ISBN 978 0 7459 5627 5
e-ISBN 978 0 7459 5787 6

First edition 2014

Acknowledgments
Extracts from The Authorized (King James) Version. Rights in
the Authorized Version are vested in the Crown.
Reproduced by permission of the Crown's patentee,
Cambridge University Press.

A catalogue record for this book is available
from the British Library

Printed and bound in the UK, September 2014, LH26

To Rachel: Wife, Scholar, and Best Friend

CONTENTS

Acknowledgments

There are many individuals who have, in various ways, encouraged and assisted me over the years with the research which lies behind this book, and I am grateful to them all. Especial thanks, however, are due to my late friend Peter Hingley, Royal Astronomical Society Librarian, and my still very active friend Tony Simcock, Archivist of the Museum of the History of Science, Oxford, for their unfailingly generous help with all the queries I have thrown in their direction; Kevin Kilburn, of the Manchester Astronomical Society, for his planetary computing skills; my late good friend Sir Patrick Moore, C.B.E., F.R.S., for his inspiration from childhood onwards; Jane Fletcher and the BBC *Sky at Night* team; and Martin Durkin, Director of WAG TV. Nor can I forget the inspiration I have received from the late Colin Ronan and Andrew Murray who (along with Patrick Moore), at R.A.S. Club dinners, knew how to combine erudition and stimulating conversation with good fellowship: a tradition carried on by present-day Club members. In particular, too, I wish to thank Ali Hull, of Lion Hudson, for all her advice and encouragement; Margaret Milton, also of Lion Hudson, for her expert masterminding of the book's production, and my copy editor, Julie Frederick, for her sensitive efficiency in weeding out the inevitable errors and infelicities of style.

Institutionally, I am indebted to the skills and assistance of librarian friends in Wadham College (Tim Kirtley and Francesca Heaney) and in Christ Church (Janet McMullin, Cristina Neagu, Judith Curthoys, and Angela Edward), in the History Faculty Library, and in the Bodleian Library, all in Oxford; and in the Royal Society, the Royal Astronomical Society, the National Maritime Museum, Greenwich, Manchester Central and Salford City Libraries, and numerous other institutions. In addition, I would like to express my gratitude to the Curators of the Collections of the Museum of the History of Science, Oxford (especially the late Francis R. Maddison, Gerard L'Estrange Turner, and John D. North, who taught me a great deal about how to examine and to learn from historical scientific artefacts), and of the National Maritime Museum (in particular the late Commander Derek Howse

R.N.). And I would also like to acknowledge my debt to Lancaster University, where I took my first degree, in History.

And as I always learn so much from my students, I would like to express my heartfelt thanks to them; and also to the members of the numerous astronomical and scientific societies to which I am invited to lecture, especially the Salford, Lancashire, the Mexborough and Swinton, Yorkshire, and the Orwell, Suffolk, Astronomical Societies, the Society for the History of Astronomy, and the William Herschel Society, all of which I have the honour of serving as Honorary President. For I always maintain that there is nothing like teaching and lecturing before live audiences to oblige one to master one's ideas thoroughly and present them with lucidity, and to defend oneself when challenged. I am also greatly indebted to Wadham College and its Chapel, and to Christ Church and its Cathedral for the intellectual stimulus and spiritual support I have found there, and to my "native" parish churches of St Thomas and St Anne, Clifton, Salford, Lancashire, where I have many friends.

But most of all, I am hugely indebted to my wife Rachel, who has worked alongside me at every stage of this book, for her manifold skills, unfailing encouragement, and infinite patience in coping with a husband whose office and administrative skills are not quite on a par with his skills as an astronaut!

Preface

Galileo is probably the most written-about figure in the entire history of astronomy. His life, and in particular his condemnation on a technical charge of heresy in 1633, has inspired poets, artists, novelists, playwrights, and hagiographers, especially in the wake of the "Romantic" movement after c.1780, and the post-Russian-Revolutionary and Nazi eras. Yet was Galileo really the "martyr" to intellectual freedom that popular legend intones?

And a century before him, was poor Copernicus – the "Timid Canon" of Arthur Koestler's excellent *The Sleepwalkers* (1959) – really the publicity-shy lone genius keeping his great thoughts to himself, and only daring to disclose them to the world when he felt death's hand upon him?

What I hope to do in *Stargazers* is not only to re-visit these stories and re-examine them within the wider context of well-documented history, but also to look at the significance of the achievements of other figures whom the popular historical perception has cast into a mere supporting role. These include Tycho Brahe, who appeared to be famous because he was an irascible Danish aristocrat, with a golden nose and a pet dwarf, who did arcane things with big instruments from his exotic island castle observatory. Then there was Tycho's "lapdog", the German Johannes Kepler, who had strange theories about occult forces, and said that the planets moved in ellipses.

What is unfortunate, however, is that this legendary history of astronomy rarely addresses awkward recorded facts: that the sun-centred astronomical theories of the "Timid Canon" Copernicus, for example, were already well known long before he died, and that in his own lifetime Copernicus was both a highly respected ecclesiastical lawyer and a medical doctor of considerable standing. And if being a "Copernican" was so dangerous, how was it that the Lutheran Protestant Kepler, who published his first overtly pro-Copernican treatise aged 25, in 1596, would go on to be employed, and respected, by two deeply Catholic Holy Roman Emperors in Prague, and would *never* be hauled up before the Inquisition?

Instead of being concerned with the supposed "confrontations" of legend, *Stargazers* looks at the bigger picture, setting the great astronomical discoveries and innovations within the wider context of the Renaissance: the Italian Renaissance for Galileo, and what I style the "Northern Renaissance" for Copernicus, Tycho, Kepler and a good few others. For the astronomical discoveries were part of a pan-European cultural movement which included not only Leonardo, Machiavelli, and Monteverdi, but also Shakespeare, Luther, and Rembrandt. And that pan-European movement was not just about art, literature, and music, but also about business, global exploration, religion, education, politics, medicine, science, and much else besides.

Nor does the tale end with the death of Galileo. The full story is much more multi-faceted than the received opinion that Galileo's condemnation somehow terminated scientific progress in Catholic Europe, thus enabling enlightened "work-ethic"-driven Protestants to bound ahead unimpeded by the heavy hand of "the Church".

Stargazers also reminds us that the Renaissance astronomical enterprise was about much more than the debate on whether the earth rotated around the sun, while the Renaissance scientific enterprise was larger still. This enterprise, indeed, included rapidly-advancing sciences such as optics, geomagnetism, experimental and theoretical physics, chemistry, terrestrial and lunar cartography, anatomy, biology, medicine, physiology, early fossil geology, geophysics, and even aeronautics.

Discoveries and innovations abounded: from Jesuit missionary priests building model steam engines for the Emperor of China, to Italian professors discovering new planetary satellites, to Dutch Calvinists wrestling with elliptical orbits, to Anglican clergymen not only founding the Royal Society of London, but also electing scientifically-distinguished overseas Catholic and Calvinist colleagues into the Fellowship.

Not only was "modern science" coming into being, but also the truly international "brotherhood" (and more recently, the "sisterhood") of science. Nationality, religious denomination, and political loyalties mattered less than did an individual's "genius", or ability to advance science yet further. As Latin was still the international tongue of learned Europe, a German could easily correspond with an Italian, and a Scotsman read a book written by a Pole.

What all these men possessed was a growing realisation that scientific advancement in all fields was not solely about big, inspired ideas; it was also about the down-to-earth recognition that any scientist was only as good as his *facts*. The "big ideas" were all well and good, but would only be of enduring value if they squared up to the reality of increasingly precise observation and measurement that could be cross-checked and confirmed by colleagues using state-of-the-art precision instruments – telescopes, microscopes, barometers, magnetic and optical devices – and rigorous experimental procedures.

So a big idea about any aspect of the natural world now had to stand up to rigorous international peer review. And for that, precision instruments were becoming absolutely crucial. For an instrument enabled a researcher to detect, measure, and quantify things in nature of which our five unaided senses were oblivious. Things such as the craters on the moon, the individual stars that made up the Milky Way, microscopic "animalcules" in body fluids, barometric pressure, and meteorological changes – and those exceedingly tiny angles that would demonstrate beyond all dispute whether or not the earth really did move around the sun.

The acid test of Copernicus's theory lay not in brilliant rhetoric or philosophical argument, but in the measurement of the exact angular position of astronomical bodies, made with instruments of increasing accuracy. The clinching physical argument was the discovery and exact quantification of those phenomena which, in 1728, would be called the aberration of light, and then, in 1836, the stellar parallax. That is why our story does not end with Galileo, but carries on for a good eighty years after his death, and ultimately, a further century after that.

During this odyssey of human ingenuity, it is hardly surprising that many ancient cultural "truisms", such as astrology and alchemy, bit the dust: truisms that made perfect sense in an earth-centred universe of planetary and starry spheres, but evaporated in the new sun-centred solar system and possible cosmological infinity of 1730.

And as the truth is often stranger than fiction, so, I would argue, the full story of Copernicus, Galileo, the telescope, the Church, and beyond, becomes even more fascinating when placed in context within the wide sweep of European Renaissance civilisation. So read on.

Allan Chapman
Oxford
August 2014

1.1 The "three-decker universe" of *c.* 1,000 BC, broadly shared by the Old Testament Jews, Babylonians, and Egyptians. Four pillars support the starry "Firmament", sometimes likened to a tent. Above the "Firmament" are waters, the source, for example, of Noah's Flood. The sun, moon, and planets move beneath the starry Firmament, and probably go under the earth when not visible in the sky. The earth is flat, and perhaps upheld by a primordial ocean: the biblical "Deeps", or the Babylonian "Apsu". Beneath it all is the "Pit", Hades, hell, or the Underworld. (Reconstruction: Allan Chapman.)

CHAPTER 1

New Brightness from Old Light.
Part 1: The Classical Cosmology

*W*hen Nicholas Copernicus was born, in Torun, Poland, in 1473, many of the leading figures of the age believed that the world was approaching its last days, and Armageddon would soon be upon us. All the signs were there. Contemporary people, for instance, did not live to the great ages achieved by Adam and Eve, Methuselah, or Abraham, and since 1346 Europe had been struck by wave after wave of the supposedly new disease, bubonic plague, which was winnowing the population away. Nor did there seem to be giants on the earth any more, as were reported in the Old Testament, with figures like Goliath, and the Anakims who had so terrified the ancient Jews. As Thomas Paynel put it in the "Dedication" to his *Regimen Sanitatis Salerni* ("Rules of Health of Salerno"), 1541, a man who now reached his forties was reputed "happye and fortunate". Not only did the total human population seem to be shrinking due to plague, but we were getting smaller in size and feebler. Who of the "present age" could compare in power of intellect with Pythagoras, Plato, and Aristotle of classical Greek times, whose writings still constituted the bedrock of learning in 1473? Where could we now find men of the spiritual power of Isaiah or St Paul, or generals of the stature of King David, Alexander the Great, or Julius Caesar? Humanity had become a puny, feeble, dull-witted, worn-out race.

The heavens themselves also seemed to provide further substantiation for this end of the world scenario. Several ominous comets were reported, and on 25 December 1471 a comet with a large tail hung in the winter skies of Europe for over a month.[1] Comets were believed, in accordance with Aristotle's physics, to be the relatively local products of noxious "effluvias" rising up from the earth into the atmosphere, and catching fire from the sun's heat; hence their perceived relevance to the human race. Could it also be that the very heavens were approaching the end of time? It was becoming increasingly clear that even the calendar was running into ever-deeper error, as dates slipped backwards against the seasons. It was becoming difficult, from the existing astronomical tables, to obtain a Europe-wide consensus for the central feast of the Christian year, Easter, the moveable date of which was computed afresh for each year from the full moon at the spring equinox.

Then, when Copernicus was nineteen years old, in 1492, a terrifying red-hot fireball suddenly fell from the skies at Ensisheim, Alsace[2] – another portent, no doubt. No one could have doubted that the devil was more active in the world now than he had been in previous centuries. Who could fail to notice the growing number of witches up to their malevolent activities across Europe, occasioning Heinrich Kramer and Jacob Sprenger to write their subsequently notorious *Malleus Maleficarum* ("Hammer of the Witches", 1487) treatise in an attempt to curb the burgeoning menace? Witchcraft, contrary to present-day belief, had never been seen as a serious problem in the Middle Ages, but by 1480 it was thought to be at the root of every mischief. In addition to descending fireballs, calendar problems, witches, and a miscellany of other portents, there were dire prophecies of the approaching end; for Jewish, Christian, and classical pagan numerologists and number-jugglers had predicted, and were predicting, that the end of time would come in AD 1500, on the basis, generally speaking, of permutations of the number three, the Holy Trinity.

To top it all, Christendom was under visible threat of extinction from "the Turk", for in May 1453 the ancient Christian Greek city of Constantinople (Byzantium) fell to the besieging armies of Sultan Mohammed II, and what was left of the great late classical and medieval civilization of the Byzantine empire was extinguished. Mohammed's armies surged north into the Greek Orthodox and Roman Catholic Balkans, and it seemed touch and go whether heartland Europe would be invaded and whether Christian civilization would survive.

This period in history, the late fifteenth century, is generally portrayed as one of "rebirth", or what nineteenth-century historical scholars would style "The Renaissance". Was not this the age, in which European civilization reawakened from its long sleep of the "Dark Ages", an epoch which had blanketed and stultified Europe across the 1,000 years that followed the end of Greek and Roman classical glory? Was this not an age, in particular, when the pursuit of science had been effectively killed off by an ignorant, totalitarian church which would condemn you to the stake if you so much as dared to think? To understand the magnitude of what happened in European civilization, and in particular, the profound changes that took place in astronomy, cosmology, and science between 1500 and 1700, it is essential that we become aware of the "big picture". For while Copernicus, Galileo, and others were, without doubt, men of genius, they were *not* the isolated figures of legend; they were *not* men who could simply see further than everybody else, or somehow grasped "the truth" while their contemporaries floundered in ignorance, nor did they stand out as lighthouses in a sea of authoritarian obscurantism and murky darkness.

Crucial to understanding the "Astronomical Renaissance" is a clear appreciation of what went before, and of the already existing firm foundations of philosophy, culture, and science upon which Copernicus and Galileo built. This was the "Old Light" from which they were to draw their "New Brightness". Even by 1500, this old light was a good 2,000 years old and, far from being obscured during the medieval centuries, had even taken on a new focus that Pythagoras, Aristotle, and Ptolemy could scarcely have imagined. Copernicus, Tycho Brahe, Kepler, Galileo, and even Newton, along with many others, would fruitfully draw upon it.

As the sixteenth and seventeenth centuries moved on, the omens of decline that haunted the imagination of the late fifteenth century began to lessen in their immediacy. The dreaded year 1500 passed without incident, as did 1533 – five times the number of the Holy Trinity plus the 33 years of age which Jesus Christ had reputedly been at his crucifixion and resurrection –

although the new breed of prognosticators and chronologists that grew up with the Reformation and Counter-Reformation after 1517 brought their own doom warnings, as we shall see in the following chapters.

Bubonic plague epidemics, though continuing to haunt Europe until they mysteriously disappeared after 1670, seemed to claim fewer lives overall. Europe's population was clearly expanding again by 1550 and would continue to do so down to our own times. Witches also came to be regarded differently, as the so-called "Age of Reason" began to view them in a way that more closely resembled the old, more reasonable, medieval view: witches clearly *existed* because they are mentioned in Scripture, but extreme behaviour, delusion, and misfortune could arise from causes other than spiritual malevolence. Burning crazed females solved nothing.

Global politics also changed radically and fundamentally between the fall of Constantinople in 1453 and the Polish King Jan Sobieski's deliverance of Vienna from further Turkish menace in 1683. Improving Western weaponry and military organization, and European domination of the world's oceans, both commercially and militarily, decisively shifted the global balance of power in favour of Europe. The future of Christian Europe seemed far brighter and more hopeful by 1650 than it had two centuries before. These circumstances created the stage upon which the Astronomical Renaissance, from the days of the juvenile Copernicus, through Galileo's 78-year lifespan, and into Sir Isaac Newton's middle age, would be acted out, and made their achievement both possible and culturally relevant.

Yet in all branches of science, great minds are not enough. One also needs perceptive eyes and dexterous hands: scientific instrument technology. Building upon a European tradition of progressive technology going back to the eleventh century – geared windmills, clocks, glass spectacles, and printing, to name but four key European inventions – the astronomers of the "long Renaissance" of 1500–1700 were able to devise a series of instruments that would transform the science of classical antiquity. They would show the world that the "moderns" – the men of 1540 – far from being runts of the litter of history, could, when empowered by a new research

4

technology, leave the ancients standing when it came to making fundamental new discoveries.

Firstly, the great three-masted ocean-going sailing ships of the Renaissance overturned classical geography by discovering continents and oceans that the ancient Greeks had never dreamed of. Next, this new world had to be surveyed, mapped, and published from the new printing presses, demanding a rapid development of practical geometry, precision mathematical instrument making, and cartography. Without these new technologies, Nicholas Copernicus and his great Danish admirer, Tycho Brahe, would never have come to the starting line of discovery.

Secondly, practical optics and the study, manipulation, and use of light advanced rapidly, especially from the late sixteenth century onwards, as the glass-maker and lens-figurer began to improve upon the thirteenth-century technology of magnifying and "visual" glass-making. This optical technology would produce two of the most radical and far-reaching inventions in the history of human ingenuity: the telescope and the microscope. When one combined individual lenses possessing the right geometrically shaped optical curves into deliberate optical *systems*, the ancient bounds of "reality" changed for ever. Two new realms of knowledge were immediately opened up: the telescopic realm of the universe, and the microscopic realm of exceedingly tiny things, both organic and inorganic. Galileo pioneered the telescope as an astronomical instrument, but he also pioneered an early microscope, and was amazed at the complex beauty of insects.

In 1665, Robert Hooke, in *Micrographia*, would sum up the Renaissance age of scientific discovery, and especially the stunning impact of the telescope and microscope upon the intellectual culture of the age. Instruments, said Hooke, were "artificial organs" that gave a new power to our natural and ancient organs of sense. By "artificial" Hooke did not mean *false* (our common modern-day usage of artificial). Rather, he used the word in its seventeenth-century sense, signifying a work of *art* or *ingenuity*, in contrast with something that occurred naturally: a clever piece of devising and contriving, such as a naturalistic oil painting or a microscope, as opposed to a natural object, such as a flower. The

5

Renaissance not only opened up new domains of light and optical wonder. It also revealed a vast new realm of natural forces, once thought to be mysterious, but now susceptible to measurement and quantification via a range of newly devised "artificial organs". By 1665, these included instruments for the physical study of the earth's magnetic field (compass and dip-needle), atmosphere and weather (barometer, thermometer, hygrometer), and of combustion, flame, and organic respiration (air or vacuum pump). Then there was a panoply of precision-engineered time- and angle-measuring devices (pendulum clock, screw micrometer, precision graduated scales) which propelled astronomy into a realm of accuracy beyond anything that Copernicus could have imagined in 1540, and which would, by 1728, provide the *physical* demonstration of the earth's motion in space, over 200 years after Copernicus devised his original heliocentric model of the solar system.

All of this took place *not* – as the familiar mantra goes – because the "Dark Ages" had ended and brave men dared to "stand up to church tyranny", but because the sheer weight of new physical discovery had revealed things that the wisest Greek philosopher and the most rationally deductive medieval schoolman could never have imagined. Many of these discoveries were actually made by churchmen, Catholic and Protestant, as well as by devout Christian laymen, as we will see in the following chapters. Honest discovery was neither persecuted nor suppressed.

The Astronomical Renaissance came about *not* from the deliberate breaking of the bounds of classical and medieval knowledge, daring radical philosophies, or conscious revolutionary zeal. It came about, rather, as a response to the floodtide of new factual data deriving from explorers in ships and from observatories and laboratories, and by a serendipitous chain reaction of ingenuity and rethinking of what knowledge was and how we could – in the words of Sir Francis Bacon – accomplish its "advancement". The physical discoveries came before the new ideas, as has largely been the pattern of science from 1500 onwards. Discoveries such as that of the American continent, the mountains on the moon, the presence of microscopic creatures in stagnant waters, and the changes in barometric pressure with approaching storms

6

compelled a rethinking of what we already knew as a result of sheer pragmatic necessity if we wanted the world to make sense. When the "big ideas" did appear, be they of Copernicus, Galileo, Newton, or Einstein, they did so because the old theories could no longer adequately explain the new body of data, and we needed to rethink reality.

If these were the circumstances that drove Western scientific culture towards a "New Brightness", then what was the "Old Light" which the men of 1500 inherited from their classical and medieval ancestors?

CLASSICAL COSMOLOGY

The earth moving around the sun, as proposed by Copernicus, the curious geometry of planets moving in elliptical orbits through the void of Kepler, and the telescopic universe of Jupiter's satellites and – perhaps – the infinitely receding stars of Galileo seemed an affront to common sense in their time. The classical cosmos of the ancient Greek and medieval scholars it came to replace was not only elegant, but was delightfully commonsensical.

It interpreted the facts of the heavens and the earth, as they were then understood (and would continue to be understood for nearly two millennia to come) in accordance with what appeared to be natural and obvious to the eye and to normal experience.

So what did the classical cosmos, as it was still studied and taught in 1500, actually look like? At no time, since early classical Greece, did educated and mathematically literate people believe that the earth was anything but a *sphere*. The story of the brave Christopher Columbus just *knowing*, from a species of superior wisdom, that he would *not* sail over the edge of the earth, and going on to defy all odds, is a modern legend. It dates from early-nineteenth-century American patriotic histories, in particular from Washington Irving's 1828 popular "biography" of Columbus, and later American anti-Christian-church writers such as William Henry Draper and Andrew Dickson White. Though for a long time enshrined in the United States elementary education system, the idea of a flat earth would have made any half-educated person of 1490 – or indeed of AD 490 – roll over laughing. In the sixth century BC, Pythagoras worked on the assumption that the earth was spherical, while Aristotle's *De Caelo* ("On the Heavens") of two hundred years later gives clear evidences of this. Did not a ship gradually disappear from view because of the earth's curvature? Was not the shadow cast by the earth upon the full moon at a lunar eclipse always circular? Eratosthenes around 290 BC even made a remarkably good estimate of the size of the earth in *stadia* (or Greek miles) from the length of the shadows cast between Syene and Alexandria in Egypt.

To the Greeks, geometry was the key to understanding astronomy, for while we transient humans lived within a world of change and decay, we could nonetheless make contact with the realm of the eternal, the perfect, and the beautiful through geometry, mathematics, and logic. Long before the time of Christ, Greek philosophers had come to realize that our minds enabled us to transcend our weak bodies and contemplate the changeless beauty of the divine principle in astronomy and mathematics.

In addition to the philosophy and theology, the Greeks invented practical astronomy, devised the earliest known scientific instruments, and, through a combination of observation, measurement, mathematics, and theoretical deduction, came up with an earth-centred or *geocentric* model of the cosmos which would endure until Galileo's time. After going through several developmental stages in the hands of Eudoxus (*c.* 380 BC), Hipparchus (*c.* 140 BC), and others, it achieved its mature and enduring form in the *Magna Syntaxis* ("Great Synthesis" or "Treatise") or *Almagest* of Ptolemy of Alexandria in around AD 150.

1.2 "Astronomy", on Giotto's Campanile in the Piazza del Duomo, Florence, fourteenth century. An astronomer, thought to represent Ptolemy, observes the altitude of the stars with a small quadrant. (Drawing by Allan Chapman.)

In Ptolemy's synthesis, as developed through his predecessors, the earth was a large sphere set at eternal rest in the centre of nine perfectly transparent "crystalline" spheres that nested concentrically inside each other rather like the skins of an onion, and which rotated around a common polar axis. Seven of these spheres carried the then known planets: the moon, Mercury, Venus, the sun, Mars, Jupiter, and Saturn, while the eighth, black sphere carried the "fixed stars" or constellations. Beyond the stars lay the theoretically postulated ninth sphere, or primum mobile ("prime mover"), which somehow regulated the motion of the others, and beyond this lay the realms of the blessed, the Christian heaven, or the endless void, depending upon one's wider beliefs.

Each of these spheres rotated at a speed unique to itself, and at a perfectly uniform velocity. To understand Greek geometrical astronomy, it is essential to realize that perfectly circular orbits upon perfect spheres, and perfectly uniform orbital velocities were logical prerequisites of the system. As the heavens were, by definition, perfect, it was philosophically impossible that incongruity or irregularity of any kind could be present in their operations.

The nearest, lunar, sphere went around the earth in twenty-eight days, the sun in 365¼, Jupiter in twelve years, Saturn in 29½

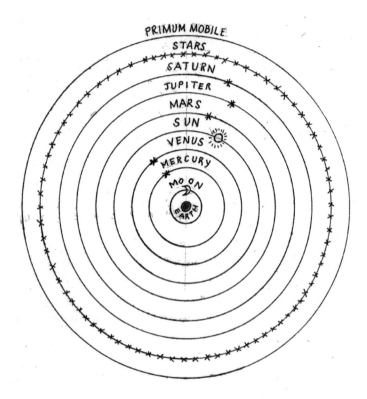

1.3 The Greek geocentric universe, with the planetary and starry spheres and *primum mobile* rotating around a spherical central earth. (Drawing by Allan Chapman.)

years, and the fixed stars in one day. All the planets rotated within the relatively narrow zodiac band of the stars, so that when one measured the planetary velocities against the star positions, the moon moved rapidly to define the lunar month – new moon to new moon – the sun went round in one year, and Saturn took nearly three decades to complete a circuit of the zodiac. Each of the planets received its motion from the rotation of the sphere to which it was attached, yet all of the perfect crystalline spheres, except the outermost one of the fixed stars, were thought to be rotating at the same velocity. This meant, therefore, that while

Saturn and the moon were probably travelling at the same speed
– in miles per hour, as it were – Saturn *appeared* to move much
more slowly because it was tracing a vastly greater circuit across the
heavens than did the moon.

Try this experiment. Go to a large field with two friends. Set one
friend at a measured distance of 10 feet from you, then ask the other to
pace out 300 feet from you. Position them so that, at the outset, the three
of you form a straight line: a radial line, with you at the centre. Then,
at a signal, ask your friends to walk around you in a circle at the pace
of one equal step per second. The friend walking in the 10-foot-radius
circle will appear to move rapidly, covering their 63-foot-circumference
circuit in 63 seconds, whereas the person 300 feet away will only have
paced out 63 of their total circumference of 1,887 feet in that time, yet
both will have walked at exactly the same speed.

This is how the ancients explained the perfect, even, synchronous
motion of the planets, while at the same time observing a variety
of different *apparent* motions. In their highly geometrized way of
thinking, this was seen as providing a key to the very distance of the
astronomical bodies, for if you could reliably measure the distance
of one body, such as the moon, which the Greeks correctly realized
was the closest, then by extension it should be possible to calculate
the distances of the rest.

Somewhere around 280 BC, Aristarchus of the Greek island of
Samos (who, among other things, developed a sun-centred model
of the solar system 1,800 years before Copernicus) proposed a
geometrical model for measuring the distance of the sun and moon
from the earth. It was based upon establishing the exact time of
half-moon, or quadrature – a very hard thing to do in practice. He
then realized that exactly at the half-moon phase the moon, sun,
and earth formed a perfect right-angled triangle with each other;
and already knowing the earth's radius in *stadia*, or Greek miles, he
proceeded to calculate the lunar–solar distance from the narrow
angle of the long right-angled triangle. Aristarchus concluded from
this that the sun was nineteen times farther away from the earth
than was the moon. (It is around 400 times farther away.)

While his figure fell massively short of the true value known
today, his *theory* was actually correct. What Aristarchus, Hipparchus,

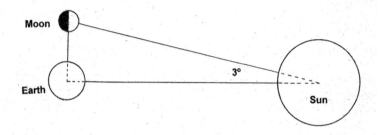

1.4 Aristarchus' attempt to measure the solar distance from the exact half-moon. (Drawing by Allan Chapman.)

Ptolemy, and all the Greeks lacked were instruments of sufficient accuracy to measure the very tiny angles involved: an instrumental problem that would still bedevil Copernicus, Tycho Brahe, and Galileo nearly 2,000 years later. The heart of the matter is that, through their grasp of geometry, their attempted observation and measurement, and logical deduction, the Greeks set astronomy on the right lines, and people were still guided by them when both Copernicus and Galileo were students. By extension, so are we today.

The actual heavens did not behave as neatly as geometrical and philosophical theory demanded. The *observed* planets of reality, as opposed to the ideal planets of philosophical theory, did *not* move at even speeds and unchanging velocities, but sped up, slowed down, and described strange loops in the sky: the *retrograde* motions, as they were technically styled. The moon was the biggest brain-teaser of all, for while it did not describe retrograde loops in the sky, it moved in an extremely complicated orbit that seemed to come full circle in just over eighteen years: what came to be called the Saros Cycle – a cycle that appeared to lie at the heart of the lunar–solar system and which produced eclipses. (This cycle was first noted by those Babylonian astronomers whose earlier work so inspired the Greeks.)

Various "mechanisms" were devised over the ensuing centuries in an attempt to explain the moon's behaviour. Could it be that

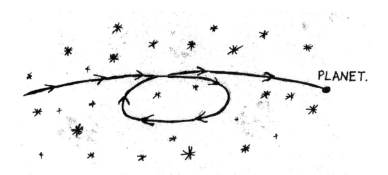

1.5 A planetary retrograde, as seen from the earth. Mars, Jupiter, and Saturn appear over weeks and months to perform strange "loops" in their orbits, when viewed among the fixed stars. (Drawing by Allan Chapman.)

while moving in a perfectly circular orbit about the earth, that orbit was *eccentric*, with its centre not corresponding to the earth's centre, thereby causing the moon to swing around us, and be slightly closer at some times than at others? Surely, if the lunar and solar orbits had been perfectly concentric, we should either have lunar and solar eclipses on a monthly basis, or not at all? Then there was the behaviour of the planets themselves, especially Mars, Jupiter, and Saturn, each of which described baffling retrograde loops at certain times in their orbits. Mars, for example, made two such loops for every one of its rotations around the earth, yet Jupiter made twelve, and Saturn nearly thirty. They seemed to make as many loops as they took years to complete a full circuit of the zodiac, as viewed from the fixed and central earth – a point Copernicus would struggle with many centuries hence. Eudoxus, Hipparchus, Ptolemy, and others all wrestled with the retrogrades, each making his own contribution to what would serve as the solution that would survive until, and beyond, Copernicus's day. By the time of Ptolemy, in the second century AD, this *epicyclic* theory had been brought to its mature development, in which a planet-carrying circle rotated around an empty point which itself rotated around a centre, such as the earth, to describe a geometrically elegant loop, or *epicycle*, all within the geometry of perfect albeit eccentric circles.

13

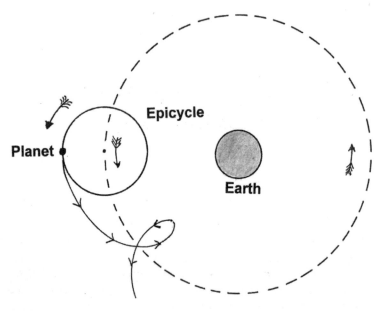

1.6 The epicycle. Two perfect circular motions – the motion of the epicycle's centre around the earth, *and* the planet's rotation around the epicycle's centre – can be made to create a forwards–backwards looping of the planet as seen from the earth. (Drawing by Allan Chapman.)

As the centuries rolled on, all those astronomers and cultures that had inherited the classical universe of the Greeks, and especially Ptolemy's great *Almagest*, began to find that the observed heavens were not squaring up to predicted theory. This discrepancy would fuel the great astronomical enterprise of medieval Arabia and Europe. Yet before examining astronomical developments during the Middle Ages, let us first look at classical ideas about the forces of nature, for they too would mould the thinking of Copernicus, Galileo, and other figures in the Astronomical Renaissance.

CHAPTER 2

New Brightness from Old Light.
Part 2: Matter, Elements, and
Forces

*S*everal Greek philosophers had speculated upon the physical properties of matter, and especially about why things on earth seemed in a constant state of change. Aristotle, around 340 BC, brought these ideas together in a system of physics that would endure at least until the time of Galileo.

THE GENIUS OF ARISTOTLE

Aristotle argued in his *Physics* that there were four primary qualities of nature: earth (solidity), water (moisture), air (wind and vapour), and fire (heat and flame). These four elements, or basic and unchanging fundamentals of nature, constantly melded together, to form all the substances we know on earth, including flesh and plant material, although natural decay, physical pounding, or intense heat invariably split them apart. These elements were in a permanent state of struggle against each other, thereby causing the seasons, storms, birth, death, and decay. If we consciously try to forget all that the last 400 years of scientific discovery have taught us, does not Aristotle's explanation seem to accord with the observed behaviour of the world about us? Are not all terrestrial things heavy, light, hot, cold, dry, or wet, and do they not constantly change, decay, or wear out given sufficient time?

This fourfold systematization of elements and natural agencies in Aristotle's physics also dovetailed into an approach to classical medical thinking that dated back to Hippocrates, a century before Aristotle, in the doctrine of the four humours. Yellow bile, black bile, blood, and phlegm, with their connections to the hot, cold, moist, and dry attributes of the four elements, would continue as a format for medical explanation until the century after Galileo's death in 1642. Being "bilious", "phlegmatic", or "sanguine" (Latin *sanguis*, "blood") could be used to designate almost everything about humanity, from a tendency to corpulence (water retention due to phlegm-dominated temperament) to depression (an excess of black bile, or "melancholia") to violence (too much burning yellow bile).

The heavens and the astronomical bodies, in stark contrast to human and earthly things, exhibited a striking permanence and immutability, as the sun's heat and light never changed from age to age, nor did the eternal cycles of the moon, planets, and stars. The reason becomes obvious once you detach your mind from modern scientific explanation and slip into classical and medieval thinking. As terrestrial change is occasioned by the warring four elements, celestial perfection is the product of a unity and harmony of substance. Everything beyond the earth was made, it was argued, from *one* single primary substance, the "quintessence", or fifth element. This quintessence was always at peace with itself.

One major reason why this way of thinking lasted for a good two millennia, in physics, astronomy, and medicine, was *not* because it was somehow enforced to stop people thinking for themselves, but because it was elegant, obvious, and deeply *commonsensical*, and seemed to best fit the then available facts. It was also a way of thinking that would have underpinned the education and much of the instinctive thinking of both Copernicus and Galileo, not only in their physics and astronomy, but also in their biological ideas. Dr Nicholas Copernicus was a university-trained physician who practised medicine for nearly half a century, and Galileo had begun his training as a medical student at Pisa before abandoning medicine for astronomy. While Galileo would rebel vociferously against the physics of Aristotle as new discoveries were being made by the early seventeenth century, this common-sense way of thinking about the structure and operations of the natural world was rooted in the very intellectual fabric of both men, as it was of their contemporaries.

It constituted their natural frame of reference, even when they rebelled against it.

Aristotle's physics not only seemed to make sense on a straightforward observational level; it was also deeply logical. His physics was only part of an all-embracing intellectual system that he devised between *c.* 360 and 322 BC, which was destined to provide the most influential and long-lasting framework for explaining the natural world, surviving into the seventeenth century – when it was attacked by Galileo and Sir Francis Bacon, as we shall see in later chapters – and beyond.

In Aristotle's system, natural phenomena were explained by extrapolating from their observed behaviour. Stones fell to the ground, for instance, because they were "earthy" and heavy, and flame rose up from a candle to escape the earthy grossness of the wax and be reunited with its light, hot, fiery primary element above the air. Rest was the state to which all earthy objects aspired, for motion was discordant and disruptive. The motion that made a stone fall to earth was a desire for rest and unity with its own kind (the earth), and was therefore a *natural* motion. But any force that made an earthy object rise up away from the earth – as with a flung stone or an arrow in flight – was an *unnatural* or *violent* motion. Thus the curved path of a flying arrow could be understood as a combination of two contrary forces: the violent force imparted by the bow, propelling it upwards, and the natural force of the earth, pulling the wooden, earthy arrow down to rest on "mother earth". The projectile's path was curved because the natural and violent motions worked against each other. As the violent force imparted to the arrow by the bow progressively weakened with distance, so the natural pull of "mother earth" gradually took over, and finally brought the arrow down to earth. In this way of thinking, "gravity" was not how we think of it, for *gravitas* signified a heavy body's tendency to fall, rather than a mathematically calculable force.

While we may find it odd to speak of inanimate objects *desiring* something, such as to be at rest, or with their own kind, the cosmos inherited from antiquity by Copernicus and Galileo was essentially *vitalistic*, imbued with innate, driving tendencies to do particular things, such as burn, move, or seek rest. It was through this innate vital tendency to act that one explained all motion.

BALANCE, ORDER, AND LOGIC

Aristotle's science, therefore, was about tracing the actions of innate, natural properties in the world, and cosmology connected sequentially and seamlessly to physiology, biology, philosophy, politics, and even art. Do not things live because they have within them a balance of natural forces – heat, moisture, and such? Is not a "balanced" political constitution superior to a chaotic one, or an elegant poem or building more pleasing to the intelligent beholder than a nonsensical scribble or a rough hut, because they all share a balance of natural forces and an aspiration to rest and tranquillity? While Aristotle's science was neither experimental nor mathematical, it was philosophically deductible from axioms or demonstrable first principles, such as hot, cold, heavy, and light. It was also elegant, harmonious, adaptive, and – at least in theory – universal in its application. Science, to the classical and medieval thinkers, did not mean the same as it means to us. Rather, the word derived from the Latin *scientia*, or systematic, organized knowledge. Even as late as 1633, when Galileo was tried before the Roman Inquisition, Aristotle's scheme was still awe-inspiring in its comprehensive power, and still furnished the very stuff out of which European university science was taught.

ALCHEMY, ASTROLOGY, AND THE MANIPULATION OF NATURAL FORCES

The philosophy of Aristotle, with its four elements, vital properties, explanations of "substance", and deductive logic, along with its medical parallels to the theory of the four humours, also underpinned much of the rationale behind medieval alchemy. Sadly, because of the ridicule heaped upon alchemy in the eighteenth and nineteenth centuries, in which it was invariably portrayed as the irrational pursuit of deranged monks and charlatans obsessed with turning lead into gold, its elegant intellectual congruence with classical Greek geocentric cosmology, and Aristotle's ideas of matter, has been ignored.

To an educated medieval person, be he an Arab or a European, the logic that lay behind alchemy was elegant, sensible, and seductive. Alchemy was seen as a philosophical and even a spiritual discipline, in which the "chymist" tried to work his way through the complex structures of the divine creation to gain insight into the mind of God. Gold-making for the sake of wealth accumulation was frowned upon by the true *adepts* whose goal was wisdom and understanding. So what were the principles upon which learned alchemy was based?

For one thing, there was the remarkable congruence between the seven planets of the heavens and the seven then-known metals that occurred within the earth – far too strong a correlation to be coincidental. Did not the metal silver correspond to the silvery moon; free-flowing mercury – the only liquid metal – to the fast-moving and elusive planet Mercury; copper to Venus; gold to the bright sun; iron to Mars, the planet of war; tin to Jupiter; and dull lead to the slow-moving Saturn – the planet of melancholy and old age?

Gold was very special, for not only was it the only metal that did not dissolve in nitric acid, but it was also a powerful metallurgical "dye", as small quantities of gold dust fused with molten copper, silver, or mercury had the strange power of making the whole metal mass look like gold. (It does: I have tried fusing gold dust with boiling mercury for a TV documentary on alchemy – a dangerous experiment which today simply *must* be performed in a special laboratory fume cupboard.) While alloying with silver or mercury, gold never lost its own basic "purity", and in the hands of a skilled laboratory operator it could be retrieved intact, and at full weight. Gold also did not tarnish, while at the same time it was capable of being beaten into fine leaves or a thin layer, or fused on to base metal using a mercury flux "butter of gold" to gold-plate a piece of brass.

One crucial component in the logic of alchemy was Aristotle's idea of how one defined something. This was done by enumerating its "accidents", or specific properties. The accidents of gold, for instance, would have included being metal of a golden colour, soft, malleable, and resistant to heat and acids. If an alchemist, therefore, prepared a metallic alloy in the laboratory that had each of these traits *except* acid resistance, then he might be well on the way to making gold from a "lower" metal such as mercury, and would look forward to achieving this goal when he finally perfected his preparation and made his compound acid-resistant – hence, possessing all the accidents of true gold. This was a fundamentally different concept of substance from that of modern chemistry, which laid alchemy open to ridicule by later ages. Yet when you enter the world and mental landscape of 1500, alchemy made sense on so many levels and was far from irrational. Alchemy permeated the thinking not only of medieval but also of Renaissance civilization. It was sufficiently commonplace in the fourteenth century for Geoffrey Chaucer to write a Canterbury Tale about it – *The Canon's Yeoman's Tale*, of *c.* 1380, in which Chaucer displays an impressive knowledge of the techniques and apparatus of alchemy. In the 1660s, by which time both Copernicus and Galileo were long in their graves, sober, altruistic, and committed scientists of the calibre of Robert Boyle and [Sir] Isaac Newton were widely respected as "adepts" in the alchemical Arts of Fire. Its images of transmutation, as a mutable base metal is made to grow and mature – almost like a foetus in the womb – and become indestructible gold, resonate with images of revival, transformation, and sought-after change for the better. Alchemy was also seen as replete with religious parallels: to spiritual rebirth and perfecting, and to Christian resurrection. George Herbert's poem "The Elixir" (1633) speaks of Christian salvation and the Holy Spirit as analogous to the alchemist's transformative agent, the elixir, or philosopher's stone, "that turneth all to gold".

Alchemy was intimately connected with astrology, for within cosmology and understanding of the forces of nature, did not the seven planets, along with the encircling twelve zodiac constellations, somehow beam their own particular powers down to the earth which lay at the very centre of the universe? Did it not stand to reason that these celestial forces influenced the elements, metals, and substances which "grew" in the earth, along with the four humours of the human body, to link the heavens with the earth through alchemy and medicine? The most famous and controversial alchemist of the

Renaissance, the iconoclastic Swiss doctor Paracelsus, asserted that the true physician must also be an alchemist and an astrologer who, in his laboratory, would manipulate the forces of the heavens acting upon the metals to produce a universal medicine. We will be saying more about astrology in Chapter 23.

Alchemy and astrology, therefore, constituted an all-encompassing force in medieval and Renaissance culture, bringing the astronomical, medical, chemical, spiritual, and transformative together in a remarkably coherent whole. While they, like Ptolemy's geocentric cosmology, were found to be scientifically "wrong" by subsequent ages, this in no way diminishes their significance as "Old Lights" which would eventually help to facilitate the "new brightness" of a later epoch.

Time, calendars, and the beginning of the medieval astronomical enterprise

It is important to understand that Copernicus did not in some way awaken astronomy out of a backward and anti-scientific "Dark Age", for the science had never ceased to be actively and intelligently practised in Europe during the Middle Ages. It is true, though, that the disruption that followed the end of the Roman empire by the sixth century AD – including epidemic diseases, harvest failures and periods of starvation, and successive waves of invasions – had confined it to pockets. Such pockets included the great monasteries at St Gallen in Switzerland, Ravenna in Italy, and Rheims in France, Vic (Vich) near Barcelona, and in York, and communities in Ireland and elsewhere in Europe. Astronomy was of the highest practical importance to the Christian church, as it had always been to the Jews and would be to the Muslims. Each of these religions required key festivals – Passover, Easter, and Ramadan – to be celebrated in given parts of the year, and as all of them involved the sun, moon, and seasons, this meant that astronomical observation, record-keeping, and computation were important to all. Medieval civilization, from the Scottish Highlands to Indonesia, needed astronomers and mathematical calculators who knew how to get it right.

It was a monk of the – probably early – Benedictine community of Jarrow, Northumbria, who, around AD 700, became the first known Englishman to teach and write upon classical astronomy, albeit in Latin. This was the Venerable Bede, and in his *De Temporibus* ("On the Times") and *De Temporum Ratione* ("On Reckoning Times") he discussed the classical, spherical earth-based cosmos and the lunar phases and tides, and gave important astronomical information about the calculation of dates and times, such as how to establish the date of Easter. These would be used for centuries to come for teaching and computational purposes, and would give Bede posthumous fame across Europe.

In an age devoid of rapid communications, fixing the correct date for the celebration of Easter, for every church across Christendom from the Isle of Skye to Constantinople, was no easy task. Such a task needed a knowledge of how lunar and solar cycles worked together, and as Easter, by tradition, had to be held after the first full moon following the spring equinox, it was important to know the equinox day precisely. That day is when the sun ascends from its winter six-month arc in the sky, crosses the "celestial equator" that divides the northern and southern hemisphere constellations, and enters its northern six-month arc, to give the longer days of summer, all of which was discussed by Bede.

This annual calculation was replete with problems. The lunar and solar cycles do not synchronize neatly together, there being twelve lunar cycles and eleven days in a solar year. Adding to the mathematical tangle was the length of the solar year itself. This was not the 365¼ days of custom, with its four quarter days neatly rounded up every four years to make a leap year, as in Julius Caesar's calendar (as measured from the noontide altitude of the sun on the longest day in June), but an awkward 365 days, 5 hours, 48 minutes and 46 seconds. This slight discrepancy of just over eleven minutes was of no real consequence in the short run, but as the centuries rolled on, glaring errors began to emerge as calendrical dates did not square with astronomical events, such as the solstices (June and December) and equinoxes (March and September). If the classical calendar fixed the date of the spring equinox at 21 March, for example, yet the observed astronomical equinox fell, let us say, on 17 March, with a Sunday falling between the dates, how did one fix the correct day for Easter Sunday, and following from it, the rest of the ecclesiastical year?

This problem got worse with each medieval century, as the error accumulated, and much intellectual energy was expended on trying to harmonize the astronomical cycles and work out a lucid mathematical expression. Several Calendar Commissions were inaugurated by successive Popes, and when the young Dr Nicholas Copernicus was invited by Pope Leo X in 1513 to give expert advice to one of them, one gets a clear indication of his international standing as a mathematical astronomer a decade before he began to work out his heliocentric theory.

All this highlights the high profile that astronomy, both practical and theoretical, had in the centuries before, and well into, the Astronomical Renaissance, and reminds us that astronomical ideas, computations, and practical skills had – of necessity – to be spread across Europe. And the Venerable Bede – the first internationally known British astronomer – was one of their earliest exponents. This classical Greek astronomy was taught across the universities of Europe by the thirteenth century, and was an established part of educated culture from Salamanca to Prague. So what did the people of the Middle Ages, and especially an educated European of 1250, know about astronomy, and how was that knowledge practised and taught?

MEDIEVAL ASTRONOMY

In addition to necessary calendrical knowledge, the astronomy of classical Greek antiquity, along with ancient ideas on physics, optics, and the medical sciences, passed into the medieval period between AD 600 and 1500, through a variety of channels. In the early centuries in the West, the ideas of Ptolemy and others came in not as complete works so much as through late classical commentators such as Cassiodorus, Boethius, and Isidore of Seville – through digests and compilations.

ARABIC ASTRONOMY

Classical astronomy and science also entered the Arab world. In the wake of Islam's sudden and violent initial expansion after AD 622, and military conquests extending from Arabia, Mesopotamia, through Egypt, North Africa, and into Spain by 711, many Muslim scholars became fascinated by the late classical, Jewish, and early Christian world that they had overrun. Astronomical, medical, optical, and other texts were translated into Arabic from their original languages – predominantly by Christian and Jewish scholars in the new Muslim-conquered territories – and became subjects of intensive study, particularly in southern Spain, the new city of Cairo, Damascus, and Jundishapur (in modern-day Iran). It was in what was termed the "House of Wisdom", in the new Muslim city of Baghdad, that an especial amount of scholarly energy came to be generated and expressed. As Islam also needed a calendar, astronomy became a subject of close study, although between AD 850 and 1250 the intellectual and physical energy which Arabic scholars devoted to the study of the heavens far outstripped the needs of calendrical astronomy. Science became an intellectual passion: in optics, medicine, natural history, and most of all, astronomy.

Having translated Ptolemy's *Magna Syntaxis* into Arabic under the title *Almagest*, by which it is still known today, a succession of Arabic scientists began both to observe the heavens and to continue the intellectual quest of trying to make the epicycles of the ancient Greeks explain the observed motions of the planets.

Arabic astronomers began to remeasure and remap the stars on the basis of the original forty-eight Babylonian–Greek constellations of Ptolemy. Having a cultural spread that extended down to India, some 20 degrees further south than any Greek or northern Egyptian could see, they could observe constellations in the southern skies that were permanently below the horizon for anyone in the Mediterranean. Abd al-Rahman al- Sufi, Abu al-Wafa Buzjani, and others produced star maps and atlases, and many of the star-names that have survived into modern astronomy are of Arabic or Middle Eastern origin – Algol, the winking "demon star" in Perseus, being one of the best known. Even our word "almanac" for a set of astronomical tables itself derives from the Arabic *al-manunkh*.

Mathematical and computational astronomy fascinated so many Arabs – Al-Battani, Al-Biruni, and Al-Zarqali to name but a few – who wrestled with mathematical solutions by which theory could be made to fit observed celestial phenomena. Nasir al-Din al-Tusi of the Maragha Observatory in Persia took Ptolemaic theory about as far as it could go by the time of his death in 1274, when he devised an ingenious "couple" or "linkage" geometrical mechanism which simulated a planetary motion that had similarities to those produced by ellipses. Johannes Kepler would return to this planetary orbit shape, albeit within a very different explanatory rationale, in 1608.

The Arabs were keen observers of the brilliant skies that arched above their domains, constantly comparing the values for such things as the equinoxes, the precession of the equinoxes, star positions, and planetary motions, with those determined by Ptolemy and passed on in classical tables. It was also the astronomers of Arabia who perfected an instrument described in principle by Ptolemy, and which would be an artefact both for astronomical observation and for computation: the astrolabe. The "pinhole" sights could be used to read off celestial angles against the graduated brass degree scale, while the rotating star map and accompanying tables could be used to perform a variety of computations.

Without doubt, the Arab world, between *c.* AD 850 and 1250, made major and significant advances in the practical business of celestial mapping based on observation with planetary motion theory, and especially in the development of astronomical geometry. Yet this development was stalling by the fourteenth century, and following the murder of the Mongol astronomer Ulugh Beg by his own sons in 1449, the last great Islamic scientific centre, the Samarkand Observatory, ceased to exist. By 1449, the academic study of astronomy was already well established across Europe, from the newly chartered St Andrews University in Scotland to Bologna, from Salamanca to Prague.

EUROPEAN ASTRONOMY

Much scholarly debate has been devoted to the factors that led to the burgeoning and widespread cultivation of classical science and scholarship in Europe after *c.* 1100. Could the medieval "climatic warm" have resulted in the population increase of the early "High Middle Ages"? Population increase, an agricultural boom, and a great expansion of economic prosperity are well-documented facts of European history for the period 1000 to 1350. Successful campaigns to expel Islamic invaders from southern Italy and Spain led to a major project for European scholars, in the new universities of Paris, Oxford, Bologna, Cambridge, and elsewhere: to translate classical Greek texts which the Muslims had translated into Arabic into the Latin of medieval Christian scholarship – a project which made hundreds of "old books" available to the burgeoning "young minds" of Europe. A very large number of the books were on astronomy, medicine, optics, and the other sciences.

By 1250 the astronomy of Ptolemy and other ancients, and, soon after, the philosophy of Aristotle, were firmly established on the curricula of Europe from Iberia to Poland. Medieval undergraduates would be taught astronomy, basic celestial mechanics, the geometry of eclipses, and plenty more besides. All would be within the common-sense science of the earth-centred universe, the crystalline spheres, and the physics of Aristotle. These young men were taught to think critically, argue, and defend a "proposition". The pervasiveness of astronomical knowledge in medieval European culture is easy to see. Not only was astronomy on the undergraduate curriculum of the universities as one of the "Seven Liberal Arts", along with geometry, arithmetic, and music (dealing primarily with the celestial–terrestrial harmonic relationship), but an early thirteenth-century Irishman, Englishman, or Scotsman (he has been claimed posthumously by all three nations) wrote an enduring astronomical best-seller that started off as a basic textbook in the science at around 1240 and was still available, in new printed editions, for years after Galileo's death. Johannes de Sacrobosco's *Tractatus de Sphaera Mundi* ("Treatise on the Sphere of the World/Cosmos") was a simplified version of Ptolemy's *Almagest*, complete with all the arguments in favour of a spherical earth and cosmos.

Outside the universities, and for an educated lay audience, one finds astronomy, medicine, and other classical sciences referred to extensively in the writings of Geoffrey Chaucer. In addition to his informed references to alchemy mentioned above, Chaucer's *Treatise on the Astrolabe* and his very scholarly *Equatorie de Planetis,* both from the 1390s, and various *Canterbury Tales* give us insights into what this poet and civil servant knew about the science of his day. Was his rapscallion Master Nicholas in *The Miller's Tale* that untypical for an Oxford (or other university) student of the age, who, in addition to plotting how to seduce his elderly landlord's pretty young wife, also read "His [Ptolemy's] Almageste", performed computations on his "astrelabie", and sang "The Virgin's Angelus"? There is no reason whatsoever to assume that Chaucer's knowledge of classical science, as passed on through European and Latin translated Arabic writers, was in any way exceptional for an educated professional man of the fourteenth century – or for the ladies in his audience.

Such knowledge in Chaucer's time would have come partly from late classical commentators, and partly from original texts of Aristotle, Ptolemy, and others, in twelfth- and thirteenth-century Latin translations by scholars such as Gerard of Cremona and Adelard of Bath. Gerard of Cremona made a major translation of Ptolemy's *Almagest* from an Arabic intermediary in 1175. Part of the wider expansion of Europe after *c.* AD 1000 included, as we saw above, the Christian reconquest of Muslim-occupied territories in southern Italy and Spain. Sicily fell to the north-European Normans between 1061 and 1091, while in 1085 Alphonso VI took Spanish Toledo and made it his capital. As both Sicily and Spain had libraries containing Arabic-translated and some Greek classical texts, north European Latin scholars began to descend upon them, learn Arabic, and initiate that flood of "new" books that surged into Europe and now became available in medieval Latin. This movement became the "Twelfth-Century Renaissance", with the springing into existence of Bologna, Paris, Oxford, then, in 1209, Cambridge, and many other early European universities.

Some other texts came in the original Greek, from Greek Christian Byzantium or Constantinople, but it was the scholars fleeing from Byzantium to the West, in the wake of Mohammed II's capture and enforced Islamicization of Byzantium in 1453, which many see as triggering the Italian Renaissance. Refugee Greek scholars began to arrive in the Italian ports, sometimes bringing their libraries with them. As most of these Greek texts had never passed through an intermediary language, such as Syriac or Arabic, Western scholars now clamoured to learn the Greek language and study them in the original tongue – pure and uncorrupted by prior translation. It was new knowledge *a fontibus*, from the sources or fountainheads.

Fundamental to the Astronomical Renaissance was Johannes Bessarion, a Greek Orthodox archbishop, who was already a resident in Rome as a Byzantine diplomat in 1453, and later became a Roman cardinal. Bessarion was a driving force – amongst other aspects of scholarship – in encouraging the study of Ptolemy in the original Greek, and it is hard to overestimate the impact he and his circle of astronomical disciples had upon subsequent scientific history – and upon Copernicus. Georg Peurbach and Johannes Müller (better known as Regiomontanus) were young mathematical astronomers influenced by Bessarion, who addressed problems in planetary motion, the calendar, and other current astronomical puzzles in a new way, on the basis of the best available Greek texts, in the decades after 1450.

If there was one way in which Arabic and European astronomy had noticeably differed between *c.* AD 900 and 1475, it was in the use of direct astronomical observation. Western astronomers had worked very largely from the surviving tables of ancient observations which had come down from antiquity, or observations derived from the Arabs, while the Arabs had reconstructed large observational instruments described in Ptolemy and other Greek writers – such as the triquetum or "three rulers", the armillary sphere, and the quadrant – and had built observatories, the most famous of which was al-Tusi's Maragha Observatory in Persia. All of the instruments in these observatories were designed for measuring angles in the sky, to monitor the motions of the planets among the fixed stars, and to compile tables that were more accurate than those of Ptolemy. To perfect Ptolemy's astronomy, and establish the exact parameters within which the celestial epicycles, "equants", and eccentrics worked, it was necessary to have data of greater refinement than that available in AD 150. Latin versions of Al-Zarqali's *Toledan Tables* (from Toledo) and the tables and mathematical models of planetary motion from al-Tusi were only two of several. These original observations, improved tables, and mathematical models would pass into the West in Latin translation, and have a serious influence upon Copernicus's own thinking from the 1490s onwards. European astronomers had observed the heavens right through the medieval centuries, but judging by written accounts and manuscript illuminations, they tended to use much smaller and hence less accurate hand-held instruments A hand-held quadrant or an astrolabe would have been used to *check* an astronomical calculation or prediction, but to undertake long cycles of primary observations, larger and much more accurate graduated instruments were needed, and these had to be permanently mounted in regular observatories.

The first major European observer was a Nuremberg merchant, Bernhard Walther, who used the profits of his business to fund his astronomical research. Between 1475 and 1504, he made regular observations of the seasonal solar altitudes, as well as the positions of other astronomical bodies. While no one claims Walther, who had been an astronomical pupil of Regiomontanus, was the first European to measure angular positions in the sky with instruments, he seems to have been the first to recognize the importance of sustained, systematic, long-term observations from one particular location, in a permanent observatory. Walther's measuring instruments were neither small nor hand-held, but quite large and set in fixed locations, including a "triquetum" or set of angle-measuring rods, an armillary sphere, and a clock. By the time of his death, in 1504, he had accumulated a systematic run of 764 measurements of the solar altitude and 615 of the sun, moon, and planets – primary, original data which could be used as a foundation for analysis.

It is impossible to understand the historical place and scientific achievement of Copernicus without reckoning in the fruits of a recent invention which had just begun to transform the nature of knowledge and the creative power of European civilization at the time of his birth: the printing press. Dating from no more than twenty years before his birth, the new technology of printing had become a major driving engine of Western culture by 1500. Printing did not merely give a standardized "typographical fixity" to the printed word – making it possible for a scholar in Salamanca to work from exactly the same text as another in Heidelberg, without the risk of manuscript error variants – it also facilitated the mass production of mathematical tables and woodcut illustrations and diagrams.

Regiomontanus, who was a great publicist for the "new" Greek astronomy in the late fifteenth century, quickly recognized the significance of the printing press, and his *Kalendarium* and *Ephemerides* tables were published in Nuremberg in 1474 only two years before his sudden death during a visit to Rome. Peurbach, Walther, Johannes Schöner, and other men influenced by Bessarion and Regiomontanus would take full advantage of the printing press to publish their ideas, tables, calculations, and pictures and descriptions of their instruments for the European world of learning. Copernicus had read, marked, and inwardly digested them all.

This was the "Old Light" from which Copernicus, Galileo, and others would draw their "New Brightness". While these men of what would become the Astronomical Renaissance of 1500–1700 would indisputably advance astronomy and science beyond what Regiomontanus, Peurbach, and Walther could ever have imagined, there is no reasonable way in which we can see them as Promethean, uniquely sighted bolts out of the blue, whose radical brilliance would disperse the dark gloom of the Middle Ages. Not only did the legacy of classical antiquity and the ingenuity of the early Arabs help to forge the new understanding; so too did the rich heritage of medieval Christian Europe.

CHAPTER 3

Nicholas Copernicus:
The Polish Polymath

*P*oland has suffered great disruption over the centuries. Being a country with few natural geographical barriers, and largely open and flat on its eastern borders, it has had to face waves of invaders. Cossacks, Turks, and the Teutonic knights all poured in during the late Middle Ages, and by the time of Mikolaj Koppernig (or Kippernic) and Lukasc Watzenrode, Copernicus's father and maternal uncle respectively, clear attempts were under way to establish a stable Polish nation under King Casimir IV of the Jagiellan family. These included trying to expel the Turks and pin down the Teutonic knights under the Treaty of Torun of 1466.

Both the Koppernig and Watzenrode families were prominent in Torun, which stood on the Vistula in Royal Prussian, Western Poland. Both had strong mercantile connections, were well off, and had played leading roles in regional politics, especially when it came to curbing the Teutonic knights. Both families belonged in many ways to Europe's late medieval and Renaissance "merchant aristocracy": self-made families of clout and culture.

Barbara, Copernicus's mother, was a young woman of standing as a member of the Watzenrode family, and the substantial house in which the astronomer was born, on 19 February 1473, is now a museum. In addition to commerce and regional politics, several members of both families went into the church in a variety of capacities. Copernicus's brother Andreas became an Augustinian canon, his sister Barbara, named after their mother, a Benedictine nun and later a prioress, and his sister Katherina married a successful merchant.

It was uncle Lukasc, his mother's clergyman brother, who would play the decisive role in shaping and establishing young Nicholas's subsequent career. In 1485 Nicholas lost his father, and uncle Lukasc stepped in. Recognizing the twelve-year-old's intellectual gifts, Lukasc set him on a journey which in many ways mirrored his own career: first to the University of Cracow in 1491, and then to Bologna in Italy to undertake what we might now call postgraduate studies. In 1489, uncle Lukasc was elected to the dignity of Bishop of Warmia, or Ermeland, thereby extending his already considerable powers of patronage. He was an early recipient of what we would call a "humanist" or original Greek and Latin languages based Renaissance education, as was his nephew Nicholas.

EDUCATION AND EARLY LIFE

At Cracow, the eighteen-year-old Nicholas was enrolled, as was natural for a medieval or Renaissance undergraduate, under the Faculty of Arts. This would have involved study of the arts of language and the techniques of understanding: grammar, rhetoric, and logic. The curriculum would also have included the four arts of mathematics and proportion: astronomy, geometry, arithmetic, and music. Between them, these Seven Liberal Arts, dating back a good 1,000 years in 1490, were designed to train and discipline the mind, to make it logical, balanced, rational, and precise: quite the opposite to the frenzied superstition and dark ignorance which are popularly perceived to be part and parcel of the Middle Ages. The teaching would have been in Latin, the learned language of historical Christendom, shared not just among churchmen but also lawyers, medical men, diplomats, and all scholars. A true lingua franca across Europe, it made it possible for an educated Pole to converse with an educated Irishman or Spaniard without any need for translation. It also allowed scholars to read each other's books with ease: a body of books, ancient, medieval, and modern, which had swelled into a cascade of new learning with the advent of printing after the 1450s.

Copernicus, like his undergraduate contemporaries across Europe, would have used his intellectual skills to study classical Greek and Roman literature, such as the *Dialogues* of Plato, the prose and poetry of the classical Roman authors, the philosophy and science of Aristotle, and the mathematical astronomy and cosmology of Ptolemy. There would have been some Roman law, and a solid foundation of Christian theology based on the Bible, the early Church Fathers, such as St Augustine, and the great medieval philosophical theologians such as St Thomas Aquinas.

The student Copernicus's encounter with classical languages and culture would have differed in several respects from that of a thirteenth- or fourteenth-century student. Quite apart from access to printed books in the 1490s and the rich body of new material which they contained, he would have been among the first European undergraduates to benefit from the sea-change in learning of which Cardinal Johannes Bessarion had been an initiator thirty years before, having access to the Greek classical authors in their pure, original language as opposed to copies which may have passed through Syriac, Arabic, and medieval Latin translation on the way. It is hard for us today, accustomed as we are to easy access, in the best translations, to the historical literature and thought of the *globe*, to realize the impact of this "shock of the new" upon the young minds of 500 years ago. Plato, Ptolemy, Hippocrates, and playwrights such as Aristophanes naturally came over differently in their own original Greek than they did in a fourteenth-century Latin translation. Learning Greek, and reading it for oneself, opened up a whole new and dazzling world.

The same applied to Latin. Since the end of the Roman empire in the fifth century AD the Latin language had undergone changes. The old words and the basic grammar remained, but the language evolved in the hands of the Spanish, Frankish, Teutonic, Irish, and British Isles scholars who came to use it for liturgical, legal, or administrative purposes. Old Roman Latin went on to help form the newly emerging vernacular languages of Europe, especially medieval Spanish, French, and Italian. In the same way that classical Greek was being rediscovered, so was the "pure" Latin of the ancient Romans; while Latin and Latin culture had never been lost during the medieval centuries, the language had changed and in many ways become simplified. Just as the New Testament Greek of St Paul or the Gospel writers had been simpler than that of Plato, so the Latin of Horace, Cicero, and the Roman "Golden Age" poets was different from that of St Jerome's Vulgate Bible of AD 386, or that of St Thomas Aquinas of almost a millennium later.

As an undergraduate in Cracow, and perhaps even as a schoolboy, this linguistic sea-change would have rolled over Copernicus with no less force than his later heliocentric universe would roll over sixteenth- and seventeenth-century astronomers – bringing challenge, but also exciting fascination. In their later generations, it would also roll over Tycho Brahe, Galileo, Kepler, Jeremiah Horrocks – and even Sir Isaac Newton. The Astronomical Renaissance was not just about astronomy. It was, rather, part of a wider Renaissance that extended to every aspect of European culture, from theology to sartorial fashion, from art and architecture to sports and games, from "High Literature" to joke books. (Cheap printing and cheap paper were putting ribald books of gags into circulation by 1530, and some of the joke scenarios, in updated form, are still with us.)

Prowess in languages formed a central part of the Renaissance academic curriculum, and Copernicus enjoyed a fluency in Polish, German, Italian, and Latin and Greek. He never seems to have taken his degree at Cracow, but that appears to have been in part occasioned by his being elevated by his Prince Bishop uncle Lukasc to a canonry of Warmia Cathedral in the autumn of 1495, although it was not until 1497 that the 26-year-old astronomer fully entered into his cathedral appointment: from undergraduate to cathedral dignitary in one jump. His installation in his canonry was by proxy, for by that time he had left Poland for the great University of Bologna in Italy, to study Canon Law.

ITALY, LAW, AND MEDICINE

Law, like languages and mathematics, was regarded as one of the great intellectual disciplines of the medieval and Renaissance curriculum. Like them, it demanded rigorous logic and exact thinking, and would have perhaps seemed closer to astronomy than it strikes us today. But when Copernicus returned to Poland in 1501, his colleagues in the cathedral chapter encouraged him to go back to Italy to study medicine. He did so until 1503, at the illustrious medical school of Padua, near Venice. Here he would have studied the medicine of Greek antiquity, Hippocrates, Galen, and no doubt Arabic clinical writers such as Ibn Sina (Avicenna), whose works were widely known in the West, and were even referred to by Chaucer in The Pardoner's Tale. Almost certainly, Copernicus would have witnessed both human and animal dissections, which were an integral part of medieval and Renaissance medical teaching, of which Padua was destined to become a world centre of excellence.

Copernicus took his Bologna doctorate in Law in 1503, though it is not clear that he ever supplicated for his doctorate in medicine. This would not have been seen as irregular 500 years ago, for taking a formal degree was less important than having received a rigorous education. After all, he never took his Cracow arts degree, and a Bologna doctorate in Law automatically proclaimed him as belonging to the elite brotherhood of European learning. In fact, many learned men practised medicine without a formal degree, not only in Copernicus's time, but for three centuries afterwards, without any aspersions being cast upon their competence. Within that world, a university-trained physician, with or without an MD degree, was respected because he had read the great classics of Greek and Latin medicine. It was not the MD's job to dispense medicines and provide hands-on therapy. Rather, he would diagnose and prognose using Hippocratic and, most likely, astrological techniques, and it would be the job of lesser men, such as apothecaries, druggists, "leeches", and surgeons, to provide the hands-on practical care, broadly guided by the physician. As these "lesser" practitioners often possessed sound practical skills and experience in the management of fevers, tumours, and broken limbs, it did not matter whether the university graduate had, or had not, gone through the formal ritual of taking his "qualifying" degree. A man who had spent twelve years in academic study and had taken a Bologna Law doctorate, as Copernicus had, was deemed to be "learned".

For all of the above reasons, the thirty-year-old Copernicus returned to Poland in 1503 to become an invaluable member of the Frombork Cathedral Chapter. While there is no evidence that he ever became a priest, he would have been in "minor orders": perhaps a deacon. But as a high-powered ecclesiastical lawyer, a physician, and a capable administrator, he would have been worth his weight in gold. Between 1503 and 1510, he often travelled as part of his Prince-Bishop uncle's entourage, making at least one visit to Germany. His fame as a physician extended well beyond his Polish cathedral city, as eminent persons living afar would – as was the accepted medical custom of the day – seek consultations by post, sometimes without a personal visit. Towards the end of his life, in 1541, he won extra medical laurels by successfully treating the High Prussian Councillor, George von Kunheim, after all other doctors had failed.

So to see Copernicus as the "timid Canon" of legend, hiding himself away while nurturing dangerous thoughts about the universe, is simply not borne out by the historical record.

COPERNICUS THE ASTRONOMER

In earlier times, learned men did astronomy in pretty much the same way as they did medicine, literature, or theology. It was part of a broad culture, and we need to understand this if we are to see Copernicus in context rather than extracting him from the world in which he lived and reinventing him as a species of inspired radical prophet of modernism. Physician, lawyer, diplomat, and administrator as Copernicus undoubtedly was, he was also deeply interested in astronomy. This may have gone back to his undergraduate student or school days, but was certainly in evidence by the time he was studying for his Law doctorate between 1496 and 1501. He had already obtained copies of Georg von Peurbach's and Regiomontanus's astronomical books, including Regiomontanus's *Epitome*, or digest and interpretation of Ptolemy's *Almagest*, in the Venetian edition of 1496. No doubt inspired by the observational practices of Regiomontanus, Peurbach, and Walther, he had acquired some instruments and begun to use them at least by 9 March 1497, when he was testing the lunar epicyclic theory by observing the moon's angular position against the bright star Aldebaran in the constellation of the Bull.

Before the invention of the telescope began to transform many aspects of astronomical practice after 1610, astronomers did not so much look at celestial bodies as make angular measurements of their positions against each other. For apart from the mottled surface of the moon, and the dazzling brilliance of the sun, all astronomical bodies appeared as simple points of light to the naked eye. The bodies themselves revealed no worthwhile astronomical information about their natures – apart, perhaps, from some puzzling coloured and variable stars – and were studied solely as fixed (the stars) or moving (the sun, moon, and planets) marker points against the black "eighth sphere" of the stars. Astronomy was not about physics so much as about geometry. The night sky presented an endless cavalcade of changeless geometrical cycles, as five "wandering" points and two spheres moved amongst the thousands of fixed starry points, or the planets amongst the stars.

The point-like appearance of the stars and planets was very convenient when it came to measuring their positions, for they could be easily centred in the middle of the small pinhole sights of an astrolabe, or a larger fixed instrument such as a quadrant or set of "Ptolemy's Rulers" – instruments based on prototypes in the *Almagest*. In this way an astronomer could make a map of the "fixed" stars, or constellations, and then carefully monitor the positions of the sun, moon, and planets amongst them. This could be done for a variety of purposes, such as establishing the positions of the winter and summer solstices or the spring and autumn equinoxes, and the inclination of the sun's orbit to the plane of the celestial equator (at around 23½ degrees). The data, once tabulated, could be used for a wide variety of purposes, including calendrical astronomy or astrology.

Significantly, one could monitor, and hopefully refine, some of the values, or "quantities", for the celestial positions that had come down to us from the Greeks. Take, for example, the very important quantity known as the "precession of the equinoxes". The spring and autumn points where the sun's annual orbit cuts through

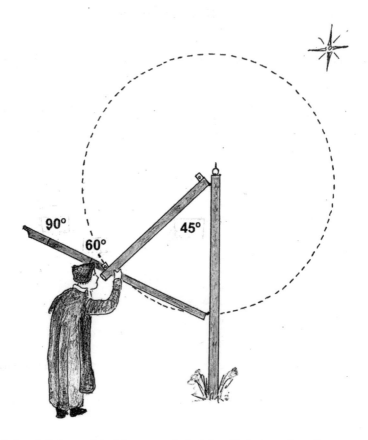

3.1 Ptolemy's Rulers exploited the geometrical relationship between the radius, chords, and tangents of a circle. The astronomer observes a star along the radial sighting arm hinged at the centre of the circle. He then slides the arm along a second arm hinged to the circumference of the same circle, and forming a geometrical chord to the circle wherever the two rods intersect. If the chord arm is graduated, then the "Rulers" can be used to measure very precise vertical angles without need for the more complex geometry required to graduate a circular scale. (Reconstruction by Allan Chapman.)

the band of the zodiac stars, the *equinoxes*, do not remain fixed throughout time with relation to any given star. Instead, equinox points slip back a tiny fraction each year with regard to the "celestial equator", or that mathematically established line around the starry sphere which corresponds to the earth's equator as projected on to the stars. (The celestial equator is exactly overhead if you happen to be on the earth's equator.)

Ptolemy and the Greek astronomers quantified this slippage, or precession, at 1 arc minute per year, or one-sixtieth of a degree of arc (or one-thirtieth of the diameter of the sun or moon). In reality

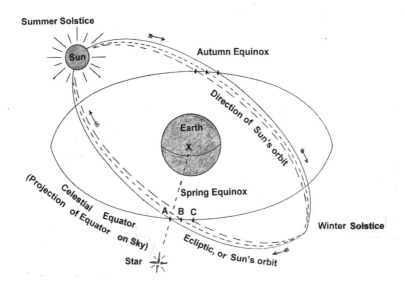

3.2 Precession of the equinoxes. In any given year, an astronomer at "X" on the earth's surface will see the sun at spring equinox near to a star, along the line of sight passing through "A". But next year, the sun's path across the sky will have fallen back – precessed – to fall behind the star to "B". And in the third year it will have fallen back further, to appear at position "C"; and so on, through 25,800 years, when it will have gone full circle to return again to "A". (Drawing by Allan Chapman.)

the angle is slightly smaller than a neat arc minute, but the problem did not become obvious for a long time. The angle is so tiny that it took decades and even centuries for the slow accumulation of the discrepancy to start throwing astronomical predictions based on Ptolemy's tables into error. The error had become so large by

AD 1000 that, as we have seen, Arab astronomers were able to recalculate the annual rate of precession to within an arc second or so of the figure that we accept as correct today.

Yet no medieval astronomical instrument, either Arabic or European, could measure such tiny angles by direct observation. What astronomers did, rather, was measure where the equinox point was on the starry sphere in AD 1000, let us say, and then compare it with the place where it had been in Ptolemy's tables some 850 years before. The angular distance in degrees separating the two points would then be divided by the number of years that had elapsed between the ancient and the contemporary observations in the sky, and the resulting angular fraction would be the annual rate of precession.

Similar long-term comparative observations were made to refine other quantities, such as the extent of the tilt of the sun's orbit with regard to its midsummer and midwinter positions with reference to the celestial equator mentioned above, and, most baffling of all, the supremely complex orbit of the moon around the earth, with all its long- and short-term cycles and eclipses. Once again, medieval astronomers attempted to do this by observing the angles between the moon and key fixed stars in the zodiac. In a nutshell, what all classical, medieval, early modern, and even modern geometrical or "astrometric" astronomers do is use the stars as fixed reference points against which to pin down the dance of the planets for any one time, using the sky as a piece of graph paper, as it were, against which to plot and quantify movements.

This is what Bernard Walther started doing in his Nuremberg observatory in 1475, and what Copernicus would do, first in Italy and then back home in Poland. It would provide the rich mathematical soil from which his heliocentric theory would spring sometime before 1514.

COPERNICUS RETURNS TO POLAND

In 1503, the thirty-year-old Copernicus's studies were over, and the lawyer–doctor–astronomer returned to Poland, taking up his canonry at Frombork Cathedral. While he doubtless had some liturgical duties in the cathedral, his principal work seems to have consisted of being the chapter lawyer, doctor, and administrator. This was probably a major reason why uncle Lukasc had spent so lavishly on his education. Among other things, Copernicus was required to act as his uncle's secretary – and physician – and travel with him on his various diocesan and other duties, including making a diplomatic visit to nearby Prussia. After his uncle's death in 1512 Copernicus seems to have stayed put in and around Frombork. He was well off, having a residence within the cathedral precincts and imposing tower premises on Frombork's defensive wall. It was from here that he seems to have done most of his astronomy: observing the heavens with his instruments, and wrestling with the increasingly pressing anomalies of the Ptolemaic system.

Copernicus's development of a heliocentric theory of the cosmos was not especially driven by practical considerations. While in 1513 he was consulted by Pope Leo X and the Vatican for advice on calendar reform, his driving motive appears to have been intellectual: a desire to make sense of the universe and devise coherent explanatory models for the dance of the planets. He was familiar not only with Ptolemy and other Greeks, but also with the subsequent work of Arabic astronomers, and may have been acquainted with Ibn Tusi's ingenious thirteenth-century modification of epicyclic theory as a way of trying to account for anomalies in planetary motion. Copernicus was also familiar with those classical Greeks who had proposed sun-centred theories, and mentions Philolaus and Ecphantus and Aristarchus, although he struck out the latter's name from the final draft of his 1543 treatise *De Revolutionibus Orbium Coelestium* ("On the Revolutions of the Celestial Spheres"), most likely on the grounds that even the pre-Christian pagans had accused Aristarchus of impiety. Copernicus did not undertake diplomatic work for uncle Lukasc and the Frombork Cathedral Chapter for nothing. He knew how best to present a complex case and sidestep potentially embarrassing associations.

Copernicus began to take heliocentricism seriously some time around, or before, 1510, for between then and 1514 he composed a forty-page manuscript essay, "Commentariolus", or "Short

Commentary", upon a projected heliocentric theory. In its essence, this put forward the same basic argument that *De Revolutionibus* would do in much more developed form and detail thirty years later. In "Commentariolus", one finds the argument that the earth goes around the sun for the first time in post-classical astronomy. Here we find the sun as the centre of terrestrial and planetary rotations: the apparent motion of the sun and stars across the sky are but an effect of the earth's own axial rotation and polar rotation, and the starry heaven is an immensely great distance from the sun. Central to Copernicus's argument is the heliocentric theory's ability to explain the planetary retrogrades, or loops, when seen against the stars. It was this final point which, in the early sixteenth century, was the heliocentric theory's only remotely strong point, although even then it was still necessary to retain epicycles to account for some apparent motions as seen from the earth, most notably those of the sun and the moon.

EXPLAINING THE PLANETARY "RETROGRADE MOTIONS"

How did the heliocentric theory provide an explanation for the retrogrades? It was all about relative planetary motions as seen against the fixed stars. Two bodies never seemed to go backwards, but always moved across the sky in the same direction: the sun and the moon.

Mercury and Venus appeared to have a sort of affinity with the sun, Mercury never moving far from it and often being hard to catch in the twilight. Copernicus never saw Mercury with his own eyes. Venus, while straying further from the sun than Mercury, was never seen at more than 45 degrees' distance, or elongation, from it. Strangely, both Mercury and Venus were best seen as "evening" or "morning" stars, either for an hour or so at most after sunset and then following the sun below the horizon, or else rising in the east before the sun and then being drowned out by the light of dawn. It was impossible to see Mercury or Venus high in the south at midnight, as one could with Mars, Jupiter, and Saturn. But why?

When it came to Mars, Jupiter, and Saturn the retrograde

loops were plain to see, and capable of being monitored precisely amongst the fixed stars. Copernicus's heliocentric system supplied an elegant geometrical model for explaining the loops, based upon the idea that the earth moved *faster* than Mars, Jupiter, and Saturn, and *slower* than Mercury and Venus, while the moon simply revolved around us as a satellite. Basically, it was all about planets seeming to catch up with or overtake the earth. If Mercury and Venus rotated around the sun, and were nearer to the sun than we were, then not only were they moving faster than us – circuiting the sun in 88 and 225 days respectively – but their orbits must have smaller diameters around the solar centre than we had with our 365¼-day circuit, or year. This clearly explained why they never moved far from the sun as viewed from the earth, for they formed the "inner" solar system.

As the orbits of Mars, Jupiter, and Saturn must be *much* bigger in diameter than the earth's orbit, could their "loops" be caused by our earthly line of sight changing as we approached these planets, thereby making them seem to slow down in their orbits and to stop as we came to occupy a radial line connecting us with the sun and the planet in question? Then, as the earth moved ahead and "overtook" them, could this make Mars, Jupiter, and Saturn appear to retrograde backwards as seen amongst the zodiac stars? This could also explain why the retrogrades always appeared to be related to the length of the terrestrial year, or our own orbit about the sun: two retrogrades for Mars's two-year orbit, twelve for Jupiter's and nearly thirty for Saturn's. It also explained why we could see the planets of the "outer" solar system – Mars, Jupiter, and Saturn – high in the southern sky at midnight, for they were beyond us, well away from the sun, and further out in space.

Yet for all of its geometrical elegance, the heliocentric system seemed to be absurd. Plainly and simply, it flew in the face of common sense in so far as the earth was *not*, by any standard of reason, flying through space *and* spinning on its axis as well. Just think: even if you were moving rapidly yet smoothly, on something like a sledge down a hillside, did not the rush of air blow your face and clothing? Even if blindfolded, were you not aware of rapid motion? And if you had a bowl of water in the sledge, before you had gone far it would have been spilled all over the place, as the water sought *rest* from the moving earthy sledge. Try jumping up or spinning in a pirouette on the sledge at speed – how many broken bones would you end up with? The earth was seen as behaving exactly like the moving sledge, as the atmosphere, the water, and one's body would seek stability and try to escape the enforced unnatural motion.

This is how Aristotle's four elements and all of his physics and theories of motion dovetailed beautifully into everyday experience. Copernicus knew that his theory was a sheer affront to two thousand years of physical science, medieval logical analyses of motion, and the whole philosophy of Aristotle, long enshrined in the teaching of Europe's universities. The universality of Aristotle's whole integrated system of teaching – from physics to medicine to psychology to aesthetics and on to poetry – represented the logical investment of Europe's universities. Academic careers from St Andrews to Naples had been built upon it. Who today would leap into print with a new theory of physics, biology, or medicine if they knew that in exchange for one purely theoretical phenomenon-saving argument, gravitational theory, cellular pathology, and the germ theory had to be thrown out of the window? You would think long and hard about it, collect additional facts, and try to strengthen your single argument before putting your career on the line. In 1514, the 41-year-old Copernicus was already approaching the top of the professional tree: as a canon lawyer, a physician with several notable patients, and a diplomatic negotiator. Heliocentricism could be professional suicide, as distinguished people across Europe gasped and came to see the eminent Pole as a fool who, as Martin Luther would allegedly put it around 1541, wanted to turn astronomy upside down.

CHAPTER 4

Copernicus Publishes His Theory: De Revolutionibus *in Nuremberg*

As we saw in Chapter 3, Copernicus's caution about publishing his theory had no direct or necessary connection with religion; rather, it was because heliocentricism flew in the face of observed physical reality as it was then understood. So the practically astute Copernicus thought it wise to share his ideas with selected friends, such as the men whom he permitted to read his "Commentariolus" manuscript and, no doubt, make their own copies. Meanwhile, he would continue to collect his own and other men's observations, think, recalculate, and gradually develop the great treatise that would demand a fundamental rethink of cosmology and physics as they had been understood since classical Greek times.

This is the reason why Copernicus took thirty years to issue a mature, yet, as he was aware, not evidentially clinching version of his heliocentric theory in 1543, by which time he was seventy. The argument that he held back from publication for so long because he feared he would be punished as a *religious* heretic is confounded by those who made prior public comment on Copernicus's theory. It is also clear that while he had been circumspect regarding those people with whom he had shared his idea, the heliocentric cat had escaped from the bag long before 1543, and had scampered around Europe. Often, it was received with respectful admiration. Did Copernicus, for instance, discuss his ideas with his good friend Bishop Johannes Dantiscus, who had visited England on a diplomatic mission? One might *speculate*, and no more, that the moving earth might have been discussed at Hampton Court, or

Whitehall Palace – among such high-powered figures as Cardinal Wolsey, Sir (later St) Thomas More, the international Anglophile Dutch scholar Desiderius Erasmus, and perhaps even H.M. King Henry VIII, who in these earlier years of his reign was highly respected as a scholar and man of letters, and who loved discussing scholarly issues with the leading minds of the day.

Bishop Dantiscus apart, we have clear evidence that heliocentricism was being lectured upon in Rome by the Papal Secretary Johann Albrecht Widmannstetter, and at the very highest level: Pope Clement VII was part of his audience. Far from a heresy-hysteria breaking out, Pope Clement was said to have been interested in the idea, for Clement was a Greek humanist Renaissance Pope. On 1 November 1536 Cardinal Nikolaus von Schönberg of Capua wrote a letter to Copernicus from Rome, in which he indicated his familiarity with the theory, as it was clearly doing the rounds of Rome and probably learned Europe. Schönberg specifically mentions that Copernicus was saying that the *sun* was at the centre of celestial rotation, and that it was the orbiting, spinning earth which created the effect of the turning sky. What is abundantly clear from his letter is that Cardinal Schönberg was an *admirer* of Copernicus, expressing his "very high regard". He wanted to know more about the theory, which he admitted he had first heard about "some years ago". Could Copernicus give him more detailed information, and might it even be possible that he, Schönberg, could commission a scribe to copy out Copernicus's text so that he might read and digest his heliocentric argument at leisure? As the cardinal makes very obvious, Copernicus's reputation as an astronomer and scholar had spread far and wide beyond Poland and, in discerning learned circles, he was already a famous man.

Copernicus was clearly so proud of Schönberg's warm and admiring letter that he would publish it for all the world to read on the preliminary sheets of his *De Revolutionibus* in 1543. This is a totally different scenario from the legend that the obscure Polish canon kept his head down and his outrageous and heretical thoughts to himself until he felt death's hand upon him.

In addition to admiring Roman cardinals, and a possibly admiring Pope, devoutly Roman Catholic Copernicus had declared fans in Wittenberg, the powerhouse of the Protestant Reformation, in spite of anything that Martin Luther or Philipp Melanchthon might have said. One cannot help but be struck by how widely news of his heliocentric theory had spread, presumably by word of mouth or correspondence, from Poland to Germany to Rome.

In 1539 Copernicus received a visitor in Frombork who had travelled from Protestant Wittenberg, wishing to meet the eminent Polish astronomer and scholar. This was the young Lutheran mathematician Joachim Rheticus. He urged upon Copernicus the need to publish his heliocentric theory in a complete and worked-out form, although by that date the *De Revolutionibus* manuscript was probably as watertight, evidence and argument wise, as heliocentricism could be made in 1539. One year later, in 1540, Rheticus published in Dantzig a forerunner to Copernicus's great work, alerting the scholars of Europe to the theory in a published form: this was his *Narratio Prima* ("First Narrative" or "Account"). The *Narratio* was only a short book, but it gave a digest of the key heliocentric arguments. It rapidly sold out, and in 1541 a second edition was printed in Basel, taking Copernicus's theory across Europe a full two years before *De Revolutionibus* would appear, and once again undermining the myth that Copernicus kept quiet about his theory until he was dying.

Copernicus did not lack friends and supporters within the Roman Catholic hierarchy. Not only was there his old friend Bishop Dantiscus, and admirers in Rome like Cardinal Schönberg and perhaps Pope Clement, but it was to another bishop friend that Copernicus handed over his manuscript of *De Revolutionibus* for printing: Tiedemann Giese, Bishop of Chelmo. He, in turn, handed it over to Protestant Rheticus for printing in Nuremberg, over 400 miles away from Frombork. The printer Johannes Petreius in Nuremberg took the manuscript, and his Protestant disciple from Wittenberg was charged with the task of seeing Copernicus's life's work through the press.

Why did Copernicus send his book miles across Europe from Frombork to the south German city of Nuremberg, especially as there were presses in Poland and other places much closer at hand? One suspects that it was because of Nuremberg's standing as one of Europe's acknowledged centres of business, finance, enterprise, and technological know-how. It was the "Silicon Valley" of late-medieval and Renaissance Europe. In Nuremberg, you could obtain a suit of armour, a striking clock, jewellery, a complex mechanical toy or a gun, arrange an international bank loan, or commission the printing of a beautiful book. Not only was Nuremberg a prestigious city to proclaim on your title page; it was also a major centre for the distribution of books and *objets d'art* across Europe, and a lynchpin in the Renaissance system of international trade fairs.

PUBLISHING *DE REVOLUTIONIBUS*

Two things happened while the book was in press. Most decisively, the 69-year-old Copernicus suffered some kind of seizure or paralysis stroke towards the end of 1542; and then Rheticus, having been offered a post in Leipzig, was obliged to leave Nuremberg with the book still in press, leaving Copernicus's other Wittenberg disciple, Andreas Osiander, to do the final editing, correcting, and proofreading. Osiander appeared to take upon himself (for there is no indication that he had Copernicus's authority to do as he did) the right to add an additional "Preface" to *De Revolutionibus*. This Preface stated that the heliocentric argument worked out in the text need not necessarily be read as a real description of the solar system, so much as a hypothesis or geometrical exercise.

Scholars have agonized over "Osiander's Preface" and why he seemed to add it in the final stages of printing. Some have claimed that it was to prevent Copernicus being condemned by the church for heresy, even if only posthumously. Yet as we have seen above, Copernicus's heliocentric cosmology had been doing the rounds of European scholars for some time by 1543, and had even been favourably commented upon, as a theory, by a cardinal. It is more likely that Osiander was trying to protect the legal and medical dignitary from ridicule. Medieval and Renaissance scholars, after all, loved playing intellectual games – it was part of that drive to display ingenuity and mental agility upon which the universities prided themselves – and in this respect Copernicus could be admired as a very clever man. On the other hand, to believe that the earth both spun upon its axis and rotated about the sun could be professionally and posthumously damaging. This is why Osiander added his own Preface.

Legend has it, but there is no decisive proof, that the stricken Copernicus was handed a newly arrived copy of his *magnum opus* on his deathbed. Perhaps he was; but before he passed away, on 24 May 1543, the devout Copernicus was probably more concerned with preparing his soul for judgment than about his posthumous reputation as an astronomer.

It used to be thought that no one bothered to read the dense and tightly argued astronomical treatise, but this was recently overturned by several scholars, most notably the distinguished Harvard historian of astronomy Owen Gingerich, who succeeded in tracking down some 245 surviving copies of *De Revolutionibus* in libraries around the world. Gingerich found that a significant minority of these copies contain marginal notes and comments, in contemporary hands, suggesting that in a good number of cases, the book was carefully pored over and annotated.

DE REVOLUTIONIBUS AND ITS RECEPTION

De Revolutionibus Orbium Coelestium carried its argument over six "books", or sections, and laid things out over a structure similar to that of the thirteen books of Ptolemy's *Almagest*. Book 1 contains an overall view of the heliocentric theory, and Book 2 a theoretical study of spherical astronomy. Book 3 is devoted to the apparent motions of the sun, and Book 4 to the complex problems of the moon; while Books 5 and 6 analyse the motions of the planets in longitude and latitude respectively as they move amongst the "fixed" stars.

No one was punished or threatened, and a second edition came out in Basel, Switzerland, in 1566. That does not mean that astronomers and scholars blandly accepted it in respectful acquiescence, for as we saw above, medieval and Renaissance scholars loved to argue and attack each other. This procedure was even built into the teaching and examination rituals of the universities, where *lectio* and *disputatio*, or statement and challenge, and the *viva voce* or adversarial oral encounters which decided whether or not a student received his degree (especially his doctorate) were – *and still are* – a normal part of British and European academic life (I passed through these at Oxford). Statements, challenges, attacks, and defences were simply part of the scholarly game.

In the immediate aftermath of the publication of *De Revolutionibus*, and also perhaps before 1543, Copernicus's book was attacked on three principal grounds. Firstly, it flew in the face of common sense and reason, for only a fool or a publicity-seeking, novelty-loving charlatan could lay claim to such a preposterous idea as a moving earth. Secondly, the whole explanatory architecture of the book silently struck at the heart of Aristotelian physics: if the earth was *not* at the centre of creation, then why did stones fall down or flames rise upwards? If you dropped a stone from a tower, why did it unfailingly fall *directly* below its point of release? Surely, if the earth were moving, should not the stone fall in a slightly different spot, the earth having moved a fraction during the stone's descent? Even worse problems could arise if you started to admit that Aristotle "The Philosopher" was in error about astronomy and physics. As Aristotelianism had been carefully built into medical, chemical, psychological, and even theological interpretations, would all these disciplines also come crashing down? Aristotle's philosophy was a carefully crafted intellectual edifice: remove one brick, and the whole could be in danger of collapse, a prospect too terrifying to contemplate.

Thirdly, there were possible theological objections, deriving from statements in the Old Testament book of Joshua and in the Psalms that made it clear that the earth was "fixed and 'stablished". In particular, in Joshua 10, when the children of Israel needed more time to gain a victory in the battle against their enemies, the Gibeonites, God held back the sun so as to lengthen the day, to enable the Jews to secure their victory. This had been a formative event in Jewish history, as God had held back the course of nature on their behalf.

EARLY CRITICS OF HELIOCENTRICISM

Copernicus's critics, such as the Roman Catholic Bartholomeo Spina and his friend Giovanni Maria Tolosani, both Dominicans, who were quick off the mark to inveigh against him by 1544, used the above arguments in various permutations, while Philipp Melanchthon in Wittenberg had even responded angrily to heliocentricism on the strength of Rheticus's *Narratio Prima* in 1540. From where things stood in 1544, they all had sound common sense, classical philosophy, and Judeo-Christian authority on their side. Tolosani, a scholar in the logical and rationalistic style of St Thomas Aquinas, accused Copernicus of fanciful thinking, mistaking arguments drawn from numbers and mathematics for physical reality, and trying to make reality conform to a novel theory. As we have already seen, Luther regarded Copernicus and heliocentricism as absurd.

Yet all of this criticism amounted to no more than academic brickbat-throwing. There was no question of posthumously proclaiming Copernicus to be a heretic, or of hunting down and punishing whoever agreed with him. It was academic foolishness, and in no way struck at the core doctrines of Christian teaching, Catholic or Protestant. No teachings or doctrines, such as Christ's Saviourship, the Holy Trinity, the resurrection, or God's love and grace towards the world, were in the least bit compromised.

What about seemingly overt challenges to Bible teaching, such as that of the sun standing still for Joshua? In the Copernican universe, things were rather more physically complex than in the Ptolemaic; for while one could rationally envisage one single astronomical body, the sun, being stayed by the hand of God for a few hours while a battle was won, it was hard to see how God could stay the sun when the object was stationary already. The Bible did not say that God stopped the earth from spinning and orbiting for several hours, as the inspired chronicler of the book of Joshua should have done had the universe been heliocentric.

ASTRONOMY AND SCRIPTURE

In this period of the early Reformation, there was no universal consensus about the exact literal interpretation of Scripture. As

Adam and Eve, for example, had only sons, Cain, Abel, and Seth, where had the women come from with whom they had sired the Patriarchs? Genesis says nothing on this matter, and no daughters are ascribed to Adam and Eve. And how, in the Genesis narrative, could God create plants and vegetation on the third day of the primal earth, while waiting until the fourth day before setting the sun in the sky? There were other well-known textual interpretation problems, including some in the New Testament, such as doubts about the Petrine authorship of the Second Epistle of Peter. Contrary to what is popularly believed, most theologians and Christian scholars have not been simple literalists or fundamentalists in their understanding of the Bible, realizing, back to the scholars of the early church, that a critical understanding had to be exercised in the interpretation of the ancient texts. In the sixteenth century, and perhaps occasioned by the pressures of the Reformation, both Catholics and Protestants were often agonizing about the interpretation of Scripture. Nowhere in the Old Testament was this more apparent than in the interpretation of the Pentateuch, the first five books of the Bible, including Genesis, which in the sixteenth century were believed to have been written by Moses. Joshua, the sixth biblical book with its account of the children of Israel's conquest of the Promised Land, including the story of the sun standing still, was accredited almost equal authority.

Both Protestant and Catholic theologians spoke of the "plain meaning of Scripture", yet this in itself could be a paradoxical phrase, for in certain places Scripture was not plain. How, for example, do you square the Psalmist's request (69:28) that his enemies "be blotted out of the book of the living" with the Bible's wider teaching to love your neighbour and even your enemy? By 1544 a millennium and a half of scholarship had been devoted to how to reconcile those passages where Scripture was *not* plain or self-evident.

One of the central intellectual tenets of Luther, Melanchthon, and other early Protestant reformers had been that the medieval Catholic Church had become too dependent upon doctrines, which in some cases used Scripture as a sort of springboard to the exploration of rather abstract philosophical concepts. This was the philosophical theology of the "Schoolmen" of Europe's medieval universities, which seemed a far cry from the needs of those ordinary Jews and early Christians who saw the Bible as a plain and straightforward guide. By the mid-sixteenth century, Roman Catholic theologians of the Counter-Reformation – which aimed to win Protestants back into the Catholic fold – were admitting that the Protestants had a point. This is why the Dominican friar Tolosani and the Protestant reformer Melanchthon could both independently accuse Copernicus of contradicting the "plain word of Scripture" concerning the matter of the sun standing still in the book of Joshua.

The Dominican's position was by no means the only one, even amongst Catholic theologians, especially with regard to interpreting poetic descriptions of grand natural phenomena in the Bible. Who could deny the monumental authority of St Augustine, who had lived over 1,000 years previously, when it came to scriptural interpretation? In his *De Genesi ad Litteram* ("On the Literal Meaning of Genesis"), AD 401–415,[1] St Augustine discusses the ancient Psalmist's statement that God "stretchest out the heavens like a curtain" (Psalm 104:2) in relation to the geometrical fact known to Greek-educated men like himself that the heavens were *spherical*. Augustine's argument, in a nutshell, is that what matters is God's majesty and creative power as demonstrated in nature, not whether the heavens are a curtain (or tent) or a sphere. Has not God given us reason and sense to fathom out the details as best we can, once we understand that he had made everything that exists?

Simple literalism was not necessary. Around 1598, the Roman cardinal, scholar, and ecclesiastical historian Cesare Boronius hit the nail on the head when he stated that "the intention of the Holy Ghost [the Bible, or Scripture] is to teach us how one goes to heaven, not how heaven [the heavens] goes [go]".[2] Scripture should not be read as a guide to scientific fact, but as a guide to salvation. It was Galileo who wrote down Boronius's epigram, and he may have heard it in conversation with the cardinal when His Eminence was in Padua in 1598. Either way, it is very clear that, at least in the Roman Catholic world, there was no simple consensus on the plain meaning of Scripture, including Joshua and the sun. We shall return to Cardinal Boronius, Galileo, and Catholic views on science and Scripture in Chapter 13.

After the passing ripple in Protestant and Catholic circles occasioned by *Narratio Prima* and then *De Revolutionibus* between 1540 and 1543–44, nothing much further was said about the heliocentric theory in a theological context. As modern scholars have amply demonstrated, however, it was in no way ignored, and was being discussed all over Europe and beyond – as we shall see. Criticisms were invariably on scientific grounds, as these grounds were understood at that time. One can *never* blame one age for lacking the insights of later centuries, especially when those insights would only be possible after fundamental innovations in precision instrumentation and research technology, followed by a succession of theoretical, conceptual, and mathematical developments arising from that technology – of which no one in 1543 could ever have dreamt. These innovations began in the 1570s and did not come to fruition until around 1730.

GIORDANO BRUNO

What about Giordano Bruno, a heliocentricist, condemned for heresy and burned at the stake in Rome at the beginning of 1600? Looking more carefully at him suggests that while he was certainly a heliocentricist, he was not a Copernican. His inspiration, rather, drew on Pythagorean central fire philosophy, and mysticism about all things rotating around sacred flames. Bruno's thought did not draw on a complex mathematical geometry as did that of Copernicus, but on other currents flowing through Renaissance Europe, such as hermeticism, magic, and occultism. Crucially, Bruno, a lapsed Dominican friar, had, in most respects, left Christianity altogether to become a pantheist, seeing, amongst other things, the sun and stars as divine intelligences in their own right. Bruno's ideas about God, and certainly about Christ, redemption, and Christian spirituality, had wandered so far from base, as it were, as to render him a prima facie heretic, irrespective of anything to be found in Copernicus. Bruno and Copernicus were coming from different directions, and addressing different issues, as contemporaries understood, and of which we also should be aware.

It would be seventy-three years after *De Revolutionibus*'s original publication, and half a century after the second edition in 1566, before Copernicus's heliocentric theory was to become a thing of theological contention, with the warning given to Galileo by Cardinal Roberto Bellarmine in 1616. Yet the question remains: why did the church take so long to get around to condemning Copernicus's ideas if, as is popularly believed, they were so heretical, and so offensive to Scripture?

Serious *official* ecclesiastical concern with heliocentricism only arose after Galileo became its advocate, in the wake of his telescopic discoveries after 1610, and may have had more to do with Galileo's distinctly controversial style amidst the post-Council-of-Trent Counter-Reformation Catholic Church, than it had with any specific points in either science or Scripture. We will come to Galileo in Chapter 9, after looking at the work of two men whose influence upon the future of both practical and theoretical astronomy would be both profound and enduring.

CHAPTER 5

The Great Dane:
Tycho Brahe Tests Copernicus

*T*yge Ottesen Brahe was an astronomical phenomenon, not only because of the profound and influential character of his scientific work, but also because of the circumstances of his life. He appeared to break many of the rules of sixteenth-century Danish society, perhaps most of all in his passion for astronomy, and his determination to devote his life to it.

Tyge Brahe, or Tycho, as he Latinized his Christian name on the world stage, was an aristocrat born and bred, descending from two ancient Danish noble families, the Brahe and the Bille, his parents being Otte (or Otto) and Beate. He was born on 14 December 1546, at his father's ancestral seat, Knudstrup Castle, Skania, in what is now southern Sweden, but was then Danish. On both sides, his family had been soldiers, diplomats, courtiers, ambassadors, and high government and church officials. The Brahes had generally been the fighting men, while the Billes had tended more to peaceful than military careers, producing senior Crown officials and archbishops in the pre-Reformation Danish Roman Catholic Church. By venerable custom in that society, great noblemen were not encouraged to devote themselves to university academic careers any more than were swineherds: Denmark had a three-layered society. There was the nobility; a relatively narrow middle class which provided the professional, lower ecclesiastical, academic, and commercial services; and at the bottom a large peasant class. Unlike sixteenth-century England, with its established customs of sometimes extraordinary social mobility (Cardinal Wolsey, for example, had been a butcher's son and risen through education), Danish society was more in keeping with wider European conventions of the time, in which a major move between classes was not easy.

Something happened to the infant Tycho that we today would regard as appalling and traumatizing – he was kidnapped, and his parents seemed unbothered by it. The kidnappers were uncle Jørgen Brahe and aunt Inger Oxe, his father's brother and his wife. (Aristocratic Danish women generally retained their maiden names after marriage.) It seems that the childless Jørgen and Inger had an agreement with Otte and Beate that if the latter produced a son first, they would be allowed to bring him up as their own heir. Tycho was born with a twin brother who died, and it seems that Otte and Beate were a trifle slow in handing the surviving baby over, so that uncle and aunt took the initiative and whisked little Tycho away. It had been a long-standing agreement, and Otte and Beate had further children. Tycho's brother Steen seems to have appeared before the kidnapping occurred, so that the future astronomer was most likely a toddler rather than baby when uncle and aunt stepped in. It was a common practice in many of Europe's aristocratic families for children to be farmed out to relatives, or even friendly non-related noble families, to be brought up as part of the household. It was probably seen as part of a toughening-up process.

EDUCATION AND MARRIAGE

Noblemen, generally speaking, did not go to school but were educated privately, although there are clear suggestions that Tycho attended a school. A bright young nobleman could learn languages, and Latin – the international language of diplomacy – as Tycho did between the ages of six (his "seventh year") and twelve, as well as classical literature, history, and some Lutheran theology, but he was not expected to write books or become seriously involved with practical activities like astronomy. Tycho, however, like most other young gentlemen, was taught basic Ptolemaic cosmology and mathematics, for that was part of general culture. In addition, a bright young nobleman would be educated in law, statecraft, and warfare, as only befitted a person born to serve king and country at the highest level. He was most definitely expected to marry within his class, and to continue the generations.

Tycho broke all of these expectations. Though not averse to fighting or swordsmanship, he fell in love with the motions of the heavens – most likely when he was only thirteen in August 1560, when he witnessed a partial eclipse of the sun and was amazed to discover that such glorious phenomena could be accurately predicted. He also fell in love with ideas, with devising things, and especially with what we would now call precision engineering and measurement; in later years, he would transform the practical business of celestial angle-measuring as he evolved a set of astronomical instruments – each design improving upon its predecessor – that would enable the science of the heavens to advance more rapidly than it had done for the previous 2,000 years. The principles Tycho established would lay the foundations of astronomy as the technologically driven science that it still is today. Tycho, the Danish lord, born to fight or to govern, was to become one of the first to recognize the importance of new, primary physical data in the advancement of science, and how better data could provide new insights into old problems. Such accurate data, it was hoped, might help astronomers to establish, as a *fact*, whether or not the earth rotated around the sun.

Whether or not Tycho's childhood training in Latin did take place in a school with other boys or with private tutors, when he was only twelve, on 19 April 1559, he became a student at Copenhagen University, where he entered upon a study of law: a basic training for a young aristocrat. In 1562, when he was in his sixteenth year, he was sent abroad to study at Leipzig, Wittenberg, Wandesbeck, and other universities – institutions, one should note, within the essentially Germanic, Lutheran Protestant north.

As a nobleman, he would not have taken a formal degree but was expected to acquire a wide range of learning in subjects such as law, history, and classical humanist scholarship, all of which would have been deemed necessary for a future senior civil servant, diplomat, or courtier. As sixteenth-century Europe was a deeply Christian society then in the throes of the Reformation, he would have been expected to gain a sound understanding of Lutheran theology, which had only recently become the Danish state's official denomination. On these travels, he was to "learn the nature of men and nations", and develop a firm understanding of how the politics – including the ecclesiastical politics – of Europe worked. Astronomy, beyond a general cultural grasp of Ptolemy, would *not* have been an especial part of his intended formal education.

On a personal level, Tycho would also break, or at least, seriously bend, the social rules by choosing a partner who was "beneath" him, in 1571. His "wife", Kirsten Jørgensdatter, was variously described as a local girl of Knudstrup or another local Brahe village, and as the daughter of a local clergyman Hans Jørgen or Jørgensen. Either way, she was most certainly not an aristocrat, and for that reason they could not formally marry: nobles could only marry nobles. Their relationship was not deemed illegitimate, however, as the ancient Jutish law of Denmark said that if a woman had lived for three winters with a man, and carried the keys of the household, as sixteenth-century wives did, then she could be publicly recognized as his wife. On the other hand, the children of such a marriage could not inherit their father's titles and social status. Tycho and Kirsten had eight children. It would not be until the couple had left Denmark in 1597, eventually to reside at the Holy Roman Emperor's Court in Prague in 1599, that their almost thirty-year union was formally recognized as a marriage.

TYCHO'S "GOLDEN NOSE"

If there is one thing that anyone who has heard of Tycho will tell you, it is that he had his nose cut off in a sword fight and thereafter wore a "golden" prosthesis. Unlike many stories of famous people, this one is true – at least in part.

Only a week after his twentieth birthday, on 27 December 1566, when Tycho was a student at Rostock University and staying with Lucas Bacmeister, Professor of Theology, he attended a wedding celebration in that city. A fellow guest was a distant cousin, Manderup Parsburg. Some accounts say that Tycho and Parsburg fell out about a mathematical proof, while others have suggested it was about a young lady. Either way, they resolved, in the best aristocratic tradition, to settle the matter with a duel. They met on 29 December, and, perhaps unavoidably in the depths of a Baltic midwinter, fought with swords in the dark. Honour seems to have been satisfied when a piece of Tycho's nose was sliced off. Tycho had been very lucky, for not only could he – or Parsburg – have lost an eye in such a fight, but the nose has two major arterial vessels serving it, so Tycho might easily have bled to death. Tycho then seems to have had a prosthesis, or artificial part, made to fill up the hole cut out by his cousin's sword.

My own medical-historical interest in Tycho's nose was especially fired some years ago when I received a telephone call from a facial repair surgeon on the staff of a major Yorkshire hospital. He was trying to develop a repair procedure using titanium implants and skin grafting, for people who had lost their noses in accidents or from other causes. His historical and clinical curiosity was aroused by Tycho. He wanted to see portraits in which the prosthesis was clearly visible – Tycho was so proud of his metal nose that he had it delineated in his subsequent portraits – and the surgeon said the Royal Society had suggested that he should contact me.

Judging from the pictures, it appears that Parsburg's sword had sliced off a lump of tissue in the region of the bridge of the nose, leaving the lower nose intact. But how could the artificial nose have been attached? Some scholars have suggested that glue might have been used; others that, considering the nearness of the nasal bone, there might have been some kind of mechanical catch clipping under the bone.

We are not sure, but when Tycho's body was exhumed from under his memorial stone in the Tyn Church, Prague, for medical examination in 1901, and then again in 2010, traces of copper were found on the adjacent skull. So could the long-lost nasal prosthesis have been of a brass-related alloy, perhaps with gold or silver additions to improve its appearance? It is interesting to note how Tycho's work, and mortal remains, still fascinate historians, scientists, and facial reconstruction surgeons to this day.

PHILIPP MELANCHTHON AND THE REFORMATION

To put Tycho Brahe into historical context, it is essential to understand what had gone on in Europe, and more specifically in Denmark, during the thirty years that had preceded his birth in 1546. The most influential event had been the Protestant Reformation. Though primarily a north-European phenomenon, it was destined to change the course of world history in the centuries ahead, to generate intense intellectual energy north of the Alps, and profound responses elsewhere. These responses, on the one hand, set the Roman Catholic Church upon its own course of self-examination and reform in the Counter-Reformation, and also, at their worst, led to internal wars, mayhem, and bloodshed, as traumatic changes often do.

In Denmark – which at this period controlled most of Norway and parts of southern Sweden – the Reformation had been sudden and socially divisive. The nobles grabbed Catholic Church property and suppressed monasteries, schools, hospitals, and all manner of ecclesiastical charities, invariably leaving the peasantry bereft of their old supports and virtually enslaved to the new lay aristocratic owners of the former monastic estates. This circumstance goes a long way to explaining why Tycho became so hated by the peasants of the Island of Hven, granted to him by King Frederick II in 1576, and upon which he was to build his great observatory, Uraniborg, or "Castle of the Heavens": Europe's first major research observatory, and a direct intellectual and technological inspiration for what would follow at Dantzig (Gdansk), Greenwich, and elsewhere in the seventeenth century. Sadly, when Tycho left Uraniborg for good in 1597, the islanders tore it apart – for building materials, and for sheer hatred's sake.

This circumstance was brought home forcefully to me in October 2006, when visiting the now conserved Uraniborg site. As I and my Danish astronomer friends were inspecting the site, a passing Hven farmer stopped his car and summoned us over. He invited us back to his spacious and comfortable farmhouse, where, as an object of decoration in the sitting room, sat a stone block, about 1-foot cube. It came from Tycho's observatory, he told us, after his island ancestors of 400 years before had destroyed the place. He said that for over 300 years the beautifully carved stone block – and I think I can identify the very instrument that it supported from a description in Tycho's *Astronomiae Instauratae Mechanica* ("The Instruments by which I Recreated Astronomy"), 1598 – had supported a swill trough in the family pigsty. He also told us that Islanders down the centuries, on seeing this and other ex-Uraniborg stones, used to *spit* upon them as a mark of their ancestral hatred of the harsh landlord Tycho.

Our unexpected host, a prosperous, educated, and extremely hospitable gentleman farmer, had not only lovingly cleaned up the block, but put it in a place of honour in his house – a stone block now rightly recognized as a physical relic of Scandinavian intellectual greatness. I relate the above incident not only to place it on historical record, but as a first-hand account of a perspective on Tycho by a man whose distant ancestors had felt the whiplash of his years on Hven, and *never* forgotten them.

Tycho's Uraniborg enterprise was largely financed by expropriated Roman Church revenues, such as those of Roskilde Cathedral, made over to him by the king. Tycho was even granted a canonry of the laicized Roskilde Chapter, complete with all its rents and revenues, for his astronomical purposes.

Separate from the religious and political impact of the Lutheran Reformation on ordinary Danes, key aspects of its theology would exercise a powerful moulding influence upon northern Europe and its schools and universities. When one notes which universities Tycho visited on his various travels over the years, one is struck by their Protestantism – Wittenberg (where the Protestant Reformation had been born in 1517), Rostock, Leipzig, Frankfurt (where he purchased books at the city's famous book fair), and elsewhere – he never seems to have studied in Roman Catholic lands. A characteristic of many of these places was the classical humanist scholarly and theological influence of Martin Luther's friend and fellow Protestant Reformer, Philipp Melanchthon. Of all the Germanic Reformers, Melanchthon had been the one most switched on to wider classical philosophical values, and had a sheer love of learning for its own sake. This new Protestant humanist scholarship was known from its founder's Christian name as "Philippianism", embedding its passionate Christian theology within a rich matrix of linguistic, historical, and even naturalistic components, and seeing the church as not only a spiritual but also a teaching institution. Did not good learning, including scientific learning, lift up the human mind to the contemplation of God? This way of thinking, as we shall see, had a powerful effect upon Johannes Kepler.

This Philippianism formed a major component of that intellectual and spiritual stream out of which Tycho drank, and perhaps nowhere is it more evident than in the opening "Oration", or plan of action, with which he began a series of deeply influential lectures, encouraged and supported by King Frederick, and which he delivered under the auspices of the university, beginning on 23 September 1574. They were probably delivered in the French Embassy, at the request of Tycho's friend and admirer Charles Dançey, France's envoy or ambassador to Denmark, because lecturing in the University of Copenhagen was the preserve of the essentially middle-class academic professoriate. Class lines and privileges were clear-cut in sixteenth-century Denmark, and while Tycho's fame as a man of learning was internationally recognized by 1574 – and many distinguished professors, students, and other academics were graciously invited to the embassy as Dançey's guests – the invitation was more in keeping with the social rules than if Tycho had lectured in the university.

What did Tycho say in these lectures, and in particular, in his ground-plan "Oration"? It was remarkably theological in the Philippian tradition. Not only does Tycho trace astronomy back to Seth and Moses in Genesis and the other early biblical books; he also sees it as useful and purposive, for it reflects God's glory, and stimulates and elevates the human intellect. It is also useful on a practical level, enabling us to measure the seasons and draw up accurate calendars. As well as going on to the later achievements of Hipparchus and the Greeks, however, Tycho provides a detailed discussion of two subjects close not only to his own heart, but also to that of European civilization itself in 1574: astrology and alchemy.

63

THE COSMIC FORCES IN RENAISSANCE EUROPE

For most people of the sixteenth century, educated and uneducated, the heavens were believed to influence things on earth, as we saw in Chapter 2. In a geocentric, common-sense physics and cosmology, it stood to reason that the earth itself, and all living things on it, synchronized with celestial events. Who could deny the empirical correlation between the tides, seasons, fecundity, weather, and states of both mind and body, and the regularly changing relationship of sun, moon, and stars? Were not planetary changes empirically related to earthly affairs, such as the malign conjunction of Jupiter and Saturn in 1563 and the plague epidemics that followed in its wake, to which Tycho drew attention? Even the most respected physicians of the age regularly employed astrology as a tool of both diagnosis and prognosis, as will be shown in more detail in Chapter 23.

Sixteenth-century criticisms of astrology were not so much about the truth of its physical reality as about its relative crudeness and need for "perfecting". Horoscopes were often wrong because the primary planetary data used in their calculation were defective, not because astrology was false – hence the urgent need for the much-talked-of "reformation of astronomy". More accurate observations would hopefully lead to the publishing of more reliable planetary tables. It was *not* about the science supposedly breaking free from superstition, as many people imagine was going on in the new science of the Renaissance, but that the new science was trying to make the "superstition" more reliable. To fail to understand this point is to ignore one of Tycho's most powerful motivations.

A point of controversy was whether a horoscope could *compel* a circumstance in the human realm, or whether it simply *forewarned* or *inclined*: this is where things become theological. If God had given human beings free will and the ability to make moral and other choices for themselves, how far did the heavens compel them? Quite acceptable to both the Catholic and Protestant Churches, and to lay scholars across Europe, was *natural* astrology, or the use of the horoscope for such things as weather prediction, medical understanding, or the elucidation of future general tendencies. This could be seen as an aspect of the bounty of God, bestowed to help the confused and suffering human race. What was condemned was *judicial* astrology, which claimed to deal in inescapable doom predictions, such as inescapable death at a future given time, for this inevitably abrogated free will, and was seen as impeding God's free grace, kindness, and response to earnest prayer. Judicial astrology was frighteningly pagan and potentially heretical in all Christian traditions. This is the wider context in which Tycho was to develop his scientific enterprise.

Complementing astrology was alchemy: the art in which Tycho was already an informed "adept" and practitioner in Copenhagen, well before obtaining royal, ex-ecclesiastical funding to build Uraniborg. He was engaged in alchemical research at the time of his first sighting the "new star" or supernova of November 1572. Like all learned alchemists, he was not attempting to turn lead into gold, but to learn the nature of substances. As we saw in Chapter 2, alchemy was intimately bound up with astrology, as all things on earth, including metals and all living things, were believed to be sensitive and responsive to celestial influence. The guiding star of much sixteenth-century alchemy was the Swiss doctor who called himself Paracelsus (or "Greater than Celsus", Celsus being the ancient Roman medical writer), who up to his death in 1541 had transformed and re-invigorated alchemical thinking with his own radical ideas on the nature of life, substance, heat, the influence of the heavens upon earth, and alchemy's potential as the key to medicine.

Tycho was in many ways a disciple of Paracelsus, and he discussed him in some detail in his Copenhagen lectures in 1574. Alchemy was replete with reproductive and fertility analogies, in its attempts to explain how things were engendered, grew, and developed. How did a seed become a tree, how did the sexual act engender humans and animals, or base metals mature into gold and silver, as alchemists believed? Were the fixed stars of the zodiac constellations the equivalent of "seeds" waiting to be "impregnated" by the fertile power of the moving sun and the planets, only to beam their special powers down to the centre of the universe – to the earth, and all that was upon it?

These Paracelsian ideas were inspiring to men like Tycho, for they seemed to hold the key to how to change the world: first, by "reforming" astronomy so as to make astrology more accurate and reliable; and secondly, by understanding the nature of substance and mutability upon earth. To a highly educated, intelligent man of 1574 this was neither superstitious nor foolish, so much as empowering. It was also godly, in the best Philippian tradition, for did not God want mankind to use its divine gift of intelligence to contemplate, understand, and use his creation?

It is tragic that so many modern writers who selectively craft the "Scientific Revolution" scenario around people like Copernicus, Tycho, and Galileo either wholly ignore all of the above, or else brush it aside as an embarrassing aberration – something to which "geniuses" had to pay lip service as a way of avoiding persecution by their backward contemporaries. Yet to separate Tycho the observatory-building, critical-measurement-making "modern" astronomer from the cosmological ideas outlined above is to take him out of his proper historical context to suit our own purposes.

What would change Tycho's world, cosmos, and prevailing intellectual climate profoundly, and pretty well completely by 1700, was a series of discoveries in astronomy and physics over the following century which would tip the balance of probability away from the geocentric theories of Ptolemy in favour of the heliocentric system of Copernicus. While Tycho would go to his grave in Prague in 1601 still firmly convinced that the earth was fixed in the centre of creation with the heavens rotating around it, the transformation of astronomical techniques and methods that he would pioneer in Denmark between 1572 and 1597 would play a major part in eventually undermining geocentricism. Figures such as Johannes Kepler, Galileo Galilei, John Wilkins, Jeremiah Horrocks, Pierre Gassendi, Johannes Hevelius, Christiaan Huygens, Robert Hooke, John Flamsteed, Denmark's Ole Rømer, and many others, became increasingly confident – without yet being able to *prove* geometrically – that the planets rotated around the sun and not the earth, while some even came to espouse the view that the universe *may* be infinite, with no centre, and with the stars scattered throughout space. By logical extension, astrology left the learned academy and gradually became relegated to the popular prognosticators and fortune-tellers, while alchemy and alchemical medicine likewise lost their rationale by 1700, as we shall see in Chapter 23.

Central to this fundamental way of thinking about the universe and humanity's place in it would be an unexpected celestial phenomenon which got all the astronomers of Europe talking and observing. This would impel Tycho to make the first of his famous long runs of meticulous astronomical observations as a way of seeking an explanation. While this phenomenon would seriously undermine key aspects of Aristotle's physics, it would do no real or immediate service to the Copernican theory either. This was the new star of 1572.

CHAPTER 6

Tycho Brahe: New Stars, Comets, and the "Castle of the Heavens"

*O*n the evening of 11 November 1572, Tycho noticed a strange object in the constellation of Cassiopeia. Suddenly, a brilliant new star blazed out in that constellation which he had not noticed previously, though this may have been caused by cloudy skies over Copenhagen, as astronomers elsewhere would claim to have seen it a few days before. Its light became so dazzling, it was said, that it was brighter than Venus, and could, on moonless nights, even cast a pale shadow under the unpolluted skies of 440 years ago. Naked-eye new stars are extremely rare, and from antiquity to the present day only a handful have been recorded by Western and Chinese astronomers. Modern astronomers call them "supernovae", or giant exploding stars, many light years or billions of miles from the earth. Tycho, like other European observers, termed it "nova stella", or a new star.

THE NEW STAR OF 1572

Rare as such objects were, sixteenth-century science had an explanation, based on the science of Aristotle. As the realm of the stars – the "eighth sphere" in Ptolemaic cosmology – was perfect, eternal, and unchanging, the so-called star must be in the earth's atmosphere rather than a true star in space, in the realm of change and decay, as Aristotle's *Meteorologica* Book 1 ("Things in the Air"), *c.* 350 BC, makes clear. In fact, so the science of 1572 argued, the "star" was probably occasioned by some sort of ignition high above the earth, as foul, stagnant airs rose up, to catch fire from the heat of the sun. So Tycho and various other European astronomers set about measuring how high up it must be.[1]

It should have been a simple matter, especially as the darkening Scandinavian winter, with its long nights and diminishing hours of daylight, made it possible to observe Cassiopeia and the new star as they crossed, or transited, the northern meridian over several months. Cassiopeia is always above the horizon in northern Europe, describing a complete rotation around the Pole Star in the course of a day, moving above the Pole Star in its "upper transit" and below it at its "lower transit", yet always in the sky. It was lucky that the star blazed forth at the onset of winter; in the latitude of Copenhagen, almost 56 degrees north, the southern transit could be observed regularly throughout the dark months in a way that would not have been possible had it shone forth in the long light days of the Scandinavian summer. Winter was ideal.

Tycho's intention was straightforward: to see if the new star displayed a "rocking" motion, or "parallax" displacement, when observed against the normal "fixed" stars of Cassiopeia over more than a hundred transits of the northern meridian when it passes directly below the Pole Star once every twenty-four hours. The moon, for instance, displayed a regular, known, slight "rock", or parallax, when observed against the fixed stars over twelve hours. As the new star, as an assumed atmospheric object, *should* have been much closer than the moon, it should have displayed a much bigger parallax rock – the moon was known to be beyond the earth's atmosphere. (This is what happens when we look at a nearby object with relation to a distant object: when we shift our line of sight, the nearby object *appears* to have moved more than the distant one – a distance-measuring technique used by the land surveyor as well as the astronomer.)

Tycho was puzzled to find, however, that while the moon – the distance of which was known fairly accurately by 1572 – displayed its usual measurable rock, the new star stayed in exactly the same place. Tycho was making those observations with a large, accurately made "sector" measuring arc of just over 5 feet in radius, with very accurately drawn degree scales: one of the most accurate angle-measuring instruments in Europe in 1572.[1]

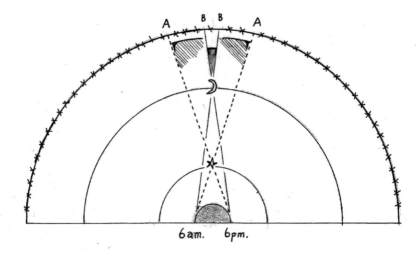

6.1 Irrespective of whether the earth or the sky rotates, the observer's position will move through 180° with relation to the stars, between 6am and 6pm. At the latitude of Copenhagen, this corresponded to a base line of just over 4,000 miles. The moon would have displayed an already-known parallax angle "rock", "B–B", in that time. Yet the New Star, instead of "rocking" through a much bigger angle "A–A" – as it would have done if closer to the earth – displayed no motion at all. This suggested that it was vastly further away than the moon, and in remote stellar space. (Drawing by Allan Chapman.)

After several weeks, the star slowly faded away – as we now know that supernovae do – but whether bright or dim, it *always* stayed in the same position with respect to the stars of Cassiopeia. Precision measurement left no alternative explanation than that the new star was *vastly* more remote than the moon, and that it was in *space*: an impossible conclusion to draw according to Aristotle's writings. Was Aristotle's physics wrong?

Science has always progressed by new, instrument-based evidences challenging older, less accurate observations and the theories built upon them. Tycho's observations of the new star of 1572 would become a *cause célèbre* in that respect, although we must not jump to the conclusion that Tycho was somehow gunning for Aristotle and the scientific classical tradition, for he was not. In spite of his colourful, not to say eccentric, career for a high-born Danish aristocrat, he was an instinctive conservative, as is abundantly evident from what he would say two years later in his Copenhagen lectures and in his published works.

Yet his observations of the new star would not be without ramifications for the Copernican theory. Not only was it very hard to explain the nature of the new star in conventional Aristotelian, atmospheric terms, but it added substantiation to the Copernican suggestion that the stars might be extremely remote. If the earth *were* rotating around the sun, should not the stars in the constellations display some sort of seasonal displacement between December and June, as our terrestrial viewing platform changed in its position in space? Should not zodiac constellations, as shapes, get slightly bigger as we moved towards them, while constellations 180 degrees away on the opposite side of the zodiac get correspondingly smaller as season followed season? For would not moving across the solar system be similar to moving across a large room with doors on opposite walls: move towards one door and it appears to get bigger, while behind you, the opposite door appears to become smaller, due purely to a line-of-sight effect? In space, as earth moves towards Gemini, let us say, should not Sagittarius, facing it across the zodiac, get smaller, and hence change slightly in angular size when measured with an accurate instrument?

Yet no matter how carefully astronomers measured the angles between stars across the seasons, they stayed *exactly* the same. Even Tycho, with his superior instrumentation, found likewise. This observed, empirical fact of geometry left one with two alternative explanations: either the eighth sphere (that supposedly carried the constellations) was relatively close, and stayed the same size because the earth was fixed, or else the stars were so inconceivably remote from the solar system that no matter how much the earth moved in the course of six months, the angular parallax, or rock in position, was so tiny that no instrument on earth in 1572 could detect it.

We might, with the hindsight of four centuries, argue that the new star, with its lack of a parallax *and* its inexplicability in Aristotelian physical terms, was somehow favourable to Copernicanism, by allowing an openness to new ideas and possibilities. In reality, we must step very carefully when trying to see the flowering of "modern" ideas in the sixteenth century. Puzzling as the new star undoubtedly was, the traditional astronomy of Ptolemy and the physics – along with the medical physiology – of Aristotle still offered a far wider gamut of explanations for natural phenomena than did the Copernican alternative.

THE COMET OF 1577

In 1577, a comet suddenly blazed across the northern skies, as a further six comets would do between 1580 and 1596. In Tycho's time, comets, like any unfamiliar or transient lights in the sky, were reckoned to be meteorological or atmospheric in their source. Aristotelian theory posited that comets, just like the one-off new star, came from rising terrestrial vapours or effluvias, catching fire high in the air. Being relatively local, it stood to reason that comets must be portents, or fiery harbingers of doom to the regions over which they flew. Tycho – now commencing the construction of his great observatory of Uraniborg on the island of Hven – began to use even more accurate instruments than he had possessed in 1572 to track the comet's angular movement amongst the starry constellations, and hopefully measure its daily parallax, and hence its distance above the earth. Once again, he found that, even when using the finest instruments ever made in the history of technology and capable of detecting an angle no bigger than a one-thirtieth part of the diameter of the full moon, the 1577 comet displayed no parallax whatsoever – nor would those of 1588 and later. Were comets, then, also in astronomical space, just like the new star?

Comets displayed another puzzling characteristic separate from those of the new star. They moved *directionally* (or in a line) amongst the stars over the weeks of their visibility, while at the same time displaying no daily parallax. How could comets move in the region of the heavens that stood between the orbit of the moon and the eighth sphere of the fixed stars? Observed cometary orbits were *not* circular, as Greek astronomical theory posited was natural for the planets, but displayed an odd variety of curves and even apparent straight lines, as they grew and diminished in brightness, sprouted and then lost their tails. Comets were sometimes fiery and menacing, arrow-straight, or scimitar-curved and murderous-looking as they hung in the sky. Few doubted that they were doom warnings.

But how could a comet presage danger for Nuremberg, Paris, or Lisbon if its lack of daily parallax indicated that it was perhaps nearer to the sun than to the cities over which it appeared to hang? Even more baffling, how could a comet move in a curious, non-circular orbit with relation to the sun without crashing through the concentric spheres of crystal which everyone for the past 2,000 years just *knew* rotated within each other, carrying the seven planets with them?

While once again this was no proof for the Copernican theory, it certainly posed explanatory problems for Ptolemaic cosmology and for Aristotelian physics. As before, Tycho was cautious about jumping to conclusions.

THE "CASTLE OF THE HEAVENS"

Intellectually cautious as Tycho undoubtedly was when it came to the wider interpretation of his astronomical measurements, what is beyond dispute is his visionary realization of the importance of accurate physical data. No one before him had pursued the goal of accuracy of measurement more wholeheartedly, nor perhaps glimpsed the idea – taken up by his disciples in the centuries ahead and which lies at the heart of all modern science – that there was no ultimate ceiling at which high-quality data collection could comfortably rest. As his ground-breaking *Astronomiae Instauratae Mechanica* (1598) spells out, in detailed descriptive text and fine technical illustrations, once an instrument had been developed, its defects should be quantified, and it should itself become a springboard to a yet more advanced, efficient, and accurate design.

Over almost thirty years, Tycho developed whole "families" of precision instruments, each succeeding generation improving upon what had gone before, eliminating errors, and getting as close to geometrical perfection as metal and human hands, eyes, and ingenuity would allow. He would do this at Uraniborg, his "Castle of the Heavens" on the island of Hven (or "Venusia" as he called it) in the narrow straits that separated Copenhagen from the western coast

73

of southern Skania: complete with those local farmers and residents who would *not* come to share the rest of the world's admiration for their new lord and master. It has been estimated that, at its height, Tycho's great astronomical and scientific establishment possessed not just astronomical instruments, but also workshops employing some of the finest craftsmen of the age, a fully equipped alchemical laboratory (always close to his view of natural processes), printing presses, a library, and an elegant residence for him and his family, pupils, and assistants: Europe's first full-scale scientific research institute and cultural centre. Tycho made a careful survey of Hven and published a map in his *Mechanica*, along with drawings of the buildings, while other artists were to execute beautiful paintings depicting the place. Art was combined with science, philosophy, and technology, while underpinning it all was the Philippian theology of mankind and our relation with God's creation.

When I visited the island in 2006, I was surprised to see how small the main stone fabric had been. The buildings had been torn down by the locals soon after Tycho left in 1597, and even when Tycho's seventeenth-century disciples Pierre Daniel Huet (who later became a Roman Catholic bishop) and then Jean Picard visited Hven in 1652 and 1671 respectively,[2] they found little more than rough ground and broken walls where Uraniborg had once stood. In modern times, the site has been carefully excavated by the Swedes – who now own the island – and the remains of the walls of the great house are marked out by a carefully trimmed shrub hedge. The "borg" or great house or "castle" itself was only a 16-metre (53-foot) square, and to judge from the surviving pictures, a cube. The pictures record the presence of great wooden pier platforms extending from the house, upon which large instruments were permanently mounted and protected from the weather by enveloping wooden triangular sheds which could be folded back when the instruments were used – wooden structures long since vanished.

Then there was Stjernborg (Latin *Stellaeburgus*), or Tycho's "underground" observatory. It was not underground in a subterranean sense, although it was partly sunk below ground level in a flat place so that it gave an eye-level line of sight to sky and horizon. Here the observers' bodies would be protected from the searing arctic winds which could blow across the island in winter, making it more comfortable to use than the above-ground instruments. Stjernborg was developed after 1584, as part of Tycho's progressive instrument technology, and in 2006 was being restored. As part of the observatory complex, there is also a man-made excavated "cave" with descending steps. This could have been Tycho's private prison, but more likely it was the ice-house: packed with snow and ice in winter, in the hope that it could act as a fridge in summer and a source of ice for cooling drinks on hot days. Ice-houses were becoming common in great residences by 1600.

MEASURING THE HEAVENS

At Uraniborg, Tycho perfected three broad classes of large observing instruments which helped push astronomical research and accurate data collection further between 1572 and 1597 than it had gone since classical times. It was all down to brilliant engineering design, magnificent craftsmanship, and meticulous error-analysis. One major class of instruments were the quadrants: great quarter-circles, with a radius up to $6^1/3$ feet, designed to measure vertical angles in the sky between the horizon and zenith across 90 degrees. Then there were the sextants, encompassing one-sixth of a circle, or 60 degrees, at a radius of 5 feet, set on adjustable swivel joints, so that a pair of astronomers could measure a lateral or slanting angle between two stars. Between them, the quadrants and sextants enabled Tycho and his assistants to measure star positions in latitude and in longitude: up and down, and sideways. Thirdly, there were the armillary spheres: great brass and steel rings with a diameter of up to 9 feet by which observers could measure celestial objects in latitude and in longitude at the same time.

Why did he need so many different varieties of instrument to measure the same angles in the sky? Simply, so that they could be used to corroborate, or cross-check, each other, and thereby reduce error margin – ways of having more geometrical bites at the same celestial cherry, as it were. Tycho was one of the first scientists in the world to realize that different instruments behaved in slightly

6.2 The principle of the astronomical quadrant. An accurately graduated 90° scale is erected in the vertical, and a moveable sighting arm enables the astronomer to measure the altitude of a star. This was invariably done with the instrument in the meridian plane, or facing due south. The quadrant could then measure altitude (or *Declination*) angles. (Drawing by Allan Chapman.)

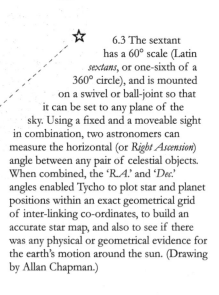

6.3 The sextant has a 60° scale (Latin *sextans*, or one-sixth of a 360° circle), and is mounted on a swivel or ball-joint so that it can be set to any plane of the sky. Using a fixed and a moveable sight in combination, two astronomers can measure the horizontal (or *Right Ascension*) angle between any pair of celestial objects. When combined, the '*R.A.*' and '*Dec.*' angles enabled Tycho to plot star and planet positions within an exact geometrical grid of inter-linking co-ordinates, to build an accurate star map, and also to see if there was any physical or geometrical evidence for the earth's motion around the sun. (Drawing by Allan Chapman.)

different ways, and by quantifying and eliminating their mutual errors, one got closest to the truth. For nearly thirty years, he tested instruments and compared their performance, looking always for consistent results. Only when one had the best possible data about the tiny movements of the sun, moon, planets, and stars could one hope to "reform" astronomy: to make astrology more reliable and calendars less prone to error, and decide once and for all what rotated around what in the heavens.

An incident took place in 1584 which casts light on two interesting things: first, Tycho's opinion of Copernicus; and secondly, how vastly superior Tycho's instruments were to those of Copernicus fifty years previously. The Canons of Ermeland, in Poland, made a gift of one of Copernicus's large wooden instruments to Tycho (an indication in itself of the friendly relations that could exist between Roman Catholic cathedral dignitaries and a Danish Lutheran layman scientist). Tycho was thrilled and honoured to receive such a memento that had once belonged to the "incomparable Copernicus", as he called him. Tycho saw Copernicus as a scientific role model: meticulous, honest, and clever. While he may have been sceptical about Copernicus's model of a heliocentric universe, he admired his working methods and superior tables of data.

Yet bypassing all the geometrical analysis and technical error comparisons, Tycho estimated that his own Uraniborg instruments could measure angles at least seven times more accurately than could those of Copernicus.[3] How could Tycho be a Copernican disciple yet not subscribe to his moving-earth theory? We shall discuss this shortly, but one very significant thing was Tycho's seeing Copernicus as a fellow great north European – indeed *Baltic* region – humanist scholar, just like himself, and perhaps like Luther, Melanchthon, Erasmus, the Flemish artists, and many other "north of the Alps" thinking men. In the next century, the Polish-German Lutheran astronomer Johannes Hevelius would admire both Copernicus and Tycho within that same tradition, as we shall see in Chapter 22.

Uraniborg was much more than an observatory, laboratory, and proto modern science research institute. It was also a scholarly nobleman's court. Tycho always surrounded himself with clever men – many of them young – as his island acted as a magnet to craftsmen, artists, and, over the decades, many scores of students: young men who would now be considered as postgraduate research students. While the more formal craftsmen-assistants would work for contracted wages, the students often came for a few months only, in very much the same way that the young Tycho, like many students of the age, would move between several universities – Wittenberg, Rostock, Leipzig, and such – in quest of a broad postgraduate education.

Their names are still preserved, along with the rest of Tycho's surviving papers, in the Royal Library in Copenhagen, where I was graciously given permission to work on the Great Dane's manuscripts in 2006. The names of these men were first published by Dreyer in 1890,[4] but without doubt the modern scholar who has done more than anyone to bring Tycho's Copenhagen Uraniborg "family" or court into the light of day is John Robert Christianson, from whose *On Tycho's Island*[5] we can trace the names, origins, duration of stay, accomplishments, and in some cases, subsequent careers, of many scores of men.

What a wonderful place Uraniborg must have been, to learn the "new astronomy" in all its ramifications. While Tycho never accepted the idea of the moving earth, on good contemporary scientific grounds, his public admiration for Copernicus as an astronomical mathematician was known far and wide. How many Scandinavians, Poles, Germans, and East Europeans (judging from their names) had been intellectually influenced by Tycho, and in turn, by his esteem for Copernicus? They were all Protestants, most likely, and many no doubt Philippian-influenced Lutherans. Among them were Englishmen and Scotsmen, such as Thomas Moffet, Daniel Rogers, and Duncan Liddel, while the Trinity College Cambridge graduate John Hamon (Hammond), who later became a British physician of eminence, spent over three months on the island in 1587 as part of Tycho's *famuli*, or circle. Even King James VI of Scotland, the future King James I of England, visited Tycho in 1590, as part of his diplomatic visit to seek the hand of his future queen, Anne of Denmark. Uraniborg was *the* place to visit if you were a diplomat or intellectual going to Copenhagen for either business or pleasure.

If you were a student or travelling scholar intending to do "postgraduate" work with Tycho for a few months, you were not only expected to assist with the observatory work, but to possess social skills as well. As a presumed young man of culture, you were expected to be able to recite the Latin and Greek authors, and perhaps sing, play a musical instrument, or discuss literature, philosophy, or theology – to be an accomplished gentleman, in fact. Such skills no doubt came in very handy during the long dark Scandinavian winter evenings, when a snowstorm howled outside, and all thoughts of observing the heavens had to be postponed.

In keeping with a great nobleman's household, Tycho even kept a jester: a man who may have been a midget or dwarf, named Jepp. In its prime, from the late 1570s to the mid-1590s, Uraniborg must have been an exciting place to be – if not a trifle over-crowded.

COPERNICUS, TYCHO, AND THE "EARTH–SUNCENTRIC" UNIVERSE OF 1584

As we have seen, Tycho's admiration for Copernicus was profound. Yet Tycho could not accept the Pole's sun-centred universe as a physical reality, for too many obstructions lay in the way. Why, if the earth spun on its axis once a day, and orbited the sun at a prodigious velocity, were we not all flung off into space? As things stood in 1584, all that Copernicanism had to offer on the plus side was a geometrical explanation for why the planets appeared to move in retrograde, while on the minus side, one had to jettison the whole of classical physics. In spite of the challenges posed to Aristotle's physics by the new star and comets, Copernicanism seemed a bad deal when it came to the number of things that could or could not be explained.

If you dismissed Copernicus's theory as an explanation for reality, it nonetheless gave astronomers a marvellous computing format. For if, when calculating tables, you suspended reality and *pretended* that that earth moved, then the process of calculation became much easier and more exact. The computational attraction of Copernicanism had long been recognized by astronomers and mathematicians even before Tycho had been born. Erasmus

Reinhold's *Prutenic Tables* (1551), for example, were computed in accordance with Copernican planetary theory (notwithstanding some Copernican-retained epicycles), and were much better than those calculated from Ptolemaic theory. If you glossed over the first of the six great books of Copernicus's *De Revolutionibus*, where he presents his heliocentric theory, and concentrated your serious reading on Chapters 2 to 6, which dealt with the motions of the sun, moon, and planets, then you had a marvellous astronomical resource. You could therefore be a disciple of Copernicus without buying into his heliocentric cosmology. This is precisely where Tycho Brahe stood.

TYCHO'S GEO-HELIOCENTRIC COSMOLOGY

In the early 1580s, Tycho began to perfect a theory which had antecedents extending back to classical Greece, as an alternative to those of Ptolemy and Copernicus. This theory, a full description of which he published in *De Mundi Aetherei Recentioribus Phaenomenis* ("On the More Recent Phenomena in the Celestial World"), 1588, combined the best of both, considering where the evidences rested at that date. He tells us in Chapter 8 that he developed this system some four years previously, which would push it back to 1584, or perhaps to 1583.

In Tycho's system which, like Copernicus's, had both classical and sixteenth-century antecedents, the earth stood motionless at the centre of the universe. Around it rotated first the moon, and then, in 365¼ days, the sun. All the other planets, Mercury, Venus, Mars, Jupiter, and Saturn, rotated around the *sun*. But as the sun itself rotated around the earth, all the planets rotated, indirectly, around the earth. It was a brilliant "compromise" theory, combining the best of both systems; yet it was more than a compromise. Tycho believed he was describing physical reality, as did thousands of other astronomers and men of science across Europe and probably at early Harvard College, Massachusetts, and Jesuit missionary scientists to China and Latin America, over the next seventy or eighty years. Its elegance and simplicity remain stunning even today, and if you suspend what was later discovered about the laws of inertia, gravity, the aberration of light, and measured stellar parallaxes after 1838, you can easily see how the Tychonic system could be an answer to an astronomical maiden's prayer. We will return to this in Chapters 11 to 14, when we examine Galileo's increasingly strident Copernicanism after 1610.

Tycho's "earth–suncentric" (or geo-heliocentric) cosmos did provoke some bitter controversy, as the Great Dane's *bête noire* Nicholas Reymers Ursus asserted (perhaps not without some justification) that he had a prior claim to it. Tycho's subsequent obsession with vilifying Reymers Ursus, even after his death in 1600, gives us an interesting insight into the intensity of sixteenth-century priority conflicts, even for men who, like Tycho, humbly and sincerely acknowledged "the help of the most High"[6] in their advancement of scientific knowledge.

DEATH IN PRAGUE

In the late sixteenth century, Prague, in Bohemia, or the then Holy Roman Empire, and now the Czech Republic, was a great seat of learning – especially for astrologers, astronomers, and alchemists, as several emperors had smiled benignly upon the new learning of the Renaissance, and none more than Emperor Rudolph II. Tycho arrived in Prague in June 1599, some two years after leaving Denmark for what turned out to be for ever.

Though Tycho had thrived under King Frederick II of Denmark, who had authorized his lordship of Hven and given him enormous revenues, his royal successor, Christian IV, cooled most noticeably towards the Great Dane. True, Tycho had become internationally famous as a scientist, an ornament of the northern Renaissance, and perhaps the most talked-about Dane in Europe; but his arrogance and rough treatment of so many people had won him numerous enemies. And Renaissance royal courts were hotbeds of plotting, flattery, and intrigue, as Galileo would find in his future involvement with the Medici and Papal Courts. For Renaissance monarchs were generally absolute rulers, and the careers of even courtiers like Tycho all too often resembled the "wheel of fortune", an analogy to which Niccolò Macchiavelli had alluded in *The Prince* (1513).

As things became less favourable at court, Tycho, perhaps strategically, left his island to reside in Copenhagen in the spring of 1597. Then, as he sensed things turning increasingly against him, he left Copenhagen in June, bound for his old Baltic university city of Rostock. He travelled in style, not only with Kristen and the family, but also with his assistants, servants, hangers-on, and tons of baggage. Over the next couple of years, he made something of a Grand Tour of the northern Germanic world, including Wandesbeck and Wittenberg, finally arriving in Prague in June 1599 to receive a warm welcome from Emperor Rudolph II.

Rudolph was to grant him a castle, Benátky, not far from Prague. Here Tycho undertook further observational work, and a great deal of analysis of existing observations, in his attempt to demonstrate that the "heavy" earth sat fixed at the centre of the universe, the sun rotated around it, and the planets in turn rotated around the sun. It was in Prague that Tycho came to employ the famous Czech instrument-maker Jobst Bürgi, commissioning from him angle-measuring instruments, some of which still survive, and an ingenious clock of Bürgi's own devising. And it was in Benátky that Tycho first met the astronomer Johannes Kepler, on 4 February 1600.

Then Tycho died suddenly. On 13 October 1601, he was in Prague to attend a banquet. It is said that he needed to "make water" during the banquet, but court etiquette required that he remain seated with his hosts. By the time protocol enabled him to rise, something serious had happened in his urinary tract, and he found he could not urinate naturally. Why he never ordered a servant to bring him a chamber pot to use discreetly while remaining seated at table is a mystery. But he did not. The now seriously ill Tycho was put to bed and developed a raging fever: a common reaction to infection or medical complications in an age still innocent of germ theory and basic hygiene, especially as it is not impossible that his doctors may have tried to insert an unsterile catheter tube into his bladder in an attempt to drain off the urine. After eleven days of suffering, Tycho died on 24 October 1601.[7]

Over the centuries, a variety of theories have been advanced to attempt to explain Tycho's death, leading to his exhumation for medical examinations in 1901 and 2010. One of the headline-grabbing "explanations" put forth to justify the 2010 exhumation was that Tycho had somehow been poisoned by Kepler to get hold of his master's observations for his own purposes. Conspiracy theorists even argued that Tycho's old friend-turned-enemy, King Christian of Denmark, had him poisoned. Could traces of poison – such as mercury or arsenic – be found in scraps of Tycho's hair, which, as pathologists know, absorbs and retains recent pre-mortem toxins? Metal poisons were indeed found in surviving fragments of the 400-year-old corpse.

Before jumping to the "Tycho was murdered" scenario, we should look at sixteenth-century medical therapeutics. In the wake of Paracelsus and his medico-chemical disciples, it was held that mercury, arsenic, and antimony were powerful fast-acting drugs, provoking such reactions as saliva production and sweating and easing respiration in a way that more traditional herbal drugs did not. By provoking these often drastic physiological responses, it was believed that they would "purge away" the "toxins" which the doctors of 1600 believed caused fever or illness, to make the patient well once more. This was why Paracelsus believed that new medicines and cures must inevitably be the products of the chemical laboratory. And these metallic compounds *could* be toxic in excessive doses.

So we must be on our guard when people assert that modern tests suggest that Tycho might have died by criminal poisoning, as opposed to, perhaps, being the victim of erroneous medical thinking, as I said in a talk on the BBC Radio 4 *Material World* programme in mid-November 2010.

Thus died the "Great Dane", who was at one and the same time a convinced geocentric astronomer, a great admirer of Copernicus, a true star of the northern Renaissance, and one of the larger-than-life legendary figures of scientific history.

CHAPTER 7

Johannes Kepler: Copernican
Astronomer of the Reformation

By the time of Tycho's death in 1601, physical science was approaching a crossroads. The mathematical, computational latter five books, or divisions, of Copernicus's *De Revolutionibus* were acknowledged by Catholic and Protestant mathematical astronomers across Europe. Copernicus's model of a sun-centred universe, as presented in Book 1, was regarded with much caution – not so much on theological grounds that mainstream biblical interpretation could not somehow deal with, but because of a glaring absence of physical evidence in its favour. It was an elegant and ingenious theory and computational device which people were willing to applaud as an intellectual creation, but no more.

While at the time of his death Tycho may have still been locked in a priority dispute for its devising with his recently deceased rival Ursus Reymers – against whom Kepler was required to write a refutation – his geo-heliocentric system simply won hands down. One thing people tend to forget today is the fundamental separation in the classical, medieval, and Renaissance worlds between astronomy and physics. So inextricably related are they in modern scientific thinking that it is all too easy to forget the reasons for their fundamental separation in 1600. In this classical frame of reference, physics was about motion upon or just above the earth: why stones fell, and how the four elements of Aristotle interacted. Physics most definitely did *not* relate to the heavenly bodies: not even the moon, which was known to be the nearest. Celestial bodies, rather, moved under a different divine force or property which suited their changeless perfection, and measurement, number, and geometry were the ways by which to understand them.

The first to seriously explore the possible connectedness of the realms of heavenly and earthly motion, and their mathematical relationship, was Johannes Kepler. Yet even for him, it was by no means an easy thing to grasp. After all, it ran in the face of two millennia of thought about the world and cosmos – not to mention common sense.

EARLY LIFE

Tycho's and Kepler's backgrounds were very different, but to see Kepler as a peasant genius dragged up from the gutter – as some have implied – is an exaggeration. The house in which he was born, on 27 December 1591, in Weil der Stadt, not far from Stuttgart, Germany, is still standing, and is a substantial town house. The Keplers, however, were a family on the way down. His grandfather, Sebald Kepler, had been an innkeeper and had even been sufficiently prosperous in his time to serve as mayor of the town. Johannes's father, Heinrich, however, was a wanderer and a mercenary soldier who, killed in some distant battle or dying of fever, simply never came home.

Johannes seems to have been brought up by his mother, Katharina Guldenmann, who, in spite of her limited circumstances, appears to have recognized his intelligence and pointed him in the direction of school. He recalled in later life how his mother had taken him as a not yet six-year-old to a high location to see the brilliant comet of 1577 – the same comet for which Tycho, on Hven in 1577, was currently trying, unsuccessfully, to measure a parallax. Then, in 1580, the thirteen-year-old Kepler was struck by the red colour of the total lunar eclipse of that year. While Katharina was to be falsely accused of witchcraft in 1617 (her now eminent son playing a major part in securing her acquittal), it is clear that she was a perceptive woman who took the trouble to show little Johannes memorable events in the sky.

A near-fatal dose of smallpox when he was a child damaged Kepler's eyesight – smallpox could even leave lucky survivors blind

– which left him unsuited to any occupation requiring acute vision. Like Tycho, he rapidly mastered Latin, and by the age of eighteen was a student at Tübingen University. It was Kepler's ambition to train for the Lutheran ministry, and under Jacob Heerbrand, an ex-pupil of Melanchthon at Wittenberg, he studied theology; under Michael Maestlin, Professor of Mathematics at Tübingen, he began to explore the world of proportions. One does not have to look far into Kepler's education and later achievement to detect those Philippian influences which also helped to frame Tycho's broader intellectual and spiritual values: Lutheran theology combined with that of Philipp Melanchthon, and Melanchthon's views on God, prophecy, nature, usefulness, and Renaissance humanist classical scholarship.

But his intention of becoming a Lutheran minister was sidetracked in 1594, when he was offered a mathematical teaching post in the Protestant school (later university) of Graz. Although he never did become an ordained minister, his passion for theology never left him, and his deep Christian faith, with its curious admixture of classical philosophy, was to suffuse everything he was to discover and write about astronomy over the next thirty-six years.

THE COSMOLOGICAL MYSTERY, 1596

It may seem odd to modern people to give a major scientific book the title *Mysterium Cosmographicum* ("Cosmological Mystery"). To our ears it carries overtones of magic, occultism, and secrecy. For Kepler, however, it was in no way strange to name his first major book thus; to a late-sixteenth-century academic this is exactly what the cosmos, and the earth's place in it, actually were.

So many writers on the so-called "Scientific Revolution" (a historians' term coined around the mid-twentieth century), especially if they are coming from an anti-religious direction, cherry-pick from the sixteenth- and seventeenth-century discoveries only those which suit their "triumph of science" agenda. In this way of thinking, Kepler in particular is a figure in need of careful editing, so that we see him as a pioneer mathematician and a mathematical physicist of genius, and the man who used Tycho's observations to go beyond the outdated earth-centred system of his Prague master, to blaze the Copernican trail where the supposedly shy and fretful Copernicus would never have dared imagine. All these Keplerian achievements are historically true, except for the timid Copernicus bit. To develop a balanced understanding of Kepler, however, we must weigh in other factors and treat them with respect, and not shy away in embarrassment.

Johannes Kepler was a mystic in the grandest tradition of Renaissance occult philosophy – *not* occult as relating to witches, spells, or fairies (as in Shakespeare's *Macbeth*), as we generally assume today, but in the way *they* used the word. The Latin word "occult" means concealed or hidden, and needing to be brought into understanding. This was the tradition in which the great occult philosophers of the sixteenth century had worked: Paracelsus, Henry Cornelius Agrippa, Giambattista Della Porta, John Dee, and many others – men of the gravest learning, whose works were held in the highest contemporary respect, with antecedents stretching back to classical antiquity.

Was not the entire creation, terrestrial and celestial, interpenetrated by all manner of unknown, "magical" forces, be they magnetism, light, colour, weight, love, good, evil, mathematics, geometry, radiant heat, or the seemingly strange powers of chemical action? This was the reason why, in that world, you could not separate astronomy from astrology, or medicine, psychology, and chemistry from alchemy. It was the job of the philosopher (or what we might call the "scientist") to uncover these secrets, and bring them into the light of human understanding. Among other things, this meant trying to make sense of action at a distance, or how "A" affected "B" in the absence of any tangible connection. Such action could include the invisible way in which a magnet affected a compass needle, or how the motion of the celestial bodies was believed to affect earthly things.

Central to this way of thinking was a belief in God and, by extension, the devil, and the vision of the human race as locked in a struggle between a hopeful salvation in Christ and a potential damnation to hell if our wilfulness, vanity, and abuse of the divine forces of the cosmos led us to be seduced by Satan's blandishments and promises of worldly glory. The message implicit in Christopher Marlowe's reworking of the Dr Faustus legend (1592, published 1604) would have been immediately comprehensible to Johannes Kepler and to men like him. Throughout all of his research, therefore, the philosopher must remain modest, prayerful, charitable, and honest, for God would only reveal his secrets to devout and honest men, and if you used your free will to steal them by guile, or accept them from the hand of Satan, then when your worldly end came, you would be dragged helpless and screaming down into the merciless fires of hell – just like Dr Faustus, in fact.

Without understanding the above circumstances, we miss the historical Kepler, and replace him with the cardboard cut-out of a modern scientist done up in a ruff collar. This way of thinking lies at the heart of *Mysterium Cosmographicum,* and his subsequent writings.

As a man who saw the hand of Providence in all things, including the divine power of numbers, Kepler was aware that the first of his great scientific realizations came to him as a moment of epiphany or revelation. On 19 July 1595, the young professor was lecturing on astronomy before his pupils in Graz. Then it struck him: if you assumed as a working hypothesis that the sun was at the centre of the solar system, you could introduce into the great spaces between the then understood planetary distances the perfect regular solids of classical Greek trigonometry. Taking the internal and external planes and corners of the octahedron, icosahedron, dodecahedron, tetrahedron, and hexahedron (cube), Kepler found that he could create a series of trigonometrical proportions based on current astronomical data that filled the spaces between each planet. For Kepler it was an epiphany (*epiphanos* in the Greek, "appearing"), because he believed that God's logic, in creating the proportionate harmonies of the Copernican solar system, had suddenly been revealed to him, appearing as did the star to the Wise Men, bringing them to the Christ child. Science, mathematics, and divine revelation were intimately bonded together.

Kepler's theory was wrong. But it was wrong for the "right" reasons, given the limited data available in 1595. We now know that not only do the "ancient" planets known in Kepler's day –

Mercury, Venus, Mars, Jupiter, and Saturn – *not* have orbits that correspond to the regular polygons, but that the planets and asteroids discovered following Uranus in 1781 do not correspond to them either. But Kepler was right in so far as he grasped the fact that planetary orbits have elegant geometrical characteristics, and would become capable of extraordinarily accurate prediction by human beings. Kepler's beliefs, and his convinced opinion of the divinely ordained mathematical logic of the cosmos, operated in such a perfect synchronicity as to make them inseparable. This point, made explicit in the *Mysterium*, would be reaffirmed in one way or another in everything else that he wrote.

IMPERIAL MATHEMATICIAN IN PRAGUE

After six years in Graz, with Reformation and Counter-Reformation pressures coming to a head in the town, the Lutheran Kepler's refusal to become a Roman Catholic was becoming problematic. It was at this juncture, in February 1600, that the 29-year-old Kepler journeyed to Benátky Castle, near Prague, to enter the employ of Tycho Brahe, working alongside Franz Tengnagel and Christen Sorenson Longomontanus, having already won for himself a considerable reputation as a mathematical astronomer.

With Tycho, Kepler was given the job of helping to perfect his new master's earth- and sun-centred theory, and in particular, was assigned the task of resolving the precise nature of the orbit of Mars, which of all the sun-rotating planets posed the biggest problems for Tycho. Kepler would have access to Tycho's observations of Mars made over several decades as the raw material for his computation: the most accurate planetary observations ever made.

Things began to move quickly, for when Tycho died suddenly in October 1601, Kepler was invited to succeed him as Imperial Mathematician. From being a mathematics teacher in Graz at the end of 1599, he became Imperial Mathematician to the Holy Roman Catholic Emperor Rudolph II, only two years later. Kepler did not enjoy Tycho's high social status or income, but he was clearly highly regarded by Rudolph and by his royal brother Matthias, for the post demanded not only a first-class astronomical mathematician, but also a discreet individual in whom the emperor could place his full trust regarding future policy decisions that might well be foretold in the stars.

The Imperial Mathematician was also an adviser on all manner of policy affairs, because astrology and horoscope casting were deemed as natural, God-given indicators by which a monarch, like any other individual, could negotiate his way through life. All that astrology needed to make it more reliable was more accurate data, and this is where Tycho's observations also had a use, which we tend not to mention today.

While still fresh in office, in 1604, Kepler would publish the first of a series of groundbreaking books that would profoundly influence future physical science. The first of these was his *Astronomiae Pars Optica* ("The Optical Part of Astronomy"), in which he not only launches into the fruits of a pioneering set of research into optics, lenses, pinhole cameras, and the reflection and refraction of light, but also into the physiology of perception: how humans actually see. There is a full account of the lens, retina, optic nerve, and similar structures of the eye. How do the physiological structures of the eye form an image? How do we see things the "right way up", whereas the lens casts an upside-down reversed image of the outside world upon the retina? This research was by no means unique to Kepler in 1604, for the Arab scientist Ibn al-Haytham (Alhazen) had dissected the eyes of oxen in Cairo 600 years before, while many medieval and Renaissance Europeans such as Robert Grosseteste, Roger Bacon, Erazmus Witelo, and Theodoric of Freiburg had wrestled with the geometry of light and how we perceive it. But Kepler places these physiological and other optical discoveries in the wider context of how lenses work in scientific practice. He even discusses, as would René Descartes thirty years later, exactly how a retinal image, conveyed into the brain via the optic nerve, somehow activates the soul, to enable us to consciously *see*: a question by no means fully answered even by modern science.

Central to the whole of Kepler's thinking was geometrical proportion, and in the *Astronomiae Pars Optica* he discusses the way in which a light appears progressively dimmer the further away we are from it. He suggests that it appears dimmer in an *inverse proportion* to our distance from the light source: in other words, there is a precise mathematical relationship between brightness and distance for any given light source, be it a candle or a star. He would soon be extending this conceptual geometry of inverse proportionate relationships to the motions of the planets around the sun, for it was to lie at the heart of those "three laws of planetary motion" which after 1620 would gradually begin to revolutionize not only astronomical but the whole of physical thinking.

In 1604, another new star – or supernova – blazed out, this time in the constellation of Ophiucus: a mere three decades since Tycho's star of 1572. As with previous new stars, such as those of AD 390, 945, 1264, and 1472[1] (and Chinese astronomers had seen a supernova in Cancer the Crab in 1054), one could hardly blame the astrologers for thinking something big was afoot, and that the heavens were giving us prior warning. Like Tycho's 1572 star, that of 1604 also displayed no discernible parallax when careful angular measurements were made, thereby placing it, geometrically speaking, amongst the "immutable" fixed stars, and casting further doubt upon Aristotle's ideas of the changeless universe.

Astrologers think in terms of numerical cycles, as do astronomers. Like a great clock, the heavens measure out epochs of time through the long- and short-term revolutions of the heavenly bodies. Leading directly from their way of thinking was the "Grand Conjunction" of Jupiter, Saturn, and Mercury, which took place just a few days before Christmas 1603. A few months later, in October 1604, the new star itself blazed out independently. Surely, all this must be a momentous portent of things to come, heralding as it did the epoch which the astrologers called the "Fiery Trigon".

Such a Grand Conjunction can be dramatic, for the planets can come so close together that they appear to form one intensely brilliant light in the sky. Kepler had read in Jewish rabbinic sources that when the messiah was due to come, portents would be seen in that part of the zodiac associated with the Hebrews, which happened to be Pisces. Lover of mathematical calculation that he was, Kepler computed that there would also have been a truly Grand Conjunction around 7 BC. Could this have been the star of Bethlehem which Matthew's Gospel tells us had appeared in the East (more accurately translated as the pre-dawn eastern sky), and which summoned the Magi to undertake their long journey to adore the Christ child – the first *Epiphany*, no less?

We now know that Kepler had been right about the 7 BC conjunction, and modern astronomers with their superior astronomical data and computation techniques, further substantiated by late Babylonian astronomical records unknown to Kepler, can confirm that there had been a truly spectacular planetary massing in the House of the Hebrews in midwinter 7 BC.

OF ELLIPSES

During the eighteen months or so that Kepler had worked for Tycho, the Great Dane had set him to work on the complex and often infuriating observations of Mars: to make Tycho's superlative observations of that planet, measured and recorded against the zodiac stars over nearly thirty years, accord with his geo-heliocentric theory. No matter how one adjusted the theoretical model, with its eccentric circles or epicycles, the observations could not be made to square with Tycho's theory. There were sometimes errors of up to 8 arc minutes (an angle corresponding to a quarter of the diameter of the full moon) between Mars's predicted and observed places.

Such a small angle would not have mattered to the late Copernicus, or almost any other astronomer in Europe in 1600, for it would have fallen comfortably within the acceptable plus or minus error of contemporary instruments. (When Tycho analysed one of Copernicus's large instruments given to him by Johannes Hannow, one of the canons of Ermeland Cathedral around 1584, he discovered an error of almost 10 arc minutes, or one-third of the moon's diameter, as we saw in Chapter 6.) Kepler knew that Tycho's superbly engineered instruments were accurate to 1 or maybe 2 arc minutes at most, and that 8 arc minutes could not be conveniently ascribed to inevitable technological error. So the 8 arc minutes must be *real*, and must be reflected in the heavens themselves.

Following from the death of the Great Dane, with Kepler having access to his observations, and not being obliged to find a way of justifying his old boss's geo-heliocentric theory, he began to speculate mathematically, and reinterpret Tycho's observations from a Copernican, sun-centred, perspective. To the deeply theologically minded Kepler, the Copernican system possessed a spiritual compatibility with the Judaeo-Christian message, as well as with pagan Pythagoras's sacred geometry, for could not one see the sun, the source of heat, light, and life, as analogical to God the Father, about whom creation turned?

At the very beginning of the seventeenth century, Kepler began to consider possibilities that would change 2,000 years of Greek astronomical theory. Within the context of Copernican theory, could not one explain the odd orbital behaviour of Mars, and accommodate the 8-arc-minute "eccentricity", by abandoning the classical Greek axiom that the planets could only rotate in circles or compounds of circles, and instead postulate that they might move in *ellipses*? In geometry, as described in his *c.* 200 BC treatise on the curved shapes produced by making straight slices through a cone, the Greek mathematician Apollonius realized that an ellipse is an enclosed oval curve contained within a cone. It is enclosed in the same way that a circle is enclosed, in so far as the beautifully curved moving line describing an ellipse will eventually meet itself to produce a continuing perfect curve. Unlike a circle, however, the ellipse does not have a single centre from which all parts of the surrounding line stand at exactly the same distance. Instead, the ellipse has two focus points around which the surrounding curved line is drawn, thereby producing a perfect oval.

The beautiful thing which Kepler found was that he could elegantly accommodate Mars's apparent 8-arc-minute irregularity if he interpreted its orbit as a single, flowing ellipse. There was no need for eccentric circles, epicycles, or any other of the mathematical devices of Ptolemaic astronomy which not only Tycho but even Copernicus had used in their different attempts to make the observed heavens conform with *a priori* geometrical rules. Kepler may have come up with the idea of an elliptical orbit as early as 1603 or 1605, though it would not be until 1609, in his *Astronomia Nova* ("New Astronomy"), that he would publish it. And his caution about publishing, just like Copernicus's almost a century before, came not from any fear of ecclesiastical persecution, but from the fact that he, like Copernicus, was a meticulous and rigorous scientist who wanted to feel sure of his evidential ground before he reinterpreted Greek astronomy. I emphasize *reinterpreted*, and not "challenged" or "overthrew", for Kepler was no more of a revolutionary by temperament than Copernicus had been, and to impose an iconoclastic radical agenda upon him, as some twentieth-century scholars have tried to do, is frankly being unhistorical.

If the planets rotated around the sun in elliptical orbits, then another problem was unavoidable: if, for example, the traditional heavenly spheres did exist, and were *spheres*, then how could Mars move in an ellipse? The idea that the spheres might be egg-shaped, nestling within one another, seemed one leap of imagination too far. So did the heavenly spheres not exist as *real*, or even as viable conceptual objects? And if not, and if space happened to be an empty place, then what made all the planets rotate around the sun with such exquisite, predictable exactitude? This was a real problem, forcing into consideration, no matter how tentatively, the possibility of there being physical *forces* acting in space that might even have some kind of parallel with the "force" or "impulse" that sent a cannon ball flying across the earth's surface, or caused a brick to descend from a tower – another example of "action at a distance" in fact.

CHAPTER 8

Johannes Kepler:
Magnets, Invisible Forces, and
Planetary Laws

*S*ince the days of classical Greece, everyone had known that physics, or impelled motion, was unique to the earth, and that astronomical bodies moved simply because such motion was innate in their perfect natures and perfect spherical geometry. It was at this juncture that Kepler began to cast around for possible explanatory devices.

One such device – and suggested in *Astronomia Nova* as nothing more than an analogical conceptual tool – was magnetism.

A MAGNETIC COSMOS?

Although magnetism had been known, studied, and experimented with in Europe since the Frenchman Petrus Peregrinus had conducted and announced his pioneering experiments in 1269, it was the English physician Dr William Gilbert's *De Magnete, Magneticisque Corporibus, et de Magno Magnete Tellure* ("On the Magnet, Magnetic Bodies, and the Great Magnet, the Earth") of 1600 which established some crucial principles for the future science of geomagnetism. For Gilbert (a Cambridge don who had also been Queen Elizabeth I's doctor) had been the first researcher to systematically experiment with spherical magnets. These magnets were found to have northern and southern poles, just like the earth – hence Gilbert's use of the Latin word *terrella*, or "little earth", to describe them. When tested with suspended sensitized needles, it was found that the magnetic "force" moved in great curved geometrical arches between the poles, although these forces were totally invisible to the eye and could only be traced with suspended needles. The force of attraction of the magnet diminished with distance, when measured by the terrella's ability to deflect a magnetized compass needle – diminished in a way that was not without a parallel to the way in which visible light dimmed with distance.

So, could the planets rotate around the sun because they were part of some sort of turning magnetic flux or tide coming from the sun which, as it weakened with distance, exerted more force on Mercury than it did on Saturn, thereby making one planet move rapidly and another very slowly against the zodiac stars? In some ways this magnetic analogy acquired more weight after 1611, when Galileo and Johannes Fabricius (son of Kepler's friend David Fabricius), and perhaps Thomas Harriot in England and others independently discovered, with the newly invented telescope, that not only did the supposedly unblemished sun have *maculae*, or spots, on its surface, but that these spots clearly demonstrated that the sun, thought to be stable, rotated on its axis in about twenty-eight days. What is more, the spots showed that the sun rotated in the *same* direction as that in which the orbiting planets moved. Was there an invisible and intangible magnetic tide swirling out from the sun to which the planets responded in a way similar to that in which compass needles responded to Gilbert's terrella?

ANCIENT TRUTHS QUESTIONED

What could this cosmic magnetic force actually be? Invisible, intangible, undetectable by any agency other than, perhaps, a sensitive magnetic instrument, this force was truly occult, hidden, or unknown, and awaiting epiphany, or to be come upon. How did it relate to light, or weight, or the intangible agencies whereby the planets beamed their celestial forces to affect the earth's weather, the tides, or the four humours of the human body (blood, black bile, yellow bile, and phlegm) – those humours which gave us our individual temperaments and inclined us to health or sickness?

It is probably not easy for a twenty-first-century person, accustomed as we are to endless new discoveries in science, to realize how intellectually unsettling the new facts which were coming to light at this time actually were. How could the short-lived new stars of 1572 and 1604, with their lack of any discernible parallax, really be in the eternal heavens, and at inconceivable distances? Likewise, there were questions surrounding the comets, whose observed and measured motions were clearly taking them between, or through, the crystalline spheres. Did the crystalline spheres not exist after all? And was space a stunning, empty void held together with strange, *occult*, invisible forces?

Add to that other scientific discoveries that had been made over the preceding century: the discovery of the American continent and Pacific Ocean, totally unknown to the ancients. In medicine there had been new discoveries in the anatomy of the heart, veins, and arteries that, while puzzling in 1600, would lead to William Harvey's 1628 discovery that the blood circulates around the body under the mechanical action of the heart. Following 1609, with Thomas Harriot, Galileo, and a host of other new telescopic astronomers, was the discovery that the moon was cratered, and that Jupiter was a large sphere with four satellites rotating around it like a miniature solar system. Then what about the stars? Could it be possible that they might even recede into infinity, as countless millions of tiny dots of light, invisible to the naked eye, had now become visible through the telescope? We will return to the telescope in Chapter 11 and thereafter.

Contrary to what we are often led to believe by many writers, these discoveries were not condemned because they contradicted religious belief. Comb the Bible as thoroughly as you like, and you will find no references to crystalline spheres, comets being in the atmosphere, the nature of the earth's surface 1,000 miles beyond the Middle East, exactly how many stars there are in the sky, or how the human body works physiologically. No: what these discoveries challenged was not Scripture but Greek science. They opened up the potentially frightening possibility that if Greek science was wrong, or limited, as opposed to being all-embracing, then how would we explain nature, the cosmos, and mankind's place within it?

97

By casting doubts on the scope of classical science, they also challenged the academic establishment, irrespective of religious allegiance, for learned professors across Europe were becoming aware that the very foundations of the logical systems upon which their astronomy, physics, and physiology were based were now under suspicion. European science was profoundly Aristotelian in 1600, and now, under the regular blows of a succession of new discoveries, the certainties of Aristotle – "The Philosopher" – were being tried and found wanting. Furthermore, apart from the prestige of the long-dead Aristotle, no professor in Bologna, Tübingen, or Paris was likely to welcome the knocking away of the intellectual support structures upon which his career and academic prestige had been built.

KEPLER'S LAWS OF MOTION

Returning to his wrestling with Mars, in the light of a perhaps crystalline-sphere-free, magnetic void of a universe, Kepler set about the hard slog of calculation, trying to make Tycho's observations fit a variety of theoretical curves, and finally hit upon the beauty of the ellipse. This appears to have taken place between 1602 and 1606, while he was working as Rudolph's Imperial Mathematician. In addition to the ellipse shape, his calculations brought him to a further conclusion: as Mars rotates around the sun in its elliptical orbit, its speed at any one time relates directly to its distance from the sun, faster when near the sun, and slower when further away, in a constantly changing yet precise calculable sequence. This would become immortalized as Kepler's first two (of three) Laws of Planetary Motion. They could be expressed as:

(1) Mars rotates around the sun in an ellipse. The sun occupies *one* of the two geometrical focal points of the ellipse. The other focal point is empty.

(2) As Mars moves, it goes faster when near the sun than when at the distant end of its elliptical orbit. Yet, for any specified period of time, let us say a month, the line joining Mars to the sun (the radius line) sweeps out equal areas of space.

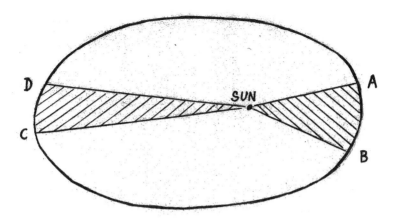

8.1 Kepler's Second Law. The earth moves around the sun in an elliptical orbit, the sun being at one of the two, offset, *foci* of the ellipse, the other *focus* being empty. The segments "A–B" and "C–D" represent equal numbers of days of the year. Yet the areas of flat space swept out over these two equal periods remain exactly the same, despite changes in the sun's motion across the seasons, as wide and narrow "wedges" of space are traversed. For the sake of geometrical clarity, the ellipticity of Mars's orbit is greatly exaggerated in the drawing; in reality the planetary orbits are very close to – but not quite – circles. (Drawing by Allan Chapman.)

What sheer geometrical elegance we find here, for no matter what force drove Mars in its orbit, the perfect shapes and proportions which it described in space were of breathtaking beauty, and only confirmed Kepler's belief that the divine mind was behind it all. And science, let us never forget, is just as much about *beauty* as is art. For what invariably gives a scientific theory its confirmatory ring of truth is its elegance and symmetry, and a deep sense of intellectual satisfaction, from Kepler's Laws of Motion to Crick and Watson's 1950s discovery of the DNA double helix and the genome.

In this respect, therefore, Kepler's work became, in hindsight, far more than just a solution to an astronomical problem: it became a milestone in human thought and creativity, producing new and wonderful insights. His first two Laws of Planetary Motion, and a mathematical solution to the orbit of Mars, along with much else not discussed in the above section, he eventually published in *Astronomia Nova*, 1609.

ASTRONOMY, SNOWFLAKES, AND SYMMETRY

Yet, one might reasonably ask, what has all this astronomy to do with snowflakes? The answer is simple: it lies in the geometrical beauty and wonder inherent in both.

In 1611 Kepler presented a scholarly New Year's gift to his friend and patron Baron von Wackhenfels, a little book entitled *De Nive Sexangula* ("On the Six-Cornered Snowflake"). This was the first serious investigation – just before the invention of the microscope – of the perfect hexagonal symmetry formed by frozen water: a study which Robert Hooke, a great admirer of Kepler, would take further in his *Micrographia* (1665). Apart from any consideration as to why water always froze into six perfect 60-degree structures with 60-degree substructures, the snowflake set Kepler upon a mathematical and physical speculation that would have profound future implications for science. Could the snow crystals be made up of vast numbers of inconceivably tiny primary units, or spherical atoms? How, mathematically speaking, could one arrange, or pack, these atoms with their points of contact with adjacent atoms, and empty interstices between? It was the beginning of the mathematics of infinitesimals.

This also opened up other lines of thinking, such as how did the perfect geometry of the heavens relate to what one might see as the perfect geometry of crystal structures, at a time when Aristotelian science drew a very clear line between the perfect heavens and the corrupt earth? Yet here in a humble snowflake was a mathematical harmony no less stunning in its elegance than the laws of planetary motion. By extension, could matter perhaps be made of little atoms locked together in mathematical harmony, rather than the earth, air, water, and fire elements of Aristotle? Atoms had scarcely figured in Western thought after Lucretius's potentially atheistical *De Rerum Natura* ("On the Nature of Things"), 60 BC, but Kepler, then Robert Boyle in the 1650s, would reintroduce them in a Christian context. "And the rest", as the saying goes, "is history."

MARRIAGE, LINZ, AND TELESCOPES

In 1597, and still in Graz, the 26-year-old Kepler had married the 25-year-old Barbara Müller: an already twice-widowed lady, with considerable property to her name. It does not seem to have been an especially happy marriage, although they did have five children, two of whom survived. Barbara died of a fever – perhaps the most common cause of death before the late nineteenth century – and in October 1613 the now 42-year-old Kepler remarried. His new wife was the 24-year-old Susanna Reuttinger, and it was clearly a much happier marriage than his first, Susanna becoming a loving stepmother for Barbara's surviving children, and she herself having six more, three of whom survived to adulthood. By this time, Kepler had moved to Linz, in Austria. Matthias had succeeded his brother Rudolph to become emperor in 1613, and with the changing currents and allegiances of Reformation and Counter-Reformation Europe, Lutheran Kepler had been permitted by Matthias to live in Linz.

Before then, though, Kepler had been able to examine an early telescope, and was clearly fascinated by the universe which it revealed. Following a correspondence with Galileo, Kepler gave glowing publicity to Galileo's discoveries, formally announced in the Italian's thought-changing little book *Sidereus Nuncius* ("The Starry Messenger"), published in Venice in March 1610, and rapidly doing the rounds of Europe. (In June 1610, Thomas Harriot in London, for example, was enthusing about Galileo's telescopic discoveries to his friend Sir William Lower at Trefenti, South Wales, having most likely heard of them from Kepler.) It was in this book, as we shall see in Chapter 11, that Galileo announced his first telescopic discoveries. Kepler, already a convinced Copernican, was delighted, and even wrote a little treatise expressing his support for Galileo, *Dissertatio cum Nuncio Sidereo* ("Discussion with the Starry Messenger"), 1610.

What is important to remember is that in 1611 Kepler was probably the leading exponent of mathematical optics in Europe, and he set about a careful examination of the Dutch telescope, commonly called "Galilean", for Galileo's instrument had the same optical configuration as the Dutch, and was also described in *Sidereus*

Nuncius. From the geometry of the lenses, Kepler described the process whereby the two lenses – the distant, convex object glass and the concave eye lens – form a visual image. He then went on to improve the Galilean design by suggesting that the eye lens, instead of being concave, should be convex, like the object lens. This gives a brighter, clearer image, and while it is upside down and hence not suitable for land use, it is better for astronomy, where an upside-down image does not matter. Although taking some years to catch on for general astronomical use, the convex "Keplerian" eyepiece

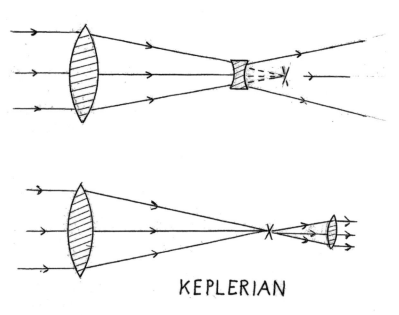

KEPLERIAN

8.2 Galilean and Keplerian telescopes. In Galileo's (or more correctly, Hans Lippershey's) arrangement, a convex "object glass" brings the light to a focal point. A second, concave, "eyepiece" lens is placed *before* the point of focus, which then directs a diverging cone of light into the observer's eye. With Kepler's telescope, however, the concave eyepiece is replaced by another *convex* lens, of shorter focal length and greater magnifying power than the object glass. This second lens is so adjusted that its own focus, and that of the object glass, coincide on a single axis. This gives a bigger, brighter image than that of the Lippershey–Galileo telescope. (Drawing by Allan Chapman.)

would become standard for observing the heavens. All this was presented in his short treatise *Dioptrice* ("Optical Studies"), 1611.

It was also around 1610 that Kepler composed a treatise that was circulated in manuscript to interested parties, though it would not be published until 1634, four years after his death. This was his *Somnium* ("Dream"). In some ways, this was the foundation text of science fiction, although many have detected strong autobiographical themes. It was the story of a young Icelander, Duracotus, who leaves home and learns about the latest astronomy. On his return home, the Icelander's mother, who conveniently has demonic acquaintances, arranges for her son to be conveyed to the moon, by passing up the shadow of a solar eclipse, to see the universe for himself. Needless to say, the moon is inhabited, and after his meeting with various lunar dignitaries, the obliging demons bring him safely home. But what is important about *Somnium* is not that it is simply a fantasy tale, but that Kepler has constructed it within the best scientific knowledge available in 1610. We shall encounter *Somnium* again in Chapter 24, when, in the 1640s, John Wilkins in Oxford, an overt admirer of Copernicus, Kepler, and Galileo, published his ideas on how humans might fly to the moon by a mechanical "Flying Chariot", or space vehicle.

KEPLER THE COPERNICAN ADVOCATE

In the *Astronomia Nova* Kepler had presented his first two Laws of Planetary Motion – as applied to Mars – regarding elliptical orbits and "equal areas". In the introduction, as we saw above, he began to inquire into what physical forces could have been at work to produce such orbits, and considered a possible William Gilbert solar-magnetic type force. Gilbert's *De Magnete*, Book VI, had also contained speculation about other possible sorts of attraction: something truly "occult" in so far as it was hidden, but not mystical, being a physical attraction. This really was sailing in an uncharted sea of possible forces in 1600, and Kepler was fascinated by these ideas. Kepler's debt to Gilbert was enormous when it comes to considering the invisible, intangible, yet exact forces that seemed to bind the universe together.

This would lead Kepler towards an early notion of gravitation, or the existence of some kind of intangible physical force acting between bodies; and while he had no idea what this force might be, or could be caused by, he fully recognized that it had nothing to do with the earth being at the centre of creation. It seemed, rather, to act between particular objects, such as the sun, the earth, and the planets, or between the earth, the oceans, and the moon (thus producing the tides). What it constituted was a speculative foundation for what, by the time of Hooke, and then Newton, would be a principle of universal gravitation. Newton's 1687 Laws of Universal Gravitation had their first glimmerings over eighty years before in Gilbert and Kepler, as Kepler in particular searched for a possible physical agent that might operate between bodies and cause them not only to move, but to do so in precise elliptical orbits and at clearly measurable and predictably changing velocities.

These ideas came to their maturity in Kepler's thinking in two major works, of which one in particular was to exert a profound effect on physical theory over the next sixty years. This was his magisterial *Epitome Astronomiae Copernicanae* ("Epitome of Copernican Astronomy"), the seven books of which were published in three instalments between 1617 and 1621. Building on the broad theoretical foundations laid down in *Astronomia Nova*, Kepler in the *Epitome* proceeds to construct a whole Copernican cosmology, and also begins to inquire into its broader physical implications. In Book I, in 1617, he starts to look at the spherical earth and its place in the solar system. He then discusses the sun as a star which only outshines everything else in the sky because it is, cosmologically speaking, so close at hand. But if the stars are distant suns, then how far away can they be? Could the starry realm even be infinite? This idea was already familiar by 1617, and had been both articulated and even illustrated in 1576 by the Englishman Thomas Digges, whom we shall meet again in Chapter 18. Kepler was not happy with the idea of cosmological infinity, partly on religious grounds.

Much of the *Epitome* is concerned with motion, and it is clear that Kepler has long since left Aristotelian ideas behind. He does not know what causes motion, in purely physical terms, but of one thing he is convinced: motion is a creation of the divine mind, and seems to be manifested through some sort of attraction between bodies. He also proceeds in accordance with the precept that "nature works by the shortest route" – the "razor", popularly ascribed to William Ockham of Oxford in the fourteenth century – whereby the simplest and most elegant solution to a philosophical problem was most likely to be the true solution. By 1620, Copernicanism was scoring a growing number of plausibility points, based on recent discoveries, although the idea that it was more reasonable to see the rotating sky as an effect of a rotating earth went back centuries before Copernicus. Bishop Nicole de Oresme, Jean Buridan and others had argued in the fourteenth century that it was simpler for God to have caused the earth to spin, and the entire cosmos to remain fixed, than the other way round. One should not leap to the conclusion that these men were proto-Copernicans: simply, they were pursuing an argument within the medieval dialectical philosophical tradition, and had no doubt that God *had* actually made a cosmologically central earth. They were exploring ideas of "impetus", relative motion, rotation, possible cosmological infinity, and even life on other worlds, of which Copernicus, Kepler and many of their Renaissance contemporaries were perfectly aware, for medieval European thought in Paris, Oxford, and Bologna in particular had been intensely adventurous philosophically and theologically.

Clear resonances of this thinking run through Kepler's writings, for in his thought astronomy, philosophy, and theology formed such an intellectual unity as to be inseparable. What is so fascinating in Kepler's thought is the way in which he can effortlessly combine hard, meticulously thought-out and calculated scientific fact with a sense of theological transcendence. In the *Epitome*, for instance, he works out, in the best mathematical terms that were available by 1620, the whole theory of elliptical orbits, and applies them to all solar-system bodies, but in particular detail to Mercury, Venus, and, of course, Mars. He also presents, as part of a wider argument, an expression of what would become his third Law of Planetary Motion, which he would publish more completely in *Harmonices Mundi* ("The Harmony of the World"), 1619:

(3) The square of the periodic times are to each other as the cubes of their mean distances.

Putting it more simply, there is always a proportionate relationship between a planet's average orbital speed and the length of its radius to the sun and the length of its orbit in miles – not an easy concept to wrestle with, I admit, especially if one has never been naturally at home with geometry and mathematics. The important thing about Kepler's work, however, in his own and down the ensuing ages, is that whatever intangible force operated across the vast and seemingly empty tracts of space *always* followed exact and elegant laws, from which it never deviated. It weakened proportionately with distance, and, wonder of wonders, had now been *revealed* to humanity. For Kepler, science was not simply about discovering how nature worked; it was also about penetrating the mind of the Creator, to "think God's thoughts after Him", as it has been put.

THE MUSIC OF THE SPHERES

This same style of thinking also ran through *Harmonices Mundi*, where he set out to understand the cosmic harmonies. Here we meet an exploration of ideas supposedly dating back to Pythagoras and later pursued by the Christian priest-philosophers of twelfth-century Chartres Cathedral in France. Kepler saw it having a direct continuing bearing on the science of 1620: namely the "Music of the Spheres".

To a civilization that saw number, prophecy, and hidden, occult secrets as divine significators that the mind of man might uncover and comprehend, the eight celestial spheres – moon, Mercury, Venus, sun, Mars, Jupiter, Saturn, and the stars – with their increasing radii and circumferences, along with the eight notes of the musical scale, seemed a parallelism too grand to be a mere coincidence. Not only had God manifested his glory in the heavens, but human minds and *souls* also responded profoundly to harmony. Music theorists from Pythagoras and Plato onwards had discussed how different sequences of notes and chords could arouse a diverse range of passions in the human breast – and in the pagan Greek

Orpheus myth, Orpheus the magical musician, with his voice and harp, had been able to charm animals, the gods, and even the dead.

Number and music sequences were also recognized by the Christian church, and when you added the *ninth* planetary sphere of classical astronomy, the so-called *primum mobile*, or "prime mover" or regulator beyond the stellar sphere, you had the perfect number, produced by multiplying the Holy Trinity by itself. The Music of the Spheres, therefore, was not simply about the heavens forming a perfect *orchestra* of motion and mystical sound, but went much further, to join with mathematics, psychology, and aesthetics to enable humans to glimpse the very mind of God in creation. This was the tradition on which Johannes Kepler drew, and upon which he would elaborate, especially in the *Harmonices Mundi*.

It is especially unfortunate that so many modern history of astronomy writers, when discussing the *Harmonices*, head straight for the book's elegantly formulated third Law of Planetary Motion, which would become the focus of attention for future scientists, while dismissing the rest as mythical nonsense. When we do this, we fail to engage with the real Kepler, and instead turn him into some sort of modern genius "ahead of his time". Yet the *Harmonices* presents a world that would have made sense to Tycho and Copernicus, and which even Sir Isaac Newton, sixty years into the future, would have found in no way alien.

In *Harmonices* Kepler returns to many of the points laid out in *Mysterium* in 1595. Can one, for example, use superior 1619 data to make a better match for the regular solids and the planetary orbits? But of particularly inspired ingenuity was Kepler's expression of the then understood planetary orbital periods and eccentricities as intervals on the five-line musical stave, which he puts forth in *Harmonices* Book IV. Here, dull and distant Saturn – the planet furthest out in the solar system as it was understood in 1619 – moves slowly over three notes deep in the bass clef, whereas fast-moving Mercury, the planet closest to the sun, rapidly glissandos across ten notes of the treble scale.

Some years ago, I transcribed the planetary "notes" from the printed music staves of the *Harmonices*, and an organist friend in Oxford first played them in sequence, and then tried to put them together to produce an orchestrated "Music of the Spheres". What a haunting, strange, and ghostly body of sound emerged, especially once the right combination of stops had been chosen. There was Saturn, breathing – almost groaning – slowly and deeply on the 16-foot Bourdon organ pedal pipes, while Mercury raced away, high and distant-sounding, on the 2-foot flute stops.

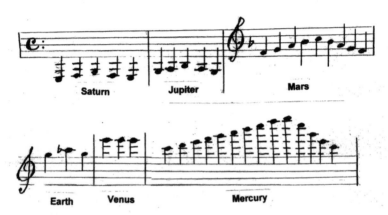

8.3 Kepler's "Musick of the Spheres", from *Harmonices Mundi*, Book V, transcribed into modern musical notation. (Allan Chapman.)

KEPLER'S TABLES IN MEMORY OF THE EMPEROR RUDOLPH

Kepler's true magnum opus was the magisterial *Tabulae Rudolphinae* ("Rudolphine Tables"), 1627, dedicated to his – and Tycho's – now deceased patron, the Holy Roman Emperor Rudolph II. The achievement of the Tabulae stood on the universally acknowledged superior observations of Tycho Brahe, completed over thirty years previously, but refined, re-computed, and presented as – for that date – a definitive set of astronomical tables, along with all their ancillary mathematical techniques for usage. Since time immemorial, let us not forget, astronomers had not simply looked at the heavenly bodies, so much as measured their angular positions with relation to each other and to the sky's coordinates, such as the poles and the celestial equator. As we shall see in the following chapters, Galileo had just brought about a new approach to astronomy, of examining the surfaces of the heavenly bodies with the newly invented telescope. In 1627, however, that new approach was still in its infancy, and very limited in its scope.

It would, therefore, be the production of superior astronomical tables of angular positions and calculation techniques that Kepler, and the vast majority of his scientific contemporaries, still saw as the road down which the "reform of astronomy" must proceed. And this reform would hopefully lead to the demonstration of the *correct* scheme of the universe: be it Ptolemaic, Copernican, Tychonic, eccentric circular, or elliptical orbit based. And this in turn would lead to the "perfecting" of astronomy, the calendar, and astrology.

This scheme, which Kepler saw coming to fruition in the *Tabulae*, was placed firmly within its perceived historical context in the fine-art allegorical frontispiece to his masterpiece. Here we have astronomical history depicted as a circular classical *tholos*, or temple. Each of its ten pillars is supposed to represent an improvement on its predecessor, starting from a rough log pillar, proceeding to crude stone blocks, then brick columns in ascending order of elegance. Copernicus has a fine Doric column, bearing a cross, to show the reformed astronomy's Christian provenance, and the architectural metaphor becomes complete with an ornate Corinthian column – the highest expression of classical architectural elegance – upon which the gorgeously robed Tycho leans, pointing above. For the unequivocal message is "with Tycho we have finally arrived". Symbolism – visual, architectural, literary, and musical – was such a deeply entrenched aspect of their culture that any educated person in 1627, looking at the frontispiece, would be able to interpret it all at a glance: how paganism had been superseded by the Arabs, then perfected by the Christians, and how the "ancients" had been fundamentally improved upon and perfected by the moderns. Without appreciating these fundamental aspects of European Renaissance civilization, we fail to do justice to Johannes Kepler.

CATHOLICS, PROTESTANTS, COPERNICANS, AND THE THIRTY YEARS WAR

Kepler lived his life against a backdrop of one of the most disturbed periods of European history, the Reformation and Counter-Reformation. More than merely the religious, there were also the political and military instabilities of the age, especially the circumstances leading up to what historians have termed the "Thirty Years War", which raged across northern Europe between 1618 and 1648. Nowhere in Europe was this instability greater than across Kepler's very own German-speaking world, consisting of those states and princedoms which now form modern Germany and Austria, and the fluctuating dependencies of the Holy Roman empire, such as modern-day Poland, Czechoslovakia, and Hungary (or Bohemia).

Throughout his life, Kepler remained loyal to the Protestant faith of his childhood, and while he may have become something of an unconventional Lutheran, with mystical Neo-Platonic tendencies, he always refused to convert to Roman Catholicism. While this may have occasioned several moves of jobs and homes – from Graz to Prague, from Prague to Linz, and on to Regensburg – he never appears to have suffered explicit religious persecution, except perhaps in the form of exclusion from the Lutheran communion of Linz because of his views on matter and spirit in the Eucharist. One should emphasize that this exclusion was *not* occasioned by Kepler's heliocentricism; it was, rather, about theological points relating to Lutheran teaching as expressed in the Augsburg Confession of 1530.

What might, in some ways, strike people today as surprising is his long and seemingly friendly employment by several very high-profile and devout Roman Catholics, such as the emperors Rudolph and Matthias, and by Albrecht, Duke of Wallenstein. It may seem odd that Wallenstein, the "star" general of the Holy Roman Catholic emperor's armies during the Thirty Years War, and a veritable hammer against the armies of Protestant princes, should have employed Kepler as an adviser, and that Kepler cast horoscopes for him. This was, however, the case.

All this opens up the wider question of why the Vatican was

warning and reining in Galileo in 1616, examining him in Rome in 1633, and condemning the Copernican theory, while Lutheran Kepler was left untouched. Galileo, after all, only declared his Copernicanism to the world around 1610, whereas Kepler's heliocentric views were published and known long before that. Why, therefore, did not the emperor, Wallenstein, or some Catholic bishop have Lutheran heretic Kepler arrested and dragged off to Rome to be burned, like the Pythagorean Copernican-sympathizing mystic Giordano Bruno had been in 1600?

It had far less to do with heliocentricism – upon which the Catholic Church had no formal opinion before 1616, and upon which the Protestants had none at all – than it had to do with personalities and styles of advocacy. Kepler was in no way strident, offensive, or "pushy" in his Copernicanism, simply presenting solid mathematical data and inspired pieces of interpretation. In the *Epitome*, in 1618–21, for instance, Kepler presents the Copernican case, along with his novel physical theories about what made the planets move, as plainly stated questions and answers. His style of argument, it has been suggested, was similar to the Christian catechism, in which the teacher would take the young believer through the church's doctrines point by point, and answer questions that might be raised. There is no bombast, no name-calling, no deriding the geocentric astronomers as fools.

Kepler appears to have been a gentle figure, who fully understood the high-profile world in which he moved, and knew beyond question that an Imperial Mathematician's job was to be a good servant, and to tender wise advice. It was *not* his place to deride and mock persons who did not share his views, especially if their social status was much higher than his own. Consequently, it appears that the great and the good could live with odd Copernican views if their holder was pleasant, courteous, and non-threatening. This was especially important at a time when Europe, and most of all the German-speaking world, was being racked with religious and military upheaval. But, as we saw in Chapter 4 with Bruno, and will see in forthcoming chapters with Galileo after 1610, these two men were *very* different personalities, as shone through in their styles of Copernican advocacy.

Yet Kepler's own deeply committed yet non-judgmental Christianity must also have been significant in that theologically lacerated age. For while a clear Protestant, he was never a bigot, seeing himself as "catholic" in the sense of ongoing historical Christianity, as expressed in the early church creeds, rather than as a radical. Nor did he seem to believe that specifically *Roman* Catholics, who, after all, shared the same Jesus and the same grace with the Lutherans, were the agents of the Antichrist, and hence must be bound for hell. Kepler's Christianity appears to have been remarkably "un-sectarian" and generous.

All this goes some way towards explaining why Protestant Kepler died in his bed, after a short illness in Regensburg, on 15 November 1630. It is sad that, following the Protestant Swedish army's destruction of the churchyard in which he was buried, we no longer know precisely where his mortal remains lie.

CHAPTER 9

Galileo Galilei: In Pursuit of Fame, 1564–1610. Part 1: Early Life

*W*e saw at the end of the last chapter how different Kepler and Galileo were as individuals. Kepler was happy to be a hardworking mathematician and teacher, devout, and instinctively mystical in his search for God and his understanding of nature. He loved the business of mathematical calculation and was content not to be too conspicuously displayed on the world's stage. Without being condescending to one of his formidable intellect, he seems to have been a thoroughly pleasant chap.

Galileo Galilei was a very different kind of man, however: seven years older than Kepler, conscious of being descended from a family that had once had more clout in the world than it did in his own day, lacking the fortune and status which he felt was his by right, unmystical, hard-headed, argumentative, and possessed of a powerful personality that did not take easily to being contradicted. Being Italian, Galileo was a Roman Catholic, although all the evidence suggests that while he lacked Kepler's subtle spiritual dimension, his religious faith was genuine, and he accepted all the key points of Catholic Christian doctrine, untroubled by either Reformation theology or contemporary scepticism. While Galileo never married, he had three illegitimate children. But there was no shortage of cardinals, and even popes, who had more.

GALILEO THE MAN AND RENAISSANCE ITALIAN

Galileo was born in Pisa, a once-independent Italian city state, but by his time part of the Florentine diaspora in Tuscany. It was said that he was named in honour of an eminent fourteenth-century ancestor, Galileo Bonaiuti, a Florentine physician and scholar of eminence. Galileo's father, Vincenzo, was a musician, lutenist, musical theorist, and, it was sometimes said, a merchant; his wife Giulia Ammannati was Galileo's mother. Northern Italy was one of the powerhouses of European wealth-generation, anchored originally in the fine wool that came from the sheep that were pastured in the beautiful Tuscan hills. It was hardly surprising that tales of nymphs and shepherds were such abiding themes in north Italian artistic culture. By Galileo's middle age, the legendary merchant wealth of northern Italy was just beginning to experience challenges from the Atlantic seaboard countries, as a maritime wealth unimaginable before 1492 began to flow from China, India, and the Americas into Spain, Portugal, England, Holland, and the Low Countries. By 1700 this global seaborne trade would have long eclipsed the traditional riches of the Mediterranean. This lay well in the future as the Galilei family contemplated their perceived former glory.

In spite of economic problems, and a tendency towards violent political gangsterism, such as that of the Medici and other powerful once-merchant but now self-styled noble families, the cities of northern Italy were proud of their self-governing, artistic, and cultural traditions. Florence, Pisa, Bologna, Milan, Venice, and Genoa were cities of painters, poets, Renaissance Christian humanists, and classical scholars, as well as of merchants. Unlike today, no one in 1600 saw any incongruity between the worlds of art, science, commerce, and the church. They were all viewed as noble expressions of wider Christian civilization; of *Christendom*.

Italy, at this point and until as late as 1871, was not a unified political entity, but a set of independent cities and states with a medley of government styles. It was just like Kepler's Germanic world, with its dukedoms, princedoms, and Prince Bishoprics, although unlike in Germany, the Reformation never gained a foothold in Italy.

Naples and Sicily in the south were poor, and had a traditional monarchy, while the "Papal States" across the middle of the Italian "boot" were the Pope's earthly domain, over which he ruled as a king, from the Vatican. It was in the north that Italy's great wealth and opportunities lay. Florence, with Pisa and Milan, were, in addition to their culture, great commercial cities famed for their merchants, entrepreneurs, and bankers as well as for their artists and scholars. Controlling much of Italy's (and southern Europe's) ocean-going trade were the rival cities of Genoa and *Serenissima Repubblica di Venezia*, the "Most Serene Republic" of Venice: proud of the blessings received from its patron saint, Mark. All these northern cities were independent and self-governing states, sometimes popular or oligarchical republics and sometimes monarchies, depending on how unstable shifting political conditions dictated. The universities of Bologna and Padua (the latter attached to Venice), especially, ranked among the great centres of Renaissance culture.

It was a deeply volatile world, perhaps best captured in the pages of Niccolò Machiavelli's *The Prince* (1513), where rags could rise to riches, and riches descend into bankruptcy and, not infrequently, to assassination. Further, it was a deeply reputation-driven world, in which otherwise good Christian men not only pursued the pagan goddess Fortuna, but would risk all for ambition and reputation. By 1600, by which time Galileo was an obscure 36-year-old professor, were there not numerous Italians who had come to enjoy golden reputations for their achievements? Apart from classical, military, or philosophical reputations, were there not dozens of contemporary men, and some women, who had won enduring fame for their spiritual and intellectual contributions – figures such as St Francis of Assisi, Catherine of Siena, Dante, Leonardo da Vinci, Michelangelo, Machiavelli, Ariosto, Lassus, and Monteverdi? In that world of reputations, did not the proud Pisan mathematician desire to win his laurels and, hopefully, dignity and ample financial security, as an astronomer and a *philosopher*, to restore the lustre and fortune of the Galilei family? To win fame as a philosopher, or great thinking man, and *not* as a mere mathematician, would be Galileo's main aspiration; for in that world, mere mathematicians were often seen as little more than the lumpenproletariat of the intellectual classes, only a couple of notches above accounts clerks, land measurers, and empiric horoscope-casters. Philosophers dealt with the weightier matters of time, space, eternity, beauty, and meaning – a distinction which he would spell out clearly to his future patron Cosimo II, Grand Duke of Tuscany, after his telescopic discoveries shot him to fame in 1610.

The image of Galileo created by Enlightenment and post-Enlightenment heroic reputation-builders is very often wide of the mark. For here we encounter the image of Galileo the victim or martyr to "the truth", who had the world-transforming courage to stand up to "blind dogmas" of the superstitious Roman Catholic Church – a victim or martyr, who just *knew* that the sun rotated around the earth by a species of uniquely far-seeing innate wisdom. These images have been hammered home visually into the Western cultural imagination by nineteenth-century artists like Cristiano Banti and Joseph-Nicholas Robert Fleury, in their imaginary depictions of a heroic Galileo defiantly standing his ground before the menacing Roman inquisitors.

To get some idea of the character and personality of the early-middle-aged Galileo, one should look at the portrait by Domenico Tintoretto of *c.* 1605–07, which now hangs in the National Maritime Museum, Greenwich. Here we see the tough, indeed hard-bitten, face of a brooding, angry-looking man with short cropped hair and close-clipped beard, in a black doublet and white collar – a face, and a personality shining through that face, which could easily be mistaken for that of a *condottieri*, or tough mercenary soldier of fortune, if one did not know it to be that of Galileo.

The Galileo of recorded history was neither a man of gentleness nor of overmuch consideration to others. Without doubt, he was a brilliant debater and an arguer – a veritable "lion amongst lambs" – who was in no way averse to hammering home his academic points with insult, ridicule, and name-calling. Strong language and insult were in some ways an accepted part of late-medieval and Renaissance argument, and one has only to look at some of the language deployed by Sir [St] Thomas More, Martin Luther, and other Reformation figures to realize that Galileo's resort to insults and even lawsuits against those who were perceived to have wronged him was by no means unique. I suggest Galileo's misjudgment of the situation lay in the *circumstances* of his use of ridicule and offensive language. While professors, mathematicians, and even religious leaders might spit insults against each other, especially if they felt sure of the political support of powerful rulers, Galileo's insults were perceived as crossing social divides. Galileo would not have been so foolish as to directly attack a cardinal or a pope, but his behaviour over the years had built up a "critical mass" of academic enemies who might be all too glad to suggest to an apparently Galileo-friendly cardinal or pope that his latest insults related to some of *their own* cherished ideas.

In that world of reputations, courtly hierarchies, favour-seeking, and gossip, in which university professors of mathematics counted for medium-sized fry at best, Galileo came to play an increasingly dangerous game in a way that Kepler would never have dreamt of. All of this came later in Galileo's career, although it constitutes the basic ground rules of the world in which he lived and moved, and is essential to understanding what happened after 1615. But let us now return to Galileo's education and early work as a scientist.

EDUCATION AND EARLY CAREER

Being the eldest of Vincenzo's and Giulia's six children – we know of Elena, Livia, Virginia, and Michelangelo – much was expected of Galileo. At first, he was intended as a priest, and received his schooling at the monastery of Vallombroso, for a well-connected church dignitary was an important asset for any family. The young Galileo seems to have been attracted to the religious life, and joined the monastic novitiate, but Vincenzo changed his mind and brought him home. It was then decided that he should train as a doctor, a profession which then, as now, carried high prestige and potential earnings, so he was sent to the University of Pisa, with its distinguished faculty, to train for a medical degree.

Medicine, it soon transpired, was not to his taste. The guiding light behind the medical curriculum was Galen, the late classical Graeco-Roman anatomical and clinical writer of the second century AD. Brilliant as Galen's work was, it had its limitations, for not only had medicine moved on over the preceding 1,400 years, but new discoveries relating to the heart, veins, and lungs were difficult to reconcile with Galen's works. Pisa appears to have had a deeply reverential attitude towards Galen – as did the other great medical schools of the day, such as Padua and Montpellier. Medicine, like astronomy, cosmology, and physics, was rooted in the classical inheritance, and in the same way that Galileo would make discoveries and formulate arguments that would ultimately undermine that tradition, so medical researchers such as Andreas Vesalius, Fabrizio of Aquapedente, and William Harvey would necessitate a fresh appraisal of how we understood the internal workings of humans and animals, no matter how much these individuals might have otherwise respected the classical giants. In the same way as telescopes, graduated instruments, and meticulous observations would start to transform the physical sciences, so painstaking dissection of cadavers, the microscope, and controlled animal and human experiments would transform medicine.

Galileo did not seem to be cut out to be a doctor. No doubt his argumentative disposition set him at odds with the Galenic academic purists (as it soon would with the Aristotelian physicists), while it is also likely that the smells, blood, and messiness of anatomical dissection in the days before formaldehyde, refrigeration, and running hot water did not appeal to his precise, mathematical mind and instinctive love of demonstrable certainties.

Vincenzo was not pleased to have his son abandon such a prestigious and lucrative profession as medicine, and was far from happy with the young man's wish to be a mathematician. In some ways, mathematics was in Galileo's blood, for Vincenzo the lutenist and music theorist had no doubt played his unwitting part in arousing in his son a love of proportions, harmonies, chords, elegance, and beauty, all of which were the stuff of Renaissance mathematics. Then Vincenzo relented, and Galileo began to train as a mathematician.

Galileo rapidly proved his worth as a mathematician and was soon lecturing in the subject at Pisa. In 1589, when still only twenty-five, he was offered the professorship. Even so, Galileo's abiding gift for getting on the wrong side of people, especially people who mattered, was already in evidence. When he was asked to give an opinion on the viability of a machine invented by the illegitimate son of the then Grand Duke of Tuscany for dredging the harbour at Leghorn, his assessment was withering, and probably unnecessarily so, in a way that appeared almost calculated to annoy. Nevertheless, Galileo's gift not only for pure mathematics but also for applied and mechanical engineering design was beyond dispute. Evidence also suggests that he was a skilled practical operator, good with his hands, and one wonders how far this may have derived, like his love of number and proportion, from musical training from his musician father. Playing musical instruments is an exceedingly dexterous business.

Legend has it, as was later passed on via his pupil and biographer Vincenzo Viviani, that Galileo's first discovery came about one evening while, still a medical student, he was in Pisa Cathedral as the lamps were being lit. According to the story, he was struck by the way in which a hanging lamp, suspended on a long chain from the ceiling, swung in exactly the same period of time no matter whether its total arc of swing was large or small. The young medical student supposedly used his own pulse to make the timings.

How much truth there is in this story is hard to ascertain, especially as that particular lamp was not set up until some years later, but it is a good example of how stories of the brilliant young physicist became part of the folklore of science, especially as the much older Galileo did important research into the isochronal, or equal-time, swings of pendulums. Did the elderly Galileo happen to mention the long-ago incident to his disciple Viviani, who then wrote it down nearly sixty years later? The dynamics of swinging and moving bodies, and what seemed to be the mathematical proportions implicit within them, captured the young Galileo's imagination early on.

Another story passed on by Viviani has Galileo dropping balls of unequal weight from the Leaning Tower of Pisa and confounding the conservative Aristotelians of the university by demonstrating that the heavy and the light weights struck the ground simultaneously, rather than the heavy objects falling faster.

According to the common-sense physics of Aristotle, the heavy object – being more "earthy" than the light one – should have sped to "mother earth" more rapidly.

Scholars are deeply divided as to when, if ever, this event really happened; or was it another example of the elderly Galileo, now under house arrest at Arcetri near Florence, holding forth to a disciple who was already establishing the canon of the Great Man's life? Galileo was certainly an accomplished raconteur and image-builder who loved telling his tale to an adoring audience. A love of argument, a natural way with words, and a delight in telling stories aimed to win over the listener are temperamental traits that often go together. While none of this diminishes Galileo's towering stature as a pioneer of physical science, we must nonetheless be cautious about some of the incidents, dates, and bias implicit in some of the heroic stories that have crystallized around his name.

Galileo was by no means the first physical scientist to consider the nature of motion, even sometimes in a not entirely Aristotelian context. Medieval Europe saw a rich tradition of "philosophers of motion" discussing their ideas, especially in the universities of Paris and Oxford. Jean Buridan, Nicole de Oresme, and Nicholas of Cusa on the Continent, along with Thomas Bradwardine (originally of Balliol), Richard Swineshead, William of Heytesbury, and John Dumbleton of Merton College, Oxford, were all making and discussing their contributions over two and a half centuries before Galileo was born. The "Merton College School" of mathematical theorists and astronomers in fourteenth- to sixteenth-century Oxford was a hive of original physical thinking, whose works were being discussed across Europe.

What interested all of those late medieval "physicists" was the relationship between impetus, motion, acceleration, and deceleration, the geometrical curves described by flying projectiles, and how the initial force that set a body flying – such as the gunpowder driving a cannon ball – diminished in an exact sequence to the attraction of mother earth that eventually brought the projectile to *terra firma*. Where did the "force" in the gunpowder, or the longbow, come from, and how could they impart a short-lived "violent motion" (away from the earth) to the projectile that was eventually overtaken by the downward-tending "natural motion" that brought it back to earth – and always over such a beautiful geometrical curve?

One thing which had especially fascinated all of these late-medieval theoretical physical philosophers, and the Merton College Geometers in particular, was what would later be called the "Mean Speed Theorem", or the calculation of the rate of acceleration of a falling body. Richard Swineshead in around 1345 had even developed one of Thomas Bradwardine's dynamical puzzles, namely, how uniformly would a heavy body accelerate if it fell down a hole that passed right through the centre of the earth? Already by that time, however, Swineshead's fellow-Mertonian, William of Heytesbury, had devised a graphic technique for calculating and expressing mean speed acceleration: probably the first use of the graph in mathematics.

What has all this to do with Galileo? This was all part of a rich late-medieval tradition, in mathematical and theoretical dynamics, to which he was a direct heir. Without doubt, the well-read Galileo was familiar with the work of his predecessors over the past 250 years, and in his own treatment of acceleration in his *Discourses Concerning Two New Sciences* (1638)[1] he would take up William of Heytesbury's Mean Speed Theorem graph (available in a printed edition of 1494, although there is no direct evidence that Galileo knew of it) and develop it for his own analytical work, with a better and firmer understanding without a doubt – but without an acknowledgment. For Galileo was no more over-zealous in admitting his influences from the past than he was in acknowledging co-discoverers in his own time, which only fuelled the many controversies which he was party to over the years. This, perhaps, is one of the reasons why he made so many enemies.

There was a difference emerging between the late-medieval physical dynamics tradition of the late Middle Ages and that of Galileo: a difference of experimental technique. Most of the late-medieval dynamicists appear to have been engaged in *thought* experiments, such as calculating the behaviour of bodies falling down holes bored through the earth – techniques based essentially on mathematical and logical extrapolation. Galileo seems to have conducted hands-on experiments, and tried to devise ways of physically quantifying acceleration in the real world. Without a shadow of a doubt, Galileo's approach to all aspects of physics and astronomy was to experiment and observe first, and theorize second, and then theorize *mathematically* – perhaps one reason why we see him as such a forerunner of what would become "Western science".

For what Galileo was doing was symptomatic of a new approach to understanding the natural world, by the use of controlled experimental conditions wherein one investigated a small part of nature in the hope of gaining insight into the whole. William Gilbert's work on the earth's magnetic field, drawn from experiments conducted on spherical "laboratory" magnets, was a case in point, as was Simon Stevin's dropping of different-sized weights from a Dutch church tower around 1586 – a historical parallel to the Galileo and the Leaning Tower of Pisa story.

In the world of 1600, an experiment was not seen as the decisive arbiter of scientific research that it would become by 1700. The very nature of experimentation was circumscribed by all manner of philosophical problems, especially in a world in which the Aristotelian *corpus* was still believed to be the answer when it came to natural phenomena. As we have already seen, in this way of thinking only the heavens, beyond the moon, were believed to be the realms of changeless perfection and mathematical exactitude, whereas in our terrestrial "sublunary" world, *motion* had to be considered as part of a semi-chaotic and certainly imperfect realm.

This would be an important component – insults apart – of Galileo's unfolding and lifelong dispute with conservative Aristotelian physicists and Ptolemaic astronomers. How could the "moderns" presume to know more than the "ancients", whose ideas had stood the test of millennia, and to what extent could hands-on, handicraft-related experiments achieve deeper insights than deductive logic and reason, which were second only to salvation, God's great gift to the human race? How could one rely on the evidence of the human senses in matters of truth when they were clearly so unreliable that two separate people might give two contradictory accounts of the same incident?

CHAPTER 10

Galileo Galilei: In Pursuit of Fame, 1564–1610.
Part 2: Inventions, Publications, and Padua

*I*n many respects, Galileo's thinking was not only deeply mathematical, but in particular was deeply mechanistic, for applied mathematics and even engineering were never far from his idea of physical reality.

EUROPE'S LOVE OF TECHNOLOGY

By Galileo's time, European civilization's love of machinery and self-acting devices was already centuries old, and pumps, cranes, complex astronomical and striking clocks, and large musical organs were an established part of everyday life. The works of sixteenth-century writers on machinery, such as Georg Agricola, Vannoccio Biringuccio, and Agostino Ramelli, would have been well known to Galileo, while wind and water mills, guns, dockyard and building-site machines, heavy metal working, and the manufacture and use of explosives would have been familiar on an almost daily basis.

There was also a growing number of precision scientific instruments, such as a wide variety of sundials – including portable ones – astronomical angle-measuring instruments such as quadrants and astrolabes, scales used by surveyors and navigators, accurate draughtsman's instruments, and spring-driven watches with tiny gears. All of them were commonplace by 1600, especially if one lived in or near to a major port. The "mathematical practitioner" was an established figure in any great city, and this included spectacle lens makers for "visual glasses" that had long been part of the European urban scene, and would help explain why, after 1608, telescopes suddenly became such talked-about and commonplace devices.

In many respects these devices represented a different type of mindset from that of the Aristotelian philosophers of the universities, with their emphasis on a primarily intellectual rather than a hands-on approach to "truth". One respect in which Galileo was remarkable was in his connection with both worlds: as a university academic it was pure truth that was his concern; yet as a practical mathematician he had one foot firmly planted in the world of the tradesman and the skilled artisan. He did not seem to be aware, from his own point of view, of any fundamental contradiction in this position, which is probably one reason why Galileo so fascinates us today. As a poorly paid lecturer, then professor, of mathematics, he quickly realized that money could be made not only by extra-curricular teaching to interested individuals with cash to spare, but that there was a great demand for precision devices which made calculation quick and accurate for non-mathematicians. This led to his first publication, in 1586, at the age of twenty-two. It was a little Italian tract, conspicuously written in the vernacular and not in Latin, entitled *La Bilancetto* ("The Little Balance"). It described a small instrument for precision weighing, in both air and in water, being a "hydrostatic balance".

Several things immediately strike us upon reading *La Bilancetto* that reveal much about Galileo. For one thing, it was inspired by a story of the great third-century BC Greek mathematician and engineer experimentalist Archimedes, whom Galileo conspicuously admired, and his physical testing of the purity of King Hiero's gold crown. It demonstrates Galileo's own meticulous instincts as an experimentalist, and it also captures something of his obvious gift for precise, lucid, and confident exposition: as a technical writer, as one might style him today. We glimpse through that clarity his power as a teacher and inspirer: all there at the age of twenty-two.

Galileo's balance, inspired by Archimedes's treatise on the buoyancy or otherwise of objects placed in pure water, was an early scientific instrument primarily intended for testing the purity of precious metals. It consisted of a delicately suspended balance beam about 4 feet long and at least two *braccia* (arms). An object to be tested was hung at one end, and weights sufficient to bring the beam into equipoise would be placed in the other. The suspended test object would then be gently submerged in a dish of water, causing it to appear lighter than the weights that still hung in air, due to the greater density of the water.

As gold had the then greatest known density, an object of pure gold would sink deeper into the water than an object of less dense silver; and if there was any copper or silver alloyed with the gold, it would register lighter than if it had been pure gold. In this way, one could establish by adjusting the weights the exact metallic purity of an object if one had quantified beforehand the respective buoyancies of gold, silver, copper, and other alloy metals. Here was experimental physics, mathematics, precision mechanics, exposition, and potentially commerce, all combined, and pointing to key traits which would unfold in Galileo's future career.

Even with his conspicuous talent, by the time of his late twenties Pisa, in spite of appointing him to the Chair of Mathematics in 1589, was getting a bit too hot for Galileo's comfort. His knack of making enemies had become evident, and he was looking for an appointment outside the Medici-dominated Florentine territories. His scientifically minded aristocratic friend Marchese Guido Ubaldo del Monte used his influence to secure the Professorship of Mathematics at the University of Padua for the 28-year-old Galileo. He would stay at Padua for the next eighteen years, until things started to get hot there as well, and he was able to use the international acclaim which his 1610 telescopic discoveries brought him to secure a prestigious appointment at the court of a later and friendlier Grand Duke of Tuscany, the young Cosimo de Medici – as the Grand Duke's Court Philosopher, no less, which placed him in a different league from that of a mere professor.

PROFESSOR AT PADUA

In 1592, Padua was not only Italy's – if not Europe's – top university for scientific and medical subjects, but being within the territorial jurisdiction of *Serenissima*, or the Most Serene Republic of Venice, it enjoyed a freedom to please itself not to be had in Archducal Florence or the Papal States. For Venice was technically a republic, and while the chief offices of Doge (or Duke, in the Venetian dialect) and senior city councillors were dominated by well-connected mercantile and professional families, one could enjoy more elbow room on the Venetian terra firma than anywhere else in Italy. Venice traditionally had bad relations with the Vatican, and was accustomed to being under interdict, or papal banishment – though that never prevented the great Byzantine Cathedral of St Mark, or the numerous city churches, from vigorous worship. With composers of the standing of Frescobaldi and Monteverdi, the "Venetian School" became one of the glories of Renaissance civilization, with spectacular musical settings of the Roman Catholic liturgy, secular songs, and even the invention of opera.

Venice, some 24 miles from inland Padua, was not just a great seaport and city renowned for its artists, musicians, bankers, and all manner of exotics (its courtesans, for example, were said to be the most sophisticated in Europe), but it was also a major European centre for engineering, technology, and ship-building. The Venice Arsenal, for instance, was one of the wonders of Europe, and a place for every tourist to visit. The arsenal has been considered Europe's first factory, in the way in which it mass-manufactured munitions for the Venetian Republic's navy, while its shipyards could turn out semi-standardized powerful war galleys almost on a production-line basis. Such war galleys were vital to the protection of Venice and her seaborne trading empire against the Ottoman Turks, and the safeguarding of Christian-held territories in the eastern Mediterranean from Algerian and other pirates. Padua was the Venetian Republic's "local" university.

Venice was also the most libertarian and tolerant of all the Italian states, and was not only very rich and enterprising, but remarkably stable politically, for what bedevilled so much of Renaissance Italy, in spite of its genius, was an all too frequent political instability.

Florence's ups and downs were legendary, as Machiavelli had described a hundred years earlier. As Italy had no coordinated military body, it was always susceptible to foreign invasion, from the French, Germans, or Austrians in particular; while the infighting of the cardinals of the Curia, and invariably elderly popes, meant that the Papal States and Rome not infrequently lurched from one political crisis to another. Yet Venice seemed stable and strong, in spite of its own internal power-broking and a wise tendency to elect old men to the office of Doge, thereby ensuring that any one Head of State did not hold power for too long.

In many ways, Padua, within the protective orbit of Venice, or *Serenissima*, was the ideal place for Galileo to live and work. One also suspects that the commercial and technological ambiance of Venice stimulated Galileo to produce new works, such as *Le Meccaniche* ("Mechanics"), *c.* 1600, and, most notably, his substantial tract *Le Operazione del Compasso Geometrico et Militare* ("The Operation of the Geometric and Military Compass"), of which an early manuscript copy survives from 1597, though later additions were made before eventual publication in Padua in 1606. Galileo's "compass" was very much a piece of pure, practical, mathematical technology. The word "compass" might appear confusing for a modern reader, for it had nothing to do with magnetic compasses. Instead, it was a type of brass mathematical instrument with a pair of hinged legs which opened like a circle-drawing compass, but it was not itself a drawing instrument. It belonged to a class of calculation instruments called sectors, each leg of which carried engraved mathematical scales and which, as an instrument type, were ancestors of the engineer's slide rule. It facilitated quick calculation of geometrical shapes and angles without requiring a detailed knowledge of geometrical theory from the user, in much the same way as a modern pocket calculator does not presume that its user can calculate long divisions or percentages on paper.

The military association of the instrument derived from its foreseen usefulness to gunners, military engineers, and designers of fortifications, not to mention civilian land surveyors. As with *La Bilancetto*, Galileo displays his talent for clear, elegant, technical writing. For as is obvious in his two instrument booklets of 1586 and 1606, and as would become evident in his future works on astronomy, mechanics, and experimental science, Galileo had a clear, practical mind, seeing mathematical and physical data as primary to our understanding of the world around us.

It was a very different sort of mind from that which delighted in subtle perceptions or abstract philosophical "quiddities", and one quickly sees both why he had not been attracted to medicine as a profession, and why – insults apart – his mind worked in a different way from that of the Aristotelian philosophers. While Renaissance doctors were building up a corpus of knowledge about purely scientific or laboratory-based anatomy and physiology, the understanding of disease itself remained an intractable mystery, and often ascended to abstruse heights of speculative thinking. Galileo's very experimental approach to physics was a world removed from the subtle interactions of earth, water, air, and fire which were the stuff of Aristotle's physics.

Galileo's *del Compasso Geometrico* was not a direct product of his formal professorial teaching at Padua, but most likely came out of his extramural or "sideline" teaching that augmented his income. His official chair at Pisa had been poorly paid at a mere 60 crowns per annum, and his new one in Padua rather better at 180 florins, rising to 320, but following his father Vincenzo's death in 1591, Galileo found himself head of a hard-up, if not dysfunctional, family that depended almost entirely on his own earnings. Giulia was now a dependent widow, and – picking upon incidental details – seems to have been a rather sharp-tongued lady. As the family breadwinner, Galileo had dowries to find for two of his still unmarried sisters, while his sixteen-year-old younger brother, Michelangelo, had to be prepared for his intended musical career. Poor Michelangelo proved incapable of obtaining a decent post in Florence or Italy, and was obliged to seek his career in Poland and Germany. Though a fine lutenist like his father, some of whose compositions have come down to us, Michelangelo's life seems to have consisted of a series of struggles with money, while his own son, yet another Vincenzo (Galileo's nephew), proved a problem – and it was Galileo, as head of the family, who was always being importuned. This explains his keenness to turn his hand to various ancillary enterprises, such as private technical teaching and inventing, and hopefully controlling the manufacture and sale of useful devices and instruction booklets. He even took in lodgers.

In Padua, Galileo formed a liaison with a Venetian lady named Marina Gamba. She seems to have been – at least in her earlier days – something of an "exotic", who, we are told, had red hair. Redheads and blondes are not uncommon in northern Italy, where travellers, merchants, tourists, and marauding armies from Austria, Germany, and even further north in Europe had long left their traces on the genetic landscape.

Galileo never married Marina, but she did bear him three children. Virginia and Livia (named after his own sisters) were born in 1600 and 1601 respectively, and one wonders whether it was the birth of a third child, Vincenzo, named after his grandfather, in 1606, that acted as the spur to bring his long-in-manuscript *del Compasso Geometrico* into print, as a way of making some extra money. After Galileo finally won his much-desired fame and respectability in 1610, he would despatch Marina back to her family in Venice, and put the two little girls into a convent. Galileo, after 1610, would use his new-found fame to obtain a status of legal legitimacy for little Vincenzo, who would become his father's acknowledged heir. In this world, after all, sons, unless they were like younger brother Michelangelo, were cheaper to rear than girls, could make their own fortunes in the world, and did not require all the expenses involved with marriageable daughters. We shall see more of Galileo's family in Chapter 13.

MIDDLE-AGED AND DISCONTENTED

By his fortieth birthday in February 1604 we see in Galileo a man who was not especially happy. He had a lot of mouths to feed, his salary was modest, casual earnings were vital, and his ability to make enemies by no means worked to his advantage. Yet he undoubtedly had warm friends and admirers, some of whom were men of real influence, such as Marchese Guido Ubaldo del Monte, and the Venetian mathematical gentleman Giovanni Francesco Sagredo (subsequently immortalized in the controversial *Dialogue*

Concerning the Two Chief World Systems of 1632), who got his salary at Padua increased from 180 to 320 florins per annum. Galileo was conspicuously brilliant. His knowledge was not confined to mathematics and astronomy; he had also delivered paid "extra-curricular" lectures on Dante's "Hell", and on the poetry of Ariosto and Tasso in Florence and Siena. He was deeply knowledgeable about music, architecture and the visual arts, and philosophy. He could also be a fine and stimulating conversationalist, especially when he felt admired rather than challenged, when he was less likely to lurch into "wolf amongst lambs" mode.

Galileo Galilei was a man of Renaissance culture in all its breadth. But he was also perennially hard-up, feeling that his talents were being overlooked by those who mattered, as the Renaissance goddess Fortuna consistently failed to knock on his door. One also suspects that he did not especially enjoy university teaching or dealing with the generality of students, particularly in the free-for-all, rumbustious student world of Padua. What he wanted was something more prestigious, more leisurely, and, one suspects, enabling him to mix with a different class of person than the denizens of a university town.

It may have been for this reason that he eventually published his *del Compasso Geometrico* in 1606, for it gave him the opportunity not only of displaying his intellectual wares for all the world to see, but also to aim them at a high-born and influential personage from whom he hoped to solicit patronage. The fulsome and blatantly flattering tone of the Dedication in the compass tract left no one in any doubt as to where he was casting his net. Its title page is "Dedicated to The Most Serene Prince Don Cosimo De' Medici", and Galileo's frankly grovelling dedicatory epistle concludes, "expect from my simple mind from time to time those mature fruits that Divine Grace has conceded for me to gather. And so, with all humility, I bow to kiss reverently your robe and pray God for your great happiness. From Padua, the 10th of July, 1606. From your Highness's Most Humble and Obedient Servant Galileo Galilei."

For the time being, at least, the wolf has assumed the persona of the lapdog, in the hope, no doubt, of a tasty archducal morsel. The *real* morsel would still be four years in coming and even then would come only in the wake of new tricks performed – with the telescope.

GALILEO'S FIRST BRUSH WITH THE HOLY OFFICE IN 1604 – FOR CASTING HOROSCOPES

When a file came to light in a Florentine academic library in 1992, many people were embarrassed, if not shocked. While the file pertained to Galileo and another Paduan professor, Cesare Cremonini, being examined by the Inquisition, in April 1604, it did not relate to the usual venerable matters attributed to Galileo and his dealings with the ecclesiastical authorities. The matter at hand was not the Copernican theory, biblical interpretations relating to a moving earth, or intellectual freedom, but the practice of astrology. Yes, Galileo, the forty-year-old Paduan academic mathematicus, not only augmented his professorial salary by lecturing on Italian poetry, designing useful instruments for artillerymen, and keeping a lodging-house, but he also ran a sideline in casting horoscopes for money.

I don't see any reason why we should find this revelation about Galileo's business acumen especially shocking. We only find it shocking when 21st-century people deliberately reinvent their modern scientific heroes as advanced thinkers born centuries before their time: or, as I have put it elsewhere, when we turn them into cardboard cut-outs of modern scientists dressed up in ruff collars. The *real* Copernicus, Tycho, Kepler, and Galileo were men firmly embedded in a historical culture which differed in many ways from our own. To understand them, and respect their achievement, we must place them in proper historical context. In that context, as we saw in Chapter 5, astrology made sound sense as a way of interpreting all aspects of the human condition, and was seen as no more of a "superstition" than "super-computer" number-crunching technology is seen by its modern-day prophets, who claim to be able to tell us what is likely to happen in twenty years' time, as dealing in arcane prophecy.

Astrology was part of the mathematician's trade, and could be a good little earner in its own right; and who can blame Galileo for "playing the market", especially when cash was short? While modern apologists from the "Galileo the modern scientist ahead of his time" school like to think he *knew* horoscope-casting was superstitious and only calculated horoscopes for gullible clients because of poverty, I am not so sure. Why should Galileo have been proof against one of the most widely held cultural assumptions of the centuries – that the heavens affected the earth and the human race? It is true that Galileo does not philosophize about astrology in the way that Kepler did, and simply calculated horoscopes when paid to do so; but that is no proof that he was axiomatically sceptical. The difference between them derives from their temperaments, for Galileo's writings do not indicate that he was ever given to mysticism or abstract speculation (a matter upon which he would differ from his future patron, Cosimo II, Grand Duke of Tuscany). Physics and mechanics were his passion – even when the heavenly machinery might be influencing the earthly elements.

The incident of April 1604 probably had its origin in the relationship between Galileo and a man who had previously been his amanuensis or secretary, Signor Silvestro Pagnoni, and had since moved on to another job, seemingly after an amicable separation. In 1604, Silvestro made a disclosure to the Inquisition. What was at issue was *not* the fact that Galileo had cast horoscopes, for horoscope-casting was accepted as a normal part of that society. What mattered, rather, was the *type* of horoscope that he was calculating: the specific horoscope which Silvestro reported to the church authorities was deemed a *fatalistic* horoscope, in so far as it predicted the death-date of an individual. As we saw in Chapter 5, this was styled *judicial* astrology, pertaining as it did to foretelling or "judging" the termination of specific human lives. In Christian theology, could God be bound by the motions of the heavens that he had created? Could God be a slave to the future like a mortal man, and hence be incapable of changing that future by an act of grace?

Clearly, the idea was unthinkable, for had not God given mankind free will so that through prayer and wise precaution we could overcome the tendencies suggested by the planets? Shakespeare hit the nail squarely on the head when, in *Julius Caesar* (Act I, scene ii),

Cassius utters the immortal line, "The fault, dear Brutus, lies not in our stars, but in ourselves that we are underlings." The heavens can guide us, but divine grace and God-given human free will ultimately decide our fates.

This was the cause of Galileo's first brush with the church authorities. It is unclear what Galileo thought about astrological fatalism, but my suspicion is that he did his horoscopes without much thinking, and that the incident would never have come to light had not Signor Silvestro, for whatever reason, harboured some animus against his old employer and ratted on him to the ecclesiastical authorities. More serious was the offence committed by Cesare Cremonini who, it appears, had argued from Aristotle against the immortality of the human soul and its survival after death: the offence of "mortalism", or atheism, which flew directly in the face of basic Christian teaching.

Not content with spilling the beans about Galileo's fatalistic horoscope prediction, Silvestro proceeded to widen his remit to personal character assassination, telling the authorities about Galileo's "Venetian whore", Marina Gamba, and other juicy morsels of gossip, such as his owning a copy of the notorious pornographic poem of the Venetian Pietro Aretino. We do not know what motivated Silvestro in his exposé but might surmise that it had something to do with Galileo's unfailing knack for making enemies.

So, was Padua getting too hot for Galileo at the time he penned his fulsome dedication to Cosimo de Medici in the compass tract of 1606? There is no evidence that he was actively evangelizing the Copernican theory around this time, and whatever enemies he had made seemed primarily to come from personal conflicts. It is true that the Inquisition had officially censured him for heresy regarding the horoscope, but it was a minor heresy and as much to do with his irregular domestic arrangements as it had to do with science and theology.

As the years rolled by, taking Galileo into his mid-forties – solidly middle-aged by seventeenth-century standards – he remained stuck as a not especially distinguished professor of a not especially esteemed subject, living in an officially censured personal relationship. He had failed to become the Dante or the Leonardo of mathematics and physics, and had Galileo Galilei died at the age of forty-five in the summer of 1609, he would have been remembered at best as a minor Italian mathematician with a few brief publications to his credit, warranting no more than a passing reference in a history of science textbook. But things were soon destined to change dramatically.

Chapter 11

Galileo Galilei: Fame at Last.
Part 1: Galileo and the Telescope

*I*n the early summer of 1609, Galileo received a report of an optical novelty contrived in Holland. Within a year, it would fundamentally revise humanity's understanding of the heavens, challenge classical astronomy, and propel Galileo to instant and enduring fame, turning his life into the stuff of legend. That novelty was the telescope. Yet before continuing with Galileo, let us first look at why the telescope appeared on the European scene when it did.

Light, lenses, and seeing distant things

It is a curiosity of scientific history that the telescope was not invented until 1608, for figured lenses, in transparent quartz and in glass, had been around for a good 300 years by 1608, not to mention concave metal mirrors. The Arabic optical theorist Ibn al-Haytham (or Alhazen in the Latin tradition) had conducted experiments with polished quartz spheres, pinhole images, atmospheric refraction, and spectral fringes around AD 1000, while a string of medieval Europeans, such as Bishop Robert Grosseteste, Roger Bacon, Erazmus Witelo, and Theodoric of Freiburg, had explored the geometry of refraction and reflection, modelled rainbows in the "laboratory", and even discovered that weak eyesight could be strengthened with polished convex lenticles of quartz or glass. Legend has it that Roger Bacon, who died in 1294, even hit upon the idea of spectacles, though the first clear references to "visual glasses" in Europe came a few years later.

Without doubt, by 1400 or 1450 spectacles were becoming fairly commonplace across Europe, and had already established themselves as the recognizable trademark of the scholar. Well before 1500, artists producing pictures of the great early Christian scholars, such as St Jerome or St Augustine, often felt obliged to show these men at their desks with a pair of spectacles to hand – in spite of the fact that St Jerome and St Augustine had lived around a thousand years before their invention. One can even trace the evolution not merely of visual glasses, but of frame designs, over a couple of centuries of Western art, from early frames in which the lenses were stitched between rings of leather and tied around the head, to the elegant "designer" thin wire frames depicted in el Greco's portrait of Cardinal de Guevara of *c.* 1600. These frames were very similar to early British National Health Services glasses, or those made fashionable by the young John Lennon in the 1960s. Once the technique of grinding glass had been perfected, spectacle lenses became quick and easy to make.

The art of the glass grinder and polisher probably grew out of the vastly more ancient art of the "lapidary" or gemstone-polisher: an art extending back to early biblical times. As European glass-making technology expanded rapidly after about AD 1100, with a new demand for church and house windows to keep the weather out and to let the light in, lens-making soon followed.

To make a simple lens, all one needed to do was take a fairly transparent flat slip of glass from the glassblower, maybe an inch across, and then gradually grind it face down into a previously prepared convex depression, about 6 inches across, in the upper surface of a strong iron plate secured to the workbench, using sand as an abrasive. When the glass had been ground to its desired curvature by turning it around in the concave plate, one would polish the resulting convex lens with successively finer abrasives, like powdered chalk and jeweller's rouge. A skilled man could easily make a decent lens in a few hours. Optical lathes were improving and quickening the grinding process by the sixteenth century.

By the time of Galileo's birth in 1564, therefore, there were glass-grinders in most of the great European cities, and by 1629, when he was sixty-five, there were enough spectacle-makers in the City of London alone to set up their own trade guild or livery company: the Worshipful Company of Spectacle-Makers. (And they are still thriving, for I have lectured to them.)

So, why did the lens or refracting telescope take so long to come about, consisting as it does in its simplest form of two plain lenses of matched focal length set at opposite ends of an otherwise empty tube?

HANS LIPPERSHEY: THE SPECTACLE-MAKER OF MIDDELBURGH

Like most world-changing innovations, even ones made by chance, the lens, or refracting, telescope entered upon the world stage because its inventor smelled a profit. According to the received story, which may or may not be true, Hans Lippershey, a spectacle-maker of German origin but living in Middelburgh, Holland, got the idea of the telescope when children playing in his workshop suddenly discovered that two lenses, held by chance at the right distance apart, made a distant church spire appear much closer than it was. Not a man to miss an honest guilder, Lippershey soon worked out which configuration of lenses worked best, and offered his invention to the States General, or Dutch government, in hope of a patent or public reward. Holland, after all, was the thrusting maritime "tiger economy" of northern Europe in 1608, and was also locked in a war of liberation from Spanish control of the Low Countries – and being able to see what people were up to a long way off could be a vital strategic asset.

Lippershey failed to get his patent, as other inventors succeeded in showing that he was not the only person to have done wonders with lenses in a tube, although he did receive a modest reward and a contract to supply the authorities with some "perspectives", or early telescopes. But the optical cat was safely out of the bag, and several sources of the time tell us that early telescopes were even on sale over the counter in Holland, Belgium, France, and elsewhere, and news of the device quickly spread across Europe. The news no doubt travelled west and south, across France and down the great commercial artery of the River Rhine, through Germany, into

Switzerland, Austria, and into Italy. This may have been how news of the distance-magnifying device first came to the ears of Galileo in Padua. Galileo did not *invent* the telescope, though he rapidly recognized its enormous potential, having learned of it.

For the first twelve or eighteen months of the telescope's "public life", the simple pair of lenses held apart at the right distance by an empty tube seems to have been used entirely for terrestrial purposes, and this had been Galileo's original interest in the novel device. The perennially hard-up and frustrated Galileo, like Lippershey, no doubt sensed both profit and a career advantage from his political masters, the Doge and Senate of the Serene Republic of Venice.

GALILEO'S *STARRY MESSENGER*

Galileo first seems to have heard of a "Fleming's" or "Dutchman's" invention in May 1609, when he happened to be visiting Venice. The first report of the device appears to have been unclear, for some believed the stories of the Dutch novelty and others were sceptical. Galileo was convinced of the truth behind the rumours, when he heard, so he later claimed, from one Jacques Badovere in Paris, confirming the reality of the invention. Galileo gives us the impression in *Sidereus Nuncius* ("The Starry Messenger"), and this may or may not have been the case, that the news reaching Italy contained no technical details of how the device worked. He then claims to have set about an original and independent investigation of how such a device might work based upon "the theory of refraction",[1] and soon produced an instrument consisting of two lenses mounted in a lead pipe – sometimes described as an old organ pipe – which made distant objects appear three times nearer and nine times bigger. Having grasped the optical principles of the "perspective", or telescope, he quickly learned how to make the instrument more powerful, and within days had one that magnified thirty times. Its principle of operation was very straightforward once the theory of image formation had come to be properly understood.

Two lenses were needed. One must be convex, or thicker in the middle than at the edges, and the other concave, or thinner in the middle and thicker at the edges. The convex lens, of about an inch or slightly more in diameter, needed to be of 2 or 3 feet focal length, which length was easily found out by the time-honoured method of holding the glass between one's fingers and moving it back and forth until it projected a sharp image of the scene before it upon a white surface. This happened because the convex lens bends, or refracts, all the light passing through it to a single point of focus. This "object glass", as it would come to be termed technically, was mounted in the tube at the opposite end to that at which the observer would place his or her eye. At the other end of the tube, the object glass would be matched with the concave "eye-piece" lens, and when both were adjusted into the correct focal position, a magnified image of a distant object would result. Galileo gives us a characteristically lucid and elegant description of this instrument in the opening pages of *Sidereus Nuncius*, as he would do again in *Il Saggiatore* ("The Assayer"), 1623.

In August 1609, Galileo went to Venice with one of his improved telescopes, and showed it to a number of Venetian dignitaries. He, like the Dutch, was well aware of the military and naval advantages of the *cannocchiale* ("little tube"), taking Venetian senators and other important people up the great campanile, or bell tower, of St Mark's Cathedral, and other towers, where the instrument caused wonder.

With Galileo's tube one could distinctly see ships so far out at sea that they would not be entering the harbour for a further two hours – an advantage not lost on the merchants of Venice. Then, in an adroit tactical move, Galileo presented his first *cannocchiale* to Venezia Serenissima *gratis*, as a public gesture of goodwill. The ingenious professor Galileo was duly rewarded for his trouble – handsomely rewarded, indeed. His professorship was confirmed for life, and his salary increased to 1,000 florins – much to the chagrin of some, when it was pointed out that a Frenchman had sold a similar instrument in Venice for only a few lire.

Of course, one should not in any way decry Galileo for being commercially and politically astute, for he was clearly a gifted self-publicist, and everyone in Venice knew the value of money, and of reputation. Such conduct was only likely to have increased the number of his enemies and detractors who might be all too willing to give him a smiling push once the great man was on the slide downwards – as he would find when he began to slide first in 1616, and especially after 1633. But in 1609, and for a few years thereafter, he was riding high, and basking in his new-found fame.

Sometime during the late autumn of 1609, he used the *cannocchiale* for a different purpose: to look at the moon. *Sidereus Nuncius* does not supply a date for this first observation of an astronomical body, but Galileo does mention a four- and a five-day-old waxing moon with sharp, clear "horns", and a sepia wash brush painting survives from what was probably 30 November 1609. Not only does *Sidereus Nuncius* describe the rough, broken, and spotted telescopic appearance of the moon, but both the sepia wash painting and printed woodcut pictures probably taken from them clearly depict it likewise. Galileo was skilled with both pen and brush when it came to illustrating what he saw.

Unbeknown to Galileo, he had not been the first to look at the moon through a telescope. The Englishman Thomas Harriot had not only observed an also five-day-old moon on 26 July 1609 with his newly acquired "dutch truncke" [*sic*], but had left a drawing of it, even specifying his time of observation as 9.00 p.m. on that same evening. Harriot published nothing, however, and made no claims on this subject, and his lunar (and sunspot) drawings only came to light in 1784. Harriot's circumstances were very different from those of Galileo, as we shall see in Chapter 19, for Harriot was not only the first recorded astronomical telescopic observer, but was also an active supporter of the Copernican theory in England.

What most struck Galileo about the telescopic moon was its sheer roughness. He tells us in *Sidereus Nuncius* that its surface seemed to be broken and jagged – especially visible when the moon was waxing and waning – as the oblique angle at which the sun's rays struck the moon threw the topographical features into a stark contrast of brilliant light and black shadow. Most of all, the terminator, which separated the light from the dark shadowy regions of the lunar surface, was remarkable, for as the terminator shadow moved from night to night across the lunar surface, so all manner of curious formations appeared. There were obvious mountains, deep valleys, flat regions (which came to be called *maria* or "seas") and odd round depressions (craters).

These discoveries flew in the face of classical views of the moon, which judged it to be a *smooth*, perhaps tarnished, silvery ball, as it always appeared to the naked eye. Galileo was not slow to pounce upon this incongruity, not only spelling out to his readers that these lunar features "had never been seen by anyone before me",[2] but also that their visible presence strongly suggested that "a great number of philosophers" had been wrong in their belief that the moon was "smooth, uniform, and precisely spherical".[3] He does acknowledge that some Greeks, such as Pythagoras, had believed the moon to be a globe like our own.

Galileo never attempted to make a map of the moon. Rather, he was more concerned with producing impressionistic pictures which hammered home the rough nature of the surface. Specific features appeared in slightly different places on different drawings, and were not always the same size: most notably the big cater, which was probably, in modern nomenclature, either Albategnius, Hipparchus, or Ptolemaeus, not far from the middle of the lunar disc. (It would be Thomas Harriot in England who became the first proper *selenographer*, or lunar cartographer, and whose fine, accurate, and delicate pen-and-ink drawings of the lunar surface still take one's breath away when compared with modern moon maps.)

Over Christmas 1609 and the early months of 1610, the planet Jupiter was brilliantly placed in the sky. By the first week of January 1610, Galileo had made "a very excellent instrument for myself",[4] better than those he had made previously, and on the first hour of the night of 7 January, "Jupiter presented itself to me." What he saw was something truly remarkable: something, as he put it, "never seen from the creation of the world to our own time",[5] for Jupiter appeared as a somewhat oblate sphere, with three, very bright, little stars close to it, two to the east, and one to the west.

Enjoying a run of clear winter's nights, Galileo tracked their positions over the next week, for the little stars did not stay put, but clearly rotated *around* Jupiter. On the night of 13 January, he caught sight of a fourth little star, on which occasion the new star and two others appeared to the west of Jupiter, and another to the east. Over the course of the next few weeks, something very interesting emerged, for the star nearest to the body of Jupiter rotated around the parent planet faster than the others, with each successive star rotating more slowly. What was also evident, in Galileo's description of what he saw and in his accompanying drawings, was that these orbiting little stars moved along an almost straight line in what appeared to be the plane of Jupiter's equator. Galileo immediately recognized the portentous nature of his discovery, for truly such things had never been glimpsed by human eyes. To understand the magnitude of that discovery, one has to be aware of what pre-telescopic astronomers believed the planets were – irrespective of whether one were a follower of Copernicus, Tycho, or Ptolemy. To the naked eye, a planet – Mercury, Venus, Mars, Jupiter, or Saturn – was a point of light, and not by definition a *world*. Yes, it is true that some astronomers, such as Tycho, had argued that brilliant planets such as Venus displayed discernible angular diameters, while others, more circumspect, had argued that this might simply be the product of light scatter, or dazzle, within the eye – which we now know to be the case. That a planet might reveal a very sharp focused *disc* was, however, entirely novel. Equally, if not more novel, was the idea that a planet might well have satellite stars, or moons, orbiting around it in orderly, exact periods of time: periods of time so very exact and predictable that some years later Galileo suggested that they might serve as a natural clock or chronometer in the sky, which sailors and cartographers might use for the fixing of terrestrial longitudes – as would indeed happen later in the seventeenth century.

Astronomers from classical times onwards had *assumed*, on the best naked-eye evidence, that the earth – or, if you were a Pythagorean or a Copernican, the sun – was the sole centre of rotation in the universe. While it is true that Copernicans accepted that the moon had an independent rotation around the sun-orbiting earth, the idea of the point-of-light planets possessing satellites also seemed absurd. But there it was; and if anyone took the trouble to learn how to look through one of the early "Galilean" telescopes, they could see Jupiter for themselves: an early example of that "see it for yourself" ethos which pervaded the instrument-based, experimental science of the seventeenth century. As Robert Hooke would put it in 1665, the human senses, when "strengthened" by optical and other instruments, could penetrate whole new realms of knowledge. This was an early example of "peer review" in fact; for in the seventeenth century, truth was coming increasingly to be seen as residing *not* in the deductive, philosophical systems of the ancients, but in public – almost democratic – yardsticks of natural truth. An early realization of this possibility could well have been in the mind of Galileo in 1610.

VENUS, SATURN, AND FURTHER TELESCOPIC WONDERS

Three years later, in 1613, Galileo returned to the telescopic appearance of planetary and solar system bodies in his *Letter on Sunspots*. Here he points out that, when viewed through his *cannocchiale*, Venus, the star of the morning and the evening, displayed a series of phases just like the moon.[6] Venus could be full, half, or a thin crescent, depending on its position with relation to the sun and the earth. Galileo realized that, just as in the case of the moon, one-half of Venus must be illuminated at any one time; but depending on where we, on planet earth, happened to be, we saw a "full" Venus when it was on the opposite side of the sun to us, a "half" Venus when it was halfway round its orbit and formed a right angle with the sun, and a thin crescent Venus as it moved between us and the sun. The crescent became progressively thinner until, when the planet was between us and the sun with its "dark" side towards us, it disappeared altogether, only to reappear and begin a new cycle of phases once it had passed to the opposite side of the sun. It moved from being an evening star, with its diminishing crescent, and reappeared a few weeks later with its crescent phase on the opposite side.

On the vast majority of occasions, when Venus passes between the earth and the sun, we see nothing, for the planet travels just above or just below the solar disk. Yet around every 112 years, the orbital tilts of the earth and Venus coincide, making Venus appear as a small black disc which "transits" the sun. The first such transit to be seen by the human eye would be predicted and observed by the English astronomers and admirers of Galileo

Jeremiah Horrocks and William Crabtree, in 1639, as we shall see in Chapter 21.

Galileo's Venus observations clearly indicated two facts: first, that Venus was a spherical world with sharply defined edges, not just a brilliant light in the sky; and secondly, that Venus rotated around the sun, and not the earth. Neither of these facts was compatible with the classical cosmology of Ptolemy and Aristotle, which still dominated physical and astronomical thinking in the universities of Europe in 1610. On the other hand, it should be noted, Galileo's Venus discoveries did not especially challenge the "geo-heliocentric" universe proposed by Tycho Brahe in the 1580s. As we saw in Chapter 6, in Tycho's universe Venus and all the other planets rotated around the sun anyway, with the sun and its planetary family encircling the earth in a year. This was a physical caveat against his staunch Copernicanism which the argumentative Galileo had tried to avoid drawing attention to, but of which his critics, and later enemies, were all too aware.

It was also in the *Letter on Sunspots* that Galileo published another curious discovery: the odd changes of shape displayed by Saturn, though by 1613 he was drawing on a run of observations that went back three years.[7] This was only four months after the publication of *Sidereus Nuncius,* at a time when telescopic wonders were cascading out of the night sky. Galileo's original Saturn observations were first related to Giuliano de Medici, the devoutly Catholic Tuscan ambassador at the Holy Imperial Court, and a prominent member of that great Florentine dynasty from which Galileo was angling for patronage. Yet while Saturn, like Jupiter, was more than a mere point of light when viewed through the telescope, it did not display a crisp disc. Instead, it seemed to consist either of one elongated, olive-shaped oval, or of a large central sphere flanked by two smaller ones forming a line.[8]

Two years later, on 4 December 1612, Galileo wrote to Marcus Welser of Augsburg. Welser was another high-profile figure in the world of Renaissance Roman Catholic intellectuals. He was a merchant banker, financial adviser to the Jesuit order, and a councillor at the same Imperial Court as Giuliano de Medici. To add to all that, Marcus Welser was a learned amateur astronomer, absolutely fascinated by the celestial revelations of the newly invented telescope, and a fan of Galileo. What Galileo told Welser, however, is that Saturn's behaviour was causing him concern, for over the preceding two years, Saturn's smaller companions or *ansae* ("handles") had gradually disappeared. Had the planet Saturn, like the embittered and deranged Greek god after whom he had been named, "devoured his own children"?[9]

What worried Galileo was the ammunition that this metaphorical devouring might supply to the conservative Aristotelian philosophers with whom he was in conflict. Here was Galileo, claiming that sense-knowledge, and the research potential of instruments, were a surer guide to natural truth than was philosophical deduction, when one of his star witnesses before the bar of the new knowledge was breaking down and disappearing for no known reason: Saturn's *ansae* had gone.

Of course, over the next few months, the curious *ansae* would reappear and return to their full strength, but Galileo, the increasingly overt evangelist of Copernicanism, did not know that at Christmastide 1612. What would come to be announced in 1659 as Saturn's *ring* (and after 1675, *rings*), would puzzle the astronomical community of Europe for half a century after they had first puzzled Galileo. Their future resolution and elucidation would have to await further developments in optics and telescope technology, until the young Dutch astronomer Christiaan Huygens, working with a greatly superior telescope to that of Galileo, would first see in 1655, and then formally announce in his *Systema Saturnium* ("Saturn's System", or "Structure"), 1659, that Saturn was surrounded by a thin, flat ring, that nowhere touched its body. The devouring and regurgitating of what Galileo called the *ansae* would come to be understood as a line-of-sight effect. When the rings appear to be tilted at an angle to the earth, then, in a poor-quality, low-magnification telescope Saturn appears as an oval, or perhaps as three spheroids in a line. Conversely, when the very thin ring is inclined towards the earth edge-on, a low power telescope cannot detect it, and Saturn appears round. Furthermore, as Saturn takes 29½ years to rotate around the sun, and the earth takes only one year, and the planes of their orbits are slightly tilted to one another, then one has a simple geometrical solution to the behaviour of the "devouring" Saturn, as an earth-based observer's line of sight across space constantly changes.

It was mentioned above that the discovery of Saturn's ring(s) was entirely a product of progressive optical technology, and this is a wonderfully prescient example of how technologically dependent modern science is. Galileo's 1610 telescope, for example, could reveal Saturn's odd shape, but nothing more. Then Christiaan Huygens's much better instrument delineated Saturn as a sphere surrounded by a single, unattached flat ring. And in 1675, Giovanni Domenico Cassini in Paris, with an even better telescope, found the ring to be split into two separate rings, one inside the other – with the "Cassini division" between them. By 1870, astronomers with even more powerful telescopes had discovered that each of the main rings actually consisted of a system of several separate concentric rings; while in the 1990s, the cameras of the Voyager spacecraft in its "close encounter" with Saturn discovered that, far from being solid, the rings were made up of *millions* of individual rocky lumps orbiting in the plane of the planet's equator in accordance with the laws of gravity. What a spectacular confirmation this provides of Galileo's argument that new natural knowledge must come from observed, instrument-based phenomena, and not from the authority of an ancient philosopher. Similar revelations, unimaginable to pre-telescopic astronomers, now emerged from the stars themselves.

CHAPTER 12

Galileo Galilei: Fame at Last.
Part 2: New Starry Wonders

*H*ipparchus, in the second century BC, had classified the stars into six orders of brightness, or magnitude, with the brightest, such as Sirius and Vega, as first magnitude and the dim ones on the edge of naked-eye visibility as sixth.

Ptolemy, in his *Magna Syntaxis* (or *Almagest*), had given the positions of around 1,000 individual stars amongst the forty-eight classical constellations visible in the northern hemisphere, and Tycho Brahe had measured 777 of them to a new level of accuracy by 1598. When Galileo, and Thomas Harriot, looked at the sky through their most rudimentary telescopes in 1609, they saw countless shoals of new stars, and their more powerful telescopes revealed yet more.

The Milky Way was truly breathtaking. When this *Via Lactica*, as the ancients called it, which surrounds the sky with a band of pale, milky light, is examined through the telescope, it resolves into a "tight mass of stars", as Galileo put it in *Sidereus Nuncius*.[1] Once again, a ×30 magnification telescope would reveal more Milky Way stars than would a ×6 magnification. But even the most rudimentary of telescopes suddenly revealed countless *millions* of stars beyond the classical naked-eye reckoning. While it is true that some medieval theologian-astronomers had speculated about the Milky Way being composed of a band of tiny stars, they, having no telescopes, could only speculate.

So did the black "eighth sphere", to which all the stars were attached, enclosing the planetary universe and rotating around a central earth once per day, which had been a truism since classical times, *not exist*? Might the stellar universe go on for ever, as the English astronomer Thomas Digges had suggested in 1576? (We will return to Digges in Chapter 18.) Galileo, I hasten to add, did not explore these cosmological possibilities in *Sidereus Nuncius*, but kept very much to clear reporting of discoveries; yet inevitably, imaginations were fired.

Even without a telescope, and using the naked eye, it is clear that star distribution densities vary considerably across the sky. Using his telescopes, Galileo began to examine a number of well-known naked-eye star clusters, in which several stars occupied a very small piece of sky. Among the first he looked at were the Sword and Belt of the ancient constellation Orion the Hunter, a brilliant constellation which dominates the winter skies, and which, in mid-winter, between late November 1609 and February 1610, when Galileo was researching and writing *Sidereus Nuncius*, would have formed a glorious sight on a clear night, as it still does for us today. The Orion constellation is even mentioned twice in the Bible, in Job and Amos, and was clearly familiar to the ancient Jews, and perhaps to the even more ancient Chaldeans and Indians, whose literatures seem to refer to it also.

To the naked eye Orion appears as a large irregular oblong asterism, across the middle of which are the three brilliant stars of the hunter's "belt", forming a straight line. Hanging below the belt, in what the ancient mythologies called Orion's "sword", is a cluster of five or six dim naked-eye stars enclosed within what appears to be a slightly cloudy envelope. When Galileo turned his *cannocchiale* to Orion, he "was overwhelmed by the vast quantity of stars" that presented themselves to his gaze. He reckoned that, in addition to the known stars of that constellation, his telescope revealed around six hundred hitherto unknown ones. To the three naked-eye stars of Orion's belt, and the six in his sword, Galileo added a good eighty more which had never been seen before.

Not far above Orion in the sky is the constellation of Taurus the Bull, and one of its famous features is the Pleiades cluster, consisting of six – or, depending on one's eyesight, seven – small stars. Another celestial gem referred to in Scripture, in the Greek author Hesiod, and other ancient sources, the Pleiades are also a conspicuous feature of the winter sky. Through his telescope, Galileo could count at least forty hitherto unseen small stars in the Pleiades, and in *Sidereus Nuncius* he illustrates the positions of thirty-six of them. Likewise, the small Praesepe cluster in Cancer the Crab resolved into over forty "starlets" in his telescope.[2]

In *Sidereus Nuncius* Galileo refrains from too much speculation regarding the nature and consequences of what he had seen through his *cannocchiale*, and largely just narrates what he – and by extension, other people with telescopes – might see. But the sheer stark facts in themselves were potentially unsettling in their repercussions for the conservative Aristotelian philosophers of Padua and other Renaissance universities. In his later works, such as the *Letter on Sunspots* (1613), *The Assayer* (1623), and most of all in the *Dialogue on the Two Chief Systems of the World* (1632), which came to precipitate his summoning before the Holy Office in Rome, Galileo does begin to probe these consequences.

THEOLOGICAL AND PHILOSOPHICAL IMPLICATIONS

All this was unsettling for the conservative Aristotelian academics, whose theories of how the natural world was constituted it came to challenge. It was not, however, especially unsettling for Christian belief in itself, except for those academic theologians who were also Aristotelians, and whose Christian understanding was intimately bound up with their Aristotelian logical philosophy – a body of men, alas, who were by no means uncommon within the upper echelons of Catholic thought in 1610. Yet, Aristotelian partialities apart, neither the Old nor the New Testament, neither Moses, the psalmists, Isaiah, Jesus, nor St Paul offer any opinions on the nature of Jupiter or Saturn, the horns of Venus, or the number of stars in the Milky Way – except, that is, from telling us that God made them all and guides them across the sky. This is a very important point that we must keep before us when discussing Galileo's science and the church; for while he would in the years ahead become increasingly confident in his subversion of academic Aristotelian science, he has no argument with either the Bible or with wider Christian teaching.

If you were a conservative Aristotelian philosopher, you had plenty to worry about when it came to thinking through the consequences of Galileo's discoveries. Why, for instance, if Aristotle's works really were the complete explanation for all intellectual and natural phenomena, could two lenses in a tube reveal things which the great master thinker, in 350 BC, had never so much as dreamt of? And what was the intellectual *status* of the new telescopic knowledge? Given a bit of training beforehand as to where to place one's eye, *anyone* could see the moon's craters, Jupiter's satellites, or the countless realms of stars in the Milky Way, without so much as having heard of an Aristotelian logical syllogism. Artisans, servants, ploughboys, and even women could see them if given the opportunity, even if these "unlearned" folk lacked a frame of reference into which to place and interpret what they saw. In much the same way, a common sailor, after two months spent crossing the Atlantic, could set his feet on the American continent, no matter how much a conservative geographer might rail that this was logically absurd because Ptolemy in AD 150 had never mentioned the existence of America.

Such questions were potentially very destabilizing for traditional Aristotelian science, and begged yet more. How far can scientific instruments expand human knowledge? Is there a limit to what we can know? Why have the ancients got so much wrong, or missed so much knowledge? How is it that we, in *c.* 1610, can put them right? Has the classical idea of a sphere of equidistant fixed stars surrounding the earth been shown to be wrong, and could the stars be scattered into the vastness of deep space? Could the earth even rotate about the sun?

Galileo, I emphasize once again, was cautious about drawing too many outlandish conclusions from what he reported, at least in the early days, though readers of *Sidereus Nuncius* or *Letter on Sunspots* did not need to be a second Aristotle for those questions to form in their minds.

CELESTIAL PERFECTION CHALLENGED:
SPOTS UPON THE SUN

What were the sunspots about which Galileo wrote and exchanged several letters with his Augsburg banker friend Marcus Welser over 1612, and which formed the body of his far-reaching book of 1613, and why did they become objects of such controversy?

Their actual discoverer is a matter of dispute, although Galileo was quick to pounce upon anyone who claimed to have discovered them before he did. In fairness, it appears that the honour of having first noticed sunspots belonged to the German astronomer Johann Fabricius (son of David Fabricius, Kepler's friend) of Wittenberg, who announced his findings in the summer of 1611. Then there was the eminent German Jesuit astronomer Christopher Scheiner of Ingolstadt, who around the same time announced his own observations in writing to none other than Marcus Welser.

Because Scheiner's Jesuit superiors did not wish his discoveries to provoke responses which might have brought criticism or ridicule upon what was, after all, a Christian missionary order, his early sunspot communications were conducted under the name of Apelles, or, to put it more fully, *Apelles latens post tabulam* ("Apelles hiding behind his picture"), after the story of the classical Greek painter of that name who reputedly hid behind his picture so that he could secretly listen to what people said about it. Scheiner was told to wait to see how his discovery was received before revealing his identity.

In addition to Fabricius and Scheiner/Apelles, there was Thomas Harriot in England, who between December 1610 and *c.* 1612 recorded making several *hundred* detailed drawings of the *maculae* or spots on the solar surface. But, as with everything else regarding Harriot's telescopic discoveries, they remained unknown until his pages were examined in the late eighteenth century, so that his work never figured in the contemporary debate about sunspots. Harriot's papers reveal that his views on the nature of sunspots were very similar to those of his fellow Copernican, Galileo.

Irrespective of who first used a telescope to see spots on the sun's disc, what is beyond dispute is that Galileo was the man who seized upon their physical significance, and extracted a good deal of polemical mileage from them. Galileo was a self-publicist of genius, and to him must go 95 per cent of the credit for seizing upon the cosmological significance of the new telescopic discoveries, and using them to advance the "new" Copernican astronomy. In some ways he over-played his genius and it is this, when expressed in his own inimitable and often provocative style, that led to his undoing after 1633. But as a genius in "the public understanding of science", he had no rival, and the discovery of sunspots provided him with a new springboard from which to launch further assaults upon the conservative academics of Padua and beyond.

Let us begin by looking first at the method by which one could most conveniently observe the sunspots. One could, of course, point the telescope directly at the sun – for this, after all, was how Harriot made his hundreds of observations of the solar disc. But Harriot was no fool, and realized that looking at the sun through a telescope could cause blindness. What Harriot did, therefore, was confine his observations to when the sun was rising, or setting through cloud. His favourite time for observing was when the sun was rising through a thick dawn mist shrouding the Thames valley – through a fairly dense natural filter, in fact. Nevertheless, this was a dangerous method, and certainly not one to be recommended, for if the sun had broken through into a clear patch of sky, it could have cost him his eyesight; mercifully, it never did. We shall meet Thomas Harriot again in Chapter 19.

There is the popular myth that Galileo went blind – that he sacrificed his eyesight in the cause of science, by looking at the sun directly through his telescope. This is pure nonsense, exploded at source for anyone who chooses to read the *Letter on Sunspots* and to compare the chronology of sunspot discovery with the other dated events in his life. Galileo relates in detail in his second letter to Welser exactly how he observed the spots. He used the telescope to *project* an image of the sun on to "a flat white sheet of paper about a foot from the concave [eyepiece] lens; upon this will fall a circular image of the sun's disc, with all the spots that are on it arranged and disposed with exactly the same symmetry as in the sun".[3] If one used a pair of compasses to draw a circle on the sheet of paper, and then adjusted the telescope so that the solar image filled the circle exactly, one could use a pen to record the exact position of each spot with perfect safety, for none of the sun's intense, focused light and heat would directly enter the eye.

Galileo was observing thus in August 1612, when he was forty-eight years old. Over the next twenty-five years, he would make a host of meticulous, keen-sighted observations and measurements in astronomy and physics, culminating, when he was seventy-three, in his telescopic detection of the moon's "libration", or slight rocking on its axis – his last great astronomical discovery. Soon after that, Galileo started to go blind, when he was in his mid to late seventies – too late for any solar observations conducted decades before to have deprived him of his vision. Yet Galileo became a popular focus for "martyr of science" myth-makers, especially after *c.* 1750.

Why, then, did Galileo go blind? A now sadly deceased surgeon friend of mine, and an accomplished amateur solar astronomer, Mr Erich Strach F.R.C.S. of Liverpool, once told me that, from a study of contemporary paintings and accounts of the elderly Galileo, he believed the astronomer may have been suffering from the onset of glaucoma: a condition caused by a build-up of pressure within the eye, and sometimes giving it a certain "stare". This condition is now treatable surgically, but was beyond medical help in 1640. Mr Strach, a very experienced medical practitioner, emphasized that his glaucoma "diagnosis" was very tentative, for no modern doctor can pronounce with certainty upon the medical condition of a person who has been dead for over 350 years, and about whom crucial ancillary information is not available. What can be said for certain, however, is that Galileo did *not* go blind because of staring at the sun through his telescope twenty-five years before.

Galileo may have come upon this observation technique through his own well-attested technical ingenuity, although as it was also the method by which Apelles or Scheiner made his own solar observations, he may have learned of it from the Jesuit Father. The projection method is still the one employed by amateur astronomers today to observe the solar spots, and to use as a completely safe and captivating astronomical teaching aid.

Christopher Scheiner, in spite of his more conservative Aristotelian views on the nature of the sunspots, spent more of his life in carefully observing and monitoring them than did Galileo, for in 1630, Scheiner brought out his curiously entitled *Rosa Ursina sive Sol* ("The Rose of the Bears, or the Sun"). It was a large, copiously illustrated and meticulous study of sunspots, in which their positions, sizes, and densities were painstakingly recorded over a quarter of a century. In many ways, it became the first great treatise on observation-based solar physics, for while no one in 1630 knew how the sun burned and radiated its energy, *Rosa Ursina* began at the bottom, as it were, by putting on record a large body of primary physical data. It also described Scheiner's telescopic projection system, and in his "Helioscope" illustrated the first use of an equatorial mount for a telescope used to track the sun in the equatorial plane, while the projected image of its current spots was recorded. We shall meet Father Scheiner again in Chapter 16.

Matters of observing technique apart, exactly why were the sunspots so controversial in 1611–13? Galileo was very much aware of their potential as ammunition against the Aristotelians, for they provided yet another example of the "mutability" of the supposed "immutable" heavens. Only a few weeks, or even a few days, of observation revealed three basic facts about the spots. Firstly, they were relatively ephemeral: coming, going, thickening, and thinning. Secondly, they all moved from the left-hand side of the sun to the right, and all the spots, big and small, moved at exactly the same speed. Thirdly, the great majority of the spots were opaque, apparently being composed of matter so dense that not even the blinding light of the sun could penetrate them. Occasionally some light-coloured spots appeared, being white in contrast with the sun's yellow brilliance; these light spots would come to be called *faculae*, in contrast with the dark spots, or *maculae*.

But what were they? Christopher Scheiner had proposed that the spots were not a part of the sun, but were line-of-sight effects generated by little planetoids moving in space and across the solar disc. The large spots were no more than the optical effect produced by clusters of these spots transiting the solar disc in our line of sight, and their ephemeral character resulted from their constantly changing positions as they appeared to group together and move apart.

Galileo was well aware that this explanation caused the Aristotelians and the adherents of Ptolemy to trip over some of their own arguments. For example, while some traditional philosophers were willing to dismiss Jupiter's moons and the newly discovered stars of the Milky Way as optical illusions, they were also willing to populate space with little planetoids passing before the sun's surface. To Galileo's credit, brilliant polemicist as he was, he advanced his case for a *spotted* sun with impeccable thoroughness.

His arguments were based on meticulous observations and careful logical *inductions* drawn from them. The spots, for instance, while appearing two-dimensional and often in irregular clumps when face-on in the middle of the sun's disc, gradually became thinner as they approached the solar edge, or limb, until they were little more than one-dimensional lines as they went around the edge. Clearly, they were short-lived blemishes or clouds of some kind upon, or very close to, the body of the sun, in much the same way as the map of Africa on a geographical globe diminishes to a line as one rotates the globe and it vanishes around the edge.

This provided Galileo with yet another argument against the Aristotelians, for not only was the sun blemished and spotted with ephemeral objects, but, equally important, it *rotated* on its axis every twenty-seven or twenty-eight days. Galileo's *cannocchiale* had provided additional evidence which now strongly suggested that the "lamp of the universe" was not fixed and stable as a rock, but was *spinning* in space. It had north and south poles and an equator just like the earth, moon, Jupiter, and Venus.

It was in the *Letter on Sunspots* that Galileo unfurled his colours as a Copernican, no doubt sensing that the new telescopic evidences pushed the likelihood of heliocentricism several crucial points beyond the elegant planetary geometry of Copernicus's own arguments.

Let us not underestimate the fair-mindedness of Father Scheiner, to whose prescient remark Galileo drew attention in his first letter to Welser on 6 May 1612. Apelles had suggested that if Venus and Mercury rotated around the sun, then we should be able, using telescopic projection, to see them transiting the sun. This was absolutely correct, for while we can, as Galileo reminded Welser, follow the whole cycle of Venusian phases, and predict when it and Mercury will pass between us and the sun, the orbital tilts of the earth, sun, and the two planets actually mean that only rarely do the planets pass directly across the sun's disc to become visible as circular black dots. Johannes Kepler was to unravel the complex geometry of the planetary solar transits in the 1620s, while Pierre Gassendi would be the first to actually see a Mercury transit from Paris in 1631, and Jeremiah Horrocks would witness a Venus transit, from the Lancashire village of Much Hoole in 1639. We will discuss them in further detail later.

Galileo the philosopher-courtier to the Medici

What is beyond dispute is that the telescopic discoveries not only inaugurated a fundamental revision in astronomical thinking; they also transformed Galileo's life and public profile. By the end of 1610 he was the most famous astronomer in Europe. The University of Padua had confirmed his professorship for life and given him a huge salary increase to 1,000 florins a year, but soon after, he had received an even better offer. The university, rightly, felt that it had been poorly handled by its new "celebrity" astronomer, when Galileo's "angling" had landed him the big fish he desired: Grand Duke Cosimo II invited Galileo to return to Florence as an academic courtier. Galileo let it be known that he did not want to be Cosimo's astronomer or mathematician, for these titles carried overtones of being mere mechanical or routine activities. No, he would be the Grand Duke's Philosopher, a title carrying ancient connotations of wisdom and high insight beyond that of any mere stargazer or land-measurer. There was very little about image, style, connotations of titles, and self-presentation that a modern PR agency could have taught Galileo.

And now, wearing fine robes and gold chains, dining at the duke's table with visiting cardinals and ambassadors, and receiving accolades not only from the learned of Europe but also from its crowned heads, Galileo had *arrived*. His new address, appearing on his sunspot correspondence with Marcus Welser by 1612, was no longer a professor's lodgings in Padua, but "the Villa delle

Selve", Florence, the residence of his patrician friend Signor Filippo Salviati. Capping it all, Galileo's friend and admirer Father Christopher Clavius SJ (Society of Jesus), of the Papal Observatory in the Vatican, wrote to him just before Christmas 1610 to say that he and his Vatican Observatory colleagues had *confirmed* the facts of his momentous telescopic observations.[4]

The telescope had brought Galileo fame at last.

Chapter 13

"No one expects the
Spanish Inquisition."
Part 1: Galileo, the Telescope, and
the Church

$\mathcal{A}$s a scientific celebrity philosopher and courtier of international standing, and basking in his fame at the illustrious Medici court, Galileo realized that certain aspects of his life had to be put in order. If he was to move amongst cardinals, ambassadors, and Grand Dukes, he had to become respectable.

MARINA GAMBA AND HER CHILDREN

Marina Gamba, his mistress of several years' standing and mother of his three children, no doubt became something of an embarrassment to a man of Galileo's new-found eminence. While princes, cardinals, and even popes had mistresses and illegitimate children, the normal practice was to keep the ladies hidden away at a distance, and pass the children off as nephews, nieces, or relatives of one's extended family. One suspects that Marina and Galileo's irregular relationship had been too open and too well known for that (especially in the wake of his denouncement for casting horoscopes in 1604), and while this may not have mattered so much for a mere professor of mathematics, it could be potentially embarrassing for a now internationally famous Medici Court Philosopher. Marina, who had been born around 1570, would now have been about forty, and was very likely not the beauty she once was (for people aged faster in that pre-modern-medicine world) and had lost her appeal as an "exotic".

There were aspects of Galileo and Marina's relationship that had clearly been kept out of the legal record right from the start, as the ambitious Galileo angled for distinguished patrons both in Venice and especially at the Medici Court in Florence. In none of the surviving baptismal records for their three children, Virginia, Livia, and Vincenzo, is Galileo named as their father. Vincenzo's baptismal record states "father uncertain", while Virginia is bluntly recorded as the "daughter by fornication of Marina of Venice".[1] No matter who Marina was, it seems that even during the years of their co-habitation Galileo had been happy for her to go on legal record as little more than an unmarried common prostitute, and mother of three illegitimate children.

One wonders what sort of relationship they must have had if, once his star of fame had risen in 1610, Galileo was willing to pack off the now early-middle-aged Marina, with whom he had had an intimate relationship of ten or twelve years' duration, back to Venice as she was now an obvious social embarrassment. What happened to her in Venice is a matter of dispute. Was she the Marina Gamba who died on 21 August 1612, or the Marina who was long believed to have married one Giovanni Bartoluzzi? Probably she was the lady who died in 1612, although we do know that a Venetian woman named Marina continued to look after little Vincenzo before he was deemed old enough to travel to Florence to join his father at the Medici Court, at around the age of eight or nine, in 1614. In 1619, the Grand Duke legitimized Vincenzo. The two girls, Virginia and Livia, were placed in a convent, where they took the religious profession names of Sister Maria Celeste and Sister Arcangela. Maria Celeste would become a model nun, a loyal and supportive daughter to her father, and enter history as "Galileo's daughter".

THE GRAND DUKE'S PHILOSOPHER

It was during his first years – or months – at the Florentine Court that Galileo embarked upon what would turn into a series of high-profile ecclesiastically related controversies. The first of these, as we saw in Chapter 12, involved the discovery and interpretation of sunspots over 1611–13, and while the exchanges with the Aristotelians began courteously, they did not stay that way. Perhaps because he was now a celebrity "philosopher", enjoying the explicit protection and patronage of the Grand Duke of Tuscany, Galileo felt more confident not only in advocating an explicit Copernican allegiance, but also in giving rein to his natural pugnacity. But Grand Dukes notwithstanding, Galileo began to find that he had powerful enemies – enemies, one hastens to add, that he need not have made, had his personal "style" and method of advancing his scientific arguments been different.

Things had begun to go wrong as early as August 1610, while Galileo was still at Padua; for, as he said in a letter to Kepler, some prominent Aristotelians had *refused* to look through his telescope even when it was offered to them. We must divest ourselves of the gift of hindsight when reviewing this circumstance, for the telescope was an instrument the like of which was wholly unprecedented in world civilization. Since classical times, the *true* instruments of the astronomer were graduated angle-measuring instruments, based on the properties of the 360-degree circle. Astronomical truth lay in measurement and in geometry: it did *not* lie in strangely magnified images of familiar bodies such as Jupiter or Saturn, sometimes complete with image distortions and false colour fringes. To many scholars in 1610–11, the telescope was a novelty at best and an irrelevance at worst.

The telescopic discoveries flew in the face of *reason* as it was then understood in science. In Aristotelian and Ptolemaic thinking, the disciplined rational intellect and the accumulated wisdom of the ages comprised the royal road to truth. Light being bent and distorted through lenses down tubes was an absurdity, and so clearly full of false information that no wise philosopher could be expected to give credence to what appeared through the eyepiece.

Some philosophers who were willing to look claimed that they could see nothing. They have my sympathy, for having built and observed with a replica Galilean telescope, I can vouch for how awkward they are to use. I once showed the moon to a group of Oxford medical students through my Galilean telescope: young men and women who were daily familiar with the use of microscopes and other very sophisticated optical and other instruments. Many of them, like some of Galileo's Paduan philosophy colleagues, took several goes, with much repositioning of their eyes, before shouting out in delight, "Yes, I've got it at last!" The ray of light emerging from a Galilean eyepiece is very narrow, and making it fall, sharply focused, upon one's retina can be quite a job, until one gets the hang of it. In 1610–11, that was only the beginning: making logical *sense* of what you saw was a wholly different matter.

What was truly remarkable were the number of Aristotelians, Jesuits, and others who not only looked through Galileo's telescope, but then went off to build their own and begin to wrestle at first hand with the implications of what they seemed to be seeing. Looking at things from their new confused and ancestral-wisdom-challenging point of view, it is not surprising that they needed time and much debate to accept the *reality* of the lunar mountains or Jupiter's moons.

One of Galileo's first encounters with Jesuit and Aristotelian puzzlement came in 1611, when he visited the Collegium Romanum in Rome to talk about telescopes and the implications of the new discoveries with the Fathers. Far from entering the lion's den, he found well-wishers and admirers there. Father Christoph Grienberger SJ, for example, was not without sympathy for Galileo's discoveries, but as part of that rigorous debate and counter-challenge way of thinking on which the Jesuits prided themselves, he argued the Aristotelian case *against*. As we saw at the end of Chapter 12, Father Christopher Clavius, one of the most distinguished astronomers in Europe, was an admirer of Galileo though he could not accept his interpretation of the rough lunar surface. The Collegium Romanum comprised men of the very highest intellect, and to dismiss them as prejudiced bigots simply fails to respect the historical context.

Yet, one may ask, did not Galileo's arguments in favour of the earth spinning on its axis and moving through space explicitly contradict numerous passages in Scripture – most notably Joshua 10, and Psalms 93:1 and 104:5? On the other hand, as we saw in earlier chapters, why did it take the Roman Catholic Church so long to get around to condemning the Copernican theory, which had been in circulation and in print not only since 1543, but from Rheticus's *Narratio Prima* of 1540 (Dantzig) and 1541 (Basel), and had even been favourably commented upon by Cardinal Schönberg in 1536, if it was so theologically offensive? One could use the device mentioned by Andreas Osiander in his unauthorized "Preface" to Copernicus's *De Revolutionibus* and assert that the book was outlining a *theoretical* model of the universe which simplified planetary calculation rather than presuming to describe the universe as it was. But all the evidence suggests that Copernicus believed that the earth *did* move, both on its axis and around the sun, as did a decent minority of both Catholic and Protestant thinkers over the seventy years following 1543 – including high-profile Protestants in Roman Catholic employ, such as Kepler.

What had changed between Cardinal Schönberg's warm letter of 1536 and the trouble that began to brew for Galileo after 1613? Galileo's personal "style" and knack for making enemies did not help; but what other changes had happened between 1610 and 1616? Perhaps these might be related to the wider European and global scene.

Vatican and wider European politics

For one thing, in Copernicus's time the Reformation, as we now call it, was still a new movement, and while bloody wars had been fought between Catholics and Protestants in Germany and parts of Eastern Europe, many hoped for reconciliation. Erasmus, the great Dutch theologian and editor of the first Greek New Testament, had friends on both sides, and while remaining a Roman Catholic, admitted that the Reformers were making some important points. Not only Martin Luther believed that the Catholic Church of 1530 needed reform; many on the "inside" did as well.

By 1610 the idea of a friendly reconciliation between Rome and Wittenberg, Zurich, or even Canterbury seemed impossible. The division was made deeper by wars and acts of violent religious genocide, such as the shameful massacre of "Huguenot" Protestants by Catholics in Paris on St Bartholomew's night, 24 August 1572. The governments of Queen Elizabeth I and James I had actively pursued, hung, drawn, and quartered English-born Roman Catholic priests who simply wanted to take the Sacraments to those beleaguered folk loyal to the "old religion" in northern and other parts of England.

After 1534, St Ignatius Loyola's missionary Society of Jesus, or Jesuits, set out to win converts back to Catholicism by ingenuity, argument, self-sacrifice, and acts of amazing bravery, in Europe and then in the Americas and China. It was a radical, independent, order of Christian gentlemen which sometimes angered the ecclesiastical "establishment" by siding with the Indian tribes-folk of Latin America against the aggressive secular forces of Spain. The New World became not merely a battleground for global politics, but also for souls, as committed Protestants in North America aspired to take their interpretation of Christianity to the native people of Roanoke, Chesapeake Bay, and then Boston, Massachusetts.

Of central significance in the period between Copernicus and Galileo's telescopic discoveries had been the deliberations of the Council of Trent, at Trento, Italy, between 1545 and 1563. During this Counter-Reformation the senior clergy of the Roman Catholic Church set about putting their own house in order, dealing with issues as diverse as clerical corruption, Christian doctrine, and the musical settings of the church's liturgy, which were often over-complicated, making it hard to follow the Latin words. Yet, while theological houses, both Protestant and Catholic, were being put in order by the late sixteenth century, the matters of debate which Martin Luther nailed to the door of Wittenberg Cathedral in 1517 had now hardened into what could at best be styled a Christian "stand-off" between two hostile sides facing each other across a chasm. A stand-off, alas, which sometimes broke down into acts of overt military aggression, such as Philip II's mercifully failed

Spanish Armada against Protestant England in 1588, and the horrors of the Thirty Years War after 1618.

By 1630, the Vatican itself was even less of a "united happy family" than it was usually. While politicking and hostilities between individual cardinals were as old as Christian Rome itself, they were exacerbated by the nationalistic political abrasions taking place between Italian, German, French, and Spanish factions within the Sacred College. By the 1620s relations had become especially strained between Spain and the Vatican. The great and ancient European royal house of Hapsburg, which ruled Spain, Austria, much of Germany, and the Low Countries, began to accuse Pope Urban VIII of pursuing policies favourable to the Spanish arch-enemy, France, and even to the Protestant King of Sweden, Gustavus Adolphus, whose armies were occasioning revolt in Holland, Belgium, and the Rhineland. Pope Urban VIII was being accused of not harrying the Protestants of northern Europe with sufficient zeal.

What may have lain behind these accusations has been a topic of much discussion among historians, but what matters is that the perception of the same inflamed Spanish and Hapsburg sensibilities in the 1620s. Cardinal Gaspar de Borja (or Gaspare Borgia), a senior Spanish cardinal resident in Rome – who on two occasions also served as Spain's ambassador to the Holy See, thereby combining in his person both high ecclesiastical and high diplomatic offices – made little effort to disguise his contempt for Urban VIII. Incidents were recorded in which the two men jostled each other, and, on one occasion, it was said, Cardinal Borja even hit Urban in the face. In 1634 things had got so bad that Urban insisted that the King of Spain withdraw Borja's ambassadorial status, while Urban hindered the cardinal's eventually successful elevation to the new dignity of Archbishop of Toledo.

All this detail about the high-level theological, political, and personal ructions that were going on across Europe, and especially Roman Catholic Europe, is necessary in order to provide some background or perspective to the "Galileo affair". It is popularly assumed that Roman Catholic Europe, and especially Italy and the Vatican, were a unified and homogeneous whole, with an absolutist pope whose word was law, and before whose authority all good Catholics meekly bowed – but history provides abundant evidence to the contrary. When new ideas or discoveries appeared on the scene, opinions about them could be as varied within the Catholic intellectual world as could be opinions about popes, personalities, or politics.

This is crucial to understanding Galileo in context, as opposed to seeing him as the brave and then persecuted champion of "truth", daring to stand up to the supposedly unified monolith of church dogma – much like the scenario portrayed in Berthold Brecht's historically biased yet formative *The Life of Galileo* (1939), in fact.

So, how did the church respond to Galileo's discoveries, and to his post-1612 openly declared Copernican allegiance?

GALILEO'S FIRST ENCOUNTER WITH
CHURCH OPPOSITION

Galileo, as we have seen – astrology and his irregular liaison with Marina Gamba apart – always enjoyed good relations with the Roman Catholic Church. While not an especially assiduous churchgoer in Padua, he had never displayed evidence of any noticeable theological unorthodoxy. It is true that there had been some growls in 1611, but that had come to nothing, although his friend Ludovico de Gigolo said that Galileo had made enemies amongst some Jesuit Aristotelians in his dispute around this time on the nature of buoyancy and the physics of floating bodies. As we have seen many times already, however, Galileo was no stranger to the business of making enemies, especially when it came to the way he drove experimental conclusions in the face of Aristotelian deductive ones. Yes, we know after 400 years of hindsight that Galileo had been right, and the Aristotelians wrong, but the truth of Galileo's various claims was by no means proven in 1620 – besides which, why make unnecessary enemies?

The controversy regarding heliocentricism in particular began in 1613, when the poet and philosopher Cosimo Boscaglia argued that the idea of the earth spinning and moving through space was contrary to Scripture. Boscaglia, one must say, accepted the reality of the new telescopic discoveries as a fact; but, like a good few others, he disputed Galileo's heliocentric interpretation. On the other hand, Galileo had a defender in an old pupil, Benedetto Castelli, who was not only an astronomer and mathematician, but also a Benedictine monk and abbot.

More worrying blasts of clerical opprobrium came in 1614 and 1615, when Tommaso Caccini, a Dominican friar, preached an Advent sermon on 2 December 1614 which openly attacked Galileo's advocacy of a moving earth. Caccini did this on the strength of his biblical text, Joshua 10, and, it was said, Acts 1:11, about the Galileans witnessing Jesus' ascent into heaven. Not long afterwards, Niccolò Lorini argued against Galileo and Copernicanism on the basis of a ruling in the Council of Trent regarding the plain meaning of Scripture. (It was not only the Protestants who were concerned with Scripture's "plain meaning", but also the Counter-Reformation Catholic Church, as it began to put its house in order.)

Then on 19 March 1615, Caccini formally denounced Galileo and Copernicanism before the Roman Inquisition. The largely Dominican-run Holy Inquisition, however – made especially notorious to history through its separate and constitutionally different Spanish division, as we shall see shortly – was a body set up to counter heresy back in 1232. Primarily, it was concerned with unbelief: with sceptics, Albigensians, Anti-Trinitarians, Jews, and, to some extent, Muslims. Christian *theology* was its concern, and science and scientific discovery were not part of its remit; it was only with the heating up of the accusations against Galileo that it became more formally involved. While the Copernican and mystic Giordano Bruno had fallen foul of the Inquisition in 1600, it was Bruno's anti-Trinitarian pantheist universalism that concerned them far more than astronomy.

Things moved up a gear when the Neopolitan Carmelite Father Paolo Antonio Foscarini published his effusively entitled Italian *Lettera... sopra l'opinione... del Copernico* ("Epistle concerning the Pythagorean and Copernican Opinion on the Mobility of the Earth"), 1615. Foscarini's *Lettera*, which was really a book, set out to defend Copernicus and Galileo's Copernican interpretation of his telescopic discoveries. It did so, very crucially, by arguing *not* that the heliocentric theory was merely a hypothesis and a calculating device, but that it described the physical truth of the universe: the earth *really did* go around the sun. Foscarini then went on to attempt to reinterpret certain key passages of Scripture which implied that the earth was *not* fixed in the centre of the universe. It was this attempt to reinterpret Scripture that was potentially most troublesome, for it could be seen as running counter to the Tridentine Council's decision about Scripture's "plain" meaning.

Foscarini seemed no less confident of his power to convince the church about the physical truth of Copernicanism than was Galileo, for he sent a copy of his *Lettera* – originally intended for the head of the Carmelite Order – to Cardinal Roberto Bellarmine in Rome. Now Bellarmine was one of the leading "big guns" in the Catholic Church's intellectual armoury: a theologian, Renaissance scholar, and thinker of the highest eminence, and a man of great personal power and influence. On 12 April 1615 Bellarmine sent a long and detailed reply to Foscarini. This letter may seem to us today excessively cautious and conservative in its interpretation; but if only we can think ourselves back into the world of 1615 and lay aside all that has been discovered over the past 400 years, we will acknowledge that it reflects a cool-headed wisdom. Should we cast aside the insights of the Church Fathers, 1,500 years of critical understanding of Scripture, much Greek philosophy, and even the wisdom of Solomon, not to mention the wise deliberations of the reforming Council of Trent, in favour of what a rather bombastic Paduan professor claims to have seen through two small lenses in a tube?

Bellarmine sets out three points for Father Foscarini to consider. Firstly, there seemed to be no problem in discussing the Copernican theory as a *hypothesis*, which is how Bellarmine interpreted Copernicus's own view (on the strength of Osiander's unauthorized "Preface"). Secondly, he reminds Foscarini that the Council of Trent forbade the interpretation of Scripture in a way "contrary to the common opinion of the holy Fathers" of the church,[2] contrary to the common-sense or plain meaning of Scripture – a point established by Trent to prevent theologians and philosophers from playing word games with the meaning of the Bible, and confusing the laity.

It is in his third point that Bellarmine is especially interesting, and in which he shows a potential for interpretational flexibility of the kind that Galileo – and, no doubt, Foscarini – were inclining to. Bellarmine says:

If there were a real proof that the sun is in the centre of the universe, that the earth is in the third sphere [or third planet out after Mercury and Venus], and that the sun does not go around the earth but the earth round the sun, then we should have to proceed with great circumspection in explaining passages of Scripture which appear to teach the contrary, and rather admit that we did not understand them than declare an opinion false which is proved to be true.[3]

Bellarmine made it clear that as the evidences stood in 1615 not only was no such *proof* available, but he could not see the likelihood of any appearing on the horizon.

The analogy of the earth being like a moving ship which appears stable and creates the illusion that the land is sliding away from it, argued Bellarmine, would *not* hold; common sense tells us that the land is stable and it is the ship that moves. Yet all sense experience tells us that the earth is *not* moving: a view implicit in the commonsensical biblical writers.

As far as Bellarmine was concerned, therefore, Galileo's discovery of the moon's mountains, Jupiter's four satellites, the phases of Venus, and sunspots might stand as fascinating newly revealed natural phenomena, but they in no way tilted the balance in favour of a moving earth. One supposes the only "real proof that the sun is in the centre of the universe" must come from astronomical geometry combined with sound philosophical deduction. But as Tycho had openly declared himself, on the best evidential grounds of the age, in favour of a *fixed, immovable* earth, one understands why Bellarmine could not foresee any new proofs appearing.

Bellarmine's letter to Foscarini gives us a good idea of how things stood in high-level Catholic thinking in 1615. It was measured, logical, concerned with solid evidence as opposed to speculation, and deeply reverent to Scripture and to the tradition of the Church Fathers. It was in no way "fundamentalist" in the twentieth-century sense of the word, and rooted not in flashes of private insight, but in the accumulated wisdom of consensually derived interpretations built up corporately within church councils and other ecclesiastical bodies, along with the universities of Christendom over 1,500 years, culminating in those of Trent, only six decades before. It displayed a potential flexibility in that it said that this is how things stand today, but if new *solid* evidences come to light, we will need a rethink. What did throw the cat among the pigeons was Galileo's own excursion into theology in 1615, especially as he, *unlike* Foscarini, had received no formal higher theological training, and was neither a priest, a monk, nor a friar.

It all began at a dinner at the Florentine Court in November 1613, where, it appears, Galileo's telescopic discoveries – and, by implication, the moving earth – were being discussed before the Grand Duke Cosimo II. Galileo had not been present at the dinner, but his Benedictine monk friend Benedetto Castelli had. On 14 December, Castelli wrote a balanced account of the discussion, along with possible scriptural interpretations of the recent cosmological discoveries, and sent it to Galileo.[4] Galileo then sent his own response, dated 21 December, in which he defended the heliocentric theory as a physical reality and *not* as a mere hypothesis, and this "Letter to Castelli" would soon form the basis of a short treatise, *Letter to the Grand Duchess Christina*, 1615, though not published as a book until the Strasbourg edition of 1636.

Christina was the widow of Ferdinando, Grand Duke of Tuscany, who in 1588 had secured Galileo's appointment to his first professorial appointment at Pisa. She was now the dowager Grand Duchess, and mother of Galileo's current patron, Cosimo II. It appears that Christina had been especially interested in what was said at the 1613 dinner discussion on heliocentricism, so it was to her that Galileo addressed and dedicated his manuscript *Letter* of 1615. It seems to have circulated around the court, and maybe beyond, and was destined to become an enduring classic statement on the relation of science and religion.

In the *Letter*, Galileo boldly nailed his colours to the mast and declared that he considered the Copernican theory to be physically true: not a calculating device, nor a phenomena-saving hypothesis, but a description of what stood and what moved in the *real* universe.

It has to be admitted that early on in his *Letter*, he spells out some home truths about Copernicus, telling Grand Duchess Christina that in his day Copernicus was so highly esteemed in ecclesiastical circles that Pope Leo X respectfully sought his opinion on calendar reform, and "the Cardinal of Capua" (Schönberg) greatly admired him. Galileo went on to mention that when *De Revolutionibus* was published in 1543, it had not only been dedicated to Pope Paul III, but that "it had been read and studied by everyone without the faintest hint of any objection being conceived against its doctrines". This is not quite true, when considering the Bartholomeo Spina and Giovanni Maria Tolosani diatribes of 1544 (which were mentioned in Chapter 4), but substantially so in so far as no official condemnation or prohibition followed.[5]

Galileo was skating on thin ice, however, when he started to talk about what the Church Fathers may, or may not, have meant in their interpretations of certain biblical passages. On the other hand, it is clear that he knew his Latin Bible well, and was certainly not *un*acquainted with the Fathers. Even so, he was *not* a professional theologian, and let us face it, professionals, in any discipline, never like being told their business by amateurs. However, Galileo's concern that modern anti-Copernican churchmen were reading physical, naturalistic, interpretations into Scripture and scriptural interpretation that were *not* the concern or intention of the original writers and commentators is not without validity. This was to constitute a pivotal argument in both his "Letter to Castelli" and its development in his *Letter to the Grand Duchess Christina* (1615).

GALILEO'S THEOLOGY OF SCIENCE

Galileo's *Letter to the Grand Duchess* makes several very important points regarding natural phenomena and scriptural interpretation, and one of the most enduringly influential for the science and Christianity dialogue was his "two books" analogy. God had written two books to facilitate the salvation of mankind: one of these was the book of God's Word, or the Bible; the other was the book of God's Works, or the natural creation, including the universe. Being the creation of the same divine author, these two books could not contradict each other. Central to Galileo's argument was that we should not assume that the plain word of Scripture was intended by the divine author to provide a simple description and explanation of natural phenomena, such as what rotated around what in the heavens.

In his advancement of this argument, he cites the Church Father whose inspired scholarship was often taken as a benchmark of authority by Catholic theologians: St Augustine of Hippo. The pagan-philosophy-trained Augustine, who had "seen the light" and been baptized as a man of thirty-three years old by St Ambrose of Milan in AD 387, had wrestled mightily with the connection between the truths of classical philosophy – such those of Socrates, Plato, and Horace – and those of Jesus Christ. Could a loving God have really condemned those wise and learned men to hell simply because they had lived 400 years before his incarnation? Rather, were not their writings perhaps a sort of pre-figurement of what would come about in the New Testament? One could argue that this way of thinking was not a million miles removed from "orthodox" Renaissance Vatican thinking, when ecclesiastical dignitaries could commission leading artists to decorate their apartments with paintings of Apollo, the pagan Muses, and Plato's Academy in Athens.

In his great Genesis commentary *De Genesi ad litteram* ("On the Literal Meaning of Genesis"), AD 401–15, St Augustine had established several precepts when it came to understanding and interpreting natural phenomena in the Old Testament – precepts which Galileo argued had a direct bearing on the contemporary Copernican debate (and which apply with no less force with regard to the six-day creation claims of present-day fundamentalists). The Mosaic books and the Psalms, for example, say that at creation God "stretcheth out the heavens as a curtain" (a tabernacle, or a tent). This is how the starry heavens can appear under clear desert skies, especially to nomadic tent-dwellers like the ancient Jews. Yet, says St Augustine, this beautiful and poetic vision of the firmament "does not contradict those who maintain the heavens have a spherical shape",[6] for the Greek geometers and philosophers had known that the earth, and heavens, were spherical for nearly a thousand years

171

by St Augustine's time. (The saint even warned Christians not to make themselves look foolish when talking with educated Greek and Roman pagans by insisting that the earth was flat.)

As St Augustine emphasizes, and as Galileo argues in his *Letter*, we must be cautious about the literalistic interpretation of biblical passages if those interpretations are likely to be shown by later experience to be incorrect in purely physical terms. As Galileo makes clear, this applies specifically to those passages which do not pertain to points of *faith*, but simply to ancillary natural phenomena, such as sunrises, sunsets, and the apparent motions of the celestial bodies. What Galileo saw as epitomizing the interpretative argument which he was advancing is laid out about one-quarter of the way into the *Letter*. He quotes "an ecclesiastic of the most eminent degree", almost certainly Cardinal Cesare, or Caesar, Boronius, who had visited Venice with Cardinal Bellarmine in 1598, where Galileo may have met him. This eminent ecclesiastic had stated that "the intention of the Holy Ghost is to teach us how one goes to heaven, not how heaven goes [or 'the heavens go']".[7]

One should not read the Bible as a textbook on astronomy and physics, but as a royal road to salvation in the presence of God – as a spiritual and a divine revelation, no less. As for the Book of Nature, we could use our intelligence and creative ingenuity to read that, and work on the premise that if the two books should appear to disagree, then we must bow to the written Word of God in spiritual matters, and lovingly and reverently reinterpret those passages passed on as simple, everyday-life images to Moses in the desert in the light of what we now know about the universe in 1615.

CHAPTER 14

"No one expects the Spanish Inquisition." Part 2: Galileo in Rome, 1616

*P*erhaps because of his apparent successes in the courtly world of Florence, Galileo decided during the latter part of 1615 that he must go to Rome to advance the heliocentric cause, and, one suspects, to thoroughly discredit his perceived enemy Father Caccini. As the Marxist historian Antonio Banfi put it in his *Galileo Galilei*, he set off for Rome with a confidence which was far from justified considering the circumstances.[1] Galileo's expectation of demolishing the opposition and triumphantly carrying the still unproven Copernican theory into the very heart of the church establishment horrified many of his friends, including Piero Guicciardini, the Tuscan ambassador to the Vatican. While discerning learned theologians considered that Tommaso Caccini had gone overboard and even made something of a fool of himself in his anti-Copernican sermon of 14 December 1613, the field was by no means clear for Galileo. The still scientifically conjectural status of Copernicanism, his layman's forays into biblical interpretation, and his not infrequently mocking tone in argument meant that Galileo never lacked for people who would leap on any chance to take Cosimo's celebrity philosopher down a few pegs.

On 19 February 1616, the Holy Inquisition appointed a Commission to look into heliocentricism, including investigating the attacks by Fathers Lorini and Caccini. On 24 February, this Commission reported adversely, stating that heliocentricism was "foolish and absurd in philosophy", and that it also contradicted the plain meaning of many passages in the Bible. The following day, Pope Paul V asked Cardinal Bellarmine to tell Galileo to abandon the Copernican theory.

It is important to remember that all of this was done in a polite and gentlemanly fashion, for, without any doubt, Galileo was by 1616 a famous international "philosopher", or man of learning, and, as far as his purely theological beliefs were concerned, a good Catholic. Even after the Index which dealt with prohibited books had formally condemned heliocentricism in early March, Galileo could meet with both Bellarmine and Pope Paul V on friendly terms, on and after 11 March. It says something for the regard in which Galileo stood that on 11 March he was granted a 45-minute-long *benignissima audienza*, or most friendly personal audience, with Pope Paul. Pope Paul assured Galileo that he was not in any danger. The following day, Galileo wrote to the Tuscan Secretary of State reporting on the friendly papal interview, and of His Holiness's assurance "that he was well aware of my uprightness and sincerity of mind", although in this letter Galileo could not avoid another grumble about being "pursued with implacable hate by my enemies", without specifying individuals.[2] What cannot be denied is that the church seems to have been giving Galileo a lot of rope, which runs contrary to the myth that it was setting out to crush him.

WHAT WAS GALILEO PERMITTED TO SAY AFTER 1616?

It was from this time, in the spring of 1616, that certain ambiguities appear to have arisen, and which seventeen years later would figure prominently at the famous trial of 1633. Exactly what had Galileo been told he could say or argue? Rumours had also got out in 1616, supposedly spread by his "implacable enemies", that the church had even forced him to repent and do penance, but this is clearly undermined by Galileo's own sense of confidence with which he returned to Florence in the summer of 1616.

Very important to that confidence was a certificate which Galileo had requested from Cardinal Bellarmine, supposedly making explicit where things stood. This certificate from Bellarmine, dated 26 May 1616, which had very obviously been got out of the cardinal at Galileo's request – if not badgering – made clear that "Signor Galileo has *not* abjured in our hand, nor in the hand of anybody else here in Rome, nor so far as we are aware, in any place whatever, any opinion or doctrine held by him; neither has any penance... been imposed upon him." On the other hand, the certificate reiterated the decision made by the Congregation of the Index back in March that the Copernican idea of a moving earth and a fixed sun that does not move from east to west "is contrary to the holy scriptures, and therefore cannot be defended nor held".[3]

The certificate is not without its own ambiguity, however. It made it clear that Galileo had been in no way punished, while at the same time holding out the possible interpretation that while Copernicus's heliocentric theory could not be "defended or held" as a physical reality in the context of the academic debates of the period, there was a suggestion that it might be discussed as a hypothesis or a mathematical model.

At this juncture, in the summer of 1616, Galileo was free to return to Florence, not much the worse for wear. While he had been firmly told not to propagate Copernican heliocentricism as a physical fact, he still felt that he might do so as a theory or as a mathematical device, and without doubt he had been treated with considerable respect by the leading figures in Catholic Christendom. Let us be honest: the church had a very strong point in forbidding the teaching of heliocentricism as a fact, for as Bellarmine had put it to Foscarini, Copernicanism still awaited firm, physical, evidential *proof.*

Say what one might about the Catholic Church, few could deny its concern with intellectual rigour when it came to precise definitions. Yes, Rome's leading theologians had been wrong in their decisions of February and March 1616; but by the best evidences of the time, and weighing in only what was demonstrably proven about the heavens at that date, they were wrong for the right reasons, and it was Galileo who was making the blind leap of faith from theory to presumed fact.

And so things would stand for several years.

OF COMETS, THE TIDES, AND *THE ASSAYER*

After his dealings with the Roman authorities in 1616, Galileo began to look for alternative ways by which to propagate his opinions. An opportunity arose when three comets appeared in the sky in 1618 – coinciding, as things would turn out, with the outbreak of the Thirty Years War.

Father Orazio Grassi of the Jesuit College wrote up and published his lecture the next year in which he concluded that comets were burning, fiery bodies, but, in the wake of Tycho Brahe's observations of the 1577 comet, that they were beyond the moon. Father Grassi's view accorded with Tycho Brahe's geo-heliocentric scheme of the heavens, which the Jesuits – like many other Catholics and Protestants in 1619 – saw as the cosmology that best fitted the physical evidences then available. Because the comets appeared to move in curved paths, more slowly than the moon yet faster than the planets, he suggested that the earth formed their centre of rotation.

This also was the explanation accepted by the great Jesuit astronomer Father Christopher Scheiner, against whom Galileo still harboured a grudge since his criticisms of Apelles's (Scheiner's) views on sunspots in 1612–13. Galileo was clearly spoiling for a fight in the Copernican cause, although since 1616 he was behaving more circumspectly and trying to fire his bullets from behind stooges. As Professor Giorgio de Santillana said in his *The Crime of Galileo*,[4] Galileo's own comments, handwritten in the margins of Grazzi's published lecture, "make a vocabulary of good Tuscan abuse", with phrases such as "unmannerly poltroon", "ungrateful boor", and "rude ruffian".

Galileo got his friend Mario Guiducci to fire the bullets on his behalf in the *Discourse on the Comets*, which came out in June 1619, although without doubt Galileo was the very solid "ghost writer" of the book. Galileo's identity as author was an open secret: perhaps substantiated by his brilliant writing style and power of argument. One figure who openly expressed delight in Galileo's albeit officially concealed return to scientific controversy was his Roman friend, Cardinal Maffeo Barberini, who came to write a Latin poem in his honour. As we saw in earlier chapters, the Roman Church was by no means the united intellectual monolith of legend, and while Pope Paul, the Aristotelians in the Index, and Robert Bellarmine may have been willing to clip Galileo's Copernican wings in 1616, other high-ranking figures such as the young Cardinal Orsini and his colleague Maffeo Barberini seemed happy, at this stage, to sit back and enjoy the fun.

Cardinal Barberini received his cornucopia of delights in 1623, when Galileo presented him with the manuscript of his next great creation: *Il Saggiatore*, "The Assayer". The polemical title suggests the precision balance used by goldsmiths to weigh or "assay" the purity of a piece of precious metal. The book clearly cast a strategic angle at the powerful Barberini family, and in its published form in 1624 would not only carry a dedication to the former cardinal (plus a clear acknowledgment to Fellow Lynx Academician, Virginio Cesarini), but also incorporate the Barberini family crest of three honeybees on its title page. I say *former* cardinal, for on 8 August 1623 Maffeo Barberini was elected Pope, taking as his papal title Urban VIII, and not only commenced, as we saw above, a nasty cycle of bad diplomatic and political relations with Spain, but apparently signalled the green light for Galileo.

Galileo must have been overjoyed at the new papal election, for Urban VIII was a very different sort of man, and promised to be a very different sort of pope, from Paul V. For while Pope Paul had not been especially concerned with scientific and intellectual issues, Urban *was*. A long-term friend of Galileo and nephew of the sympathetic Cardinal Francesco Barberini, he was a patron of the Florentine Academy of Lynxes learned society, of which Galileo was a member, and was very much a "Renaissance pope". It was said that *Il Saggiatore* was read at the Pope's dining table and commented upon most warmly, and as was mentioned above, it inspired His Holiness to compose a classical-style Latin poem in its author's honour. So, with his admiring friend now on the throne of St Peter, Galileo might perhaps have been forgiven for feeling that the Copernican heliocentric prohibitions dating from Pope Paul's reign might now be revoked.

What did *Il Saggiatore* say? Let us begin by mentioning that, like his sunspots book and *Letter to the Grand Duchess*, *Il Saggiatore* was couched in the epistolary format, being addressed to the "Very Reverend Monsignor Don Virginio Cesarini", a high-ranking papal official who would become chamberlain to Pope Urban's household in the Vatican. In 1616, it had been at Cesarini's house in Rome that Galileo had openly debated and advocated the Copernican theory, with apparent approval. Galileo was clearly revelling in his new, high-placed, advanced-thinking ecclesiastical friends, and no doubt hoping that the limitations placed upon the discussion of heliocentricism in 1616 might well be lifted.

In *Il Saggiatore* he sets the ball rolling by making reference to his *Starry Messenger* and *Sunspots* discoveries. Then he backs up Guiducci's criticisms (which Galileo had actually written, but to which Guiducci had obligingly added his name as author) of poor Father Grassi on the 1618 comets. Galileo could never resist giving a few extra kicks to someone whom he believed he had trounced already.

The supreme irony was that, when it came to the comets, Father Grassi, in his analyses of their motions, had come much closer to the truth in his 1619 lecture than Galileo had in his vociferous attacks. While comets do *not* go around the earth, they nonetheless do move in curved orbits, and – as their relatively slow motions and indeterminate parallaxes suggest – they are vastly further away than the moon, in interplanetary space, indeed. Galileo, on the other hand, dismissed comets as insubstantial, vaporous bodies scarcely worth serious astronomical attention, only making it clear that great men can get it badly wrong, especially when out to discredit a rival. Yet, while his book may have delighted Pope Urban, Cardinal Orsini, Monsignor Cesarini, and others, it certainly lost him friends and made him enemies in the Jesuit Order – enemies who would come back to haunt him in Rome in 1633, by which time even Pope Urban was beginning to find his old friend increasingly troublesome.

From the seventeenth century onwards, scientists and scholars have seen *Il Saggiatore* as a landmark document in the history of scientific thought, and rightly so. Comets, polemics, and insults apart, it sets out a rationale for scientific research which accords with how science has evolved from Galileo's day to ours. At the heart of that rationale was mathematics, for the natural world and the universe beyond were governed by great mathematical principles, or what would later be seen as *laws*. Whether you wanted to understand the force of the wind, the acceleration of falling bodies or projectiles, the tides, or the motions of the planets, the truth could only be found in numbers and proportion. Precise measurement must lie at the heart of all scientific research, and instruments were the key – just like the assayer's precision balance – to physical truth, and mathematical calculation would finally elucidate the nature of things.

Things seemed to be taking a turn for the better, as 1623 gave way to 1624, and the sixty-year-old Galileo entertained great hopes of his old admirer, now occupying St Peter's throne in the Vatican.

TROUBLE, TRIAL, AND CONDEMNATION: 1633

Everything appeared promising during the spring of 1624. Galileo was granted six long audiences by the Pope, who spoke of him as this "great man whose fame shines in the heavens and goes far and wide on earth".[5] Between 1624 and 1632, Galileo in Florence was undertaking pioneering research into physics and motion, but always with the prospect of a Copernican heliocentric "proof" not far from the front of his mind Galileo no doubt lived in the confident hope that the limitations placed upon the discussion of the Copernican theory in 1616 would soon be rescinded altogether, or at least moderated. It was in this hope that he set about writing what would become his celebrated, controversial, and eventually condemned *Dialogo sopra i due Massimi Sistemi del Mondo, Tolemaico et Copernicano* ("Dialogue concerning the Two Chief Systems of the World, Ptolemaic and Copernican"), in Florence in 1632. He couched it in the popular dialogue, or discussion, form, not only because it gave him an opportunity to place words in the mouths of characters with whom he agreed or disagreed, but because the dialogue had an intellectual lineage extending back to the iconic Socratic dialogues of Plato.

Galileo tells us in the Preface to his preliminary section "To the Discerning Reader"[6] that many years before, he had discussed heliocentricism and the earth's motion "in the marvellous city of

Venice" with his high-ranking and deeply learned friends Giovanni Francesco Sagredo and Filippo Salviati (from whose Florentine Villa delle Selve he had composed his *Sunspots* treatise in 1612–13), both men being safely dead by 1632. Both are presented as open-minded to these ideas. These discussions also included a "Peripatetic Philosopher" or Aristotelian, who was blind to the "truth" and could see no further than his master Aristotle. This third man is not named, but for the purposes of the *Dialogue*, and needing a dogmatic foil for Salviati and Sagredo, Galileo gave him the distinctly loaded name of Simplicius. This was, no doubt, borrowed from the real-life sixth-century AD Greek philosopher Simplicio, who in his day a thousand years before had been a noted commentator upon Aristotle. But in Italian, Latin – or English – the name carried overtones of being a fool.

In his felicitous, seductive, and often amusing literary style – for Galileo could never be boring or dull on paper, or, one suspects, in conversation – he unfolds the discussion across four daily episodes set in Venice. The first day begins with considerations about Aristotle, divine and human understanding, and even the idea of life on the moon. But it is on the second and third days that things begin to warm up. Here – on the second day – Galileo examines the viability of Aristotelian orthodoxy, arguments regarding the earth's rotation, the physics of moving bodies, the power of mathematics, sensory knowledge, and the nature of relative and absolute motion. Then, on day three, he re-examines the evidences for terrestrial and celestial motions which he looked at twenty years earlier in *Sidereus Nuncius* and *Sunspots*. There follows a discussion of the stellar universe and, reminiscent of 1615 and the Castelli and Grand Duchess letters, a return to the matter of the literal and figurative reading of Scripture. The fourth day returns to the subject of the tides, first discussed in his 1616 essay to Cardinal Orsini, and their role in attempting to substantiate heliocentricism.

Much of what Galileo put into the *Dialogue* was not new; there were no *new* physical evidences to discuss. There had been no more groundbreaking telescopic, or as yet, dynamical discoveries since 1613, and Galileo's 1616 tide theory hardly constituted a powerful argument, especially when weighed against Kepler's lunar alternative. On the other hand, the old facts and arguments were re-combined in a masterly, compelling, and readable way.

What is obvious in the *Dialogue* was Galileo's blatant bias. For instance, Salviati, the Copernican advocate, and Sagredo, the supposedly impartial arbiter in the discussion, are clearly on the same side, while poor Simplicio is trounced time and again. Galileo is obviously sparing with the truth in speaking of the *two* chief systems of the world, Ptolemaic and Copernican, for he omits any serious discussion of the Tychonic geo-heliocentric system – the system of the heavens that best fitted the available facts in 1632, and the one generally subscribed to by the Jesuits and other astronomers. A discussion of the Tychonic system (outlined in Chapter 6) would have muddied the waters for Galileo and made a decisive Copernican kill more problematic. These, along with other indications of bias or gratuitous offence, would all tell against him when Galileo was brought up before the Roman Inquisition in 1633.

The *Dialogue* was finished by the spring of 1630, and Galileo travelled the 200 miles to Rome with the manuscript, seeking the *imprimatur* of the church to have it printed and published. It was truly a case of a celebrity on the move. The new Grand Duke of Tuscany, Ferdinand II, who had succeeded Cosimo, lent his own personal litter and bearers, and on his arrival in Rome, Galileo moved into an elegant suite of apartments in the Villa Medici, the residence of the Tuscan ambassador, Francesco Niccolini, who *also* happened to be an enthusiastic "fan" of Galileo.

It says much about Galileo's high standing in ecclesiastical circles in May 1630 that while protocol directed that his manuscript had to receive the authority of a church censor, the well-disposed Pope Urban VIII appointed Niccolò Riccardi, of the Order of Preachers, a high-ranking Vatican official famed for his charm and easy-going disposition, to examine the *Dialogue*. Riccardi did not appear to have been especially knowledgeable about astronomy, and while doing his best to give an honest appraisal, the poor man seems to have been bullied rather shamefully by Galileo and others, until at the end of July 1631 he gave his *imprimatur* and the book was allowed to go to press in Florence. His yielding to Florentine pressure to license the book was to seriously damage Riccardi's future career in the Vatican, when things went wrong in 1633.

The *Dialogue* was finally published in Florence in February 1632, complete with its allegorical title page of astronomers in debate, and its dedication to Ferdinand II, Grand Duke of Tuscany. After some initial approbation, trouble soon set in. Firstly, the publisher was ordered to suspend sales; then on 1 October 1632, Galileo was summoned to Rome to be examined. Shocked by the furore that had now broken out in the Vatican, Galileo claimed that his age, sixty-eight, and poor health made him incapable of undertaking the 200-mile journey at the onset of winter. But no excuses were to be tolerated, not from eminent Florentine doctors, or even from the Grand Duke; so Ferdinand II finally loaned Galileo his luxury litter to carry his philosopher to Rome in early 1633.

What was it about the *Dialogue* that occasioned such an incredible backlash, transforming, in a few weeks, Archduke Ferdinand's pampered philosopher and intellectual gladiator from an admired friend of the Pope to the stunned old man now too shocked, sick, and broken to travel, yet still ordered by the Inquisition to do so?

Even so, upon arrival in Rome, the still uncomprehending controversialist was treated with great respect and lodged in fine style, being given a suite of rooms in the Florentine ambassador's residence at the Villa Medici. It says much for his obedience as a good Catholic that, instead of fleeing north to Switzerland or Protestant Germany when the summons came, as he could have done, Galileo dutifully travelled south to the Eternal City. Perhaps he was hoping that his old friend and now ex-"fan", Pope Urban, would change his mind and forgive him; or that Grand Duke Ferdinand, the Florentine ambassador in Rome, or other high-placed friends would get the whole business sorted out and quashed. If he did, then Galileo had seriously miscalculated.

Pope Urban VIII was clearly angry with Galileo. In the world of Vatican Court politics, Galileo's enemies, including the Aristotelian philosophers in the Jesuit Order and elsewhere, probably rubbed their hands and smiled when they read the *Dialogue*. Here was the rope by which they could – metaphorically speaking – hang the mischievous Florentine astronomer at last. In 1633, the Papal

Court, just like the royal courts of Spain, France, Austria, Florence, and England, was a hotbed of intrigue between competing interest groups – a point eloquently argued by Mario Biagioli in *Galileo, Courtier* (1993).

Galileo's enemies had two sorts of ammunition they could now throw at him. Firstly, there was the precise nature of the limitation on heliocentric teaching that Cardinal Bellarmine and the commissioners had placed on him in 1616. There seem to have been slight differences in wording between the certificate given to Galileo by the cardinal in May 1616 and what went on the official record. Could Galileo discuss heliocentricism as an abstract model or theory, or could he not discuss it at all? Of course, in practice everything hinged on goodwill, tolerance, and admiration. These were strongly in evidence when the new Pope Urban was praising *Il Saggiatore* in 1616, and enjoying Galileo's company in the Vatican for several years thereafter. But by the autumn of 1632, they had clearly gone, and Urban was now angry with his old friend.

Secondly, it is difficult not to see the *Dialogue* as a polemical text, for it is scarcely even-handed. As we saw above, it practically ignores the *third* great world system, that of Tycho Brahe – the system favoured by the Jesuits and which, in 1633, made it possible to reconcile the telescopic discoveries of 1609–13 with the broad principles of Aristotelian physics and philosophy; the ideal middle way, in fact. While Galileo tries to float some new, post-1613 arguments, such as his theory of the tides – explaining only *one* tide per day – he still has no more solid evidence than he had in 1616. Add to that the obvious, deceased, big Copernican guns of Sagredo and Salviati, and the intellectual and dialectical battery which they direct against poor geocentric Simplicio. Simplicio, the man with the value-laden name, is pretty well backed into a corner at every turn in the discussions.

It is hardly surprising, therefore, that Pope Urban felt angry. Galileo would not have been so foolish as to openly annoy his old admirer, yet the *Dialogue*, in many ways, was a gift to those who had little love for him. It could be agreed that it was *heretical*, in so far as it could be construed as being in breach of his intellectual "bail" conditions imposed in 1616, although *heresy* was a portmanteau word covering several graduations of culpability. The denial of basic Christian teaching was *prima facie* serious heresy, and could bring one to the bonfire – such as the pantheistic views held by of Giordano Bruno which led to his burning in 1600. On the other hand, Galileo's heresy was one of disobedience: of openly teaching something he had supposedly been explicitly told not to teach. At no point in his trial was his basic doctrinal sincerity as a Catholic Christian even called into question. One might suggest that he had been disobediently naughty rather than incorrigibly wicked.

The broad respect in which he was held was reflected in the treatment he received. When his trial commenced, on 12 April 1633, his Dominican interlocutors rose courteously and bowed – a gesture which Galileo reciprocated: so far, all very gentlemanly. But the anger against him soon became more obvious. Irrespective of whether Galileo had, or had *not*, been even-handed in his discussion of the cosmological models, his use of designations such as "dumb idiots" or "mental pygmies" for Simplicius and the Ptolemaic geocentricists made an accusation of bias inescapable.

Galileo still persisted in saying he had *not* been teaching the Copernican theory as fact, so much as a hypothesis, in spite of being under oath. One of Galileo's main points of defence was that following the 1616 "brush", the full extent of the limitations placed upon all discussion of heliocentricism had not been communicated to him by Bellarmine, as he made clear to the Dominican Brother Vincenzo Maculano de Firenzuela. Galileo was later examined on 17 April.

One of the judges in Galileo's trial was Cardinal Francesco Barberini, the Pope's nephew, who was not without sympathy for Galileo. Brother Maculano, who himself seems to have harboured no personal wish to destroy Galileo by risking a perjury accusation being made against him, then spoke privately to Cardinal Francesco. Could Cardinal Francesco not have a word with Galileo? He did, and on 28 April he was able to report that Galileo now "recognized that he had gone too far and erred in his book".

After a variety of comings and goings, discussions and considerations, the judges wound up the case over 21 and 22 June 1633. Three essential points were made in the final summing-up and sentencing on the 22nd. *One*, Galileo was declared a heretic, for continuing to advance the heliocentric theory. *Two*, he was sentenced to imprisonment, although this was, after one day, commuted to house arrest at Arcetri, near Florence. *Three*, his *Dialogue* was banned.

THE FINAL YEARS: GALILEO AT ARCETRI

As a great admirer of Galileo and defender of the right to freedom of thought and speech, I find it hard to see the events of 1632–33 in simple hero versus persecutors terms. That Galileo went "too far" and pushed the boundaries of his world – and ultimately paid the price – cannot be denied. On the other hand, Urban VIII and other dignitaries of the church displayed an arrogance and a personal fury against an old friend which were far from becoming in a humble shepherd of Christ's flock.

Yet, at no stage in his career had the obviously brilliant and charismatic Galileo lacked friends and admirers, even after Pope Urban went up in fury. On his release from Rome, he was invited by his friend Ascanio Piccolomini, Archbishop of Siena, to have what might be called a recuperative holiday with him on his way to Arcetri – another indication of the very *un*monolithic nature of the ecclesiastical hierarchy, and something of a mark of disapproval of what had taken place in Rome.

Galileo's daughter, Sister Maria Celeste, who was to stay loyal to her father down to her own early death in 1638, and her fellow nuns were rapturous at Galileo's arrival in Arcetri, not far from their convent. Here, with his son Vincenzo, other family members, and his seventeen-year-old pupil and future biographer, Vincenzo Viviani, he was to spend the last nine years of his life. It was here at Arcetri that he returned to scientific research, discovering with his telescope the axial "libration" or rocking of the moon, not long before blindness closed his eyes for visual research, as well as sketching a design for how to use swinging pendulums to make the rather erratic clocks of the day keep exact time. In 1638, he completed what would become his celebrated *Discourses Concerning Two New Sciences*, which was destined to become one

185

of the foundational texts of experimental physics. The *Discourses* would be published in Leiden, Holland, in July 1638, at the famous Elzevir Press. At Arcetri Galileo also received visitors, such as, as was later claimed, the English philosopher Thomas Hobbes and the poet John Milton, who would later immortalize the "Tuscan astronomer" in the English-language epic *Paradise Lost*. Modern scholars are now more inclined to think that it was Galileo's son whom Milton met.[7] In Chapter 24 we will meet the English clergyman-astronomer John Wilkins who, although he never met Galileo, revered him from the north, and who would in 1638 and 1640 write books on Galileo, Copernicus, and Kepler for English-language readers.

THE SPANISH INQUISITION

What about the Spanish Inquisition? In many ways, this was a different body from the Holy Inquisition that had operated under broad Roman control across Catholic Europe since 1232. Spain's Inquisition was a uniquely Spanish institution, having been founded by Ferdinand and Isabella, the first monarchs to rule over a unified Spain, in 1479, with the specific aim of targeting resident Jews, Muslims, and unbelievers, to create a fully Christian Spain. The Spanish Inquisition enjoyed a unique and intimate connection with the Spanish crown, and did not take lightly to outside interference, even from the Pope – and that was in addition to the very bad relations existing in the 1630s between Pope Urban and Cardinal Borgia. So, what happened to Galileo regarding the Spanish Inquisition?

A few years ago I was talking over tea in an Oxford Senior Common Room with a distinguished Renaissance Iberian historian who had just returned from working on a sixteenth-century archive in Madrid. Knowing my interest in Galileo, he happened to mention a packet of documents that he had encountered by chance, and which had been mis-filed. They related to the Papal Nuncio's (Papal Messenger's) instructions in 1633 to communicate Galileo's condemnation in Rome to the Spanish authorities, and see him formally condemned in Spain as well.

This perceived impertinence angered the Spanish Inquisition, and when the formal document announcing Galileo's condemnation was nailed to the door of the great Gothic cathedral of Cuenca, some 84 miles from Madrid, an official of the Inquisition promptly tore it down. Of course, this was in no way an indication that the Inquisition had any sympathy whatsoever with Galileo, Copernicus, or heliocentricism. What it indicated, rather, was that Spanish royal, ecclesiastical, and national sensibilities had been outraged by this insensitive Vatican intrusion into Spanish domestic affairs, especially at a time of bad diplomatic relations. Yet the irony remained that the Inquisition refused to condemn Galileo in Spain.

Which only goes to prove, as the BBC TV *Monty Python* sketch put it, "No one expects the Spanish Inquisition".

CHAPTER 15

Jesuits Galore: The Telescope Goes Global

*I*t is often believed amongst north Europeans and Americans that missionary activity on a global basis began with the Protestants. Yes, the Protestants were to do, and continue to do, wonderful Christian missionary work. Just think of the Methodist missions, across Great Britain, North America, and Australasia, or early-nineteenth-century Harvard College graduates taking the gospel to Polynesia; of the London-based Society for the Propagation of Christian Knowledge (1698), the London Missionary Society (1795), or Victorian Church of England missionary bishops getting out to Africa, India, and Indonesia.

Yet, it is a historical fact that Roman Catholics were actively evangelizing well before the Reformation. One such was the Spanish scholar-priest and mathematician Ramon Lull, who suffered martyrdom in North Africa in 1315, in his attempt to take the gospel to the Islamic world.

When Ignatius Loyola – later St Ignatius – founded his Society of Jesus, or Jesuit Order, in 1534, a new force was about to be let loose in the world, and a new type of missionary was to be born. St Ignatius was a scholar, soldier, and nobleman, who had come to a new and powerful Christian faith as a result of receiving a near fatal wound in a siege, going through a long and reflective convalescence, and having a series of powerful spiritual experiences.

The Order which he created would have a number of interesting features, for his men would be gentlemen, scholars, utterly determined in their faith, and as tough-minded as they came – priests capable of holding major university appointments, possessing the social skills and tact that enabled them to move easily among royalty, whether it were a European king, a South American tribal leader, or an emperor of China at the exotic court of Peking. They were to be educated, suave, and polished, adapting to the mores of the culture in which they found themselves; yet chaste, devoted to a life of poverty, renouncing personal property, and actively concerned with the poor. If their social role demanded it they dressed splendidly, such as at the Imperial Court in Peking, where they were often granted mandarin rank – but they wore rough hair shirts beneath their gorgeous silk robes, as a constant reminder of who their real King was.

The Jesuits were focused *thinking* men. Within a few decades of the founding of their Order, there were not only eminent Jesuit theologians, but also jurists, constitutional lawyers, diplomats, philosophers, academics, physicians, and scientists. So many young men flocked to join St Ignatius that by the 1560s the Order contained over a thousand, and was growing fast. Among the scientists, there were lots of men interested in what we would now call physics, as well as geologists, medical researchers, explorers, surveyors, and cartographers – and lots of astronomers. One reason why Galileo had so many encounters, for good or ill, with Jesuits was because they were, by 1600, the intellectual elite of Catholicism. Jesuits had played a major role in devising the new Gregorian calendar in 1582, and directed the new Collegio Romano observatory in the Vatican City after its foundation in 1580. They were prominent in Bologna, Vienna, Augsburg, Munich, Prague, Salamanca, and all those places in Catholic Europe where scientific ideas were on the move. Their primary rationale was Aristotelian, being attracted, like so many scholars from the thirteenth century onwards, by the elegant systematization and dialectical force of Aristotle. A training in Aristotelian thought could make you a deadly opponent in debate, where an adroit arguer could easily move from philosophy to theology to physics to cosmology.

The Jesuits were a spiritual and an intellectual *corporation*: wholly international by 1610, and including English, Scandinavian, and German Fathers, many of them converts; while by 1660 they had become truly *global*, with Jesuit missions as far afield as India, Peru, Chile, Mexico, California, Poland, Indonesia, and China. Many, in the sometimes hostile distant lands, suffered martyrdom; many still do.

In spite of all their seeming focus, the Jesuits were full of surprises, and not infrequently angered Europe's Catholic establishment, not to mention certain popes. While loyal and unswerving sons of Catholic Christendom, they were nevertheless their own men. They repeatedly displayed an exasperating trait: serving Christ, standing up for the poor, and speaking the truth, rather than cosying up to secular worldly wealth and corruption – even when they were on open display in the Vatican itself. The Spanish scientific missionary to South America, José de Acosta, for example, angered the powerful Spanish and Portuguese empire-builders and slave-dealers by condemning their brutal treatment of the native Indian population. While the Jesuits became the Roman Church's intellectual big guns, they were not infrequently its loose cannon as well.

TYCHO BRAHE AND THE TELESCOPE GO TO CHINA

It was in China that the Jesuit mission had a truly stunning history, for in the realm of the Celestial Empire, astronomy and high-level precision technology became major instruments in the cause of Christian evangelism.

One of the defining features of Jesuit missionary activity was to look for particular needs in the prevailing culture, and how they could supply that need. Missionaries should find out how they could make themselves useful, and use that need as an avenue for Christian evangelism. Very often, this involved being open-minded, flexible, and able to adapt to local ways. Learn the language as quickly as you can, try to get through to the top dog, respect the indigenous culture, and work the Christian message into that culture. Whatever you do, don't, for heaven's sake, talk Latin, and try to turn Peking into Rome. It is hardly surprising that Protestants accused them of using "Jesuitical cunning".

When Father Matteo Ricci and his brethren reached Macao in China in August 1582, after a time in India, he soon learned that they were in for a long wait,[1] for was not the Ming emperor, Wan Li, lord of the universe, and were not Italians or Germans no more than strange barbarians coming to be bedazzled by the splendour of Chinese civilization? At first, the local elites mistrusted them, despite their initial "going Chinese" and donning the saffron robes of Buddhist monks. They found it hard even to rent accommodation for their mission – until they hit upon the idea of living in haunted houses, where they were left in peace.

The missionaries were finally summoned to enter the imperial presence in Peking in 1601, by which time they were confidently speaking the language and behaving like accomplished Sinoized barbarians, with Father Matteo styling himself Li Ma-teu (no doubt from Matteo, or Matthew). And one thing which the Fathers quickly picked up on was the inadequate state of the Chinese calendar – the correction of which would be child's play for an educated European with Western instruments and a volume of Tycho Brahe's astronomical tables, such as was available in any good bookshop in Europe by 1620. The Jesuits went well prepared, and in their correspondence with home – conducted via the merchantmen that came to buy porcelain and other exotica for rich European clients – they made sure that missionary needs were soon supplied.

While we now know that Chinese and Korean astronomers had been carefully observing the heavens and compiling detailed lists of lunar phases, eclipses, and "guest stars" (supernovae) for nearly 4,000 years by 1620, the Chinese had never developed a theoretical, mathematical astronomy, such as had been built up since Greek times in the West. Instead, their astronomy was essentially arithmetic, taxonomic, and empirical. While Chinese astronomers had determined the length of the solar year to an extraordinary level of accuracy, by observing and averaging, the prediction of phenomena involving long and complex lunar and solar cycles such as eclipses were often unreliable.

This chaos was more than just a scientific calendrical problem: it was also a threat to the emperor himself. A Chinese emperor was thought to be a divine being, who must *know* how to order the heavens, for if he could not control the realm of the stars and planets, how could he ensure peace and abundance on earth?

Eclipses in particular could be embarrassing, for if the emperor did not know exactly when a malignant dragon might descend to eat up the sun, how could humans be properly prepared when it came to scaring it away?

The Holy Fathers were quick to pick up on this and other problems. The department of the Chinese state which dealt with the heavens was the Astronomy Bureau, which had a fine observatory on top of a bastion on the walls of Peking. The instruments which it contained in *c.* 1610 were large equatorial armillaries, or big graduated bronze rings adjusted to the celestial equator and other key sky coordinates, along with several large shadow dials for measuring the sun's daily altitude. These large angle-sighting instruments, it must be emphasized, were constructed to the highest standards of China's legendary fine metallurgical craftsmanship.

Yet, one thing which must have exerted an enormous braking effect upon the historical development of Chinese astronomy was their division of celestial angles in accordance with a 365¼-digit circle, each digit precisely corresponding to a single day's journey of the sun's annual circuit of the stars. The number 365¼ is a fiendishly awkward one to divide into even fractions, and Chinese mathematics had nothing like the convenience of 180, 60, 30, and other numbers into which the 360-degree circle so elegantly divides – a 360-degree circle, one must point out, that the Greeks inherited (or borrowed) from the Babylonians. As a consequence, China never developed an analytical geometry whereby the conceptual world of theoretical angle manipulation could be used to interpret and intellectually model the universe as a sort of *machine*, as the Greeks did. This was another thing which the Jesuits were quick to pick up on, and see where Western science could supply a need to the emperors.

Although Father Matteo Ricci took Western astronomy to China, it was his successors who got inside the Chinese mandarin "establishment": Fathers Emmanuel Diaz, Johann Terrenz Schreck (Terrentius), and especially Johann Adam Schall von Bell and Ferdinand Verbiest. Schall von Bell was a German from Cologne, and one suspects that he, like so many of his brethren, had "style" and an instinctive eye for opportunities. Not only did he show that, using basic Western angle-measuring instruments in conjunction with Tycho Brahe's published tables, one could put the calendar in order with relative ease, but he was also an influential teacher of European astronomy both to the astronomical mandarins and to high-born and influential Chinese nobles and intellectuals.

He certainly showed the Chinese astronomers Galilean telescopic views of Saturn's "protuberance" (rings), Jupiter's moons, the Milky Way, and other phenomena, and before its condemnation in the Galileo affair, he also taught the Copernican theory. Father Adam's didactic frame of reference remained Tycho Brahe's geo-heliocentric system, which in 1640 was still the best cosmology on offer for combining explanations of the complex planetary motions with Aristotle's physics. At least before 1633, he was a clear admirer of Galileo and his telescopic discoveries, and his *Yuan Chin Shao* ("The Far-Seeing Optic Glass") of 1626 not only described Galileo's telescopic discoveries, but even contained the first picture of a European telescope to be published in a Chinese book.[2]

Jesuit astronomers in China, however, were not there simply to do science, although Schall von Bell and his colleagues followed the protocol and wore official silk robes (over hair shirts), complete with pigtailed hair. They were there to win souls for Christ: that was always their agenda, even if sometimes it may have appeared somewhat hidden. Their policy was actually straightforward: go for those at the top, the intellectuals, mandarins, courtiers, and, hopefully, even the emperor himself. When these folk accept Christ, then in a society as monolithic as imperial China, everyone must follow suit, from the scholar in his study to the peasant in his paddy-field. The way you won the top people over was by associating Christianity with wonders never revealed to the wisest Oriental sages, and by solving pressing problems.

One senses that a knack for showmanship and pulling off dramatic demonstrations came easy to the Jesuit Fathers; a not infrequent technique used by the Jesuits was to issue what might look like prediction challenges to the Chinese astronomers. For example, Father Adam not only predicted the solar eclipse of 1 September 1644 with spot-on accuracy, whereas those made by the *Da tong* and Islamic calendars had been up to forty-five minutes in error, but he crowned his achievement by projecting a telescopic image of the sun-eating dragon on to a sheet of paper for the benefit of the staff of the Chinese Astronomy Bureau.

Another strategy lay in getting through to the young, through education; and both Schall von Bell and Verbiest angled to exert an educational influence upon princely children in the royal household. Father Adam and his fellow priests were suddenly in serious danger of their lives in 1664, when a backlash against Christian influence at the royal court, and especially, Christian influence upon the boy-emperor K'ang Hsi, was unleashed. The mandarin Jesuits were arrested, imprisoned under appalling conditions, loaded with chains, and sentenced to death. Shortly before their executions were due to take place, in 1665, the Celestial City was shaken by a succession of violent earthquakes, and, it was said, a comet and fiery portents blazed in the sky. The Jesuits were reprieved. Father Adam died of natural causes, two years later, at the age of seventy-five. The Lord clearly looked after his own. Father Adam – who lived for forty-seven years in China – like many of the Jesuit missionaries, went to the East for life, as it were, growing old and dying there, while they used astronomy and Western science as the tools through which, they hoped, the Celestial Empire would be brought to Christ.

Father Adam's successor was a Flemish Jesuit, Ferdinand Verbiest. Father Ferdinand was in China at what would transpire to be a time of much greater political stability. The young Emperor K'ang Hsi turned out to be a remarkable gentleman, who not only liked Verbiest personally, but even enjoyed him as a conversational companion. K'ang Hsi was not only a highly intelligent individual; he also displayed a real curiosity towards things Western – including Christianity. He was also clearly fascinated by Western science, technology, and inventions, and quickly realized that the congenial barbarians who came from beyond the sunset might well have something interesting to say.

Going back to Matteo Ricci's time, it is clear that the Chinese elite were fascinated by Western self-acting devices. Spring-driven automata, and most of all, clocks, captured the Chinese imagination: especially beautiful clocks that rang bells, played tunes, simulated the motions of the heavens, or incorporated moving human figures. The Jesuits were not slow in acting upon this. Chinese delight, and the missionary priests' letters back to Europe, soon ensured a supply of horological and other mechanical novelties. The "self-ringing bells", as the Chinese used to call them, turned out to be perfect ambassadorial luxuries.

Of course, China itself had not lacked ingenious artisans who had, over the centuries, built mechanical wonders. The famous Su Song water clock, of AD 1088, which had been as big as a house and had even incorporated a rotating stellar globe, was a notable example. Yet all of these Chinese devices, like the great bronze circles in the Imperial Observatory, were specialist "one-offs", and were seen as adjuncts to the imperial persona in so far as they were concerned with the divine harmonizing of heaven and earth. Unlike the West, China did not possess an innovation-driven free market economy which catered not only for the elite, but also for many social gradations below. In Europe this had led to a configuration of gearwheels and ratchets in a church tower that in 1340 had been part of a machine as big as a garden shed becoming sufficiently miniaturized, standardized, and relatively "mass-produced" by 1640 to allow its presence on middle-class mantle shelves and even in middle-class pockets.

The Chinese nobility loved the "self-ringing bells", or striking clocks. Father Verbiest was soon importing other ingenious Western machines by the 1670s, including a harpsichord, a small organ, novel firearms, meteorological instruments, a microscope (the Jesuit mission already had telescopes), and other optical devices for the delectation of K'ang Hsi and his courtiers. The ever-resourceful Father Verbiest, knowing of Greek and more recent European steam novelties, even built a simple steam engine for the emperor. It was an "aeropile", standing upon three wheels. Pressurized steam from a boiler blew through a pinhole to turn a little fan, or simple turbine, which, through a gear transmission system, turned the wheels and moved the little vehicle. Of course, it was only a toy, yet, like a striking clock, the steam car was capable of making a Chinese emperor gasp with wonder. How *clever* these Christians were.

Then, three years after escaping execution, Verbiest, like Father Adam before him, offered another astronomical challenge to the Court Astronomers. Could they predict the *exact* length of the shadow cast by the sun at noon for a specified day in February 1669? For a western European astronomer with a good set of mathematical tables, it was child's play. For the mandarins of the Astronomy Bureau, it was a matter of checking old records, precedents, and making educated guesses, for as we saw above, Chinese astronomy never developed a coherent mathematical theory of the heavens. Father Verbiest won hands down, which only strengthened Jesuit standing in the eyes of K'ang Hsi.

Especially significant, astronomically speaking, was the commission which Verbiest received, probably in the late 1660s, to re-equip the Imperial Observatory with Western-style angle-measuring instruments carrying 360-degree scales with which to rectify the ailing Chinese calendar and keep it in permanent adjustment, and to instruct the mandarins of the Astronomy Bureau in their correct usage. It was a formidable cultural coup by any standards, and a spectacular indicator of Jesuit initiative.

The instruments were perfect expressions of Jesuit diplomatic adroitness, for they were carefully designed cross-cultural hybrids. Their purely scientific parts were taken straight from the designs laid out for Tycho Brahe's Uraniborg instruments in his *Astronomiae Instauratae Mechanica* (1598), of which the missionary priests possessed a copy in their own library in Peking. These included the dimensions for the armillary sphere, sextants, and quadrants of the new Peking instruments, which were the same as for Tycho's pieces, while their 360-degree scales, geometrical single arc-minute (or one-sixtieth of a degree) divisions, and precise sighting arms all clearly indicated their Tychonic provenance.

On the other hand, the heavy bronze stands upon which the Tychonic technical parts were mounted were pure Chinese high art. Exquisite lions, noble rampant dragons, flaming pearls, and other celestial imperial motifs are all there: all in fine bronze, cast and executed in accordance with the very highest standards of Chinese technical excellence. Verbiest was careful not to imply that he was in any way superseding Chinese astronomical culture, so much as making it even more magnificent.

Someone, either Father Verbiest or perhaps even K'ang Hsi himself, had an idea for which I, and many other Western historians of science, have been deeply grateful. The Jesuits next produced an exquisitely detailed set of 103 Chinese wood-block "xylograph" printed illustrations, showing up to 117 instruments, on high-quality rice paper, each one a foot square, which not only depicted the new instruments, but also displayed the stage-by-stage process of their manufacture. These Peking pictures are probably as near as we will ever get to knowing the detailed processes by which Tycho Brahe's own instruments were made: a knowledge that was clearly still around in European scientific circles in *c.* 1660, but which has since been lost – creating thereby the ironic circumstance that we need to go to a set of technical drawings produced by Jesuit astronomers for the emperor of China in Peking to gain an insight into what Tycho's men were doing in Uraniborg, Denmark, over eighty years before – a scenario which I have described as "Tycho Brahe in China".[3]

These landmark plates in the history of precision astronomical technology tell us about much more than just the science, for they are public proclamations. On the one hand, they further substantiate our existing knowledge that K'ang Hsi was fascinated by technology and technical processes, for it is hard to imagine that imperial pride in his new observatory was not a major motive in their production. They are unique artefacts in the history of Sino–European relations. On the other hand, I suspect that Verbiest recognized their excellent publicity value for the Jesuit mission to China back in Europe. Though the bibliographical history of the loose sets of prints in Europe is complicated, they were entitled *Astronomea Europaea: Liber Organicus* ("European Astronomy: Book of Instruments"), and carry the date 1674. The French Jesuit and colleague of Verbiest, Father Philippe Couplet, returned to Europe and published the Latin text, but reproduced only one of the original set of 117 plates. This was the picture of the entire Peking Observatory, with all the instruments in their working positions. Couplet's book was entitled *Astronomia Europaea sub Imperatore Tartaro-Sinico... ex-umbra in lucem revocata...* ("European Astronomy, brought from the shadow back into the light for the Emperor of Tartary and China called Cam Hy [K'ang Hsi]") (Dillingen, 1687).

I should mention that only a few sets of the original Chinese plates now survive in European and American collections: in places such as the School of Oriental and African Studies and the British Museum, London, and the Bibliothèque Nationale in Paris. In 1976, I was able to secure a mint-condition set for the library of the Museum of the History of Science, Oxford. Of course, most of the original instruments still survive in remarkably good condition, despite having been exposed to the elements for 350 years in their original location in the Peking Imperial Observatory, now a museum.

What do the pictures tell us about Jesuit astronomy and physics in Peking in the days of K'ang Hsi? Very significantly, they provide a pictorial step-by-step guide as to how to design and build Western scientific parts for a 6-foot-diameter bronze equatorial armillary for measuring both up and down (declination) and east–west (right ascension) angles in the heavens. They begin by showing how to lay down a 6-foot prefabricated brick mould into which the molten metal is poured. Next, the cold rings are sawn, filed flat, polished, then spun on a large man-powered lathe to ensure their perfect circularity. Then, the gleaming rings are graduated into 360 degrees with large beam-compasses, using Greek geometrical techniques, following which the individual degrees are subdivided into tiny intervals, exactly after the manner of Tycho Brahe. This particular construction sequence ends by showing the finished armillary sitting on the ground, ready to be hoisted up on to its beautiful Chinese mount.

Of course, the 117 individual plates show other Western instruments as well, such as large quadrants and sextants, again modelled on those of Tycho, and there are Western physics plates depicting such things as the equal swings of pendulums (first discovered by Galileo) and European optical and other scientific instruments. These plates for the emperor of China are probably the most detailed examples of science, engineering, and technology "teaching by pictures" to come from the entire seventeenth century, East or West, demonstrating not only the assiduity of

Father Verbiest and his colleagues in teaching, but also of K'ang Hsi in learning. The unspoken but obvious subtext was "*This* is what Christianity will enable you to do."

Yet there was one aspect of Western technology which greatly interested K'ang Hsi but puzzled him as a *Jesuit* skill: heavy artillery manufacture. How could these men, who spoke of a God of love, and lived such self-disciplined, charitable, and ascetic lives, know so much about state-of-the-art weaponry? It is a question that has fascinated not just Chinese emperors but also Christians themselves, from early Christian times right down to today. Greek Orthodox monks experimented with Greek Fire as a defence against Islamic attacks upon medieval Byzantium; Friar Roger Bacon describes gunpowder mixes; and tradition says it was a German Franciscan monk, Berthold Schwarz, who invented the gun – and so on down the centuries, to the Scottish Presbyterian minister Alexander John Forsyth who invented percussion lock guns around 1807, and on to present-day parsons who collect guns and, not infrequently, steam engines as well. (I have known several over the years – and share their fascination.)

The fascination, I would suggest, stems not from any particular desire to spill blood, but from a love of complex technical devices and procedures: devices and procedures which were abounding in late-medieval and Renaissance Europe. For men – and, in more recent times, women – of God come in all shapes and sizes, and do not of necessity see any incompatibility between their faith of love and a delight in things that go bang, shoot bullets, or blow up. A seventeenth-century Jesuit missionary priest who could replicate Tycho Brahe's Uraniborg in Peking, predict eclipses, demonstrate and sometimes construct "self-ringing bells", magnify insects with lenses, play an imported harpsichord or organ, and build a working model steam car for the delight of the emperor could also cast and fire a cannon. Artillery was simply part of the portmanteau of technical skills that European Christians possessed.

Such awe-inspiring technology was clearly sanctioned by a God whose providential concern for his missionaries' lives led him to shake the Imperial City with earthquakes and fiery celestial portents shortly before the priests were due to be executed – a providence which Father Verbiest and his Jesuit brethren would have seen as genuine and true in the fullest sense, no matter how people may sneer today. They saw themselves as the latter-day equivalents of St Peter and St Paul, taking the gospel to distant lands, but whose "signs and wonders" were not healing miracles so much as useful technical skills that would have been unknown to the first apostles.

We know that Father Verbiest had many conversations about religion, and that K'ang Hsi was very curious about Christianity. While he never became a Christian – a circumstance which, had he done so, would have altered the course of subsequent world history – he was willing to tolerate it. In 1692, four years after Father Verbiest had died following a horse-riding accident, and at the request of Father Thomas Pereira, K'ang Hsi not only gave imperial permission for Christian missionaries to preach in China but also decreed their protection from persecution. A serious obstacle to conversion appears to have been Christian and Confucian differences about ancestor worship. On the other hand, it appears that Christian conversions had already been taking place before this time, for not only had the Jesuits won a sprinkling of converts around the court, but there had also been Dominican and Franciscan missions to China as well as that of the Jesuits, though they had lacked the Jesuits' access to the upper echelons of Chinese society.

Jesuit missionary astronomers and scientists continued to direct the building or importing of more modern instruments, but the Order came to be largely suppressed in Europe during the late eighteenth century, leading to the withdrawal of the mission. Though a later emperor proscribed Christianity in 1723, the seeds which the Jesuit Fathers planted represent the real beginnings of Chinese Christianity.

JESUITS IN THE AMERICAS

The Jesuits' mission to China is perhaps the best known, in so far as it overtly used science, and astronomy in particular, as an adjunct to evangelism; yet there were other Jesuit priests sent to various parts of the world who accomplished major scientific work in addition to their religious activities.

We have already encountered Father José de Acosta who in the late sixteenth century ruffled Spanish colonial feathers by standing up for the rights of the indigenous populations. Yet Father de Acosta, during his mission to Latin America between 1572 and 1587, was captivated by the new natural phenomena that he encountered and which had no direct parallels back in Europe. These included the complex tidal and meteorological systems of the Pacific Ocean, and especially the frequent earthquakes that occurred around the Andes. Unlike the familiar earthquakes of the Mediterranean, those of Latin America seemed unassociated with active volcanoes. These published observations have led to Father José being called "the father of geophysics". As was to emerge as a thorny point with Galileo fifty years later, de Acosta argued that we must *interpret* Scripture when it seemed at odds with scientific phenomena unimagined by the ancient Jews.

While lacking the high culture and drama of the China mission, those Jesuits sent to Latin America achieved extraordinary things, especially in cartography and exploration. The Moravian Father Samuel Fitz produced the first scientifically accurate map of the Amazon in 1707 – a project demanding the highest levels of astronomical, geo-magnetic, and hydrographical knowledge – in the midst of adventures that almost killed him: fever, accident, and nearly having his head bitten off by an alligator. Yet Father Samuel never lost sight of his main mission: his Christian ministry to the remote tribes of Amazonia.

It was Jesuit missionaries who went out to take Christianity to the South American tribes, entered truly unknown territories, and sometimes met very dangerous local people, who first explored and mapped the great South American river systems such as the Amazon, Paraguay, and Orinoco. Father Jacques Marquette was to do the same for the Mississippi in North America, paddling 2,500 miles down from Lake Michigan to the Arkansas River, observing, charting, and surveying the vast interior of the northern continent. Intellectual curiosity never lay far behind evangelism, and making themselves useful and relevant to distant peoples, be they Chinese emperors or Brazilian jungle-dwellers, was part of the broader Jesuit strategy. The last thing that the Jesuits set out to do was "ram religion down the natives' throats"; they were far too intelligent for that. No, their strategy was to win local respect, by trying to advance agriculture, cure disease (wherever that was possible in 1660), improve calendars and daily life, and argue the native peoples' case against colonial exploiters.

Why was the early European name for the South American rainforest plant yielding quinine "Jesuits' bark"? Guess who brought news of its medicinal properties to Europe. For sheer courage, daring, self-sacrifice, and focus, these missionary-explorer-scientists leave the fictional Indiana Jones at the starting line.

None of this tells us anything about Jesuit astronomers and scientists within mainland Europe – where they abounded. So, we must now move on to see the contributions made to science by Roman Catholics, lay and ordained, during and after the time of Galileo, the telescope, and his trial.

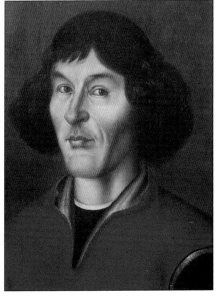

Nicholas Copernicus. (1580, Town Hall, Toruń.)

Tycho Brahe. (*Mechanica*, title page.)

Johannes Kepler. (Unknown artist, 1610.)

Cardinal de Guevara. (Note his "fashionable" spectacles.) (El Greco, *c.* 1598.)

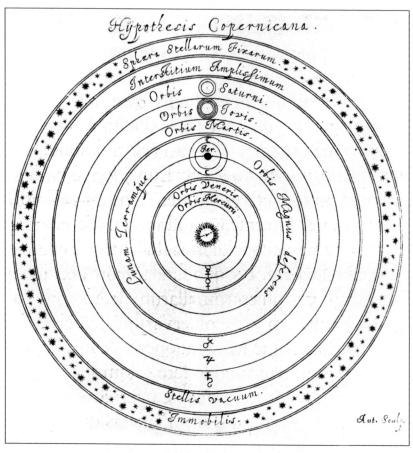

The Copernican universe, 1543. The planets rotate around the sun. (*De Revolutionibus*, 1543.)

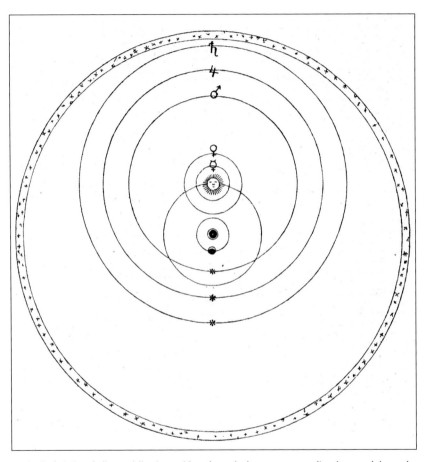

Tycho Brahe's "geo-heliocentric" universe. Note that only the moon rotates directly around the earth. Mercury, Venus, Mars, Jupiter, and Saturn rotate around the sun, while the sun and all the planets then rotate around the central earth. (Tycho Brahe, *De Mundi aetherei recentioribus phaenomenis*, 1587–88).

Tycho's quadrant of 5 cubits (6$\frac{1}{3}$ feet approx.) radius. The man on the right-hand side uses an adjustable sight to look across the quadrant and measure the altitude angle of a star seen through the narrow wall aperture on the left. For the purpose of this illustration, Tycho has filled in the blank wall supporting the quadrant with scenes of his laboratories and observing platform at Uraniborg. (*Mechanica*, 1598.)

Kepler, *Rudolphine Tables*, frontispiece, 1627. Kepler depicts "Astronomy" as a circular Greek *tholos* or temple. The earliest pillars at the back are rough wood, brick, and stone, leading, via Hipparchus, Ptolemy, the medieval Arabs, and Copernicus, to the perfect Corinthian architecture of "modern" astronomy, as epitomized by Tycho Brahe.

Galileo the "bruiser": not the face of a gentle or compliant man. (Domenico Tintoretto, 1605–07.)

Galileo's moon drawings, from *Sidereus Nuncius*, 1610. Note that Galileo is less concerned with topographical accuracy than with depicting the rough lunar surface.

The more familiar portrait of Galileo in old age. (Justus Sustermans, 1636.)

Two of Galileo's telescopes, preserved in the Museum in Florence. The larger telescope is about 30 inches long.

Father Christopher Scheiner, SJ, and his Jesuit assistant measuring the positions of spots on a projected solar image. (*Rosa Ursina*, 1626.)

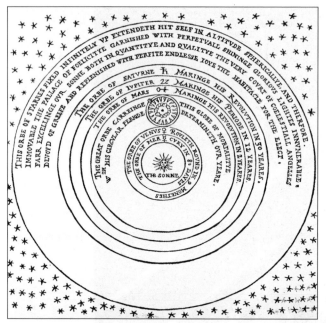

Thomas Digges's Copernican heliocentric universe. Note how he depicts the stars, as *not* on a sphere, but as receding to infinity. (*A Prognostication Everlasting*, 1576.)

Thomas Harriot, assisted by Christopher Tooke, observes the 5-day moon at 9 p.m., 26 July 1609, from Syon House, Brentford, near London. (Rita Greer's 2009 reconstruction from Harriot's description.)

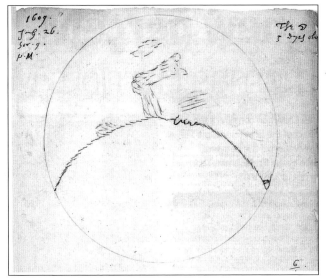

Harriot's 26 July 1609 moon drawing. Note his concentration on the rough appearance of the "terminator" separating the light from the shadow areas. (Lord Egremont Collection, Petworth House Archives, HMC 241/9 fol. 26, West Sussex Record Office, Chichester.)

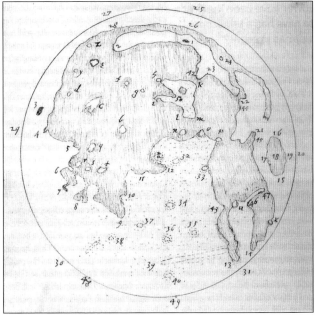

Harriot's whole moon map, *c.* 1612. This map's meticulous detail demonstrates his skill as a topographical surveyor. (Lord Egremont Collection, as above, fol. 30.)

Johannes and Catherina Elisabetha Hevelius observing the celestial angle between a pair of stars with the large sextant. This is the earliest known picture of a woman actually "doing science". (*Machina Coelestis*, 1673.)

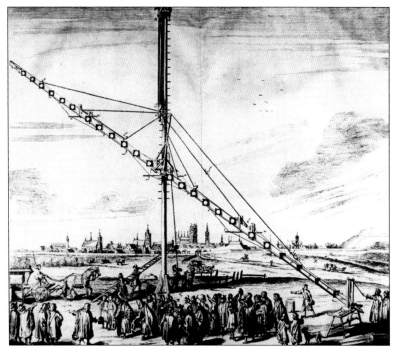

Hevelius's 150-foot-focus telescope, outside Dantzig. (*Machina Coelestis*, 1673.)

Father Pierre Gassendi (after Louis-Édouard Rioult).

Father Ferdinand Verbiest SJ, depicted in his Chinese mandarin robes, with Western instruments. (Copyright University of San Francisco Ricci Institute, 2008.)

William Crabtree observes the transit of Venus, 24 November 1639. A telescope, in the right-hand window casement, projects the solar and Venusian images on to a sheet of paper. (Ford Madox Brown, *c.* 1878, Manchester Town Hall.)

Jeremiah Horrocks 1639 transit of Venus memorial window, St Michael's Church, Much Hoole, Lancashire, 1859.

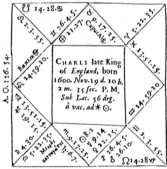

Horoscope drawing for King Charles I. Seventeenth-century horoscopes were set out within a series of squares. The zodiac was divided up into 12 inter-connecting triangular spaces, into which the planetary "aspects", or positions, could be written in symbolic shorthand. (William Lilly, *Merlinus Anglicanus* [almanac], 1652.)

The Rt Revd Dr John Wilkins. (By Mary Beale, *c.* 1670. Warden and Fellows of Wadham College, Oxford.)

John Wilkins and his protégé Robert Hooke ascend from Wadham College quadrangle in Wilkins's "Flying Chariot", *en route* for the moon. The Chariot appears to have been intended as a small ship, with clockwork-powered wings. (Reconstructed and drawn by Allan Chapman, 1976.)

Frontispiece, John Wilkins, *Discourse concerning a new world…*, 1640. Note that the sun proclaims himself to be the source of *lucem*, *calorem*, and *motum*, or light, heat, and motion. All the planets rotate about the sun, while the stars, instead of being equidistantly located on a "sphere", are scattered, perhaps to infinity, throughout space. Below are Wilkins's heroes, Copernicus and Galileo. "What if it were like this?" asks Copernicus, in Latin, and Galileo, holding his telescope, replies "Here are his eyes," and his companion, with ascending eagle, whispers "If only there were wings!". (Warden and Fellows of Wadham College, Oxford.)

Bernard le Bovier de Fontenelle, *Entretiens sur la pluralité des mondes* ("Conversations on the plurality of worlds"), 1686. Fontenelle and the Countess behold the heliocentric heavens. Note: not only does Jupiter – fifth planet out from the sun – have its four "Galilean" satellites first seen in 1610, but Saturn also displays the five moons subsequently discovered by the much more powerful telescopes of Huygens and Cassini.

Sir Francis Bacon. (Frans Pourbus, 1617, Palace on the Water, Warsaw.)

Robert Hooke. (Portrait reconstruction by Rita Greer, 2003, from two detailed "pen portrait" descriptions of *c.* 1680.)

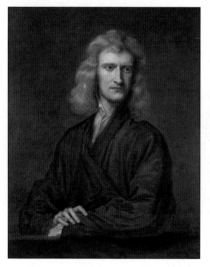

Sir Isaac Newton. (Sir Godfrey Kneller, 1689.)

The Revd Dr James Bradley. (Robert Murdock Wright, after Thomas Hudson, *c.* 1750. Master and Fellows of Balliol College, Oxford.)

CHAPTER 16

Galileo and Science in
Roman Catholic Europe

*I*t is widely believed that the condemnation of Galileo in 1633 caused the Roman Catholic Church to shut down free thought across Europe, and, most especially, to halt scientific inquiry. Popular mythology apart, it is important to look at how much astronomy and other science was actually being done in Catholic Europe, before, during, and after the "Galileo affair", who was doing it, and how it was being received.

THE CALENDAR AND THE CELESTIAL MACHINERY

We have seen how important the calendar was to Christians, who all needed to celebrate the pivotal festival of the faith, Easter, on the same day. In the Middle Ages, this had meant getting Irishmen, Poles, Sicilians, and others scattered across Europe to calculate the heavens using the same mathematical criteria. By the sixteenth century the problem had become global, for how did you ensure that when you celebrated the resurrection on Easter morning in Macao, China, Goa, Sri Lanka, Mexico City, or on the shores of Lake Michigan, you were doing so on the same day as it was being celebrated in Rome or Salzburg – and with longitudinal local time-zone differences to be taken into consideration?

As we saw in Chapter 2, there are few convenient round numbers as far as the motions of the heavens are concerned, as solar, lunar, and stellar rotation cycles are replete with all manner of awkward fractions. While a variety of Papal Commissions had looked into

Europe's inheritance of Julius Caesar's calendar over the Middle Ages, the calendar reform ball did not get rolling until Pope Leo X, in 1574, sent out an invitation to resolve the calendar problem once and for all. The man who most rose to this challenge was a German Jesuit astronomer and mathematician of the Collegio Romano (now the Gregorian University), Father Christoph Schlüssel – known to history by his Latinized name Clavius – who developed an earlier plan by the Neopolitan physician-astronomer Aloysius Lilius. By 1582, Clavius had formulated a series of calculations based upon observed data which enabled him to present a series of numerical fail-safes, through which one could apply corrections to the calendar as the decades and centuries rolled by. This ensured that errors accumulating due to the irregular numbers could be cancelled out at regular intervals, to put the civil calendar back into synchronicity with the heavens.

From his analyses, and being fully familiar with problems inherent in the ancient leap year system, where the day added every fourth year was slightly too long, Clavius proposed an ingenious computation. The every fourth year leap year system leads to the addition of 100 days every 400 years, whereas Clavius found that it was necessary to add only 97 days every 400 years. This could be accomplished by *not* adding a day to new century leap years that were *not* divisible by 400. Thus, 1600, 2000, and 2400 could be leap years, whereas 1700, 1800, 1900, and so on could not be. Thus, 97 was intercalated within 400 by dropping three leap years every four centuries: a simple yet elegant and accurate numerical rule.

By 1581, the civil and ecclesiastical calendars were at variance with the observed heavens – with the observable and measurable summer and winter solstices and the spring and autumn equinoxes – by a whole ten days. The astronomically observed equinox of 1581, for example, fell on 11 March rather than the 21st, when it should have been observed: an error which had built up by regular, tiny increments since Julius Caesar's astronomer, Sosigenes, had set up the present calendar system back in 46 BC. This ten-day discrepancy played havoc with the calculation of the date of Easter, which could only be celebrated following the full moon after the spring equinox. If, for example, the full "Easter" or Paschal moon fell on 16 March, did you calculate Easter from the true equinox of 11 March, or the "calendar" equinox of 21 March? To bring Julius Caesar's now badly erroneous, nearly 1,600-year-old calendar back into line, Clavius's new calendar simply lost ten days in October 1582. You went to bed on the night of 4 October – and woke up next morning on 15 October. Although the reformed calendar project had been inaugurated by Pope Leo X, it was brought to fruition during the reign of his successor, Pope Gregory XIII: hence its name, the "Gregorian calendar".

Crucial to Father Clavius's work was the need for a pretty exact value for the length of the year. Before telescopic measuring instruments made it possible to calculate the *exact* altitude of the sun at the solstices, after 1670, it is interesting to know how Clavius derived this figure. Of course, he would have had access to classical, Arabic, and Western observations that were easily available in Latin. But, as Clavius was working a century before the Greenwich Royal Observatory brought in the new telescopic precision angle-measuring instruments in 1675, all of these old observations would still have been made either with naked-eye measuring instruments, or with large shadow scales – none of which were reliable to more than a few angular arc minutes. So Clavius probably used long runs of these naked-eye angular observations, and averaged them to distil out a more refined figure.

There was one class of building of which Europe possessed *hundreds* by 1600, which could easily be turned into accurate solar midday angle-measuring observatories: large churches and cathedrals. Italian churches were especially appropriate, with their cavernous classical basilica interiors and relatively small windows to prevent the scorching summer sun from overheating the interiors. Such interiors could also be dark, unlike those of the great Gothic churches of the north, where vast windows designed to catch every photon of weak winter sunshine often made their noon-day interiors ablaze with light.

If one drilled a discreet hole high up in the south-facing wall of a great Italian church, it could be made to admit a thin, brilliant pencil of sunlight that would fall on the marble floor, maybe 100 feet or more away, exactly at noon. And if one observed the daily

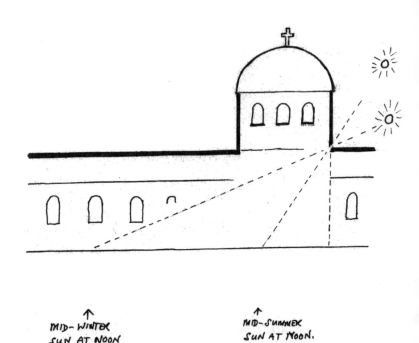

MID-WINTER
SUN AT NOON

MID-SUMMER
SUN AT NOON.

16.1 The interior of a great Italian church, looking *eastward* (towards the altar), at noon. Sunlight floods through a tiny aperture high up in the south-facing part of the dome support. This aperture admits a narrow shaft of noontide sunlight, which falls down to the pavement, on a north–south meridian line, extending across the width of the church. By utilizing the mathematical geometry of right-angled triangles, Renaissance priest-astronomers were able to make exact measurements of various details in the solar orbit, from which highly accurate calendrical data could be extracted. (Drawing by Allan Chapman.)

position of solar light as it fell on the floor each day of the year, one could establish exactly the longest and shortest day positions: or the summer and winter solstices. This could be done as a simple geometrical function, using the properties of right-angled triangles. The slanting ray of sunlight coming in through the small hole becomes the hypotenuse, or long side, of a right-angled triangle, with the cathedral wall and the spot where the ray hits the floor as the other two sides, to form an elegant Pythagorean proportion.

Of course, these proportions would change with the sun's

daily altitude, which was the very scientific point upon which the instrument capitalized. Between Christmas and midsummer, for example, the daily hypotenuse ray of sunlight would become shorter and more acute, from the low, slanting winter sun to the high midsummer sun. And the exact reverse would occur between midsummer and Christmas. Yet the light would *always* fall *exactly* upon the same meridian, north–south, line at midday. Knowing the exact latitude of the church – which was easy for a skilful priest-mathematician to establish – one could place marks on this meridian line to denote the sun's precise position for every day of the year. And at a projection distance of 50 or 70 feet, the sun's daily elevation changes were discernible to perhaps half an arc minute.

These giant sundials – for that is exactly what such an arrangement produced – were named *meridianae*, or giant meridian lines, and from the resulting runs of accumulated solar position data, a skilled astronomer could extract all manner of calendrical information relating to the length of the year.

Yet, one might ask, why did Father Clavius and his colleagues not simply use clocks to establish the precise length of the day and year? After all, if clocks would soon be sent as gifts to the emperor of China, why go to so much trouble in measuring the sun's daily position instead of just checking the clock? The answer is simple. For while the clocks of 1580 could ring bells, move automata, and tell you when it was dinner time, they were not sufficiently accurate to mark tiny *fractions* of time. To get such a level of accuracy, an astronomer had to go to the sun and the stars, directly – hence the great church *meridianae*.

The first great *meridiana* to be constructed was in the church of Santa Maria Novella, Florence, in 1574, in direct response to Pope Leo X's calendar reform initiative of that year. It was designed by Egnatio Danti, inspired by a prior, yet less accurate, *meridiana* laid out in Santa Maria del Fiore a century before. Father Danti, who was a Dominican, would further lay down an even larger *meridiana* in the Cathedral of San Petronio, Bologna, with a midwinter solar projection of an incredible 170 feet. Others would be built in other churches in Europe, as a way of keeping the post-1582 "Gregorian" calendar in check. Egnatio Danti would eventually become Bishop of Alatri. (The modern American scholar John Heilbron has published a masterly study of these *meridianae*.)[1]

It was from observations made with *meridianae* and other instruments that Father Christopher Clavius developed the astronomical criteria that made the new calendar possible. Clavius seems not only to have been the Renaissance church's "star" mathematical astronomer, but also a remarkably open-minded and imaginative man even into old age.

CHRISTOPHER CLAVIUS AND GALILEO

In 1610, the 73-year-old Clavius became fascinated by Galileo's telescopic discoveries as announced in *Sidereus Nuncius*, and confirmed some of them by learning how to look through the awkward optical tube. In 1611, the year prior to his death, Clavius applauded Galileo's work before a special Convocation of the Collegio Romano, convened to honour the Tuscan astronomer, before a dazzling assemblage of academic clergy, writers, philosophers, cardinals, and even royalty. There were many men like Clavius who, while remaining unconvinced by Galileo's anti-Aristotelian explanation for the surface-spotted sun or the reality of the Copernican universe, still respected his achievement enormously, and were fulsome in their praise. With so many friends in high places, and with the veritable floodtide of admiration and regard that his telescopic discoveries had brought him by 1611, it is a shame that Galileo continued to make unnecessary enemies.

Of course, I am not for a moment suggesting that Galileo should have trimmed or glossed over "the truth" for good fellowship's sake. Yet responding *graciously* to men who, while stating that they do not accept your Copernican heliocentric arguments nonetheless make clear their admiration for your wider achievement, is *not* being obsequious. It is common sense and good manners.

While we now know that Galileo had been right in his heliocentric interpretation of his telescopic discoveries, things were by no means so clear-cut within his lifetime, as we have seen. In their defence of Aristotelian physics and the Tychonic (not Ptolemaic) cosmology, the astronomers and philosophers within the church still appeared to have the scientific *evidential* ace-card firmly within their hands in 1640. Had Galileo's undisputed scientific genius been combined with a less dogmatic and abrasive manner, the future of Western scientific history could have been profoundly different.

ROMAN CATHOLIC CLERGY IN OBSERVATIONAL ASTRONOMY AND EXPERIMENTAL PHYSICS

While it is true that ecclesiastical decisions made in Rome between 1616 and 1633 placed clear limitations upon the discussion of the heliocentric theory, they had no discernible effect upon aspects of clerical astronomical research. The church's scientific men took up the telescope with alacrity, and used it to pioneer several new branches of the science.

It is unfortunate that in his disputes with Galileo, Father Christopher Scheiner, SJ has been historically sidelined, on the *assumed* ground that, though a clever man, he was blinded by church dogma from seeing "the truth", and deserves only to be remembered as a sort of discredited foil to Galileo.

Yet who and what was "Apelles", as he styled himself in his correspondence with Marcus Welser in 1611? I suspect that Scheiner chose his pseudonym from the early disciple "Apelles approved in Christ", to whom St Paul sends a greeting at the end of his Epistle to the Romans (16:10). (On the other hand, he may have borrowed the names from the ancient Greek painter, Apelles of Cos.) In 1611, this 38-year-old German Jesuit theologian, mathematician, and scholar was still based in Ingolstadt. After several high-level academic and spiritual appointments in Austria and the Germanic world, he went to Rome in 1624, and it was here that he developed a line of research that went beyond his initial work of 1611, making a sustained study of the sun and solar research technology, and launching a full-scale assault upon the Copernican theory.

Scheiner stood as a living refutation of the idea that an argued rejection of the heliocentric theory as an authentic description of cosmological reality somehow meant that one was scientifically backward. While he lived and worked within a broad, yet evolving, Aristotelian scheme of explanation, and while he respected Copernicus as an astronomer – without accepting his heliocentric theory – Schneiner nonetheless became a pioneer of telescopic astronomy. It was in Rome, between 1626 and 1630, that he composed his monumental *Rosa Ursina sive Sol*, published in Bracciano, in a sumptuous and beautifully illustrated folio volume extending over 780 pages.

When I first examined the Bodleian Library, Oxford, copy of *Rosa Ursina* as a doctoral student over thirty-five years ago, it brought home to me that this was the foundational text of what would become the science of solar physics. Before looking at its content, I was struck by its odd title – literally, "The Rose of the Bears, or the Sun" – and the elaborate frontispiece, which shows bears engaged in various activities, with a grinning bear projecting an image of the sun onto a white screen.

The secret, I discovered, lay in Scheiner's patrons: the powerful Orsini (Ursini) family, whose Italian name can also mean "bear" (Latin *ursus*). And as *rosa* is Latin for rose, or a rose garland, Father Christopher was presenting a garland of astronomical roses to his patron, Paolo Jordanus Orsini II, Duke of Bracciano, and equating him and his family with the sun – a piece of brazen flattery, even by the "over the top" book dedications of the Renaissance, yet explaining the various activities of the bears represented in the frontispiece.

Quite apart from any lack of generosity of spirit Scheiner may have shown to Galileo, *Rosa Ursina* contained the first sustained set of solar studies ever made. Galileo's sun studies were done over a few months or years, and Thomas Harriot's, David Fabricius's, and other astronomers' studies likewise; for once you had demonstrated that the sun was spotted, and that it appeared to rotate upon its axis, what else was there to do, given the simple refracting telescopes of *c.* 1620?

Scheiner *did* take things further, however. He observed the sun by projection over an eighteen-year period, and began to notice interesting features. He was able to obtain a better value for the period of the solar rotation, at between 26 and 27 days, from the motion of the spots (the modern value for the "synodic" or exact 360-degree rotation as viewed from earth is 26.24 days). By tracking their apparent angle of inclination, he established the positions of the sun's north and south poles, as well as the angular difference or tilt between the solar and terrestrial poles in space. Scheiner made careful studies of the "life cycles" of sunspots and of the relation between their "umbral" (dark) and "penumbral" (lighter) zones; how they form and break up (often looking like archipelagos, or groups of related islands on a world map), but rarely last much longer than a month. And as Scheiner, Galileo, Harriot, and others had noticed back in 1611–12, sunspots always rotated in the same east–west direction. As the dark spots were styled *maculae* in Latin, so they called the strange whitish areas which appeared on the sun *faculae* – "flares", or "little torches". Yet the relationship between the dark and light spots would have to wait for the late-nineteenth-century science of spectroscopy before much elucidation was possible.

In some respects, Scheiner did with the solar surface what Tycho Brahe had done for the starry heavens: observe, measure, and record them on a regular basis, for regular observing yielded a much richer body of primary data. Very significantly, Father Scheiner left clear descriptions of the instruments with which he worked, and in one fine-art engraving in *Rosa Ursina*, he shows a young Jesuit assistant making careful measurements of the relative positions of sunspots on a telescope-projected image of the solar disc, as directed by a senior colleague seated at a desk.

Rosa Ursina contained a detailed engraving of an instrument which was destined to become something of a prototype design for a telescopic mount. This was Scheiner's *helioscope*, or sun-scope, and what makes it significant is that his description constitutes the first ever account of an equatorial mount for a telescope. It is true that he may have been guided or inspired by a prior suggestion by Kepler, but the helioscope is a real-life working instrument. For in an equatorial mount, the telescope does not sit upon a tripod or pillar, requiring the user to constantly raise, lower, and move the instrument east to west to make it track an astronomical body across the sky. Instead, the telescope is attached to an "equatorial axis", or a firm wooden beam inclined to point exactly to the Pole Star, and delicately pivoted top and bottom, so that the beam – and the telescope – can rotate smoothly and exactly in the same plane of the sky as the sun. Consequently, if the telescope is focused upon the sun on any given day, then all the astronomer needs to do to track it from rising, to noon, and to setting, is to apply the correct pressure upon the axis, to make it turn at exactly the same speed as the sun. No further "fiddling" is required.

Of course, this is an ideal way to mount a telescope for high-precision purposes, such as when measuring sunspot changes on a daily basis. I myself once built a replica of Father Scheiner's helioscope mount, and can vouch at first hand how much steadier the sunspot images are, and how easy it is to measure their positions when the telescope is so adjusted that a projected image of the solar disc falls on a prepared white paper screen. By the nineteenth century, the "equatorial" had become the standard way of mounting nearly all large, precise telescopes, only to be superseded in the early twenty-first century by automatic computer-controlled mounts.

Scheiner describes his helioscope and other instruments in Book II of *Rosa Ursina*, for like Tycho, Galileo, Verbiest, and others, the Jesuit realized that a scientist must provide a full account of the instruments with which he is working, so that colleagues elsewhere might replicate, check, and advance his work: the very stuff of how to do good science, in fact. As Kepler had done in *Astronomiae Pars Optica* (1604), and *Dioptrice* (1611), so Father Scheiner discussed optical and other instruments, new telescopes, and the physiology of the eye in the *Rosa*.

By 1630, and with eighteen years of solar and other astronomical study behind him, Christopher Scheiner had come to accept that sunspots were either on the sun's surface, or else in the solar atmosphere, and were *not* little planetoids orbiting it, as he had believed in 1611. One also senses that, while still basically Aristotelian, he had come to accept on evidential grounds explanations that were not part of Aristotelian orthodoxy. In addition to his new views on sunspots, he appears by 1630 to have abandoned the view that there were solid planetary spheres in the heavens: a corollary, in many respects, of Tycho Brahe's geo-heliocentric system which could have led to spheres colliding with each other.

Even so, down to his death in 1650, Father Scheiner remained a convinced geocentricist who, rather sadly, still felt obliged to attack his old foe, the now deceased Galileo, in his *Prodromus pro sole mobili et terra stabili...* ("Introductory Treatise in Favour of a Moving Sun and a Fixed Earth") which was published posthumously in 1651.

FATHER PIERRE GASSENDI: ASTRONOMER, PHYSICIST, THEOLOGIAN, AND ANTI-ARISTOTELIAN

In many ways Pierre Gassendi, who was ordained in 1617 when he was twenty-five, stands as a powerful refutation of the myth that the Roman Catholic Church killed off independent scientific thinking. This ingenious and forthright Provençal French academic priest – he came to hold the Chair of Mathematics at the prestigious Collège Royale in Paris as well as the Provostship of Digne Cathedral – should have been in hot water, ecclesiastically speaking, right from the start. But he was not.

For one thing, he became increasingly and openly sceptical of several aspects of the Aristotelian philosophy, in spite of vain attempts by the Paris Parliament to enforce Aristotelianism by law after 1624. The system of physics which Gassendi erected in its place was a modified and Christianized atomism, deriving from Epicurus and other pre-Aristotelian classical Greek pagans and religious sceptics. The key difference was that whereas Epicurus and other classical atomists had argued that the world as we know it was formed by the blind chance of atoms assembling and disintegrating, Gassendi saw the mind and hand of God as the guiding force behind the atoms, instead, that is, of the four eternal Aristotelian elements – earth, water, air, and fire – which Gassendi saw as no more than gross groupings of primary atoms.

"Gassendian atomism" was to exert a major influence on the physical and chemical ideas of the deeply devout Irish-English experimentalist, the Honourable Robert Boyle, whose *Sceptical Chymist* (1661) developed the concept of the atom as the fundamental building block of all matter, and as the source of chemical change. Like the Catholic Gassendi, the Protestant "lay bishop" Boyle saw a God-directed, *Christian* atomism as opening up a path for a profoundly influential new way of thinking about matter.

In addition to being an influential physical and theological theorist, Father Gassendi was an ingenious experimentalist. One thing he wished to test was one of the arguments deployed by the Aristotelians against a moving earth. Surely, if our globe were rotating on its axis, and one dropped a ball from a high tower, then the ball must fall to the east of its point of release, the earth having turned somewhat during its descent? As everyone knows, however, a falling object fell straight down, in a vertical line, allowing the reasonable conclusion that the earth was "fixed and 'stablished".

Now theoretical dynamists, such as those of Merton College, Oxford in the fifteenth century, had asked how an object would fall if it were part of a smoothly moving object, such as a ship in calm sea. In October 1640, Pierre Gassendi, perhaps using his connections with the French admiral the Prince de Condé, performed the decisive experiment on board a fast-moving oared war-galley in a flat sea outside Marseilles harbour. Releasing a ball from the speeding galley's mast at the right moment, he saw the ball fall exactly at the foot of the mast, and not behind it. Simply, the ball had taken on what we recognize as the inertial velocity of the galley, and fell with relation to it, rather than to the earth. So, could it be that an object dropped from a tower fell directly below it because it was being carried along by a *rotating* earth? Gassendi did not need to trumpet the argument, so much as let people draw their own conclusions.

Father Gassendi was also a dedicated astronomical observer, and on 7 November 1631, he made astronomical history when he saw the planet Mercury pass across – or transit – the sun's disc, on the basis of a calculation by Kepler. Gassendi did this by projecting the solar disc on to a sheet of paper, in what, by 1631, was the standard method of observing sunspots. As he told the Lutheran minister Professor Wilhelm Schickard of Tübingen, he was amazed at the sheer *smallness* of Mercury, which he had taken for a tiny sunspot until its rapid motion confirmed its planetary status.[2] Up to this time it was assumed that the planets must be quite large, as were Jupiter and Saturn; yet Mercury appeared only as a tiny round dot against the sun.

Gassendi was a native of Champtercier, near Digne-les-Bains, and today Digne is rightly proud of its eminent scientific priest son, so much so that, in 1992, the 400th anniversary of his birth, the Musée de Digne on the Boulevard Gassendi mounted a new exhibition about him. As none of his instruments survived, I was honoured when the Musée authorities approached me regarding the construction of exact working replicas. Fortunately, detailed original descriptions existed in the six volumes of the Latin *Petri Gassendi Diniensis Opera Omnia* (Paris, 1658), to which I had easy

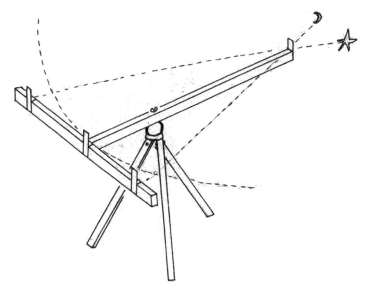

16.2 Pierre Gassendi's "Astronomical Radius". The Astronomical Radius was a popular instrument in Renaissance Europe. It worked on similar geometrical principles to "Ptolemy's Rulers" (Figure 3.1). The long rod acts as the radius to a circle, and the shorter "T" rod as a tangent to the same circle. Gassendi and an assistant would have measured the angle subtended between a pair of astronomical bodies by sliding brass sights along the tangent rod, as viewed against a fixed brass sight set at the end of the long rod. The graduation spaces between the sliding sights of the short, tangent, rod would then have been calculated against the known, fixed length of the long rod. In this way, the geometry of complementary right-angled triangles could be used to derive the number of degrees and minutes of arc between the objects in the sky. (Reconstructed from Gassendi's description by Allan Chapman.)

access in Oxford libraries. In consequence, I reconstructed his two main angle-measuring instruments.

The first of these was his 1619 *radius astronomicus*, of 7 Paris feet (2,273 mm): a configuration of two beechwood beams jointed to form a "T" shape. Along the short arm of the T was a set of delicately subdivided graduations, which, when used in conjunction with three brass sights, could be employed to measure horizontal angles in the sky, such as between the moon and a planet. I reconstructed, made, and graduated this instrument in Oxford, then despatched it to France.

The second instrument was Father Gassendi's 5 Parisian feet (1,624 mm) wooden astronomical quadrant. Because of its large size, instead of building the instrument in Oxford, I produced a set of full-sized, highly detailed engineering drawings, from which a French craftsman could then build it. Like the prototype, I gave it a full set of accurate Tycho Brahe degree graduations, which the Digne craftsmen could copy directly on to the brass scale.

With this instrument, Gassendi could measure vertical angles of celestial objects, and when it was used in conjunction with the radius, he could map the constellations – just as Tycho Brahe had done.

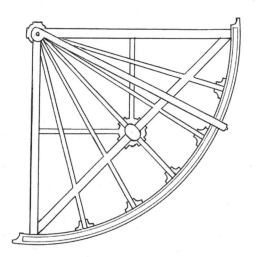

16.3 Gassendi's quadrant of 5 Parisian feet radius for measuring altitude, or *Declination*, angles. (Reconstructed from Gassendi's description by Allan Chapman.)

Gassendi's work, in astronomy, experimental physics, and atomism, ran right through the age of the "Galileo affair". He openly supported Galileo, advocated experimental empiricism against Aristotelian authority, disputed with his fellow French Catholic radical physicist, René Descartes, and died peacefully and undisturbed in 1656, respected across Europe by Catholics and Protestants alike.

GIOVANNI BATTISTA RICCIOLI, SJ: COPERNICANISM ANALYSED AND FOUND WANTING, 1651

No student of the Astronomical Renaissance can dismiss the formidable intellectual achievement of Father Riccioli's *Almagestum Novum* ("New Almagest"), 1651. Like so many of his Jesuit colleagues, Riccioli displayed a staggering range as a physical scientist, being a meticulous observer and experimentalist, a penetrating theorist, and a brilliant mathematician. To dismiss his defence of geocentricism as mere conformity to church dogma is simply laughable, for in Riccioli we encounter one of the greatest scientific intellects of the mid-seventeenth-century Catholic Church.

A native of Ferrara, and a graduate of its great university, Riccioli entered the Society of Jesus in 1614, when he was sixteen. As a scientist he corresponded with Roman Catholics like Giovanni Domenico Cassini and Athanasius Kircher, and staunch Protestants such as Christiaan Huygens and Johannes Hevelius. As a magnificent folio volume of around 1,500 pages, *Almagestum Novum* is an astronomical treatise of truly biblical dimensions.

Across the *Almagestum*'s ten magisterial "Books" (or chapters), Riccioli examined all aspects of astronomy as it was then understood, including comets, the stars, and astronomical distance measurement. But it is Book 9, on the structure of the universe, and in particular the fixity or mobility of the earth, which is the most historically significant, and to which he devotes over 300 pages of text laid out in over 100 arguments for and against.

Riccioli – geocentricist and anti-Copernican though he may have been – was *not* defending Ptolemy. No one was at that time, and Galileo had discussed the Ptolemaic system in the 1632 *Dialogue* almost as a straw target, easy to demolish. The post-telescopic cosmology of choice was now the geo-heliocentric system of Tycho Brahe, which could explain all the new telescopic discoveries *without* postulating a moving earth. Father Riccioli defended a modified Tychonic theory, in which Mercury, Venus, and Mars orbited the sun, while the sun in turn orbited a fixed earth. Riccioli only differed from Tycho in so far as he reckoned that Jupiter and Saturn revolved directly around the earth. (The discovery of Uranus, Neptune, and Pluto lay centuries ahead.)

In this system, all the telescopic discoveries could be neatly dovetailed into the "common sense" geocentric arguments. In addition to a variety of arguments based on the dynamic behaviour of projectiles and falling bodies, however, Riccioli discussed a potentially *anti*-Copernican consequence of post-telescopic discovery. Many post-1609 astronomers had noticed that instead of the stars being *points* of light, the early telescopes often showed them as tiny yet distinct *discs*, and various astronomers had tried to measure their exact sizes.

One of the main arguments advanced by the early Copernicans for why no six-monthly stellar parallax could be detected from a moving earth was that the stars were so remote in space that no graduated measuring instrument could detect an angle so small. If, however, the stars were large enough to display telescopic discs, yet were too remote to have a discernible parallax, then geometrical calculation suggested that they must be unimaginably large. This would make the sun look like a drop in the cosmic ocean, with each star actually bigger than the then reckoned size of the entire universe. An absurd conclusion.

Of course, what no optician at that time understood was the way in which point sources of light are not only refracted but also *diffracted*, or scattered, to form false discs: a phenomenon explained 200 years later by Sir George Biddell Airy in England. The nineteen-year-old English astronomer Jeremiah Horrocks had established the spurious nature of these star "discs" in 1637, although his discovery was not published until nearly forty years later. We shall meet Horrocks again in Chapter 21.

In 1651, and for some time afterwards, the arguments for a fixed earth in a "Tychonic" universe still won on points of observed fact. We cannot blame men like Clavius, Scheiner, Riccioli, and many other honest astronomers for being led by the then best available evidence.

In addition to defending geocentricism, *Almagestum Novum*, in Book 4, contained one of the early pioneering studies of moon mapping. We will return to Father Riccioli, Father Francesco Maria Grimaldi, and other Catholic and Protestant founders of lunar cartography and topography in Chapter 22.

RENÉ DESCARTES AND HIS DISCIPLES: COPERNICANS BY IMPLICATION

Much scholarly ink has been spilt in an attempt to pin down René Descartes's exact religious beliefs. He has been called a deist and a freethinker – he was certainly the latter, in the very noblest sense – and lived for many years in Calvinist Holland. Never did this Jesuit-educated north French gentleman philosopher cease to describe himself, and behave, as a Roman Catholic; and when he died rather suddenly in Stockholm in 1650, he was engaged in giving philosophy lessons to the young Queen Christina of Sweden. She would abdicate her legally Lutheran throne in 1654, and soon afterwards convert to Roman Catholicism. As her personal tutor, Descartes may have been the only Roman Catholic with whom the queen had had sustained intellectual contact.

Descartes was not an astronomer, but the system of physics and natural philosophy which he began to build in the 1620s was quintessentially Copernican and heliocentric, and would come to have an incalculable impact upon pre-Newtonian physical thinking. It was also fundamentally materialist, seeing matter in motion as forming the foundation of the universe. Like so many post-Tychonian thinkers, Descartes wrestled with how the planets might move if there were no crystalline spheres. "Cartesian physics", as it came to be called, adopted the premise that mechanical action – things pushing things *ad infinitum* – lay at the root of physics. This was the "mechanical philosophy" of Descartes, and people sometimes saw it as analogous to clockwork.

Though rejecting Gassendi's system of atoms, and controverting with him about them, Descartes nonetheless filled the whole of creation with *corpuscles*, or units of super-fine matter, that swirled in streams of *vortices*, or what one might envisage as whirlpools within whirlpools of corpuscles, each pushing the other, in the same way as gear-wheel teeth or a row of railway waggons push each other to transmit motion. This was happening throughout the whole length and breadth of the cosmos.

Mechanical rotation was implicit within the system: from the field of a magnet, to blood moving around a living body (Descartes was an early convert to William Harvey's blood circulation theory), to the planets rotating around the sun, and the sun rotating on its axis. Of course, God was the supreme cosmic engineer and Prime Mover, and in some respects Descartes drew upon medieval imagery of God the Clockmaker, setting the whole engine of creation running.

Of course, Descartes's system was not without profound theological implications, for if God's cosmos was a perfect, well-oiled machine, how could he intervene within it, such as to answer prayers? Surely, were not the complex mechanical vortices which caused the storm that blew the ship inexorably towards the rocks, or the organ failure that slid a sick child towards death, integral parts of the greater mechanical whole? How, then, could God intervene to save lives when people prayed to him? Was not the Creator locked for ever out of his creation due to its sheer mechanical perfection? Questions such as these prompted accusations that Descartes was a deist, whose God might be the supreme Creator, but who was now afar off, either uncaring or impotent. Descartes and his disciples wrestled mightily with the logic of this argument. Yet Descartes had a clear conception of the immortal soul and *mind* as well as of the machine, though it was largely his disciples who took up the explanatory torch following their 54-year-old master's sudden death in 1650: men such as the Dutchman Arnold Geulincx, who suggested a "two clocks" analogy.

Imagine two clocks designed to keep perfect time. When the fingers of one clock point to 12, its synchronized companion strikes its bell twelve times. Could a mechanical innocent be blamed for thinking that the fingers of one clock mysteriously cause the other to ring twelve? So, could not an all-knowing, omnipresent God have built a universe with all manner of preordained fail-safes? Could a sudden life-saving calm or healing action that followed the stricken mariners' or distressed parents' prayers really have been due to God's creative foresight, so that when the prayers were uttered, the long-foreseen, planned, and synchronized new mechanical actions simply clicked in? These questions of free will, determinism, prayer, and providence are still very much with us today, although it was Descartes's mechanical cosmology which first gave them urgency and an attempt at coherent expression.

By 1665 the debate in cosmology was not so much about Copernicanism as about Cartesian *mechanism*. Descartes's system, like Aristotle's, was capable of providing a universal explanatory rationale, from the acceleration of falling bodies to the motion of comets and the transmission of starlight – to say nothing of its impact upon biological and physiological thinking, morality, and ethics. Implicit in Descartes's system was the premise that the earth rotated around the sun as part of the planet-carrying vortex swirl. By logical extension, could not similar planetary vortices be moving around the stars, which, by 1650, were generally coming to be seen as very distant sun-like bodies?

In 1686, the young Jesuit-educated French scholar and astronomer Bernard le Bovier de Fontenelle published his *Entretiens sur la pluralité des mondes* ("Conversations on the Plurality of Worlds"), which popularized both the Copernican and Cartesian systems in France and beyond. Within an easy conversational setting, a charming philosopher explains the wonders of the new cosmos to a young marquise. Its principal plate has become an astronomical classic, for there they sit, in the grounds of her beautiful chateau: he periwigged, and she elegantly decorous, with a crucifix conspicuously displayed above her low-cut bosom. Above them is a glorious depiction of the new universe: a fiery sun, with the six known planets rotating around it. Jupiter is a sphere with four satellites, and Saturn not only displays his rings, discovered by Huygens and Cassini, but also his five recently discovered satellites.

Fontenelle pays no lip service whatsoever to the Catholic Church's condemnation of Copernican heliocentricism half a century before, and even explores the already often-discussed idea of life on other worlds – hence the *plurality*, or presumed abundance, of new worlds scattered throughout telescopic space implicit in the title. Of course, as Fontenelle made clear, these planetary beings were not *humans,* not being descended from Adam, but were separate divine creations specific to their worlds.

Fontenelle's book was translated into English in 1687 and again in 1691, plus other European languages, and became a best-seller. It was charming, erudite, and bang up to date, and not only discussed the very latest cutting-edge ideas in astronomy in a way that a non-scientist could understand, but was not polemical, offensive, or gauntlet-throwing. Quite simply, it was intended to be read and enjoyed by Catholics and Protestants alike. And what did the French and Italian ecclesiastical authorities do to suppress Fontenelle's book? Nothing whatsoever.

FROM ASTRONOMY TO MEDICINE TO FOSSIL GEOLOGY: SO EXACTLY *HOW* WAS CATHOLIC SCIENCE SUPPRESSED?

These last two chapters claim no more than to scratch the surface of front-rank, cutting-edge scientific research conducted by Roman Catholics in the age of Galileo and the decades thereafter. Let us now make a rapid survey of some other ordained and lay Catholic scientists of the late seventeenth century.

In addition to Pierre Gassendi, France had other ordained scientists such as Friar Marin Mersenne, not to mention a veritable galaxy of Catholic lay scientists. There was the Italian-born Giovanni Domenico Cassini, who, migrating from a chair at Bologna, became effective Director of King Louis XIV's Paris Observatory and a leading member of the Parisian Académie. Cassini was the "big telescope" astronomer who, in 1675, discovered the division in Saturn's "ring" which still bears his name. He then went on both to undertake and to direct fundamental research in telescopic astronomy, geodesy, geophysics, and global cartography, and found the French-naturalized Cassini dynasty which directed the King's Observatory and much French physics down to the Revolution in 1789.

Following upon the 1644 air weight and pressure discoveries of the Galileo-admiring Italian physicist and engineer Evangelista Torricelli, the Frenchman Gilles Personne de Roberval would pioneer work on the properties of the "Torricellian vacuum", an early barometer, in 1647 – research which would be taken much further by the devout Protestant Honourable Robert Boyle in Oxford after 1658.

Within the very heart of the Catholic academic establishment at the University of Bologna, the Jesuit-educated layman doctor Marcello Malpighi would make some ground-breaking discoveries in physiology. A pioneer in the use of the newly invented microscope – the "telescope of the realm of the minute" – Malpighi made major discoveries in the microscopic structures of embryos, the structure and chemical pigmentation of the skin, the cardiovascular capillaries, and the relation between the blood, air, and tissue in lungs. These experiments were conducted upon frogs and other animals, yet from them Malpighi drew clear parallels to the structures of humans, to finally demonstrate the blood "circulation" route as originally proposed by William Harvey in 1628. Far from his bold curiosity about the mysterious insides of God's living creatures getting him condemned, Pope Innocent XII in 1691 invited Professor Malpighi to come and reside in Rome, as papal physician.

Niels Stensen, or, in its Latinized form, Nicholas Steno, was a Danish Lutheran who, at the age of twenty-nine, in 1667, converted to Roman Catholicism. Living in both Protestant and Catholic countries, he was especially significant as a pioneer of fossil geology, arguing on anatomical grounds that fossils were the remains of long-dead animals and were *not* merely twists in the rock. It is true that his main scientific work was performed before he became a priest in 1675, but his vocation in no way invalidated his earlier work in crystallography, geology, and comparative anatomy: a thing made clear when he was made an auxiliary bishop in 1680. Devoting himself largely to theology after his ordination, Steno lived a life of ascetic poverty, ministering to the poor, later coming to be venerated as a saint, and being beatified by Pope Paul II in 1988. It is interesting to think that in a few years' time this far-seeing geologist and scientist is likely to become *Saint* Nicholas Steno.

Nor should one forget the above-mentioned Athanasius Kircher SJ, who across his seventy-eight years made major contributions to astronomy, optics, magnetism, and microscopy – and even invented the magic lantern, which is the ancestor of the slide projector.

One could go on and on, even before 1700. After 1700, one encounters globe-trotting astronomers such as the eighteenth-century Father Maximillian Hell, Father Stephen Perry (who died of dysentery returning from an astronomical expedition in 1889, after insisting that he be permitted to take the Eucharist to sick prisoners on Devil's Island), and Angelo Secchi, founder of spectroscopic star classification between 1863 and 1868: all Jesuits. The discoverer of the experimental and mathematical basis of inheritance, which laid the foundations for modern genetics, was a scientifically trained Silesian Augustinian friar and later abbot, Gregor Mendel, who continued a rich tradition of monastic science going back to the Middle Ages.

When one gets into the twentieth century, one finds the flow of Catholic scientists, lay and ordained, continuing apace, especially in astronomy and physics. Continuing from the nineteenth century, for example, was the internationally renowned Jesuit solar and astrophysical observatory at Stonyhurst College, Lancashire; while the old Vatican Observatory, in its attempt to escape the increasingly polluted skies of central Italy, largely relocated to Tucson in the 1980s, beneath the pristine skies of the Arizona desert. (I have had the honour to talk to – and even broadcast with – the former Vatican Observatory Director Father George Coyne SJ, not to mention holding discussions and sharing lecture platforms with other present-day priest-scientists.) Father Sabino Maffeo SJ, in *In the Service of Nine Popes: 100 Years of the Vatican Observatory* (1991), gives an excellent history of the Observatory's work over the centuries, but especially in the century following 1880.

Expanding-universe cosmology began with the calculations of Father Georges Lamaître at the Roman Catholic University of

Louvain, Belgium, between 1927 and 1930. Lamaître, who was wrestling with the complex mathematical implications of Einstein's "curved" space-time relativistic universe, came to conclude that everything in the universe as we know it probably started from an exploding "primal atom". When he communicated his work to the Cambridge Quaker astronomer Sir Arthur Eddington, early in 1930, Eddington immediately recognized its importance, and published Lamaître's work through the Royal Astronomical Society. Some atheist cosmologists resented the unintended possibility of a "creation" that one might choose to read into the physics – especially as it was the work of a Roman Catholic priest – and Sir Fred Hoyle would come to dismiss it as no more than a "Big Bang".

Over the last two chapters it has not been my intention to specially plead for the Catholic Church, and as an Anglican myself, I have no especial pro-Roman axe to grind. But historical fact is historical fact, and to understand Copernicus, Galileo, the telescope, and the impact of the "new astronomy", one must try to do so within the wider context of science within the Catholic world. Here, instead of a cessation, we see a continuous stream of scientific activity extending from medieval Europe down to present-day Tucson, Arizona. This might help to put the 1633 trial of Galileo into perspective, irrespective of what our personal religious beliefs, if any, might be.

CHAPTER 17

Copernicus, Galileo, and the Protestants of the "Northern Renaissance"

*I*t is generally believed that the opposition to Copernicus, heliocentricism, and Galileo came overwhelmingly from within the Roman Catholic Church, and that the Protestants were open-minded, and welcoming, to the new ideas. This way of thinking has a tangential relation to the "Protestant thesis" of scientific development, which saw scientific progress as a product of the so-called "Protestant work ethic", along with modern banking, big business, individualism, and the ability of the underdog to get on in life without being somehow held back by the perceived malign and intellectually regressive influence of Catholic theology.

GLOBAL TRADE AND ASTRONOMY

The biggest caveat about the Protestant thesis comes from the plain, unvarnished historical record. Not only did merchant and credit banking, international corporate business, complex wind- and water-powered industrial machines, printing, and the universities of Europe all come into being during the pre-Reformation Middle Ages, but, as we have seen, so did the Astronomical Renaissance. If one is looking for the causes of the gradual economic decline of Italy and Europe's Mediterranean world after *c.* 1660, one should remember the global commercial shift in spices and luxury goods that began to move cutting-edge business initiative to Holland and

England in the wake of the opening up of the Atlantic and Far Eastern sea trades after 1600. This, combined with the decline of Spain's initial dominance of the Americas, played a far bigger part in the cultural rise of Protestant northern Europe than did the absence of any ecclesiastical censorship.

How did the Protestant lands of the north respond to heliocentricism, Galileo's discoveries, and the new astronomical, physical, and conceptual technologies? Let us begin by remembering that both Copernicus and Tycho Brahe, not to mention other astronomers whom we will discuss shortly, were part of what might be seen as a "northern" Renaissance, which came a few decades after, and complemented, its more famous Italian cultural forebear. What were the particular achievements of this northern Renaissance? It was just as brilliant as that of the south, though sometimes taking different emphases. Take the Protestant Reformation itself as an example, with its stress on getting back to the earliest biblical sources: with printed vernacular translations of Scripture, and its new theological ideas. Or consider the growth of secular printed vernacular literature, spanning a range of styles from cheap joke books to Shakespeare's plays; or Dutch painting's domestic and urban scenes, "Delft Ware" fine pottery, or major innovations in ocean-going ship-building.

Such innovations were driven by a market economy of burghers, citizens, and even prosperous artisans. Of course, all these factors had operated in Italy too, though the Mediterranean economy began to feel the pinch as the long-haul ocean voyage oriented north and generated an unprecedented boom economy. One could say that by 1620 Holland had become the world's first "tiger economy". Coming to terms with Copernicus (himself a Baltic northerner), heliocentricism, Galileo, and the "Dutch spyglass" or telescope was no more than an integral part of it all.

Biblical interpretation was also an integral part of the bigger northern Renaissance picture, for whether you were a Roman cardinal reading your Bible in the Vulgate Latin or a Hamburg burgher with Luther's German translation, the biblical message remained exactly the same. The problems of interpretation remained as well, for the Genesis creation narrative, the Psalms with their "fixed and 'stablished" earth, and God's holding back the sun for Joshua were the same for Catholic and Protestant alike.

In many ways, the new astronomy contained more potential hazards for the Protestants than it did for the Catholics. In their dismissal of church tradition and certain aspects of philosophical theology, along with their stress upon the primacy of the plain meaning of Scripture, the Protestants had less room for manoeuvre than did the Catholics. This became even more problematic if one subscribed to a tradition of biblical understanding that placed all parts of Scripture on an equal, plain-meaning footing, in which Christ's teachings of love, grace, and compassion must be understood as evidentially equal to God's creation of a rock-solid earth.

This was most likely one of the reasons why Andreas Osiander, in his unauthorized "foreword" to Copernicus's *De Revolutionibus*, stated that the book should not be read as an actual description of the universe, so much as a "hypothesis". Osiander was an early follower of Martin Luther in Wittenberg, and would have been all too aware of the biblical interpretative problems involved, not to mention the heliocentric theory's difficulties on a common-sense level.

HUMANISM AND THE HERMITIC PHILOSOPHY

In addition to the new Protestant theology, two other powerful intellectual currents influenced Protestant thinking, no less than Catholic. One of these was the "humanism" of the Renaissance, while the other was hermeticism. Both drew heavily upon classical pagan thinking, yet also needed to be understood within a Christian context, be that the context of Counter-Reformation Rome, Geneva, Wittenberg, or even Oxford.

Renaissance humanism – *not* to be confused with the anti-religious sense in which the term is used today – was rooted in the rediscovery of the original Latin and Greek languages and authors, a fascination with the sensuous in art, and a belief that one could access the wisdom of Plato or Cicero by rediscovering their ancient tongues, and penetrating beyond the "bad" or "dog" Latin of the medieval centuries to the "fountainhead" of European high civilization. This pagan learning was to be understood in tandem with Christianity, with "Christianizing" of the wisest of the ancients, to produce some odd-looking combinations: with Apollo, the Muses, and Zeus somehow co-existing, at least metaphorically, with Moses, the Gospel writers, and St Paul. These are odd combinations to us, but not necessarily to the classically and Christianity-steeped minds of 400 years ago.

Hermeticism is much less familiar to modern readers, largely because, unlike Michelangelo's paintings or Shakespeare's Roman plays, it is now effectively extinct, and appears irrational and incomprehensible. Hermeticism was about the interconnected, vital, hidden, and "occult" forces that were believed to bind all things together: the forces which made fire melt iron, caused the tides, made people happy or sad, made the lodestone point north, and turned the heavenly spheres around the earth. How could one thing send an invisible force to produce a response in a distant thing, such as the passage of a ray of starlight, or how did one of Cupid's mysterious darts make William fall in love with Jane? Nowadays, we explain most of these phenomena through mathematically and experimentally based "modern science", but things were different in 1600. The great prophets of the "occult philosophy", or of "natural magic", were sixteenth-century scholars like Henry Cornelius Agrippa, Paracelsus, Marsilio Ficino, and Queen Elizabeth I's friend and adviser Dr John Dee. Hermeticism came from the legendary mythic Graeco-Egyptian-Jewish past: from Apollo and "Hermes the Thrice-Great Magician", and from the deep secrets which the Egyptians had allegedly imparted to the children of Israel when in bondage in that land, secrets passed on through concealed traditions, secret texts, the mysteries of the Jewish Cabbala, and the Brotherhood of the "Rosy-Cross", or Rosicrucians.

Humanism, magical hermeticism, and Copernican heliocentrism melded into each other to constitute an aspect of the broader "world views" of the age. Copernicanism sometimes had an appeal to men with a hermetic cast of mind, and perhaps the most notorious of these was Giordano Bruno, who was drawn to the idea of a Pythagorean "central fire" (the sun), around which all things moved, along with number magic, secret mathematical truths accessible only to the cognoscenti, and an infinity of worlds. Oxford University's Dr Robert Fludd shared some of these ideas, seeing the human mind as connected to a "world soul" that ascended through a series of divine mathematical harmonies to suffuse the cosmos. Yet Fludd, who died in 1637, soundly rejected the Copernican theory on philosophical grounds, and was attacked by Johannes Kepler in *Harmonices Mundi*.

Kepler, as we saw in Chapters 7–8, was a Copernican, Protestant mystic who, in his *Mysterium Cosmographicum* and *Harmonices Mundi*, had returned to the ancient Greek and medieval concept of the Music of the Spheres. This mysterious occult harmonious voice of the divinely mathematical cosmos formed a central tenet of hermetic thinking, and its adherents were not infrequently drawn to Copernicanism.

Another component of this way of thinking further melded into the "new astronomy": its concern with newly revealed long-concealed truths, puzzles resolved, and intellectual and spiritual "keys" found that would unlock the deep secrets of God. The Latin word for key, *clavis*, often appears in the literature generated by this style of thinking, along with the discussion of ancient prophecies about to be fulfilled, scales falling from eyes of the wise, and images of men carrying lanterns, discovering profound secrets in dark places. It was a tradition that often saw the Jews as entrusted with God's deepest secrets, which helps to explain why Old and New Testament prophecies, numerological permutations implicit within the biblical books of Isaiah, Ezekiel, Daniel, and Revelation, and Jewish Cabbala held such a fascination for hermetically inclined mathematical philosophers.

Of course, not all the men of the "new science" were attracted to this way of thinking. There is no evidence that it ever interested Galileo, though Kepler was firmly hooked. The very Protestant English Copernicans Jeremiah Horrocks and William Crabtree, whom we will look at in Chapter 21, seemed, if anything, to display contempt for, rather than an interest in, the occult, as did the Huygens brothers in Holland. Yet the stridently anti-Catholic Sir Isaac Newton, between the 1670s and 1710s, devoted more energy to "unlocking" the deep secrets of the occult than ever he spent on the laws of gravity: that is, if his surviving manuscripts are anything to go by.

What is crucial to bear in mind is that the men of the Astronomical Renaissance were deeply concerned with religious and spiritual issues, knew their Bibles intimately, and believed not only that they were living in an age of amazing discoveries, but that these discoveries, far from being chance affairs, were part and parcel of a providence which God in his wisdom was now revealing to mankind. Of all the biblical prophecies signifying the impending end of time, perhaps none was more apposite than Daniel 12:4: "Many shall run to and fro, and knowledge shall be increased." Were not men now running all across the planet, and was not new knowledge growing faster than at any previous time in history?

PHILIPPE VAN LANSBERGE AND VERNACULAR DUTCH COPERNICANISM

A good many of the intellectual currents discussed above can be found in Lansberge. Though spending much of his adult life at Goez in Holland, he was born in Ghent, Belgium, in 1561, being Galileo's senior by three years. A deeply committed Christian and a Calvinist minister, Lansberge nonetheless had also come to be fascinated by Neo-Platonist humanism, alchemy, and other strands of hermetic thinking, all of which he came to associate with Copernicanism. Leiden, with its world-famous university and medical school, at which Lansberge had both studied and taught, was a lively centre of activity not only in all the sciences, but also in theology, Neo-Platonic humanism, and hermetic philosophy. There was also active discussion about the heliocentric theory.

There were those who were willing to use Copernicus's scheme as a mathematical computing device, yet rejected it as a real description of the universe, whereas others were willing to consider it as a physical reality. Nicolaus Mulerius and Willem Blaeu argued that a moving earth was at odds with both the physical (as experienced by humans) and moral arrangement of the universe: at odds not just on scriptural grounds, but because it seemed an affront to the divine order. Willem Blaeu, the famous Amsterdam-based cartographer and cosmographer, had, as a young man, spent time working with Tycho himself at the "Castle of the Heavens". These men of the northern Renaissance were no less given to discussions of a moving earth and of humanist and occult philosophies than were the scholars of Padua or Bologna.

Yet one thing was coming into increasingly sharp focus by the early seventeenth century: the amazing power of mathematics to describe, predict, and verify natural forces, and Galileo was by no means fighting a lone battle in this respect. There were, in addition to Italians, Dutchmen, Belgians, Germans, and Englishmen – Jesuits, Dominicans, and various types of Protestants – all actively involved in this area by the early seventeenth century. For as Lansberge would reiterate in his *Cyclometria Nova* ("New Measurements of the Planetary Cycles"), 1616, in a modified phrase from the Platonists, "God always cyclometrizes", or geometrizes.

Amongst all the debates within the Protestant Low Countries about the moving earth, Lansberge had been a cautious convert to heliocentricism. An earlier declared supporter had been the Flemish mathematician and engineer Simon Stevin, yet as Herwart von Hohenburg had supposedly told Kepler in 1598, Lansberge was working on a cosmological system in which the earth had a daily rotation, but not an annual solar one.[1] By 1616, however, Lansberge had been won over to Copernicanism, as he made evident in his Latin *Cyclometria*, which he would make accessible to vernacular Dutch readers in his *Bedenkingen*, or "Considerations on the Daily and Annual Rotation of the Earth", in 1629.

Not only had much careful thought and calculation lain at the heart of his "conversion", but so had his theology, along with his Neo-Platonist numerology and hermeticism. It was at this juncture that astronomy and Renaissance hermetic *alchemy* fused together. At the heart of alchemical theory was the belief that the cosmos was vital and alive with divine forces; it was through this innate vitality that the hermeticists explained chemical and biological change, astrological influence, and the engendering of all life from "seeds". Axiomatic to this way of thinking was the sheer vital power of the earth as a planet. How could the living, vibrant, life-bearing earth be *stationary*, for the defining characteristic of life was *movement*?

This may seem a strange argument in favour of Copernicanism to us today, but as we have noted time and again over the previous pages, one cannot see the scientists of four centuries ago as "just like us" but wearing period costume.

In his grand project for the "reformation of astronomy" (in the tracks of Luther and Calvin, who had set out to "reform religion") the Copernican convert Lansberge became mystified as to how his "master", Tycho Brahe, had rejected Copernicanism as a physical reality. Surely Tycho was not only a great astronomer, but also a deeply learned alchemist and hermetic philosopher – as his extensive laboratories at Uraniborg, depicted as a backdrop to his *Mechanica* (1598), make explicit. How could Tycho, the "Reformer" of astronomy and accomplished alchemist, have failed to realize that the vital earth *must* be both rotating around the sun and spinning on its axis?

Both the Copernican astronomy and alchemy of Lansberge are presented as profoundly Christian: as part of the new revelation, in fact. In his vernacular *Bedenkingen* he develops an interesting *spiritual* cosmology based upon hierarchies of three – the number of the Holy Trinity. The tripartite division of the cosmos had a pagan ancestry extending back to Aristotle's *De Caelo* of *c.* 350 BC, but especially influential was the threefold division of the heavens as mentioned by St Paul in his second letter to the Corinthians (12:2) of *c.* AD 50.

Here, St Paul speaks of a man, perhaps in a vision, being borne up to the "third heaven", where deep secrets were imparted to him. This celestial arrangement was generally interpreted within an essentially Aristotelian and wider classical scheme in which the first heaven was the earth and air; the second was planetary space; and the third, the "Empyrean" heaven of God, beyond the sphere of the fixed stars, contained the "habitacle of the Elect".

Philippe Lansberge reinterpreted this scheme along Copernican lines, in which the first heaven was the solar system, extending from a central sun to Saturn. The second heaven now became the sphere of the fixed stars; while the third remained God's Empyrean, beyond the stars. Within the Christianized Neo-Platonic and hermetic scheme, the Trinity could be equated to the sun (Father), Moon (Son), and Air (Holy Ghost). It is fascinating to see how many seemingly diverse "schemes" melded together in this way of thinking: classical, pagan, Jewish, occult, numerological, mathematical, and all beneath what was seen as the sanctifying umbrella of the Christian revelation.

Though coming to admire Copernicus, Lansberge always appeared to entertain a caution about the astro-philosophical writings of his fellow Protestant mystic Johannes Kepler. In particular, he could not accept Kepler's elliptical orbits. Most likely, this rejection came from Lansberge's philosophical loyalty to circularity and uniform velocity as the only possible motions for objects in the first heaven of planetary space. While this may have been well and good for a philosophical scheme, it became a major shortcoming in his *magnum opus*, the *Tabulae Motuum Celestium Perpetuae* ("Perpetual Tables for the Motions of the Heavens") of 1632.

These otherwise excellent tables, drawing heavily on the observations of Tycho Brahe (and probably his own), were fundamentally flawed by his failure to employ ellipses as part of the mathematical machinery for calculating Copernican planetary positions. This failure would earn Lansberge severe condemnation from the young English astronomer Jeremiah Horrocks when he was trying to calculate the orbital elements for a possible transit of Venus across the disc of the sun in November 1639, as we shall see in Chapter 21. Horrocks, in the written account of his observations of the Venus transit – which actually took place on 24 November – further attacks Lansberge's disciple Martinus Hortensius, primarily on the grounds of not recognizing the importance of elliptical orbits in planetary table computation.

On the other hand, that Hortensius comes across as a deliberately controversial and even pugnacious figure is only to put it mildly. His intention was to promote Lansberge, who had died in 1632, as *the* true reformer of astronomy, and he is clearly gunning for all rival claimants – whether dead or alive. The Danish astronomer Peder Bartholin Kierul, for example, leapt to the defence of his fellow countryman when Hortensius not only criticized Tycho Brahe's geo-heliocentric system, but even began to pick at his formidable legacy as an observational astronomer. While Hortensius had been active as an observational astronomer since he was twenty, in 1625 it was frankly risible to assert that Lansberge had been in any way a rival to Tycho as an *observer* – especially as Lansberge had lacked Tycho's superbly accurate instruments.

Kepler is also attacked by Hortensius – as was pretty well everyone whom he perceived as a rival to Lansberge's status as astronomy's reformer. Had not Lansberge laid the new astronomy on two pillars: establishing the motion of the earth, and measuring the true sizes of the planetary spheres? Lansberge had done neither – nor in his lifetime did he appear to have made such a claim – as Jeremiah Horrocks was all too aware by 1640, when he laid into Lansberge, Hortensius, Johannes Longomontanus, and a figure we will meet very soon, the Frenchman Ismaël Bullialdus in his *Venus in Sole Visa* (posthumously published, 1662), which described the 1639 Venus transit. What Lansberge himself would have made of Hortensius's claims made posthumously on his behalf is a moot point.

What strikes one immediately in all of this discussion is the regular use of the word "reformed ", for these Dutch, Flemish, and Danish Calvinists and Lutherans were not committed followers of the "reformed" Christianity for nothing. "Reformation" was to be something of a *leitmotif* for the men of the northern Renaissance, for their concept of necessary change, regeneration, and new growth spread out from their vernacular Bibles to connect with their ideas on politics, commerce, language, global exploration – and astronomy. It was an idea intimately linked to *wisdom* as revealed in the Old and New Testaments and the Apocrypha: the way towards the "pearl beyond price", for which a knowing man would sell all he had. Just as Solomon's wisdom had hewn out her seven pillars in Proverbs 9:1, so the "reformed" astronomy must do likewise, for Hortensius tells us that Lansberge had grounded his new astronomy upon *two* wise pillars.

CHRISTOPHORUS WITTICHUS: COPERNICUS AND THE BIBLE IN PROTESTANT HOLLAND

One Dutch Calvinist minister and academic theologian who defended not only Copernicus but also the materialist philosophy was Christophorus Wittichus of Duisburg University in the 1650s. What is striking when looking at Wittichus's arguments about understanding the Bible and science is their close similarity to arguments advanced by Galileo in his *Letter to the Grand Duchess* (1615), his Roman Catholic clergy friends, and even to Cardinal Boronius's argument that the function of Scripture was to teach us how to go to heaven, rather than teach us how the heavens go.

This Dutch Reformed theologian effectively says that we cannot read our Bibles as a textbook of physics and astronomy, for that was not God's intention. Only reason and the disciplined use of the intelligence which God gave us can be used as a guide in natural philosophy or physics. Consequently, texts which contradict natural knowledge, such as the sun standing still in Joshua 10:12, must be reinterpreted spiritually or metaphorically, for while Jehovah is a God of power and miracles, he is not a God of un-reason. Wittichus even suggests that some of the attacks on the new science of Copernicus and Galileo might well be the work of the devil himself, trying to lead us astray – a fascinating interpretation of the place of good and evil in the scientific realm, indeed.

ISMAËL BOULLIAU: CALVINIST TURNED CATHOLIC COPERNICAN

Ismaël Boulliau, or Bullialdus as he Latinized his name, was born in Loudon, western France, in 1605, into a family of French Calvinists. His father Ismaël was a successful lawyer and an amateur astronomer, which no doubt helped to stimulate his eldest son's astronomical interests, although we have no indication as to what Ismaël senior thought about Copernicus.

At the age of twenty-one, young Ismaël converted to Roman Catholicism, following it up some years later by getting ordained as a priest. Spending much of his working life as a scholar-librarian at the Royal Library in Paris, he made no bones about being an admirer of Copernicus, Kepler, and Galileo, and, along with his fellow priest-astronomer Pierre Gassendi, he openly supported Galileo and his ideas. Boulliau's first astronomical publication, *Philolaus* (1639), took its name from the ancient Greek disciple of Pythagoras, Philolaus of Tarentum, who had speculated about the earth not being at the centre of all things in the universe. In 1645, he published his most influential work, *Astronomia Philolaïca*, which elaborated on the *Philolaus* idea of a de-centralized earth.

At a time when a number of European astronomers admired Kepler, yet still felt uneasy about the reality of elliptical orbits and variable speeds for planets – for such a notion still ran contrary to 2,000 years of classical astronomical wisdom – Boulliau expressed his approval. Yet, while he was willing to accept such orbits and planetary motions, he was cautious about accepting Kepler's physics, or *source* of planetary motion. In particular, Boulliau was sceptical about the nature of the planet-moving force emitted by the sun which lay at the heart of Kepler's scheme of celestial mechanics. Kepler saw this force as behaving rather similarly to light, which radiated from a source, and dimmed in an inverse square relationship to the distance travelled. Surely, Boulliau argued, if such a planet-moving force radiated in straight lines from the sun, then it too, like light, must observe an inverse square law, and weaken the further it travelled into space?

It was not for nothing, therefore, that Sir Isaac Newton acknowledged Boulliau's realization in his *Principia Mathematica* (1687). Yet instead of pursuing this mathematical point about radiating forces, and pre-empting a concept of gravitational force forty years before Newton, Boulliau completely dismissed the whole idea of the sun emitting a planet-moving force. Instead, he argued, the sun and planets rotated under forces innate in themselves, not because an external agent impelled them.

Boulliau's planetary theory brings home to us, in so many ways, the sheer multi-layered and cross-current-strewn nature of the Astronomical Renaissance. Far from its being a direct progression "onwards and upwards" from ignorance to truth, as some writers imply, one finds what from our standpoint might appear a mass of contradictory ideas existing side by side in the same mind. One finds men who could defend a de-centralized earth moving in an elliptical orbit around the sun, along with a concept of the reality of mathematical and physical truth, yet who could still see "innate" forces at work in nature; from why fire was hot, to how the planets moved.

Far from these new astronomical and wider scientific discoveries destabilizing their religious faith, they added a new dimension of spiritual understanding which complemented their physical understanding. Were not these new discoveries – covering as they did a spectrum of achievements in astronomy, anatomy, geography, physics, optics, chemistry and applied technology – divine *revelations* no less momentous than those revealed in Scripture?

In many ways Boulliau epitomizes the sheer intellectual richness of that age, being a Calvinist who became a Catholic yet continued to admire the great Protestant thinkers of the age as well his fellow Catholics thinkers, lay and priested. His friendships included the Catholics Gassendi, Mersenne, Galileo, and Blaise Pascal, and Protestants such as Christiaan Huygens, to say nothing of his obvious respect for the deceased Kepler.

His declared Copernicanism and Keplerianism notwithstanding, it is interesting to note that Father Boulliau was never punished by his own adopted Roman Catholic Church, in spite of the fact that his pro-moving-earth *Philolaus* was published a mere five years after Galileo's condemnation, and his clearly Kepler-sympathizing *Astronomia Philolaïca* only twelve years after.

It also says something for the international openness of science in that age, and for the warm regard that Catholics and Protestants could have for one another – even when ordained priests and ministers – that in 1667, the newly established Royal Society, in very Protestant London, elected Father Ismaël Boulliau to join its Fellowship as an eminent and internationally renowned French man of science. And he would be followed by others.

CHAPTER 18

Copernicus Comes to England

*A*s an island, England, Wales and Scotland had remained mercifully untouched by the religious wars and invading armies on the Continent, which had played their part in forming Flemish, Dutch, German, and Scandinavian identities. For the Protestants of those countries, the success of the "reformed" Christianity of Luther and Calvin was seen as a providential sign. Had they not withstood the mighty armies of Spain in the sixteenth century, determined as those armies had been to bring the troublesome Protestants of the "Spanish Netherlands" back under Roman spiritual and Spanish political control? And had not God's own soldier, King Gustavus Adolphus of Sweden, scattered the armies of Antichrist – at least, until Gustavus's martyr's death in battle in 1636?

While post-Reformation England was a tough, hard-fighting rival of the Dutch in the northern Renaissance's commercial "war" to dominate the Far Eastern spice trade, the English, nonetheless, saw themselves as the political and spiritual allies of the Protestant Dutch. Whether you were a Calvinist burgher of Amsterdam or an Anglican director of London's newly royal-chartered East India Company, you shared an enemy in the Pope.

On the other hand, not all the peoples of the north were Protestant. Holland, Flanders, Germany, Poland and the Baltic states and "Great Britain", as it was styling itself after the unification of the English and Scottish crowns in 1603, still had lots of Catholics living in their midst; people, generally speaking, who had for conscience' and culture's sake simply refused to convert to the new "reformed" creed, but were increasingly seen as potential traitors waiting to strike. The vast majority of these "papists" were traditional, peaceable, and law-abiding folk: they were a plentiful minority in parts of Holland, modern Belgium, Germany, and England, while in Ireland they remained the majority. The assassination of the Protestant Dutch Prince William the Silent in 1584 and the mercifully foiled Guy Fawkes plot of 1605 only served to feed the anti-Catholic hysteria. A defining moment in English cultural identity came about in 1588 when a clearly pro-Protestant deity repeated the Exodus 15:10 deliverance by destroying the Pope's and the King of Spain's Armada: "Thou didst blow with Thy wind, the sea covered them: they sank as lead in the mighty waters."

All this detail is essential to understanding the wider forces that were driving northern Europe, especially by 1620. These in turn moulded the way these societies responded to Copernican and Galilean ideas, to say nothing of their responses to classical humanism, Neo-Platonism, and hermeticism. So, how did the new astronomical ideas fare in England?

It has sometimes been argued that Copernican and Galilean ideas fared better in England and Holland because these predominantly Protestant countries were somehow more liberal than those "dominated" by Roman Catholicism. As we saw in previous chapters, however, the Catholic Church had no science-related policies whatsoever until the Galileo affair of 1616–33, and after that, I have failed to find any evidence of a single Catholic Copernican going to the stake. I cannot deny that over the relatively absolutist reigns of Henry VIII, Elizabeth I, James I, and Charles I, England sometimes resembled a police state. One might be able to proclaim that the earth revolved around the sun without anyone batting an eyelid: but just try asserting freedom of political or religious conscience – and prepare to say goodbye to your head, as Sir (later Saint) Thomas More discovered to his peril in 1536.

THE FIRST ENGLISH COPERNICANS

Politics apart, what were English and "Great British" reactions to the new astronomy? The first scholar to mention the Copernican theory within the British Isles was a Welshman. Dr Robert Recorde came from Tenby in South Wales, and by 1556 was a graduate of both Oxford and Cambridge universities, a Doctor of Medicine, and an early English-language science author. In that year (only two years before his death), Dr Recorde published his *Castel of Knowledge*, which was intended as an English primer in astronomy and mathematics, written in the style of a master and pupil discussion. While the essentially Ptolemaic *Castel* was in no way a defence of Copernicus, it did contain a passing reference to the heliocentric theory that was not dismissive.

Much more confident and committed was Thomas Digges, less than a couple of decades later. To understand Digges and English (and Welsh) "Elizabethan Copernicanism" in context, it is necessary to say something of the proliferating fascination with what contemporaries styled "the Mathematicks" across the period. English-language books on geometry, surveying, navigation, and gunnery were becoming good business, and one senses that Robert Recorde had been aware of this growing market potential.

One suspects that the booming literacy which came in the wake of William Tyndale's translation of the Bible into English in 1526 and Archbishop Cranmer's *Prayer Book* of 1549 started a trend for self-improvement reading. English-language books on medicine, surveying, book-keeping, and geometry were in big demand, and in 1570 Henry Billingsley translated Euclid's *Elements of Geometry* into English. This epochal translation of the Greek text was accompanied by a carefully argued English "Mathematical Preface" by the leading English mathematical scholar of the day and friend of the queen herself, Dr John Dee.

SURVEYORS, CARTOGRAPHERS, AND INSTRUMENT-MAKERS

Before returning to Dr Dee and his mathematical friends, we must consider an unexpected consequence of the English Reformation after 1533. When King Henry VIII sold off all the monastic lands – about one-third of the best land in England – to help shore up his shaky finances, England experienced a "land grab". As much of the land was being sold off relatively cheaply to realize cash quickly, all who had some pounds to spare were buying their very own bits of England. Tenant farmers were gentrifying their families by purchasing their farms, and even shepherds and small shopkeepers were after a few acres.

As the once monastic estates were being fragmented into numerous smaller holdings, two professions were all set to make a killing. One, of course, was the lawyers; the other, the still emerging profession of the surveyor, land-measurer, and cartographer. Jack the yeoman farmer on his way to becoming Mr John the landed gentleman naturally wanted a proper set of deeds, drawn up by a solicitor, confirming his possession. Next, especially if he were socially ambitious, he wanted a "Trewe Plot or Topographicall Description" (a commonly used sixteenth-century phrase) – an accurate map – of his new acres.

Consequently, surveying flourished, with a growing need for instruction manuals and angle-measuring mathematical instruments by which the apprentice could learn his craft. So rapid was this escalation of increasingly accurate local, and then regional, mapping that by 1577 Christopher Saxton was surveying and publishing detailed maps of the English counties, as were John Norden, John Speed, and others. All of this was driven by commercial market pressure, fuelled by an expanding class of gentry, navigators, merchants, and speculative overseas investors. Maps of the English counties, then of European countries, and world atlases showing the discoveries of Columbus, Magellan, and Sir Francis Drake were becoming major cultural icons. Amsterdam and Antwerp were the acknowledged centres of fine world cartography by 1600, with scholar-craftsmen-businessmen like Gerardus Mercator and the Dutch Blaeu family. Earlier in the sixteenth century, instrument designers and fine craftsmen in brass and silver, such as Nicholas Kratzer in Munich and Thomas Gemini at Flanders, came to settle in England; while a growing body of Englishmen like Richard Chancellor and Humfrey Cole were producing quadrants, astrolabes, and draughtsmen's and navigators' instruments to be sold to paying customers.

It was Leonard Digges, father of the first "declared" English Copernican Thomas Digges, who became a major exponent of practical mathematical teaching from the 1550s. The Digges family were Oxford-educated Kentish gentry who shared a passion for astronomy, "the Mathematicks", and instruments and practical inventions. In 1556 Leonard published his highly influential *Techtonicon* ("Measuring"), which set out to instruct the land surveyor and liberate practical technology "locked up in strange tongues" for English readers.

Especially significant was Leonard Digges's *Pantometria* ("All Measurements"), which lay in manuscript at the time of his death in 1558, and which his son Thomas edited and published in 1571. *Pantometria*'s plain English text, illustrated by detailed woodcut plates, provided a treasure-house of useful mathematical techniques and instruments, perhaps the most significant of which was Leonard's *theodolitus*, or theodolite – a piece of apparatus destined to transform *all* accurate surveying, and become the quintessential surveyor's instrument; an instrument destined to map not only England, but the planet.

The Digges were members of a circle of mathematical and astronomical friends centring upon Dr Dee – who became young Thomas's mentor after his father Leonard died. This circle included, at various times, Henry Billingsley, Richard Hakluyt, Sir Walter Ralegh, the craftsman William Bourne, and the young Thomas Harriot. It was a socially well-connected circle, with friends in the universities, the City of London, and the Royal Court, including Lord Burghley (the queen's leading ministerial adviser), and even Queen Elizabeth herself.

What did the learned Dr Dee himself think of Copernicus? It is impossible to say, and scholars have speculated along a variety of lines. Did Dee's well-known involvement in hermetic alchemy incline him to a central sun, as some have argued? His younger English contemporary Dr Robert Fludd, as we know, saw hermeticism as fundamentally *geocentric*, with all its hierarchies rooted in a central earth. The jury is still out regarding Dee and Copernicus.

What cannot be denied is that members of the Dee circle discussed Copernicanism. Thomas Digges wrote about it in two influential works, to become the first Englishman to take and defend an unequivocally Copernican heliocentric stance.

THOMAS DIGGES AND THE ORIGINS OF
ENGLISH COPERNICANISM

Although Robert Recorde had displayed a cautious interest and a certain open-mindedness towards the heliocentric theory, Thomas Digges was the first Englishman to think through its problems and implications, and to openly advocate it in print in the early 1570s. He did so in two very significant works.

The first of these, published in 1573 when he was thirty, was *Alae seu Scalae Mathematicae* ("The Steps of Mathematics"), a treatise inspired by Tycho Brahe's new star, which appeared in Cassiopeia in 1572. In this work Digges suggested that the new star might be used as a physical test for the truth or otherwise of the Copernican theory. If astronomers carefully monitored slight changes in the star's brightness, a periodicity might emerge which could suggest the earth was moving around the sun: approaching and receding from the star. But the "supernova" faded away over a few months before any such thing could be attempted.

An integral part of this technique, discussed in the *Scalae*, was trying to measure a parallax for the star, though this also failed to establish anything definitive. However, where the work was particularly significant, and helped to establish Thomas Digges's international standing as a mathematical astronomer, lay in his emphasis on the need for accuracy in making observations with angle-measuring instruments. Digges describes an instrument known as a cross staff, which was an arrangement of graduated wooden rods, which he had used to measure the new star's position vis-à-vis its adjacent stars in Cassiopeia. He conducts a rigorous analysis of the instrument's divided scales – devised by Richard Chancellor – and sighting errors, and points out how these errors must be compensated for if critically accurate results were to be obtained.

Tycho Brahe in Denmark was developing similar ideas, as we saw in Chapter 6, and he and Digges, independently, were at the forefront of a new approach to astronomy: based less upon arguments and philosophical ideas and more upon a new appreciation of accurate instrumentation combined with disciplined observing techniques. Both Digges and Tycho, just like John Flamsteed and Robert

Hooke one hundred years later, realized that exact measurement was the only way to establish for certain whether Copernicus had been right or wrong.

Thomas Digges's other overtly Copernican work appeared in 1576, and was a new, revised edition of his late father Leonard's *A Prognostication Everlasting* of 1555–56. Leonard's *Prognostication* had been a set of mathematical and navigational tables, but what made Thomas's 1576 edition so important from the Copernican point of view was his supplement *A Perfit Description of the Caellestial Orbes*, occupying only a single sheet.

Upon this supplementary sheet was a detailed illustration of the Copernican solar system, the sun at its centre, with Mercury, Venus, earth (encircled by the moon), Mars, Jupiter, and Saturn in correct sequence. Where Digges went beyond Copernicus was in his treatment of the starry realm: instead of showing the conventional single sphere of fixed stars, he showed the stars receding away into three-dimensional space, and into the corners of the printed page. The accompanying description carried this text: "This orbe of stares fixed infinitely up extendeth itself in altitude sphericallye... the palace of felicitye farre excelling our sonne both in quantitye and qualitye the very court of coelestial angelles... the habitacle for the elect." In Digges's scheme the stars receded into three-dimensional infinity.

It is true that medieval scholars, such as Thomas Bradwardine in 1326 and Cardinal Nicholas of Cusa in *c.* 1460, had speculated about a possibly infinite universe, but Digges was certainly the first to provide an illustration, and to add an English language commentary. In some respects Digges's scheme begged questions about the location of heaven itself, and where the "habitacle for the elect", to which saved Christian souls ascended, actually was. There is not the slightest suggestion that Digges was being irreligious in his cosmology, although he was suggesting that heaven could well be a lot further away than on the other side of the black starry sphere which since classical times, it was believed, separated the mundane from the divine realms. The conventional scheme for creation, with heaven lying beyond the sphere of stars, was still compatible with Copernicus's cosmology of 1543.

While Thomas Digges was no doubt acquainted with medieval discussions about an infinitely powerful creator God making an infinite universe or even an infinity of universes if he chose to do so, some people have suggested that Digges may have had other reasons for suggesting that the starry realm receded beyond the vision of the human eye. These hinged upon the so-called "Tudor telescope".

WAS THERE A TUDOR TELESCOPE?

Experimental and theoretical optics was seen as a subject of intense fascination to sixteenth-century European scholars, in a tradition extending back to Bishop Robert Grosseteste in the twelfth century, through Alhazen (Ibn al-Haytham) in Cairo, and on to Ptolemy. Light, lenses, concave and convex mirrors, refraction, reflection, rainbows, the source of colours, mock-suns, magnifying glasses, and early spectacles had long been part of Europe's intellectual culture. Optics was seen as intimately connected to religion in so far as it dealt with the coming of the divine light of God to illumine the world, and also initiated human visual perception.[1]

The astronomical group centring upon John Dee had a well-documented interest in light, and especially in optical devices: devices which coalesced with hermetic philosophy and "Natural Magick", or what we might call natural wonders. Book 17 of Giambattista della Porta's *Magia Naturalis* (1558) dealt with "strange glasses" or optical devices, and his work was well known across Europe, and subsequently translated into English.

Had members of the Dee circle, and Leonard Digges in particular, invented a form of telescope enabling him and Thomas to see things invisible to the unaided eye? In consequence, had this enabled him to see stars so dim as to be invisible to ordinary vision, forty years before Galileo saw them with his *cannocchiale*, as described in his *Sidereus Nuncius* (1610)?

There are certainly some very suggestive remarks in the writings of Leonard and Thomas Digges. The most significant of these appear in the "Preface", which Thomas Digges wrote for his deceased father's *A Geometrical Practical Treatise named Pantometria*, published in 1571, some thirteen years after Leonard's death. Thomas had been only fifteen when Leonard died, but it is clear that he had been a highly precocious lad, fully acquainted with his father's research. Thomas tells us that Leonard, working in the tradition of Friar Roger Bacon of 300 years before, had invented an optical configuration of "glasses concave and convex of Circulaire and parabolicall forms using for multiplication of beames sometime the aid of Glasses transparent".

By refracting and reflecting the incoming light, this device had enabled Leonard to see details of buildings and of life in a village "seven Myles off" across the Kentish Downs. More baffling, however, was a device which not only enabled one to see an individual house in such a village, but to "discerne any trifle, or read any letter lying there open, especially if the sunne beames may come upon it". Even modern electronic surveillance technology would be hard pressed to read a letter lying open in a room at a distance of 7 miles. What were the Digges doing?

The best indication that we have comes from an undated document in the Lansdown Manuscript in the British Library, sent by the instrument maker William Bourne, who was connected with the Dee circle, to Lord Burghley, Queen Elizabeth I's chief adviser.[2] In this treatise, Bourne describes what he understood to have been Leonard and Thomas Digges's optical experiments. It appears that two concave mirrors were used. One mirror caught the light from the outside world and sent it into a second "very large concave looking glasse". The rays coming from this second glass would naturally come to a focus, and if an observer placed his eye at that focus, then he should see a magnified image of the outside world.

Yes, it does work, as I have tried it for myself; and you can try too. Simply take a fairly large magnifying shaving mirror, and set it upright on a table facing a distant object. Then take a second concave mirror – such as a ladies' make-up mirror – and place the second mirror so that it catches the light coming out of the big mirror. Then move your eye towards and away from the smaller mirror, until you hit the point at which the light coming from both mirrors forms a focus. There you should see a magnified image. It will not be very good, and will probably be blurred and distorted, but it *will* be a magnified image of a distant scene. I find it impossible to believe, however, that such an arrangement could make distinct the houses of a village at 7 miles' distance, let alone enable me to read letters or identify coins.

I will also concede that if such a device were pointed to the sky on a starry night, then one could see lots of stars; but how many

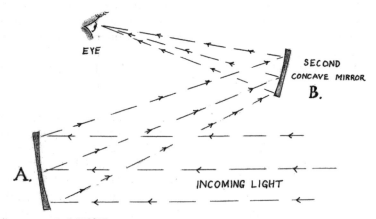

18.1 A suggested configuration for the Digges "telescope", using two slightly offset concave mirrors. The first mirror "A" directs incoming light into the second mirror "B", which sends it into the observer's eye. If one adjusts the mirrors to their correct focal lengths, a magnified, upside-down image of a distant scene can be produced, albeit distorted. One can replace the second mirror, "B", with a *convex* one, to obtain a distorted "right-way-up" image. (I have even obtained *very* poor-quality telescopic images by using the inner and the outer curves of a highly polished chromium-plated spoon, to act as convex and concave mirrors.) The reconstructed optical configurations are similar to those of the Galilean and Keplerian refracting (lens) telescopes. (Reconstruction by Allan Chapman.)

would be genuine stars, as opposed to secondary or tertiary optical reflections, remains a moot point.

We must also be cautious when reading the word "glasse" in

Tudor documents, for the word could mean either a transparent spectacle lens or a polished metal looking-glass. It is worth noting that when, in Exodus 38:8, the ladies of Israel donated their "looking-glasses" (the translation of the 1611 Authorized Version of the Bible) to be melted down to make a ceremonial vessel for the sanctuary, that vessel was to be of *brass*. In 1611, optical science had yet to develop an exact terminology.

The idea of a "Tudor telescope", based on the Digges and Bourne sources, has resurfaced several times in history, and most recently in 1990, when my late friend Colin Ronan argued for it in his Presidential Address to the British Astronomical Association. Colin Ronan even suggested that, considering England's deteriorating relations with Spain, Lord Burghley had slapped a "Top Secret" order upon it – driving knowledge of the proto-telescope underground.

I was always sceptical of this argument. Not only are such secrets hard to keep – poor-quality blurred images notwithstanding – but in the decade following the Spanish Armada threat in 1588, when England stood in grave danger of invasion, Thomas Digges was serving as a senior magistrate responsible for the defence of sections of the Kent coast. In a 1599 document (subsequently printed in 1686), then intended for the eyes of his superiors in London, and now preserved in the Bodleian Library, Oxford, are Digges's proposals for keeping the coast secure, recommending such measures as the strategic positioning of militia troops, signal beacons, and arms dumps. There is no mention at all of using optical devices for seeing the enemy while they were still far out to sea.

I will not deny that Leonard and Thomas Digges had – inspired by Friar Bacon and other authors – produced an interesting optical *arrangement*, but that it was of any value scientifically I seriously doubt. Nothing clinches this argument better for me than the case of Thomas Harriot, who, as a young man in the early 1580s, had been an active member of the Dee circle. As we will see in Chapter 19, Harriot was the first person on record to point one of the new "Dutch Spyglasses" or telescopes at an astronomical body in July 1609. What he saw on the moon and the sun clearly fascinated him, with not the slightest hint that he had any previous experience of distance-magnifying optical devices.

By way of a coda to the "Tudor telescope", however, we should remember that the occult philosopher Dr Dee also used a "glass" or piece of dark polished material to see angels and deep divine and hermetic secrets. This was his "Skrying glass", which Dee employed, along with his medium Edward Kelly, to converse with angels and other aerial beings. "Distant seeing" to a scholar living in that world did not necessarily mean the same as it does to us today.

Dr William Gilbert and the motion of the earth

We first encountered William Gilbert in Chapter 8, when his magnetic research was taken up by Johannes Kepler in order to explain planetary motion. What led this eminent Cambridge don, distinguished physician, and then doctor to Queen Elizabeth I herself down these paths, and on to developing a cosmology that was transparently Copernican in its postulates and assumptions even if this was never explicitly stated?

It all began with what might be termed Dr Gilbert's "hobby". When he was not running the finances of St John's College, Cambridge, as Bursar, or "physicking" his patients, he had long been conducting experiments into the nature and behaviour of the earth's magnetic field: to found the science of geomagnetism, no less. This was not, I hasten to add, a new study, for experimenters back to Peter Peregrinus in the thirteenth century had been conducting controlled experiments with magnets. As an experimentalist, Dr Gilbert began to work with a *terrella*, or "little earth" – a lump of magnetized ironstone, carved by a mason into a perfect sphere; an experimental earth, from which he came to extrapolate physical phenomena which could be applied to the real earth.

Using a *versorium*, or delicately poised magnetized needle, he found that the terrella did exhibit characteristics that were identical to those of the earth, for it had north and south magnetic poles, and curved magnetic meridians that arched between the poles, just as navigators sailing in polar and equatorial waters had discovered.

This led him, in Book IV of his masterpiece *De Magnete* ("On the Magnet") of 1600, to suggest that the earth rotated around its poles, *contra* the teachings of Aristotle and the ancients, but in line with Copernicus's theory.

Gilbert died in 1603 – probably suddenly, at the age of fifty-nine, at a time when a major plague epidemic was raging – leaving another major book in manuscript that was eventually published in Amsterdam in 1650. While not openly declaring for Copernicus, the heliocentric model of the cosmos lay at the heart of all of Gilbert's physical assumptions contained in *De Mundo Nostro Sublunari Philosophia Nova* ("A New Philosophy concerning our Sublunary Earth"), 1650. Gilbert spoke of the planets, perhaps ten years before the telescope revealed them to be spherical worlds, *not* as lights attached to crystalline spheres, but as inherently magnetic bodies moving in the void of space under their own and each other's magnetic influences. Central to Gilbert's argument in *De Mundo* was the abolition of the Aristotelian elemental concept which postulated that the "sphere of the Moon", or the lunar orbit, divided the cosmos into two physically and materially separate regions. These were the "sub-lunary" sphere of the earth and its four endless-change-producing elements, and the "super-lunary" realm of astronomical perfection. Instead, Gilbert saw the earth, moon, and planets as all made of a unified magnetic material, so that they acted continually upon each other – a physics considerably in advance of Copernicus, but one which appealed to the mystical Kepler.

SIR THOMAS GRESHAM'S COLLEGE AND SIR HENRY SAVILE'S PROFESSORS

Between 1597 and 1619, astronomical study in England made great institutional advances. The first came in 1597, with the establishment of Gresham College, Bishopsgate, London; and the second when Sir Henry Savile founded his two new professorships at Oxford. Sir Thomas Gresham had been one of the most successful English financiers of the sixteenth century, dying in 1579; when his widow died in 1596, leaving no legal heir, their great quadrangular mansion in the city of London, along with a hefty endowment (including monies accruing from Gresham's Royal Exchange), became an academic foundation. Part of the endowment was to pay for the salaries and in-house accommodation of seven bachelor professors.

In 1619, Sir Henry Savile, a Yorkshire knight, mathematical scholar, and Warden of Merton College, Oxford, founded two professorships that still carry his name today. Like two of the Gresham chairs, one was in astronomy and the other in geometry. The Gresham–Oxford Savilian collaboration, informal as it was, would be long and fruitful. Henry Briggs, for instance, was Gresham Professor of Geometry, then in 1619 became the first Savilian Geometry Professor. John Greaves was a friend of both Henry Briggs and John Bainbridge, and towards the middle of the seventeenth century became successively Gresham and Savilian Professor of Geometry. Sir Christopher Wren would likewise hold the Gresham and then the Savilian astronomical chairs.

Gresham's vision was not to create an Oxbridge-style student-based college in the City, so much as what might be considered the world's first college of adult education. The seven professors were required to put on their lectures at advertised times, and *anyone*, from a visiting duke to a butcher's apprentice boy, could come in, sit down, and listen. The statutes also required that the professor must repeat his lecture on another occasion in Latin, for the benefit of visiting scholars who spoke no English – and it was totally free *for all*.

The professorial lectures covered a variety of subjects, including law, medicine, language, and divinity, though of especial importance to the Astronomical Renaissance were the lectures delivered from the Chairs of Astronomy and Geometry. While Ptolemaic astronomy and Euclidean geometry formed the basis of these lectures, as they would have done in the English, Scottish, Trinity College, Dublin, and European universities, the professors clearly enjoyed a good deal of intellectual freedom regarding what they taught. And while the early professors, such as Edward Brerewood and Edmund Gunter, may not have been "committed" Copernicans, we know that at the time when the Tychonic geo-heliocentric theory answered most questions, the Copernican theory was nonetheless discussed in public lectures. Edmund Gunter was also a pioneer of calculating instruments, such as "Gunter's Scale", and like his colleagues had a commitment to teaching and publishing useful mathematics.

Professors Henry Gellibrand and John Bainbridge seem to have been cautiously interested in Copernicus's theory, while Henry Briggs and Samuel Foster were more actively inclined to the idea of a moving earth. By the 1650s and 1660s, when Sir Christopher Wren and Robert Hooke held Gresham chairs, all evidence suggests that they were openly and actively Copernican. All of this, let us remember, was not confined to the academic closet, but was available to any Londoner, or visitor, who close to enter the college hall, sit on a bench, and listen.

It is true that, especially in the winter, people coming into the lecture hall were sometimes more interested in warming up by the fire (and perhaps falling asleep) than in hearing a learned discourse on the heliocentric theory, but that is the risk you take when you open up to all and sundry. What an amazing educative resource Sir Thomas Gresham had provided, and which his City Trustees *still* provide down to this day, as I know from experience, having been a Gresham Professor myself.

Most of Gresham's science professors were also actively involved in fundamental research in astronomy, mathematics, and physics. Mention was made above about Edmund Gunter improving mathematical calculating techniques, but even more significant was Gresham professorial research into geomagnetism. By 1620, for example, it was known that the earth's magnetic field acted not merely laterally, as when the compass pointed north, but also vertically, the latter being known as the magnetic "dip", and measured by a newly devised "dip needle". When one integrated the lateral and "dip" magnetic bearings, one could get some impression of how the magnetic field operated globally. Captains heading for Hudson's Bay, the northern Muscovy Sea, the Spice Islands of Indonesia, China, and the Pacific were being encouraged to make as many astronomical and magnetic observations as possible to collect primary data. What the professors and City merchants hoped was that navigation might be made more scientific, and hence safer.

The Elizabethan navigator William Borough, for example, made careful measurements of the compass needle's variation from true north from the garden of his house at Limehouse, London, finding the variation angle to be 11¼ degrees to the *east* of north. Over forty years later, in 1622, Edmund Gunter repeated Borough's observations, also from Limehouse and nearby Deptford, only to find that the variation now stood at 6 degrees from true north. Gunter's professorial colleague, Henry Gellibrand, repeated the compass observations from the same locations over 1633–34, finding that the variation had further diminished over the decade. By the early 1660s, other scientists found that the compass pointed exactly due north in London, only to move gradually to the *west* of north, where it still rests today.

The behaviour of the magnetic compass needle fascinated the astronomers of the early seventeenth century, and nowhere more than in Gresham College, with its connections to the City of London and its prosperous seaborne trade. Edmond Halley, a City of London native who became an Oxford Savilian but not a Gresham Professor, was destined to develop the science of geomagnetism to a new level by the 1670s. Collating long runs of magnetic observations made over a century, Halley hypothesized that the earth's magnetic field could be caused by the slightly different speeds of rotation of the earth's outer mantle and an inner core. This was an astonishingly modern idea, which took it as axiomatic that the earth not only rotated upon its axis, but also rotated around the sun, with the orbiting moon in attendance, to create a complex system of gravitational pulls.

The Copernican theory was openly discussed by the Gresham College professors, while Sir Henry Savile stipulated that his professors after 1619 should teach the ideas of Copernicus, along with the theories of other modern astronomers in their Oxford lectures – not, by any means, to be crusading Copernicans, but to review the merits and demerits of the theories then on offer.

Looking at London, Oxford, Cambridge, Leiden, Amsterdam, Copenhagen, and various German universities in the early seventeenth century, one finds a spectrum of opinions on Copernicus. Some men were staunch Copernican advocates, while others favoured the geo-heliocentric systems of Tycho, or Riccioli. What is supremely important to understand is that the "System of the World", as they called it, along with its biblical implications, plus Cartesian physics, was discussed openly by Protestants and Roman Catholics alike in what resembled a free market of ideas. If anyone – other than Galileo – got into trouble for any of this, I have yet to hear of it.

The Revd William Oughtred

Born in 1575, Oughtred was the son of a working scribe – or document copier – of Eton, Buckinghamshire (now part of Berkshire). Winning King's (or Queen's) Scholarships both to Eton College and to King's, Cambridge, he settled into the life of a Cambridge don, until receiving the church living of Albury, near Guildford. There he remained vicar of the parish for the rest of his seventy-five years, even avoiding sequestration during the Cromwellian period when the Church of England was officially abolished.

Yet Oughtred had a profound effect upon several generations of English mathematicians and astronomers, including Seth Ward and Sir Christopher Wren – an influence that spread not only via his published works, but also through his personal teaching and extensive correspondence. It was said that this devoutly learned Anglican parson was a supporter of Copernicus. What cannot be denied is that many of his pupils became so – maybe not a *creedal* Copernican in the way that Galileo became, but certainly recognizing Copernicanism's strong likelihood, at a time when all the Copernican "evidence" came from analogy and elegance rather than from mathematical demonstration.

What was so striking about Oughtred was that in England he came to typify "the Mathematicks", with all its love of practicality, instruments, devices, and inventions. His son Ben even became a watchmaker.

Having seen how Copernicus fared in England, let us turn to how Galileo was received in England and Wales.

CHAPTER 19

Thomas Harriot Sends Galileo to Wales

$\mathcal{W}$e have seen how the science of optics had roots extending back to classical antiquity, and how medieval Arabic and European philosophers explored the properties of early lenses and mirrors, and developed experimentally based explanations for rainbow colours and why we have twilight. The "Tudor telescope" apart, how did the post-1608 "Dutch spyglass", *cannocchiale*, "cylinder", or telescope ("seeing from afar") – the "proper" telescope, as it were – first come into the British Isles? Let us begin by looking at the life and work of the first man to observe the heavens through a telescope, and who did so four months before Galileo.

MASTER HARRIOT OF OXFORD

The ancestry of Thomas Harriot is something of a blank. We do not know the names of his parents, or his father's occupation, although Thomas does seem to have had a sister. We do know he "matriculated" or became a member of Oxford University on 20 December 1577, was born sometime in 1560, and was a native of Oxfordshire. To qualify as an undergraduate student, he must have had a prior firm grounding in Latin, probably Greek, the Bible, and broader classical culture, for these formed the bedrock of an academic education in Elizabethan times.

In Oxford city there were a few good private "grammar" schools – specializing in training boys in Latin grammar – though such a lengthy schooling would presume parents, relatives, or a patron who had some cash to spare and who valued the potential that a good education could confer upon a bright youth. It is likely, then, that his family did not need to send him out to work, as was the lot of most children.

In 1577, the seventeen-year-old Harriot entered St Mary's Hall, Oxford, a daughter house of Oriel College, with its own premises, facing the great porch of the University Church of St Mary the Virgin across the High Street. (St Mary's would be absorbed into Oriel in 1902, and nowadays Harriot is proudly claimed as an "Oriel man" by members of that college.) At St Mary's, Harriot would have received the full classical education, with its stress on fluent Latinity, along with training in Protestant theology, some civil law, and the arts of rhetoric and argument. A Renaissance education placed great stress on the student's ability to master complex ideas and to "defend" a position in debate – crucial skills, especially if one planned on entering the legal profession, the church, or Parliament. Like university graduates across Europe, he would have been taught mathematics, geometry, and Ptolemaic astronomy: the famous "sciences of proportion". It was these mathematical sciences that especially captivated Harriot, and in which he would become eminent.

It was most likely owing to his youthful reputation as a mathematician that Harriot came to the notice of Sir Walter Ralegh, himself an old Oriel man, and eight years his senior (born 1552), and already by his late twenties enjoying a reputation as a daring naval commander, a charismatic leader, a scholar, a ladies' man, and as Queen Elizabeth I's favourite courtier. Ralegh was also keen on the exploration and possible colonization of the eastern Atlantic seaboard of North America. Such a colonization could be of enormous strategic importance to England if it could be realized: partly as a potential market for English manufacturers, and a possible source of great wealth, from mineral exploitation, animal skins, and naval timber, hemp, tar, and other supplies. The still unexplored North America could well contain a waterway flowing all the way through the continent to the Pacific, giving England a fast route to the spice islands of Indonesia. An American colony could provide bases for English privateers engaged in guerrilla warfare against the already mighty Spanish empire in the Caribbean.

Ralegh, who as we have seen had associations with Dr John Dee's mathematical circle of friends, needed mathematically and cartographically literate sea captains in his wider circle, and it was in his capacity as a teacher of such skills that the young Harriot entered Ralegh's service, and was given an elegant set of rooms in Sir Walter's great Thames-side London mansion, Durham House. It was no doubt through his employee-cum-friend relationship with Ralegh that Harriot entered that world of Tudor astronomers and mathematicians that we encountered in the previous chapter – Dr Dee's circle – and it is by no means unlikely that he met the queen herself.

So keen was Ralegh to establish good relations with that part of North America named in honour of the queen – Virginia – that two young men of the Algonkian nation, Manteo and Wanchese, even agreed to return to England with Ralegh's expedition to help with the language and cultural understanding. The "American language" was entirely incomprehensible to Europeans, deriving as it did from a wholly separate linguistic root, with no connections to the classical or Germanic tongues. Its wide range of sounds and voice intonations totally baffled European ears, and as Manteo and Wanchese were to lodge at Durham House, and become curiosities in their own right to the court and citizens of London, it was the universally learned Mr Harriot who was given the job of making sense of what they said. And he made an excellent job of it.

Manteo in particular emerged as an enthusiastic foreign visitor, amazed at the size and complexity of Elizabethan London, obliging, persuadable, and rather enjoying his celebrity status as an American "savage". He and Wanchese were probably the first Americans to set foot on British soil. Harriot not only learned their language, but developed a special script in which to write it. He even produced a translation of the Lord's Prayer in the "American language". Manteo would come, voluntarily, to receive Christian baptism.

A COPERNICAN IN NORTH AMERICA

When Sir Richard Grenville, under Sir Walter Ralegh's auspices, set sail in the *Tiger* for Virginia in April 1585, Harriot sailed with the expedition, and repatriated Manteo and Wanchese to their indigenous communities in the Roanoke area. All this was seen as a preliminary to establishing a permanent English settlement in Virginia, and the expedition on which Harriot sailed was intended primarily to be a survey voyage, to make friendly contact with the natives, buy land from them, and conduct a thorough survey. It was to be a scientific expedition, no less, in which Harriot was the "scientist" and John White the artist and draughtsman.

Ralegh's intention was *not* to seize land from the native people. All the evidence available suggested that North America was vast, richly resourced, and only thinly populated. Why, then, should not English Christians purchase what was seen as unoccupied land from local tribes for landless Elizabethan settlers to farm? Ralegh undoubtedly was a swashbuckling curse to the Spanish empire in Central America, but he was not a cruel man, and had every desire to treat the Indians fairly and honestly. The same applies to Thomas Harriot.

Harriot's *A Briefe and True Report of the New Found Land in Virginia* (1588) may have been in part a roseate sales prospectus aimed at potential Virginia colony backers in the City of London, but more importantly, it was a pioneering ethnological document. It not only described and contained surveys of sections of the Virginia coastal region, showing Harriot's clear association with the Digges–Dee practical cartographic tradition, but, through his growing mastery of the Algonkian language, Harriot was able in part to enter the mental world of the Indian people. As the colonizing intention included a desire to take the Christian faith to the Americans (but not to *impose* it), Harriot was fascinated by Algonkian religious beliefs, their moral sense, and their ideas of good and bad, heaven and hell. When a good Indian died, Harriot recorded, he followed the sun into a sort of paradise in the west, whereas a wicked person was condemned to the pit of Popoguso. How far Harriot was inadvertently reading his own Christian ideas of eternity into his interpretations of native culture is hard to say, but what is certain is that this young Oxford-educated astronomer was, amongst his other talents, a pioneer ethnological researcher. He even recorded, when a violent storm blew up the coast, scattering the English ships riding at anchor, that he was told it was the work of the storm god Huracan. Perhaps this is the linguistic root of the meteorological word "hurricane".

THE FIRST SCIENCE LECTURE ON THE NORTH AMERICAN CONTINENT?

One thing that Harriot records in his *True Report* marks him out as a founding father of scientific education on the North American continent. At some stage during his year in Virginia he gave what was a sort of lecture demonstration of European science and technology. It included:

> *Mathematicall Instruments, Sea Compasses, the virtue of the Loadstone in drawing yron, a Perspective Glasse whereby was shewd manie strange sightes. Burning Glasses, Wilde-Fire woorkes, Gunnes... Spring Clocks that seem to goe of themselves, and manie other thinges that we had.*[1]

This was delivered to an indigenous native American audience, presumably in Algonkian, for he points out that his listeners were awestruck by the devices he showed them. The spring-driven mechanical clock, the "tick" of which seemed similar to the human heartbeat, and the way in which magnets attracted iron were among the things that most fascinated his audience. Most curious of all were the optical devices, with their seemingly strange distorted images, magnifications, and even frightening properties; to say nothing of the burning glass which could make the sun cause a fire at the operator's will.

It was these optical devices that led some modern defenders of the Tudor telescope to suggest that not only did Harriot have an optical arrangement similar to that alluded to by Leonard and Thomas Digges in 1571, but that he took such a device to America. I entertain great doubts on that matter, as I indicated in Chapter 18. The strange sights and images which seemed to perplex and even alarm the Roanoke locals, I suspect, were probably no more than the facial and other distortions that anyone can see in a convex or concave mirror. It is simply that Europeans were accustomed to such sights, whereas the "Virginians" in 1585 were not. On the other hand, Thomas Harriot's lecture demonstration of 1585–86 should be enshrined in the North American consciousness as the first modern scientific lecture to be delivered on that continent – and to an indigenous American audience in their own language to boot.

We do not know for certain what Harriot may have told the Algonkians about astronomy. If, perchance, he did say anything, he would have told them the cosmology of Ptolemy that he would have learned in Oxford. After all, Tycho had not yet published the mature form of his geo-heliocentric cosmology at the time of Harriot's setting sail for America in June 1585, although he may – and this is purely speculative – have mentioned Copernicus, especially in the light of his acquaintance with Digges and others.

On 27 July 1586, the *Elizabeth Bonaventure* on which Thomas Harriot was sailing arrived safely in Portsmouth. As far as I am aware, he would never go to sea again, except crossing over to Ireland. What is more, the English hopes for an American colony would be put on hold for some years, as most shipping for strategic reasons was confined to home waters during that intensifying crisis which led to the Spanish Armada of 1588. It would not be until the establishment of the Jamestown settlement in Chesapeake Bay – to the north of Roanoke – in 1608, and then that of the Pilgrim Fathers at Boston, Massachusetts, in 1620, that things would take off again, and I am not aware that Harriot had any involvement in either.

THOMAS HARRIOT: FRIENDS, PATRONS, AND FINANCING RESEARCH

In the decades following the Roanoke expedition, Harriot clearly prospered. He and Ralegh became firm friends, and Harriot the bachelor mathematician devoted his time to the advancement of mathematics, becoming a celebrated English pioneer of algebra and binomial theory, and inventor of the algebraic symbol > < for equality. These techniques would take mathematics into new realms, and give it formidable analytical powers that would prove vital to the mathematicians of the seventeenth and ensuing centuries. Harriot seems to have enjoyed a quiet life, and to have displayed no great worldly ambitions. He never lacked for influential friends, and became what might be called a very comfortably off single gentleman.

Sir Walter Ralegh – always free with other people's property, which was not an unusual trait at the Tudor Royal Court – was generous to Harriot. In the English attempts to forcibly Protestantize Ireland, for instance, Ralegh seized Roman Catholic Church property at Waterford, County Cork, acquiring lands once owned by the monks of Molana Abbey. He then passed the estate on to Harriot, who in turn sold it for £200 in 1597.

Sir Walter, even after being banished from court awhile after getting Bess Throckmorton pregnant and secretly marrying her, had always been close to the queen. However, when Elizabeth I, the Virgin Queen, died in March 1603, shortly before her seventieth birthday, the Tudor Royal line ended, and she was succeeded by a distant nephew, King James VI of Scotland. The new king, from the royal house of Stuart, became James I, thus combining the crowns of both countries to form "Great Britain" or the "United Kingdom".

The 36-year-old King James I was a notable scholar and an accomplished linguist and Protestant theologian. It rapidly became apparent that he could not stand Sir Walter, and before 1603 was out, Ralegh had been put on trial for his life for a frankly trumped-up offence, subjected to one of the most shameful "show trials" in British legal history, sentenced to death, inexplicably reprieved on the very scaffold, and condemned to lifelong imprisonment in the Tower of London until such time as the king chose to resurrect his death warrant.

In spite of having lost his power and once opulent revenues, Sir Walter's regard for Master Harriot remained undiminished, and according to Harriot's seventeenth-century biographer John Aubrey, he recommended him to Henry Percy, Ninth Earl of

Northumberland, when both noble gentlemen were in the Tower of London. Harriot may have entered the earl's service soon after Ralegh's fall in 1603, although Northumberland was imprisoned on suspicion – through his conspirator younger brother, Thomas – of involvement in the Guy Fawkes plot of 5 November 1605. As Thomas Harriot himself spent three weeks under arrest, was cross-examined, but later released, at the same time, one might assume that he was already on friendly terms with Northumberland by November 1605, for the very efficient "security services" of the day to have hauled him in at all.

Henry Percy of Northumberland, born in 1564, was an exotic. One of the richest noblemen in England, with vast estates in the north-eastern counties, he was a scholar, an imputed sceptic, a daring thinker, a lover of the new scientific knowledge, a man who spent a colossal £50 per annum on books, and was nicknamed the "Wizard Earl". He was delighted with his "coup" of Master Harriot, who would become, along with Walter Warner and Robert Hues (Hughes), one of the earl's "Three Wise Men" trio of gentlemen philosophers.

Although writers describe Harriot's annual stipend from the Earl variously at £80, £120, £200, and £300, what cannot be denied is that Harriot was now very comfortably off. He had an income which most cathedral dignitaries would not have turned their noses up at, a fine residence in the grounds of Syon Park, Brentford, London, the earl's southern estate, and a place to stay in Threadneedle Street in the City of London. This was in addition to whatever other gifts from Ralegh he still retained. Harriot probably became one of the richest mathematicians in Europe. (By way of comparison, when Wadham College, Oxford, was founded in 1610, the Fellows, or dons, received £20 per annum each, and the Warden, or Head, £100.)

What did the earl expect from a man paid such a huge salary, with a string of fringe benefits? Very little, in practical terms. Yes, he may be called upon occasionally to give specialist advice pertaining to politics or the Northumberland estates; but his real job was simply to be clever, and to bring credit to his patron. This was not dissimilar to Dr Dee's relationship with the late Queen,

Galileo's with the Grand Duke of Tuscany, or Kepler's with the Holy Roman Emperor. When the earl also ended up in the Tower, after 1605, it was expected that Harriot and his fellow "Wise Men" would visit and wait upon him there.

How could Harriot and others visit Northumberland and Ralegh, during their long incarceration in the Tower of London as state prisoners? How could Ralegh and the earl see so much of each other in prison? To understand this, it is necessary to recall that a high-status prisoner would not have been chained up in the rat-infested dungeons of popular legend. Rather, they could take what were effectively suites of secure rooms, with a right to the "liberty of the Tower", or the ability to come and go within the precincts, but *not* to leave them. Such prisoners – upon their oaths as gentlemen – could go for walks, play bowls on Tower Green, attend St Peter's Church in the precincts, dine, perform alchemical experiments, have visitors from tailors, booksellers, and friends, and even have the wife and family move in and live a domestic life within the Tower. Lady Ralegh and son "Young Wat" moved in, with a cook and servants. When Sir Walter was not dining with the governor, working in his laboratory, or chatting with the earl and Thomas Harriot, he was writing his monumental *History of the World*. None of these luxuries came cheap, and rich prisoners paid through the nose for their privileges, but it was a far cry from the verminous dungeon. However, the ever-present threat of the king suddenly deciding to activate your death warrant never went away.

OPTICS AND ASTRONOMY

During the late 1580s to his death in 1622, Harriot became financially secure, with plenty of time to devote to primary research. In addition to his work on algebra and binomial mathematics, Harriot belonged to that class of philosophical gentlemen across Europe engaged in optical research – as one might expect from his early association with the Dee–Digges circle.

He undertook detailed investigations into the nature of light-scatter and the formation of rainbows, for example. He conducted research into the refractive indices of various substances, using a hollow glass vessel into which various liquids were placed. In 1601, he had developed a theory of reflection which is now known as "Snell's Law", after the Dutchman who independently discovered it in 1621: that when a ray of light passes from a thinner to a denser medium – such as from the air into a piece of glass – the angle to which it is refracted from the point at which it enters the glass is in exact proportion to the angle at which the ray first struck the glass.

Harriot was an assiduous practitioner of all the branches of astronomy as they were known in his day. John Aubrey would record that Harriot "had seen nine Cometes, and had predicted Seaven of them, but did not tell how",[2] while he was to leave several high-quality angular measurements of the brilliant comet of 1618, made with a large "Astronomical Radius" arrangement of wooden rods with sliding brass sights. Harriot was also fascinated by the ancient Greek idea – established in the Western mind by Lucretius in his *De Rerum Natura* ("On the Nature of Things") of *c.* 60 BC – that instead of the world being made up of Aristotle's four "elements", it was constituted of "atoms".

It is possible that he *may* have co-discovered the *non*-circular nature of the planetary orbits about the sun. In February 1610, his friend and protégé Sir William Lower, while urging Harriot to make a proper list of his otherwise unannounced discoveries, wrote to him, saying "… long since you told me as much [of Kepler], that the motions of the planets were not perfect circles" and that the planets made their "revolutions in Ellipses".[3] One wonders exactly how long since? Had Harriot come to this conclusion about orbital non-circularity from his own astronomical observations and analyses, or had he picked up the idea from his correspondence with Kepler? Harriot conducted an extensive correspondence with fellow mathematicians, both at home and abroad. As we saw in Chapter 7, Kepler had begun to consider the possible existence of elliptical orbits as far back as 1605, and could well have exchanged thoughts on the idea with Harriot in a letter before publishing it in *Astronomia Nova* in 1609. Either way, this serves only to confirm Harriot's status as a mathematical scientist of international standing.

Thomas Harriot's failure to publish anything after the *True Report* of 1588 was clearly an irritation to his friends as he grew older, and they saw discoveries which he had made and discussed with them being independently made and claimed by others, with Harriot simply sitting back and saying nothing. Few silences could have been more baffling to them than Harriot's silence about what he saw through his new Dutch spyglass during and after the summer of 1609.

HARRIOT AND HIS "DUTCH TRUNCKE"

It is not clear who invented the first simple refracting telescope, but it was the enterprising Middelburg, Holland, spectacle-maker Hans Lippershey who tried – and failed – to secure profitable patent rights from the Dutch States General in 1608. Consequently, the simple device, consisting of nothing more than a pair of matched convex and concave "spectacle" lenses in a tube, could be made and sold by anybody once the basic optical principles became known.

It was most likely through some Dutch commercial connection that Harriot obtained his prototype "dutch [sic] truncke" or "cylinder", as he called his first and as yet un-christened telescope during the early part of 1609. On the evening of 26 July 1609, at 9 p.m., and in the gloaming of a summer's evening, he directed this ×6 magnification instrument towards the five-day-old crescent moon. The resulting drawing is still preserved in the West Sussex County Archives in Chichester, along with Harriot's other astronomical and related manuscripts. On this dated sheet of paper is the earliest telescopic sketch of the moon.[4]

The sketch shows what later lunar cartographers would call the Mare Crisium, Mare Tranquillitatis, Mare Foecunditatis, and rough patches on the terminator (the line separating the dark from the illuminated parts of the lunar phase) which correspond to the Theophilius and Cyrillus formations. No significant crater detail appears on this first drawing, while the five-day moon is shown as oddly truncated and rather banana-shaped. The reason for the odd shape drawn by Harriot is obvious to anyone who is familiar with looking at the moon through a telescope, especially if that person has built a working replica of the Lippershey-type telescope, which both Harriot and Galileo used. Such a telescope gave only a tiny field of view, and was unable even to show the complete *half* moon without cropping off the cusps, or points of the crescent. As Harriot, the one-time Virginia surveyor, was concerned with the detailed middle part of the lunar image, he did not bother to add the cusps to his sketch, especially as – in his simple optical device – they would have contained no detail and would probably have appeared as no more than featureless white glares.

It is here that Thomas Harriot becomes irritating for the historian, for how soon after this first sketch, of 26 July 1609, did he wait before drawing his wonderfully detailed whole-moon maps, which are still preserved in the Chichester Archives – maps, like his first sketch, drawn on foolscap sheets, inside compass-scribed circles of about 6 inches in diameter? These whole-moon maps, which are cartographically much superior to anything that Galileo ever drew after 30 November 1609, are *undated*. On the other hand, documentary evidence suggests that Harriot did not begin to draw his whole-moon maps until after 17 July 1610, by which time he almost certainly had seen Galileo's rather crude woodcut lunar drawings in *Sidereus Nuncius*, which we know was being read in London by that date. They were also drawn with a very sharp-cut pen, with carefully numbered features, though unfortunately no key to what the numbers meant survives amongst his papers.

Why were Harriot's moon drawings so cartographically precise, whereas Galileo's post-November 1609 sepia paintings were not (a point I mentioned in Chapter 11)? I think the answer lies in the two men's very different personalities and intellectual agendas. As we have seen, Galileo was a passionate Copernican, out to proselytize the heliocentric cosmology, and the obviously rough and mountainous lunar surface gave him a stick with which to beat the Aristotelians.

Harriot, by contrast, while equally convinced of the Copernican case – in his espousal of Keplerian elliptical orbits he was an even more "advanced" Copernican than Galileo, who rejected ellipses – was not trying to convince anybody. Yes, Harriot openly discussed the Copernican theory with friends and fellow astronomers and mathematicians, but he was not out to change the world. Besides, he was by instinct a cartographer and fine draughtsman, and I suspect what appealed to him about the telescopic moon was its superabundance of fine detail which needed to be exactly delineated. As a well-to-do private gentleman, with two very high-profile friends on "death row" for treason in the Tower, and having himself been cross-examined and released in 1605, my guess is that Harriot had no desire to make himself conspicuous.

THE TELESCOPE, KEPLER, AND GALILEO
GO TO WALES

It is my opinion that the impact of the lunar surface discoveries arrived in Carmarthenshire, South Wales, well ahead of, and independently of, Galileo's published discoveries which reverberated across Europe after March 1610. They arrived at Traventi (now Trefenti) at the house of Harriot's mathematical friend, protégé, and great admirer, Sir William Lower, who had married Penelope, the step-daughter of the Earl of Northumberland.

This fact is established from the surviving correspondence that passed between Harriot and Lower following the arrival of the "dutch truncke".[5] It is clear that Harriot had set his technician, Christopher Tooke, the task of replicating the Dutch instrument, and that he had soon done so successfully. Almost certainly, telescopes would have been taken to the Tower of London, so that Harriot, Northumberland, and Ralegh could view the moon; while Lower's letter from Trefenti of 6 February 1610 makes it clear that Harriot had sent a selection of telescopes to South Wales at least a whole lunar month before, because that same letter contains what would become two classic early impressions of the telescopic moon – a letter which Baron von Zach, who first examined the Harriot papers in the 1780s, mistook to be by Northumberland. Lower says that the lunar surface reminded him of the complex topography of the earth, as depicted in "the dutch [sic] books of voyages". He continues, "In the full she appears like a tarte that my cooke made me last week. Here a vaine of bright stuffe, and there of darke, and so confusedlie al over. I must confesse I can see none of this without my cylinder [telescope]."[6]

The correspondence that passed between Lower at Trefenti in Carmarthenshire and Harriot at Syon Park is fascinating when it comes to considering the spread of the new discoveries and ideas of the Astronomical Renaissance. For one thing, the responses to the early telescopic images indicate amazement, strongly emphasizing their novelty: surely, had there existed a viable "Tudor telescope", Harriot and his friends would have shown much less surprise, if any at all.

If one looks at the non-telescopic content in Lower's letters – and sadly, Harriot's letters to his friends in South Wales have not survived – it is interesting to note what is most occupying their minds. Not a mention of Galileo, for instance, during the first weeks of 1610, for *Sidereus Nuncius* was still being written; nor would Kepler's *Dissertatio*, which also mentioned the Galilean discoveries, emerge from the Prague presses before May 1610. What interested them most were the mathematical possibilities implicit within Kepler's theory of elliptical orbits, as announced in *Astronomia Nova* (1609), and already doing the rounds of the English astronomers; and, from the admiring Lower's comments, Harriot's possible original insights thereon.

It is clear from his letters that Lower was a Copernican, and mathematically very learned. He was not the only person around Trefenti to be that way inclined, for he mentions two men, a Mr Vaughan and a Mr Protheroe, and maybe others. Infuriatingly for the historian none of these gentlemen are accorded Christian names in Lower's letters, and Vaughan and Protheroe happen to be common Welsh surnames, which makes them hard to pin down as individuals in local Welsh, academic, or wider records. But as Lower, like Harriot, had been educated at Oxford, and there were plenty of Welsh men around Tudor and Stuart Oxford, I had a look in university and college registers for any chance connection. I found nothing solid, but there were certainly Vaughans and Protheroes of Harriot's and Lower's undergraduate generations, and some from South Wales. Jesus College, Oxford, had been founded in 1571 with the explicit intention of educating young Welshmen for the church and learned professions, while Welsh names are to be found on the books of Christ Church, Brasenose, and other colleges.

In the light of the above, and the information contained in Lower's letters to Harriot, two historical claims might be advanced. Firstly, Sir William Lower may have been the first to have received a telescope as a Christmas, or maybe a New Year's, gift (having been observing for over a month by 6 February 1610). Secondly, "We Traventine [Trefenti] Philosophers", who met at Lower's house to discuss Kepler and look at the moon through a telescope, might qualify as the earliest amateur astronomical society to meet in the British Isles.

Lower's letter of 6 February 1610 makes no mention whatever of Galileo or his discoveries. This also suggests that Lower was using the "New Style" calendar which began the year on 1 January (as the ancient Romans had done) rather than the "Old Style" which began it on Lady Day, 25 March. Six months later, in his letter to Harriot dated "Longest Day 1610" (21 June), Lower is agog about Galileo and telescopic wonders unnoticed by Harriot or the "Traventine Philosophers" in the previous winter, but to which Galileo had drawn attention. These new wonders included, in addition to the lunar topography, Jupiter's four moons and the large number of stars visible in the Pleiades cluster – three new wonders, unimagined by astronomers of previous ages, yet made visible through Christopher Tooke's copied *and improved* replicas of Harriot's original "dutch truncke". Nor did the wonders include the additional wonder of elliptical orbits.

It is likely, however, that news of Galileo's discoveries reached Lower and the South Welsh "Traventine Philosophers" some weeks ahead of any actual copy of *Sidereus Nuncius*. Most probably, they did so through now lost letters from Harriot mentioning the discoveries of "Galileus" (as they called him), gleaned from letters from Kepler or other Continental mathematicians. But, as is clear from letters exchanged between other British astronomers – such as the correspondence between Sir Christopher Heydon and William Camden of 6 July 1610 – the Galilean discoveries were being discussed in learned circles by the summer of 1610.

Any talk of new stars seen in the Pleiades or in Orion's Sword *must* have depended either upon reports received from the Continent, or, perhaps, on independent observations made by Harriot or

Lower and his Welsh friends in the previous winter: observations of which there is no conclusive written record among the surviving documents. Yet it was impossible to verify such astronomical phenomena in the summer of 1610 (or the summer of any other year for that matter), for the constellations of Taurus and Orion – in which the Pleiades and Orion's Sword are to be found – are occupied by the sun and drowned out by brilliant light during the summer months, being only visible in the night sky during winter.

Following his initial lunar observations in 1609, and his correspondence with Lower over the ensuing months, Harriot does not appear to have done much telescopic astronomy until after July 1610, by which time he had not only heard about Galileo's discoveries, but was probably already in possession of a copy of *Sidereus Nuncius*. What is remarkable, and probably says much about Harriot's personality, is that he expressed only *admiration* for Galileo, without the slightest trace of jealousy. Lower likewise, in addition to trying to cajole Harriot into laying claim to some of his optical and other discoveries, expressed only admiration for the achievements of *Galileus*.

HARRIOT'S FURTHER TELESCOPIC RESEARCH

After Harriot's initial lunar observations of July 1609, and correspondence with Lower and the Traventine Philosophers over the following winter, it was the news of Galileo's wider discoveries, such as of Jupiter's moons and of the new fixed stars, that brought him back to telescopic astronomy. It was probably during this period, from the summer of 1610 to 1613 or so, that he surveyed and drew his meticulous whole-moon maps. By December 1610, when the planet was getting well placed for observation, he was observing the moons of Jupiter.[7]

Where Harriot certainly made a major co-discovery was in the existence and nature of sunspots, as was mentioned in Chapter 12. Whether he, Galileo, Johannes Fabricius, or Christopher Scheiner actually saw them first is unclear, though Galileo was quick off the mark to rubbish the other Continental claimants, while knowing nothing of Harriot's observations. Harriot himself made no claim, but his observations are clearly laid out: "1610, Syon. December 8th. The altitude of the sonne being 7 or 8 degrees. It being frost & a mist I saw the sonne in this manner", which passage accompanies his drawing of a spotted sun.[8]

Over the next year or so, Harriot was to record over 450 solar observations and make some 200 separate observations of the spotted sun, covering 73 foolscap pages in his surviving manuscripts. He watched spots appear, change shape, break up and disappear, and just like Galileo would do, concluded not only that the spots were physically on the sun's surface, but that the sun had an axial rotation. Modern mathematical astronomers have calculated that a solar rotation of 27.154 days can be derived from Harriot's values, which is remarkably close to our modern value of 27. 2753 days.

Scattered throughout his manuscripts, some of which were published for the first time in 1832, modern scholars, such as the late Professor John D. North,[9] have identified no less than six telescopes owned by Harriot, with magnifications extending between ×6 and ×50. Many of these were probably made by Christopher Tooke, with whom he sometimes co-observed. We should also remember that Christopher Tooke was the first known Englishman to actually make telescopes, the founder of what would become a British great optical tradition.

DEATH BY TOBACCO?

Although as a young man Harriot had written the Lord's Prayer in the Algonkian language, in later life his name was often associated with religious scepticism, as were those of Ralegh, Northumberland, and other "exotic" Elizabethans and Jacobeans. Such religious sceptics asked questions about how God could have created everything from nothing, or where the women came from who married the sons of Adam and Eve yet are not mentioned in Genesis. If one were interested in classical Greek atomic ideas, as Harriot was, then the question arose of whether a Supreme Being guided every single atom, or whether everything was down to blind chance.

No matter what Harriot might actually have believed about some of these subjects in middle life, several documentary glimpses that we have incline to the view that he returned to some sort of traditional Christian belief in the last decade of his life. These hints derive from statements made to the eminent Swiss Protestant physician, Sir Theodore Mayerne, the king's doctor, whom Harriot consulted about a growth which appeared in his nose around 1612, and which was probably a major contributory factor to his death in 1621.

Mayerne seems to have quizzed Harriot about his beliefs prior to treating him, for the devout royal doctor, one of the most astute clinicians in Europe, was initially cautious about treating a man with a reputation for being a sceptic. Mayerne seems, however, to have been fully satisfied when Harriot assured him in 1615 that he believed in "one all-powerful God", and not only took him on as a patient, but even seems to have become something of a friend.

As a young man, probably in Virginia, Harriot, like his friend Ralegh and a good few others, had become fond of "drinking" tobacco smoke, as they then called smoking. Elizabethan doctors even hailed it as a new wonder drug, the dry smoke being seen as countering dangerous moist humours in the body. However, it is likely that thirty years of heavy puffing of strong tobacco in his clay pipe (for various sources mention Harriot's love of the weed), and possible exhaling down his nose, may have had something to do with the appearance of the *noli me tangere* ("touch me not") type of tumour in his nose. Mayerne, for all his learning, could provide Harriot with little more than what we would now call palliative care, for surgery was out of the question. What is surprising, perhaps, is the number of years that Harriot survived after the growth's original appearance. Possibly it was a pre-cancerous growth that became malignant and metastased through his lymph system, as unchecked cancers tend to do.[10]

Thomas Harriot, the first telescopic astronomer, pioneer ethnologist, Copernican, Keplerian, admirer of Galileo, who first sent telescopes to Wales, sometime sceptic, yet probably returning to the Christian fold in his fifties, died in London on 2 July 1621. He received full Christian burial inside the local parish church of St Christopher-le-Stocks, in the very heart of the City. The church burned down in the Great Fire of 1666, and while Sir Christopher

Wren built another on the site, that in turn was demolished in 1781, to make way for further extension to the adjacent Bank of England. Luckily, however, a copy of the inscription on Harriot's gravestone survived, and in the early 1970s a new plaque carrying that inscription was unveiled inside the bank. It is ironic that Thomas Harriot, who had always had a way with money and who died a relatively rich man, may well still lie somewhere below the nation's bullion reserves.

CHAPTER 20

Sir Francis Bacon: The
Experimental Lord Chancellor

*I*t is impossible to appreciate the broader impact of the Astronomical Renaissance without seeing it within the wider context of the Scientific Renaissance taking place in Europe between 1500 and 1700. One seemingly unlikely man was destined to have an impact upon that movement which was so profound that modern experimental science still lives with his legacy today. This was the lawyer Sir Francis Bacon, later ennobled as Viscount Verulam of St Albans, and Lord Chancellor of England. Unlike most of the other figures we have encountered so far, Bacon had received no scientific or mathematical training beyond what he may have picked up as a Cambridge undergraduate in the 1570s. His training, like the greater part of his subsequent professional life, had been in English Common Law, diplomacy, and statecraft. How, therefore, did he come to play such a decisive role in science – a role that helped to frame the policy of the Royal Society after 1660, won him applause across Continental Europe in the eighteenth century, and led to his being styled the father of inductive experimental science and the founder of the "Baconian Method", no less? Let us begin by reviewing the formative influences acting upon him.

Francis Bacon, younger son of Sir Nicholas Bacon, was born on 22 January 1561, at York House on the Strand, London. As Keeper of the Great Seal of England, his father was a significant public figure who, like his wife Anne, placed great emphasis on education. Not only was the lawyer Sir Nicholas highly educated, but so was Lady Anne, who came – like the young Queen Elizabeth herself –

from a tradition of well-educated elite Tudor gentlewomen. The staunchly Protestant Bacons not only knew their classical tongues, literature, and history, but also their Reformation theology and the way in which that theology moulded King Henry VIII's and King Edward VI's new polity of England.

All of these concerns were passed on to their son Francis, as well as to his older siblings, and would stay with him to the end of his days. With residences in St Albans and in London, the Bacons were well off. Young Francis was initially educated at home by private tutors, usually young clergymen of Puritan inclination, before being sent to follow his older brothers to Trinity College, Cambridge, when he was a mere twelve years old. This was not because he was reckoned any more of a prodigy than most other young undergraduates, however, for it was common for bright youths to go up to Oxford or Cambridge in their early teens. The Master of Trinity, the future Archbishop of Canterbury, agreed to be young "Frank's" tutor. Here he would have studied the "Seven Liberal Sciences" of antiquity: the "Trivium", comprising the three linguistic "sciences" of Grammar, Rhetoric, and Logic, and then the "Quadrivium", or the four sciences of mathematical proportion – Astronomy, Geometry, Arithmetic, and Music.

After Cambridge, he went to France for a couple of years, to work on the staff of the British ambassador, and to learn the languages and customs of the states of Europe; then he came to Gray's Inn, in the Temple, London's legal quarter, just west of the City on the north bank of the Thames. Here he became a barrister and law lecturer. Bacon practised at the Bar, sat in Parliament, and served on various commissions during Queen Elizabeth's reign, but never secured a government job – at least, not until the queen died in 1603, and her successor King James I ascended the throne. Then, under James, Bacon came to hold several high legal appointments, before becoming Lord Chancellor, and the nation's senior judge, in 1618. So where, one may ask, did Bacon's career as a great inspirer of science come from?

English Common Law and Experimentation

It came from a direction which had also helped to frame Galileo's mindset, and which had been a theme running through the age: a growing disillusionment, or exasperation, with the philosophy of Aristotle. More specifically, it was with Aristotle's natural, or scientific, philosophy, where the great Greek had set about devising explanations for natural phenomena, such as how the earth and heavens and the forces of nature acted upon each other. To Bacon's pragmatic way of thinking, the trouble with Aristotle's "natural philosophy" was that it was static. It answered its own questions, within its own terms of logical reference, and could never break out to explore pastures new. In Aristotle's system, a piece of observed natural phenomena became an axiom, and hence formed the basis of a logical deduction. The logical fruits of these deductions could themselves form the theses, or foundation points, for further deductions, and on ad infinitum, making it possible for the logical philosopher to build up chains of deductions from a very limited number of observed axioms. *Scientia*, and our knowledge of the natural world, could all too easily be lost in a stratosphere of logically connected speculations that were ultimately self-referential, and which were not susceptible to external challenge. While these speculations – about the heavens, heat, cold, light, weight, magnetism, or mechanical force (energy) – could provide elegant castles in the air, they taught us nothing about nature itself, nor could they guide us in the business of advancing, or progressing beyond our present knowledge.

Even as a very young man, however, Bacon was interested in ideas that were capable of moving forward to form new ideas in response to new pieces of evidence. To such a frame of mind – as Bacon's contemporary Galileo was discovering – the Aristotelian system could be exasperating. As we saw in earlier chapters, that discontent with Aristotle's system could spring from different sources. In Galileo's case, perhaps, it came from a love of applied mathematics and a delight in challenging set ideas. For Kepler, it came from a mathematical divine mysticism; and for Thomas Harriot, from geographical and other discoveries undreamt of by the ancients. In Bacon's case, it drew its power from the English Common Law.

Coming as he did from a legal and courtly family, and as a result of his experiences at Gray's Inn and as a working courtroom barrister and an M.P., Bacon was deeply aware of the openness to challenge and constant organic development of English law. English lawyers and judges did *not* come to their decisions after referring to a set of *a priori* rules laid down in advance, but through a deeply pragmatic, constantly evolving case-law system. Precedent, responding to new evidence, and mastering a vast, sprawling corpus of case histories, each based upon judicial decisions taken about *individual* cases, was the stuff of a law student's studies, and a working barrister's practice. No two cases were the same, and every case, in whatever branch of law it might be – property, land, ecclesiastical, inheritance, and so on – contained subtly different factors that had to be weighed in when coming to a decision. Each new case would then be put on record as a guide to deciding future cases.

The "High Court of Parliament", in which Bacon sat as an M.P. representing several constituencies over the decades, worked exactly along the same lines: debates, challenges, arguments, pushing and pulling with government ministers and even the Queen herself, as Right Honourable Members argued for their constituents' interests against what the government might want. By ancient custom going back centuries even by Bacon's time, the government could not tax the English people unless Parliament agreed to it. Just like today, Parliament was individualistic, often rowdy, independent-minded, and hard to control.

Both courtroom law, before a jury, and Parliamentary procedure could be tricky for control freaks to deal with, for both had a habit of going their own way. The law, in all of its doings, was deeply pragmatic and empirical, and dominated by evidence and the fruits of changing circumstance – a world removed from the tidy-minded axioms of Aristotelian natural philosophy. It was through the seeming hurly-burly of the *Lex Communalis*, or Common Law, that the English thought of themselves as a *free* people, unlike the peoples of Continental European countries, where very different legal systems operated: a point hammered home by Bacon in his various statements on constitutional matters. The Common Law existed for a purpose: to secure justice and the freedom of the English people in a world of constantly changing circumstances – and adaptability was the key to its success.

Learning the law involved building up a fluent and responsive mastery of hundreds of key facts in many hundreds of cases and statutes already on record by 1580. This was, after all, the foundation of the very empirical nature of the English legal system. New cases *tested* existing law, and in the deeply adversarial context of the *Lex Communalis*, when the courtroom barrister on each side based their arguments upon the recorded precedents of earlier cases, it could be highly *experimental*. No one could be sure in advance which legal counsel would cite the decisive precedent or argument which would tip the verdict one way or the other. Memory, fluency, speed of thought, and even courtroom theatre all played their part, for the successful advocate was a skilled operator who knew how to use his materials to the best advantage.

The more one looks at how the English legal system worked, the more one recognizes within it those intellectual traits and habits which Francis Bacon wanted to see practised in natural philosophy. Should not the Natural Philosopher be guided by broad principles drawn from observed physical facts, just as the lawyer found his guidance in case precedents? Should he not be skilful in the manipulation of his evidence in specific cases to expose the truths of nature, in the same way that a cross-examining barrister got the truth out of a sidestepping witness on the stand? And should not the Natural Philosopher – be he an astronomer, chemist, physicist, or physiologist – go to his materials with a wider good in view: to advance natural truth and the felicity of the human condition, in the same way that a public-spirited lawyer aspired to advance moral and constitutional truths? Very conspicuously, I believe, it was through the experimental character of adversarial law that Bacon saw his experimental scientific method beginning to emerge.

CROSS-EXAMINATION AND REVEALING HIDDEN
KNOWLEDGE

The very business of cross-examination as a way of exposing concealed truths played a large part in Bacon's thinking. The highly Protestant Bacon lived in an age of brutal Roman Catholic recusant hunts, as well as attempts to murder the sovereign; and with Guy Fawkes in 1605, a plot was "hatched" to blow up not only King James I, but the whole of Parliament and the judiciary as well in one vast explosion. As a high-placed counsel, Bacon would have been fully familiar with the techniques of cross-examination which the state permitted to be used against traitors (but not in non-treacherous cases): torture within the Tower of London. It was not for nothing that Bacon spoke of the Natural Philosopher putting "Nature to the Torture" in scientific research. Was not Nature a reluctant witness whose deepest secrets had remained well concealed since time immemorial, and which must now be extracted in the torture-chamber of the laboratory? In the same way that the extracted secrets of a state traitor might be used to protect the security and continuing prosperity of the English state, so could not the new truths extracted in scientific research be used to improve the human condition?

This all became part of that vision of the power of science, pursued jointly for "the Glory of God" and for the "Relief of Man's Estate" – *pure* and *applied* science, no less – which Bacon was to style the *Instauratio Magna*: the "Great Revival", or new beginning. This was a vision and an imaginative enterprise that would inspire and energize Bacon's disciples in the Scientific Renaissance and beyond, to fundamentally re-invent classical *scientia*, or organized learning, and to give birth to *science* as we now know it – *science* as a discipline that aimed at precision, extracting new facts from the heavens and the earth, and making them universally known. It would also form a harmonious marriage with *technē*, or skilled mechanical technique, to hopefully improve the human condition. Very significantly, this came to be seen as a profoundly *Christian* enterprise, and in many ways a Protestant one: related to the wider and hopefully universal redemption that began with the Reformation.

THE MAKING OF A NATURAL PHILOSOPHER

We saw above how Francis Bacon's unease with Aristotelian natural philosophy probably began when he was a very young Cambridge undergraduate. However, in many respects, his vision was brought to intellectual maturity in those hiatuses in his professional legal career occasioned by failure and disappointment. In spite of his acknowledged brilliance, and excellent social connections, Bacon's professional career as he envisaged it did not take off until he was at a stage of life which, in seventeenth-century terms, was considered as bordering on the elderly.

Why Bacon failed for so long to obtain his sought-after lucrative government legal appointment is still a bit of a puzzle to historians. Yes, he was said to be rather cold and haughty in his bearing – but so were many other government lawyers. And yes, as an M.P. he had spoken out in Parliament against a large taxpayers' subsidy to the queen in 1593, which had angered Her Majesty; while evidence from contemporaries such as Simonds D'Ewes suggests that Bacon was homosexual or bisexual. Perhaps it was a combination of all these, but not until after Queen Elizabeth died in 1603 and was succeeded by King James I did his career begin to take off.

The years from 1580 to 1604 (made King's Council) and 1607 (appointed Solicitor General) or so may have been frustratingly unproductive professionally – in spite of his acknowledged brilliance as both a courtroom barrister and a Parliamentary orator – yet the enforced leisure which they gave him enabled Francis Bacon to think deep and long and hard about matters in science, natural philosophy, literature, and the wider world of ideas. He was becoming a natural philosophical, scientific, and literary lawyer.

Although one can trace the emergence of Bacon's ideas from surviving letters and notes from the 1580s onwards, it was in 1597 that he first mounted the stage of published philosophical and literary men, with the first edition of his famous *Essays*. The slim volume of ten essays would grow over the years to encapsulate his wit, wisdom, and insight on a range of topics, including such titles as "Of Gardens", "Of Atheisme", "Of Friendship", and "Of Marriage and Single Life", eventually reaching a total of fifty-eight essays in the edition of 1625. The *Essays* would act as a forerunner for the major natural philosophical works to come, announcing to the world that, in addition to his legal brilliance, Mr Bacon – for he was not knighted until 1603 and ennobled until 1618 – was a Renaissance thinker of the very highest order.

It would be over the decade 1603–13 that Bacon's ideas about the natural world and how we should study, understand, and utilize it, took shape. These years saw the publication of the first, shorter, English-language version of his monumentally influential *The Advancement of Learning* (1605), subsequently expanded in the Latin translation, *De Augmentis Scientiarum* (1623), and the outlining of his later scientific treatises.

But then that long-awaited professional success and recognition intervened. King James I started to take increasing interest in the forty-odd-year-old lawyer, and whatever Queen Elizabeth's prejudices against Bacon may have been, the new king did not appear to share them. James, as a Renaissance monarch, prided himself on his love of learning and scholarship no less than Elizabeth had done, though it is true that King James's scholarly tastes were decidedly more traditional and more reverential towards ancient wisdom than those of Francis Bacon. His Majesty did not find Bacon's ideas easy to comprehend, and on one occasion, King James likened Bacon's philosophy to the peace of God, in so far as it "passeth all understanding".

BACON THE LAWYER

Under King James, Bacon's long-languishing public legal career truly took off. For one thing, he had won some initial attention from the king in his constitutional legal observations concerning the uniting of the English and Scottish kingdoms after 1603: the birth of "Great [or Greater] Britain", and the "United Kingdom", as England's long-standing sovereignty claims upon Wales and Ireland were now extended to Scotland, as both sovereign lands now shared the same king. Bacon's sage legal advice on points of constitutional law in particular was admired by the king, his natural philosophy apart, and he was to serve on several important commissions. Then, in 1607, as we saw above, Bacon at last became a high-powered government lawyer upon receiving the office of Solicitor General. Luckily, the office seems to have been something of a well-paid sinecure in which underlings executed the routine business of this important government department, leaving Bacon ample time to pursue his literary and philosophical interests.

On he continued to rise, one high office succeeding another: Attorney General, Privy Councillor, judge, and finally, in 1618, Lord Chancellor: Great Britain's most senior judge. As Lord Chancellor, ennobled as Viscount St Albans and known also as Lord Verulam (from Verulamium, the original Roman settlement at St Albans), Bacon presided in the House of Lords, sat in judgment upon the most important legal cases, tendered personal and constitutional advice to King James – and made a lot of enemies.

He had been in office as Lord Chancellor for less than four years when his arch-enemies, Sir Edward Coke and Sir Lionel Cranfield, instigated impeachment proceedings against him. Bacon and Coke had crossed swords on a number of constitutional matters, most notably on the extent of the Royal Prerogative, and its subjection or otherwise to the Common Law; but what Bacon's enemies finally nailed him with, in 1620–21, was a technical charge of corruption. It concerned the granting of lucrative government patents, or privileges, to favoured persons, and in one case in particular, it was shown beyond all doubt that the Lord Chancellor had received what was politely styled a *present*, or more bluntly, a *bribe*, from a City of London livery company.

The giving of gifts by litigants to learned counsel was common practice in the early seventeenth century, and while fully acknowledging the present, Bacon emphasized that it in no way affected his judgment. It was, rather, a mark of respect to a learned lawyer, and this was almost certainly true, for Bacon's integrity was well known. On the other hand, the receipt of the gift was technically a criminal act, and Bacon's enemies, scenting blood, were unwilling to give any quarter. He was subjected to formal impeachment, sacked in disgrace from the Lord Chancellorship, arrested, imprisoned in the Tower, and fined a staggering £40,000: a sum which Bacon did not remotely possess. Most significantly, he was permanently banned from judicial and public life.

Mercifully, King James remitted the imprisonment and the £40,000 fine, but the disgrace he could not alleviate. Bacon's enemies had won, for professionally and publicly speaking Lord Verulam was a ruined man. However, even in this final humiliation, he returned his attention to that natural philosophy and the advancement of learning that would immortalize him.

BACON'S SCIENTIFIC IDEAS

The elements of English common legal thinking examined above can be traced in Bacon's natural philosophical writings. Those elements include the primary importance of a careful taxonomy and classification of natural phenomena, with lists, categories, and sub-categories, in pretty much the same way as a law student would have organized the salient details of hundreds of legal precedent cases and laid them all out neatly for cross-reference. Bacon was now engaged in the forensic analysis of natural phenomena, which, just like courtroom cross-examination, or even torture, was intended to get to the bottom of a given puzzle, and reveal the truth.

This process should be accumulative or progressive, as one revealed natural truth led to another, to advance the sum total of knowledge, forever onwards to new realms of understanding, insight, and usefulness. In just such a way the often brutal cross-examination of captured individual traitors led to the rounding-up and examination of yet more plotters, until the whole complex structure of a constitutional crime had been exposed, enabling efficient counter-measures to be taken. (This is just what happened following Guy Fawkes's arrest on 5 November 1605.)

As good law and government aspired to render the human condition more just and more felicitous, so the careful application of natural philosophy to the human condition should "relieve Man's estate", and make life better. Medicine, agriculture, and navigation for the "augmentation" of trade and social wealth in particular were earmarked as areas amenable to natural philosophical progress. Of primary importance was the acquisition of *wisdom*, with all its Judaeo-Christian resonances extending back to Solomon, Job, Ecclesiastes, and the Apocryphal books in the Old Testament. Bacon knew his

Bible well, and was acutely aware of the hand of God running through history. His dynamic vision of the interconnectedness of Providence, progress, and natural inquiry was fundamentally different from the essentially static natural philosophy of Aristotle.

These ideas were clearly beginning to form in Bacon's mind by the early 1590s, as is evidenced by various early surviving statements. He makes it clear that he has no time either for the scholastic philosophies, or for the "alchemists" or followers of Paracelsus, and their endless fruitless attempts to re-make matter in the laboratory. Both drew upon Aristotle: either his philosophical procedures or his four-element model of substance. As early as 1592, Bacon was associating natural philosophical, or scientific, knowledge with *power*: or the ability to bring about change.

In his recorded contribution to the Gray's Inn Christmas celebrations of 1594, Bacon defended "philosophy" – not Aristotle's, but rather associating "philosophy" with the conquest of nature in a distinctly empirical, investigative, and utilitarian fashion, mentioning especially the importance of a library, a garden (for botanical research), a "goodly huge cabinet" or museum of scientific specimens, and a well-equipped research laboratory. What his fellow Benchers at Gray's Inn thought about this vision is uncertain, though it has a remarkable similarity to the fictional research institution "Salomon's House", on the island of Bensalem – with all its linguistic allusions to Old Testament Wisdom, in Solomon and Salem – that he would describe in his great posthumously published work of fiction *The New Atlantis* (1627): the book that would inspire the founding of the Royal Society in 1660.

It was in the original, English-language edition of his *The Advancement of Learning* that Bacon announced his natural philosophical agenda to the wider world of learning, and commenced his *Instauratio Magna* or "Great Revival". In its two sections Bacon set out the need to re-establish knowledge on new and reformed principles, as well as reviewing the current state of modern learning. Written very much within the literary and intellectual conventions of Renaissance Christian humanism, it addresses the perceived weaknesses of contemporary scholarship.

It focuses upon what might be called its circularity, its deference to assumed classical omniscience, its use of words and language as a way of answering questions rather than looking at the world afresh and searching out new facts, and its failure to challenge conventional assumptions. Just like the apostate Israelites, who deserted the worship of Jehovah to bow down before the golden calves of their Canaanite neighbours, so we also bow down to intellectual "idols" instead of pursuing truth.

In the *Advancement*, Bacon specifies four such "idols" which lead us astray: the idols of the Tribe, the Palace (or Market Place), the Cave, and the Theatre. Broadly speaking, these idols are about accepting as true what all men conventionally believe and are told, while the idol of the Cave harks back to Plato's analogy of the cave in his *Republic* (Book VII). If a race of people were born and bred in a cave, would they not assume that the flickering shadows cast by the firelight were reality, in much the same way that we do with Aristotelian explanation? What a shock the cave-dwellers would have if they dared to emerge into broad daylight.

SCIENCE AND RELIGION

It was during the dozen or so years after 1600 that the *Instauratio Magna* began to take shape in Bacon's mind, and many of its emerging details can be traced in Bacon's correspondence with his close friend Tobias (Tobie) Matthew.[1] Matthew, son of the Archbishop of York, had converted to Roman Catholicism and was obliged to live abroad, spending much time in Italy, from where he was fortunately able to pass on information about Galileo, the early telescopic discoveries, and the debates about Copernicanism to his lawyer friend in London.

In his exchange of ideas with Matthew, the very Protestant Bacon – whose friendship with his now exiled Catholic convert friend nonetheless continued as normal – had much to say about religion and scientific inquiry. It may seem strange at first sight, however, to find Bacon saying that science and religion should be kept apart. Surely, how can one "glorify God" through scientific discovery if the two must be kept separate? What Bacon is talking about here is not whether one should attempt to find Christian inspiration in the creation, so much as the dangers of dogmatic bickering. Not only were England and Europe still in the throes of Reformation and Counter-Reformation disputes, and providentially averted invasions and terrorist acts, but Protestants (like Catholics), also bickered amongst themselves. Should, for example, the church be governed by bishops or elders; should worship settings, such as the Prayer Book, be imposed on *all* English and Scottish Protestants; should Roman Catholic techniques of biblical interpretation be used by Protestants; and how far should one use the Bible as a guide to interpreting natural phenomena?

These matters – along with a good few more besides – were already making fur and feathers fly in Rome, Amsterdam, London, and elsewhere, and were setting Christian against Christian. To Bacon's thinking, therefore, one should not allow the *Instauratio Magna* to be derailed by permitting it to become the victim of *sectarian* bickering – a crucial point, and one which in the decades and centuries ahead would enable Jesuit scientists to communicate amicably with Anglicans, Presbyterians with Jews, and atheists with everybody.

BACON'S "GREAT REVIVAL" AND HIS "NEW METHOD"

It is one of the ironies of history that Francis Bacon's intellectual masterpiece, and one of the formative books of Western scientific thought, should have appeared before the world at a time when its author's professional and personal life had crashed into the pit of impeachment and total humiliation. But that is what happened with the *Novum Organum*, or "New Method" (1620), which was intended to be a keystone in his "Great Instauration" or "Great Revival" of learning movement.

It was written in Latin, and strategically aimed at the international world of learning – as was the second, and much amplified, edition of his *Advancement*, or *De Augmentis Scientiarum*. In *Novum Organum* Bacon brings together the themes that had been maturing in his mind for thirty-odd years, to establish a coherent method by which natural philosophy could be advanced and transformed. Complementing the *Organum* in many respects was his posthumously published *Sylva Sylvarum* (1627) to which we will return below. (*Sylva Sylvarum* is an allegorical title; its literal Latin meaning is "Wood of Woods" or, figuratively, "Abundance of Abundances", teeming as it does with hundreds of questions about nature.)

Fundamental to that method was its forensic, accumulative, and *active* nature, which stood in distinct contrast to the *contemplative*, *passive* philosophy of Aristotle. This was the method of *induction*, which had its intellectual origins in the Common Law procedures of cross-examination. How, then, did the logic of induction differ from that of the Aristotelian method of *deduction*?

In Aristotelian *deduction*, logic was used to establish axioms or premises of universal truth. Why, for example, when I drop a brick, does it fall to earth? Answer: because bricks are "heavy", being made of "earthy" material. Bricks (or other weighty objects) fall because they possess a *gravitas*, or weight, which draws them to "mother earth". One proceeds from the observation of a particular, such as a falling brick, to deduce from it characteristics that must be shared with all heavy objects, to form a general axiom about weight. Where can Aristotelian logic take you beyond that, apart from observing similar characteristics in everything that falls? Deduction provides a complete answer, and even absorbs further questions, such as what is the nature of acceleration and inertia, and why pendulums swing.

Baconian *induction*, however, demands a much more radical, inquisitorial, and ongoing approach. Induction demands that first of all you set about collecting as many precise facts relating to the phenomenon under study as you can, in a way similar to that used by a treason lawyer when forming a precise understanding of a state crime. If, for example, you want to investigate weight, and why bricks fall, you must study the exact fall patterns of many objects. Then you go beyond that, to observe the motions of swinging, inertial, and resistance-impeded objects, such as pendulums, or the paths described by flying cannon balls. And then, perhaps, you investigate such things (as Bacon mentions in *Sylva Sylvarum* Book VIII, item 704) as what is *attraction*, and does *gravity* work between different kinds of things or is like attracted to like, such as gold to gold, or lead to lead? Then you might even ask, as Robert Hooke and Sir Isaac Newton would come to do, why the moon does not fall down upon the earth, but instead goes around it in an elliptical orbit.

In the inductive method, you never end up with a "pat" or closed answer. Instead, you try to draw your wider conclusions from the behaviour of a host of seemingly disparate phenomena. When combined with mathematical analysis (of which, one must admit, Bacon had no real comprehension), the inductive method could lead you step by demonstrated step from a falling brick to the Laws of Universal Gravitation – across the solar system, and beyond. It was a style of thinking about nature – and applied science-based technology – the implications of which Bacon could not have imagined in his day: from why a brick falls, to the science of physical dynamics that produced the pendulum clock by the 1660s, to gravitation theory by 1687, and, in the twentieth century, the application of gravitation theory to the 1977 launch of the Voyager II spacecraft which flew past and photographed the planets of the outer solar system – in accordance with exactly the same laws of gravitation that make the brick fall.

The *Novum Organum,* (like *Sylva Sylvarum*) also emphasizes the importance of physical, factual, *experimental* evidence for the foundation of a new philosophy. Nature had to be tested and the test results used to form the basis for an inductive approach, for Bacon's "philosophy" had no place for abstract speculation. Once again, one is struck by the forensic legal parallel.

In the six parts of the *Novum Organum*, Bacon set out an agenda for "natural philosophy" which was to have many resonances with how "science", as we now call it, would subsequently develop. There were, in addition to induction and experimentation, discussions of a progressive and accumulative approach to natural knowledge: the sciences would have to be studied individually, with a concern for practical application, to form what we now call a "science-based technology". Bacon had long been struck by how inventions had transformed the human condition, in particular the magnetic compass, the printing press, and gunpowder.

Those "Ten Centuries" of things to investigate outlined in the *Sylva Sylvarum* would come to inspire later generations: key problems or potential breakthroughs in knowledge that demanded systematic experimental investigation, rounded up in convenient hundreds. These included that old favourite, the nature of heaviness (gravitas) and lightness (levity); the nature of heat and cold, magnetism, light, and colours; the basis of chemical action; medical recipes – and a lot more besides. Bacon, with his fascination with useful things, recommended writing down in public "registers" the operational bases of all useful trades and crafts, and declared war on "secret" or obscurantist knowledge. This was one reason why he disliked the alchemists.

His vision for universally accessible knowledge, in all its branches, from the courses of the tides to the "art and mystery" of the blacksmith's trade, was truly astonishing. While he got much wrong, and was even ignorant of many branches of contemporary science – such as mathematical physics and astronomy – he acted as natural philosophy's "bell-ringer", who gave the signal for all the other "wits" to come together and take part in the great venture of the new philosophy. Englishmen, Frenchmen, Italians; Protestants, Catholics; carpenters, learned physicians, churchmen, scientific instrument makers, and lawyers – all had their *co-operative* parts to play in realizing natural science's Great Revival.

The *Novum Organum* and *Sylva Sylvarum* did not merely discuss experiments as generalities, but also reported many that had actually been tried, including some by Bacon himself. Experiments on magnetism, heat and cold, light, chemical action, and heaviness had all been tried over the years by Mr Lord Chancellor Bacon, Lord Verulam, personally: the lawyer in the laboratory.

Following its publication, copies of *Novum Organum* were sent to scholars across Europe, and we know for certain that one was despatched to Kepler. Some, like King James, were rather puzzled by it, and it would take some years before the radical impact of its message began to fundamentally change European natural philosophical thinking. This was starting to happen by the 1640s, especially in the north German Palatinate and elsewhere.

It may seem ironic that a man who was in no way mathematically inclined, although fully respecting the significance of Copernicanism, Kepler, Galileo, and the telescope, should have come to play such a leading role in bringing about the wider Scientific Renaissance. But he did, and over the following centuries the "Baconian experimental method" would inspire a remarkable diversity of scientists worldwide in pretty well every field of science where experiment, instrumentation, and practical technological application were fundamental. Without Bacon, the "Astronomical Renaissance" would have lacked a major dimension.

BACON'S DEATH

Bacon had clearly desired some sort of natural philosophical research academy to be created in England, and while his personal resources were inadequate to endow such an enterprise, he had hoped that chairs might be created in Cambridge and Oxford Universities. Though his health had begun to decline, his death seems to have been relatively sudden when it came, at the house of Lord Arundel at Highgate, London, on 26 April 1626. The unseasonably cold spring may have played a part, although the later seventeenth-century biographical writer John Aubrey claimed that Bacon's final illness was brought on by performing an experiment to see if snow could be used to preserve the meat of a chicken.[2]

I have always felt that the life of Francis Bacon had the quality of a Shakespearian tragedy: a high-status, precocious child, whose adult career was nonetheless frustrated for nearly thirty years, before he rapidly ascended to dazzling heights, only to crash in ignominy; an ill-starred visionary philosopher, whose ideas were destined to change the world, yet who died – if Aubrey's story is to be believed – as a result of performing a refrigeration experiment with a dead chicken. Shakespeare pre-deceased Bacon by a decade; otherwise I could well have imagined a play entitled *The Tragicall Historie of My Lord Verulam of St Albans*.

The Lancashire "Puritans" and the Catholic Squires: Catholic and Protestant Scientific Friendships in Northern England

*A*ll the astronomical and scientific innovation that we have encountered so far in the Astronomical Renaissance took place in an urban setting: cathedral cities, great universities, royal courts, and prosperous merchant cities such as Venice, Florence, and London.

Yet something fascinating and unpredictable took place in a corridor of land across north-west England between 1635 and 1644 – a corridor bounded by Liverpool in the west and Leeds in the east; between Burnley in the north and Salford and Manchester 30 miles to the south. In this region of what in that pre-industrial age was predominantly moorland, marshland, the Pennines, and some narrow swathes of good farmland, astronomical research was being undertaken by a group of young men which, plainly, advanced the "new astronomy" from where Copernicus, Tycho Brahe, Galileo, and Kepler, had left off.

It may seem incredible that a group of Protestant and Roman Catholic friends and correspondents, only one of whom was known to have taken a complete university course, and none of whom ever held any kind of academic position, should achieve what they did. But of that achievement there is no doubt, for the meticulous documents which they left behind and which were later published by the Royal Society give us the plain facts.

Within their surviving papers is an abundance of telescopic astronomy. There is also a wrestling with, testing, and demonstration of Keplerian elliptical orbits; an original application of Keplerian theory to explain the shape of the lunar orbit; insights into early gravitational attraction; and observations and discussions about sunspots and the sun's rotation. Running through the letters, notes, and observations of these men is both a detailed critical familiarity with, and a declared admiration for, the works of Copernicus, Tycho, Galileo, and especially Kepler.

On 24 November 1639, two of these men, Jeremiah Horrocks and William Crabtree, would cautiously predict, and successfully observe, the first ever recorded "transit" of Venus, or passage of the planet across the disc of the sun. Horrocks's account of this observation, and the profound conclusions for the future of planetary orbital theory which he drew, would first circulate in manuscript, and then be sumptuously published in Dantzig, Poland, two decades after his sudden death in 1641.

By the 1670s, these men, most of them long dead, would be familiar names in the Royal Society, in Dantzig, Leiden, Paris, and other centres of astronomical innovation. The first Astronomer Royal and Director of the Royal Observatory, Greenwich, the Revd John Flamsteed, would speak of them not only as the founding fathers of British astronomy, but as the true heirs of the Continental giants.

WILLIAM CRABTREE OF SALFORD AND HIS FRIENDS

Modest is how these men's circumstances might best be described: comfortable, but by no means wealthy. They were a mixture of pre-industrial local merchants, yeoman farmers, and county gentry. They were hard-up county gentry, however; the declared Catholicism of one family, the Towneleys of Burnley, had led to their losing much of their ancestral wealth in "recusancy fines". Another family, the Gascoignes, of Thorp-on-the-Hill, Middleton, near Leeds, were ancient Yorkshire Catholics, whose exact position by 1640 is somewhat uncertain. Both of these once-prominent county families, on opposite sides of the Pennines, were now adopting a policy of keeping a low public profile, in the years leading up to the outbreak of civil war between king and Parliament in 1642. The Towneleys had certainly suffered because of loyalty to their ancestral Catholic faith, though whether the Gascoignes had suffered, or had legally conformed and become "Church Papists" – willing to attend their Anglican parish church services occasionally as the price for being left alone by the authorities – is not clear.

It has been suggested that the Towneley and Gascoigne concerns not only with science and astronomy, but also with antiquarian and historical scholarly studies, developed as a "contemplative" occupation for intelligent gentlemen now excluded from the traditional public life of their caste: magistracies, militia commissions, and seats in Parliament.

As a Lancastrian and a Salfordian myself, these "north-country astronomers" have fascinated me since boyhood. The sheer incongruity of their circumstances, their independence from the usual lines of patronage, and their seemingly effortless social intermixing intrigued me. Their very existence and co-operation challenged the usual theories of social and religious division which were supposed to prevail in pre- and post-Civil-War England. I am instinctively drawn to documented circumstances where fact challenges theory. But who was William Crabtree and what did he do?

It is largely through Crabtree's surviving letters, subsequently published in the Royal Society's *Philosophical Transactions* and elsewhere,[1] that much of the north-country astronomers' activities take shape. William Crabtree was a textile dealer, or "clothier", of Salford, Lancashire, which even in pre-industrial times was an already ancient borough standing on the north bank of the River Irwell, with Manchester – another small borough – on the south bank. Domestic textile manufacture was a major local trade, often seasonally combined with tenant farming. As a merchant clothier, Crabtree would have bought in yarn, supplied it to his spinners and weavers in their cottages, collected the finished cloth "pieces", and sent them off by trains of packhorses to London for sale.

London, however, gave him vital connections with the wider world, and we know it was from there that he acquired the books, lenses, and other devices of which he spoke in his letters. He was on friendly terms with Dr Samuel Foster, Professor of Astronomy at Gresham College, London, with whom he corresponded, and whom he had no doubt met on business trips to London.

Crabtree was not a university graduate, although he had attended the Manchester School, which in his day – Crabtree was born in 1610 – was a grammar school attached to the then Collegiate Church, later Manchester Cathedral. He must have acquired a good knowledge of Latin, astronomy, mathematics, and geometry, however, judging from the Continental authors whom he cites in his correspondence.

Crabtree was a comfortably off local merchant, and married into the similarly circumstanced Pendleton family. William and Elizabeth's house at Broughton Spout, Salford, is still lived in to this day. The astronomical genius of the north-country group was the young Jeremiah Horrocks, of Toxteth, Liverpool, who probably encountered Crabtree during stopovers with his undergraduate chum Mr Worthington of Manchester, on his way to and from Cambridge University. Their correspondence between 1636 and 1640 would prove pivotal to the further development of the new astronomy.

JEREMIAH HORROCKS: THE BIBLE CLERK OF MUCH HOOLE

Education was remarkably well spread around Tudor and Jacobean England, and the already ancient universities of Oxford and Cambridge (England's only two universities until 1828), true to their medieval ancestry, admitted large numbers of young men from modest backgrounds on scholarships. The popular myth that these universities were for the "toffs" is blown apart by sheer weight of evidence, for Oxbridge's "elitism" only belonged to the nineteenth and early twentieth centuries.

The bright sons of yeomen farmers, urban tradesmen, county professionals and clergy, and even some clever "paupers", formed the rank and file of the student body, as they did of the numerous endowed grammar and boarding schools. Whether you were a medieval bishop or a post-Reformation land speculator, you were fully aware of the need to maintain the supply of bright young men to keep the church and state afloat. Many a judge, bishop, senior civil servant, or even enterprising first-generation nobleman had risen from the farmyard or behind dad's shop counter. For then as now, education opened doors. When writing their wills, these "rags-to-riches" men invariably displayed great generosity towards their old Oxbridge colleges. Their cultural descendants still do.

Jeremiah Horrocks entered Emmanuel College, Cambridge, in 1632, at thirteen or fourteen years of age. Modern research has shown that he was by no means the first Horrocks, or on his mother's side, Aspinwall, to make the long tramp south from Liverpool to Oxford or Cambridge. An academic education was almost a "tradition" for the clever members of these families of farmers, urban craftsmen, and watchmakers – yes, *watchmakers*, for commercial watchmaking was already an established cottage industry around the Liverpool area by the time of Horrocks's youth. His uncle James Aspinwall was a watchmaker, while one of his grandfather Thomas's watches of 1606 is preserved in the Prescott, Liverpool, Museum. So, one might say, astronomy, mechanics, and ingenuity were in the family blood.[2]

What turned the young undergraduate into an astronomer of genius we do not know, but surviving in Trinity College, Cambridge, library is a copy of Philippe van Lansberge's *Tabulae Motuum*, autographed by Horrocks, and including a list of thirty-one books with which he was already acquainted. All of them were in Latin, and all except one by Continental European authors. By 1636, when he probably first met Crabtree in Salford, he was already an accomplished mathematician, the owner of a simple telescope, and an ardent Copernican, Galileian, and Keplerian.

Over the next few years, their letters would fly thick and fast, exploring cutting-edge issues in the astronomy of the day. These letters between the teenager now back home in Toxteth and the Salford cloth merchant displayed a sophistication of thought about astronomy, books, and wider culture that would have done credit to a pair of Court Astronomers in Florence or Prague.

ASTRONOMICAL RESEARCH IN RURAL LANCASHIRE
AND YORKSHIRE

In the 1630s, Lancashire was a remote, thinly populated county, and even its biggest towns, such as Manchester, Liverpool, Bolton, and Preston, would have contained only a few thousand souls apiece. Yorkshire was a bigger and more populous county. Its intellectual energy was well established, and while the north-country astronomers were men of exceptional achievement, a growing body of historical research is revealing that the provincial shires were places of great intellectual vitality. In Chapter 19 we saw evidence of an early astronomical "club" in South Wales in 1610; the profusion of grammar schools and of rural clergy and Oxbridge-educated professionals who wrote books on theology, classical studies, medicine, archaeology, and natural history suggests that a remarkable intellectual vigour co-existed with the cowsheds and maypoles of rural Britain.

Letters were the creative means of exchange, yet we know that the considerable body of surviving correspondence that passed between Crabtree, Horrocks, Gascoigne, and Towneley was only a fraction of the total. We know that some letters were lost in the Civil War, and some in the 1666 Great Fire of London, when the shop of Mr Brooks, who was to publish some for the Royal Society, went up in flames. Enough survived for Horrocks's Emmanuel College contemporary, the Revd Dr John Wallis, now Savilian Professor of Geometry at Oxford, to publish a substantial volume, *Opera Posthuma* ("Posthumous Works"), for the Society in 1672–73, including Horrocks's surviving mathematical essay on the lunar orbit theory. John Flamsteed saw more surviving material, including some of William Gascoigne's instruments, when visiting Towneley Hall in 1672; Flamsteed printed yet more in Volume III of his *Historia Coelestis Britannica* ("The British Account of the Heavens"), 1725, for he saw these men as the founding fathers of "modern" British astronomy. The Revd William Derham F.R.S. published whole and selected sections of further letters of the north-country astronomers that had come to light in the Royal Society's *Philosophical Transactions* in a series of papers between 1711 and 1719. Several more had clearly been found by 1841, when Professor Stephen

Peter Rigaud of Oxford included some Gascoigne pieces in his *Correspondence of Scientific Men of the Seventeenth Century* (1841). One suspects that had all their manuscript writings survived, they would have filled several substantial printed volumes.[3]

Original ideas and brilliant perceptions about the heavens abound. Their sources of inspiration are clear as daylight: Tycho Brahe, who placed astronomy upon a modern observational foundation; Galileo, with his telescope (none seem to have heard of Harriot); and their adored Kepler. Kepler was the man who made the Copernican theory viable, and Kepler's insights into planetary motion, orbit shapes, optics, and the nature of perception secured him their highest esteem. The seemingly erroneous tables of Lansberge, Ismaël Boulliau, and Martinus Hortensius were their *bêtes noires*.

While there is no evidence that Horrocks ever read Bacon, his approach to scientific knowledge was remarkably similar: jettison the tables and accepted guidelines, and address oneself to the heavens and nature, direct. Make new, original observations, determine the error parameters and limitations of your instruments, and apply compensating corrections to your results. Check, and repeat your observations as often as you can, and even (clearly from Kepler's optical writings and those of Edward Wright in particular)[4] determine the perceptual eccentricity of your own eye. Don't be led astray by other people, and even test yourself. Absolutely central to this process was instrumentation. Accurate instruments provided the physical acid test for a theory, for it was through measured natural phenomena, combined with mathematics, that one would uncover the true nature of God's creation: powerful thinking for an eighteen-year-old.

The greater part of the correspondence, 1636–40, centres primarily on Crabtree and Horrocks. But then, sometime in 1640, and probably through the agency of the brothers Charles and Christopher Towneley, they made the acquaintance of William Gascoigne in Yorkshire.

William Gascoigne (1612–44): Yorkshire
County Gentleman, Astronomer, and Inventor

In a letter of 1 August 1671, John Flamsteed would describe Gascoigne as, "as ingenuous [*sic*: i.e. ingenious] a person as the world has bred or known".[5] Praise, indeed, from an astronomer of such international standing as Flamsteed.

We saw above that William, the son of Henry Gascoigne, was descended from an ancient Yorkshire gentry family. We have few sources for his early life, and they are very brief. Perhaps the most reliable comes from a letter written by Gascoigne to the Revd William Oughtred in 1640, in which he says he had attended Oxford – probably in the early 1630s – yet found it "destitute of mathematical learning". This is an odd circumstance, considering the known activity of the Savilian Professors of Astronomy and Geometry. There is no mention, however, of Gascoigne's name in the lists of Oxford alumni, although he may have been an unmatriculated (unregistered) "sojourner", or visiting gentleman without a formal collegiate association, who simply spent some study time in Oxford – a route sometimes followed by Roman Catholics.

Another piece of information comes down to us at second hand, written down many years later. The source is the prolific seventeenth-century biographer and gossip John Aubrey, who got it, probably in conversation, from Sir Jonas Moore. Here, the reference is somewhat tangential, as Moore and Aubrey were discussing Jesuit experiments in flying. It seems that "Father Grenberger [Grienberger] of the Roman college found out a way of Flying" and subsequently taught it to "Mr Gascoigne".[6] Tangential and unsubstantiated as this tale was, neither Moore nor Aubrey clearly saw any incongruity in associating Gascoigne's name with a prominent Jesuit astronomer at the College in Rome. It was not unusual for an English Catholic gentleman to gain part of his education on the Continent, and undertake periods of study at the English College in Rome.

Sir Jonas Moore was in as good a position as anyone to know things about Gascoigne, for he was a Lancashire lad, from near Burnley, who in the 1640s came to know Christopher Towneley.

Born in 1617, young Jonas Moore became a civil engineer, mathematician, and tutor to James, Duke of York, the future King Charles II's younger brother, and in 1685, King James II. As a Royalist dignitary at the Restoration of the monarchy after the Civil Wars, Moore was knighted by King Charles in 1663, and would become John Flamsteed's patron and the driving force behind the founding of the Royal Observatory, Greenwich, in 1675. Moore, very much aware of the achievement of the north-country astronomers, would begin to collect up their surviving papers and anecdotes after their deaths.

In addition to Crabtree's and Gascoigne's own letters, and Moore's remarks, a third source was Sir Edward Sherburne's "A Catalogue of Astronomers, Ancient and Modern", included as an appendix to his translation of the Latin astronomical poem *The Sphere of Marcus Manilius* (1675). Sir Edward was a Roman Catholic gentleman of Stonyhurst Hall, Lancashire (which became Stonyhurst College in 1794), a declared Royalist who fought in the Civil Wars, and was subsequently knighted by King Charles II.

Sherburne displays an interesting mix of traits. He was a Catholic who, like many others, was loyal, and *not* sympathetic to foreign-inspired fanatics like the English convert Guy Fawkes had been. Such Catholics could enjoy civil friendships with Protestants, especially when they shared powerful, non-sectarian interests, such as astronomy and literature. In addition to passing on material about Gascoigne, Sherburne discussed and openly admired the unequivocally Protestant William Crabtree, Jeremiah Horrocks, and others.

THE TOWNELEYS OF TOWNELEY HALL

Sherburne attributes considerable importance to the role played by the staunchly Catholic Towneley family – his gentry neighbours in the Pendle district of north-east Lancashire – in the encouragement of the north-country astronomers. In the 1630s, these included the brothers Charles and Christopher Towneley – both of whom fought on the Royalist side in the Civil Wars. Charles Towneley and William Gascoigne both fell on the same day, 2 July 1644, in the

Battle of Marston Moor, with brother Christopher luckily surviving unharmed, but being taken prisoner by the Parliamentarians. The brothers were men of wide culture, with scientific, literary, and "antiquarian" (historical and archaeological) interests. Christopher would have a major influence upon his orphaned nephew, Richard, who would play a leading role in the encouragement of the arts and sciences in Lancashire and West Yorkshire in the next generation. This would include, for example, the building up of a large private library, museum, and collection of scientific instruments at Towneley Hall for observing the heavens and performing physics experiments, as well as collecting together some of the surviving papers and instruments of Crabtree, Horrocks, and Gascoigne. On 27 April 1661, for example, the 32-year-old Richard Towneley and his friend the Protestant Cambridge-educated Halifax physician, Henry Power, would carry a newly invented barometer to the top of the nearby Pendle Hill, noting that the mercury level in the tube fell a whole inch between the bottom and the top of the hill.

The Towneley brothers appear to have brought Crabtree and Horrocks into contact with William Gascoigne, and that contact had become sufficiently well established by 30 October 1640 not only for Crabtree and Gascoigne to be corresponding in a friendly manner, but for Crabtree to have recently visited him in Yorkshire.[7] Other letters pass on the regards of Mr Horrocks, suggesting a real friendship and mutual regard. This was a friendship not only between an Emmanuel College educated Anglican "Puritan" and a devout Protestant merchant – Horrocks and Crabtree – but also between a possibly Jesuit-educated Yorkshire squire of Catholic ancestry and an ancient Lancashire Catholic family – Gascoigne and the Towneley brothers, not to mention the admiration of a Royalist, Catholic Lancashire knight, Sir Edward Sherburne, who would later publish his own encomium on the Protestant astronomers.

Religious and social caste differences apart, what did these men do that was so outstanding and original?

ASTRONOMICAL RESEARCH AND DISCOVERIES, 1635–41

While Charles Towneley, his son Richard, and his brother Christopher, with Edward Sherburne, were active scholars, observers, and "facilitators" of the new science in the north, it was Jeremiah Horrocks and William Gascoigne who were the original and creative driving forces of the group. The achievements of these men could well have changed much in the science and technology of the age had they not died so tragically young. What they shared, but had come upon wholly independently, was a passion for optics and accurate measurement, which they saw as the key to fathoming the universe.

JEREMIAH HORROCKS: THE ENGLISH KEPLER

Probably since his days in Cambridge, and certainly by 1636, when he first began to correspond with Crabtree, Jeremiah was trying to find a clear way forward in the new astronomy, and was not merely a convinced Copernican, but also a Keplerian. Kepler's elliptical orbits and wider physical (but I suspect not Kepler's metaphysical) theories seemed the way ahead. Horrocks was also becoming frustrated, as we saw above, with Lansberge and the other planetary table compilers, whose inaccuracies had so often led him astray. If the universe were an expression of God's glory, then how could it contain errors?

Though Horrocks gives no evidence of ever having read Bacon, his solution was the same: go to nature direct, not via intermediaries. That meant measuring the celestial angles afresh, as did Tycho. Unlike the Great Dane, the teenage Horrocks lacked financial resources. This circumstance, however, only acted as a further spur to his ingenuity, for Horrocks, like Harriot and Gassendi, constructed an "Astronomical Radius", or cross staff, using two straight wooden rods jointed to form a "T" shape, 3 feet in length.

As you place your eye at the end of the long rod, and look down it, your eye acts as the centre of a circle to which the wooden rod becomes a radius, with the short "T" piece forming a tangent to the same circle. If you then make a pair of brass pointers that can slide along the short "tangent" arm, you can adjust them so that they "enclose" an angle in the sky: such as the angle between a star and a planet.

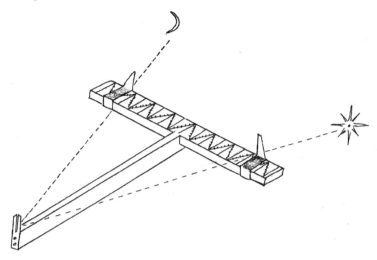

21.1 Jeremiah Horrocks's Astronomical Radius. This worked on similar principles to Gassendi's (Figure 16.2), but was held up to the eye rather like a crossbow, the brass sights "enclosing" a moon–star angle on the graduated "T" bar. (Reconstructed by Allan Chapman.)

Without getting into deep geometrical water, it is possible to convert the brass sight openings on the rod to an exact angle, using a table of trigonometrical tangents. With this instrument Horrocks measured many hundreds of celestial angles, using the tables of Bartholomeo Petiscus to convert the proportions to exact angles. From angles observed with this instrument, Horrocks concluded by 1637 that the moon's orbit around the earth conformed to an ellipse, as defined by Kepler's Laws. This was a momentous physical discovery by any standards, and went a long way towards explaining why the moon's eighteen-plus-year orbital cycle around the earth – the cause of the eclipse cycle – was so fiendishly complicated. Yet no one, except Crabtree, was to hear of it during Horrocks's lifetime.

Tabulated and analysed observations with this "radius" instrument further enabled Horrocks to derive important facts about the solar system. Did Jupiter's and Saturn's slightly variable orbital speeds when together in the same part of the sky mean that they might be exerting a physical effect upon each other (gravitation)? Why were the planets' orbits tilted to each other, yet in the same approximate plane as they rotated around the sun?

Horrocks was further fascinated by the geometrical optical properties of pinholes. For instance, if you knew the exact diameter of a small hole made in a thin piece of metal, you could calculate the diameter which it subtended at a given distance from the eye. Using this principle, he looked at the planets through a pinhole, to try to work out their angular diameters, hoping to relate them to their then understood distances from the sun, in the hope of ranking the planets by physical size in the solar system.

He also observed slight seasonal variations in the apparent solar angular diameter, thereby suggesting that the earth rotated around the sun in a Keplerian ellipse: as did the moon around the earth. This was the genesis of the complex "three bodies problem" – sun, earth, and moon – of Newtonian gravitation, no less. Newton would acknowledge Horrocks in *Principia* in 1687.

Horrocks also owned a modest telescope, for which, he told Crabtree, he had paid a half-crown – or one-eighth of a pound sterling. As with the rods of his "radius" and holes in pieces of metal, Horrocks would use it to reveal wonders.

By watching the dark edge of the moon instantly snuff out the light of dim stars of the Pleiades cluster as it passed across or "occulted" them on 19 March 1637, Horrocks drew the radical conclusion that the stars as seen from earth were but points of light and did *not* subtend tiny discs, as was generally believed.[8] Likewise, no matter how far from the naked eye you might remove the pinhole in a card, the star you are observing through it will *always* remain a point of light, and will *never* fill the pinhole. (Try the experiment for yourself – I have.) Horrocks argued, therefore, that the apparent roundness of bright stars as seen by the naked eye was caused by light scatter within the physiological optics of the eye. He was correct.

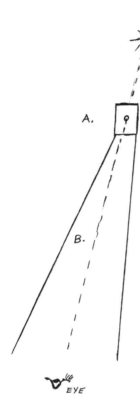

21.2 Horrocks showed that no matter how bright, once stripped of its glare a star remains a mere point of light when viewed through a pinhole in a card or piece of metal foil, suggesting that it is vastly remote. (Reconstructed by Allan Chapman.)

What was to project young Horrocks to posthumous immortality was his correct prediction that on 24 November 1639, Venus would pass across, or "transit", the sun's disc. He came to this conclusion after averaging out calculated values for the planet's exact position, from his own and other astronomers' observations, as it moved between the earth and the sun.

The transit day was a Sunday, and he made the observation from the village of Much Hoole, some 8 miles from Preston, Lancashire, where he was then working, most probably as a Bible clerk to the incumbent Reverend Robert Fogg. In his letter to Crabtree describing his observation, Horrocks alludes to what were probably ecclesiastical duties at the parish church of St Michael, though at twenty he was too young to have been ordained: one needed to be twenty-three for that.

The transit, which began just before sunset, was observed only by Horrocks and by Crabtree in Salford. Such was the body of primary astronomical data that Horrocks extracted from it that he wrote it up as a book, *Venus in Sole Visa* ("Venus seen on the Sun"), which was eventually published by the admiring Johannes Hevelius in Dantzig in 1662. In it, Horrocks was able to correct our knowledge of Venus's orbital data, and demonstrate that Venus herself – when divested of her shining clothing and silhouetted on the sun – was much smaller in physical size than everyone believed, when comparing Venus's diameter with the known solar diameter.

Horrocks would have liked to own a "micrometer" of the kind invented by William Gascoigne, or so Crabtree told his new Yorkshire friend in 1640. But he never got the chance. He died suddenly on the morning of 3 January 1641.

WILLIAM GASCOIGNE: INVENTOR OF THE MICROMETER

In his letters to William Oughtred, and especially those of 2 December 1640 and (undated) February 1641, Gascoigne stated that his scientific passion was for astronomy, optics, and the exact mathematical behaviour of light and lenses.[9] By the late 1630s, he was involved in true cutting-edge innovation: how to combine precision mechanical engineering with optics for the purpose of measuring the exact angular sizes of astronomical bodies. While the telescope had been around for thirty years by 1640, no one had yet solved the problem of how to measure the angular sizes of astronomical bodies when viewed through the telescope, and it was a problem that had a direct bearing upon the proof and physical demonstration of both the Copernican and Keplerian theories of the solar system and of planetary motion. Gascoigne addressed himself to this problem.

The sun and moon always appear the same size in the sky to the naked eye. Yet if the moon is going around the earth in an elliptical orbit, and the earth, likewise, is orbiting the sun in an ellipse, then the varying distances of these bodies must, inevitably, make them change their apparent size slightly, depending on whether we are at the "near" or the "far" end of the oval orbit. These orbital differences are very slight, however – for both the lunar and terrestrial orbits are fairly close to being circles – and their elliptical nature was far from easy to detect physically.

One could measure the seasonal changes in the solar diameter between winter and summer by means of a "camera obscura". Simply pass sunlight though a pinhole and notice the solar image circle projected on the facing wall. At a carefully measured projection distance of 30 feet or so – inside a dark barn – one can detect tiny size differences between June and December, and likewise for the full moon. We know that Horrocks experimented with such projection techniques in his own work on the elliptical orbit. However, if one could measure the angular size of the moon as seen through a telescope, then one had a much higher order of precision. How could this be done? Several astronomers from Galileo onwards had tried to insert measuring scales inside their telescopes, and only obtained a dark blur.

It occurred to Gascoigne, probably in late 1639 or early 1640, that if he replaced the "negative" or concave eye lens of the Galilean telescope with a "positive" convex lens, of the type described by Kepler in 1611, then the focus of both telescopic lenses would fall on *exactly* the same point inside the tube. The idea seems to have "clicked" in his mind, when an obliging spider spun its web exactly in the correct spot – at the foci of two lenses – of an optical experiment he had set up. What he saw was a sharply focused black line in the telescope's field of view: a fixed marker, or measuring point, no less.

Then Gascoigne's instinctive genius as an optical and mechanical engineer clicked in. Why not insert *two* sharp edges in the telescope's field of view, whose positions could be exactly controlled by two very fine-pitch screws? In this way, he could make the sharp edges approach and recede from one another, making it possible – for example – to sandwich the full moon between them. From his technical knowledge of optics which need not concern us here, he would use the screw counts to measure the lunar image diameter in

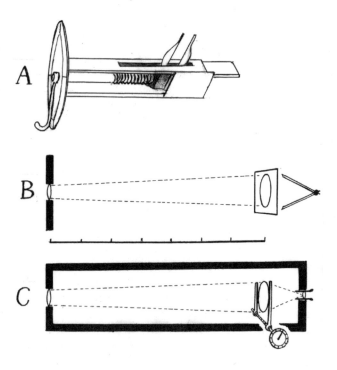

21.3 William Gascoigne's micrometer

"A" shows a brass box, perhaps 4–6 inches long, containing a pair of carefully cut fine-thread screws (probably made for Gascoigne by a local Leeds watchmaker). A pair of "nuts" run along these screws, and upon each nut is soldered a "knife edge" vertical brass pointer. When the screws are turned the nuts move, carrying the pointers towards and away from each other. The circular brass dial is engraved with fine graduations, against which the whole, and fraction, screw-turns can be counted. This micrometer is to be inserted in the telescope eyepiece. "B": A (6-foot)-focal-length lens projects an image of the sun or moon. The longer the focal length of the lens, the bigger will be the resulting image. A pair of dividers can be used to strike off the edges of the solar or lunar image. When the size of this image in inches is next divided into the focal length of the lens, the simple geometry of circles and triangles enables one to calculate the *angular* size of the image with respect to the focal length.

"C": Gascoigne then inserted his precision screw micrometer inside his telescope at the exact spot where the object glass and Keplerian eyepiece images coincided to a common focus. Then, by looking through his eyepiece, he saw not only a sharp image of the moon (or sun, if looking through dense cloud), but also saw his two micrometer pointers standing upright in sharp silhouette in the same field of view. Next, Gascoigne gently turned his micrometer screw (or screws) until he "enclosed" the moon or sun, a "knife edge" pointer on each side.

All that he now needed to do was to note the exact number of screw-turns registered on the dial, and use simple arithmetic to convert screw counts to inch-fractions. And from that, he could calculate the lunar or solar angular diameter to the unprecedented accuracy of a few arc *seconds* (3,600th parts of a degree). Gascoigne's micrometer was destined to become an established research tool in science. I have reconstructed and built two fully working instruments from his description, used in conjunction with long-focus Keplerian telescopes, and can attest to the accuracy of his design. (Drawing by Allan Chapman.)

the telescope tube, to an accuracy of nearly one-thousandth of an inch. Using optical geometry, Gascoigne could then convert the tiny fractions of an inch to tiny *angle* fractions, to compile an exact record of the seasonal lunar or solar diameter changes, and relate them to predicted Keplerian elliptical orbit criteria. It was a spectacular example of using a new piece of precision technology to test a mathematical theory. Gascoigne's measuring-screws device would be immortalized as the "micrometer", and would come to be used not only in astronomy, but in engineering, microscopy, and elsewhere, until mechanical methods of precision measurement were replaced by laser and computer instruments in the late twentieth century.

It is hardly surprising that when Crabtree told Horrocks of the micrometer device which he had seen on his visit to Gascoigne in Yorkshire, "it quite ravished his mind from itself and left him in Exstasie between admiration and amazement".[10] Crabtree was so keen to own a micrometer that he asked Gascoigne, "Could I purchase it with travel or procure it with gold?"[11] Both Horrocks and Crabtree, as well as their friends at Towneley Hall, recognized the significance of the micrometer. This new-found capability of measuring tiny telescope angles accurately was useful not only for testing elliptical orbits; the micrometer could also be used to measure the tiny angular diameters of the planets themselves, as part of a wider process of determining the size of the solar system and the bodies within it. Gascoigne himself, for example, used his micrometer to measure the angular diameters of Venus, Mars, and Jupiter in 1640.

Some years ago, friends on the staff of the then Royal Greenwich Observatory, Herstmonceux, kindly used the observatory's powerful computers to calculate the sizes of these same planets as they would have appeared on the dates when Gascoigne had observed them. Gascoigne's values for the angular diameters of these tiny sources of light were within 20 to 40 per cent accuracy – and made with the world's first micrometer.[12]

JEREMY SHAKERLEY AND THE NORTH-COUNTRY ASTRONOMERS' LEGACY

Horrocks, Crabtree, Gascoigne, and Charles Towneley were all dead by either natural or military causes by the end of July 1644. Christopher Towneley, however, survived, and was able, in a more limited way, to maintain his family's tradition as patrons of science and learning in north Lancashire, as well as stimulating and helping to direct his young nephew Richard.

Mention should be made of one other young astronomer of the Burnley area "Towneley circle": a Protestant lad named Jeremy Shakerley, born in 1626. Shakerley's first love was astrology, but this love soon died after he encountered the ideas of Horrocks, Crabtree, and Gascoigne, in surviving books and manuscripts that Christopher Towneley, along with Jonas Moore, were beginning to accumulate by the mid-1640s. We can trace Shakerley's relationship with astrology and the beginning of his interest in the "new astronomy" from nine of his surviving letters written between 1648 and 1650, addressed to the London astrologer William Lilly from whom he was seeking metropolitan patronage, and later ones to Henry Osborne and John Matteson. They are preserved in the Bodleian Library, Oxford.[13]

It is hard to deny that young Shakerley was a rather ungrateful fellow, judging from his disparaging remarks about Christopher Towneley who, in the wake of Marston Moor, was living in very reduced circumstances. Yet Shakerley's "client" relationship with him is clear, as his letters are headed "Carre Hall", which was Christopher's Pendle home after the Parliamentary seizure of Towneley Hall.

Ingratitude notwithstanding, the content of the letters is fascinating, for they discuss not only technical points of astrology, but even meteorological phenomena seen in the vale of Pendle, such as the "Mock Suns", or "sun dogs" in April 1649, which the locals attributed to occult causes, but which Shakerley knew were simple optical phenomena.

What is truly remarkable about Shakerley is that in 1649 he became the first astronomer to sing the praises of Jeremiah Horrocks in print, ranking him only just below Kepler and Bullialdus. This was in Shakerley's polemical *Anatomy of "Urania Practica"* (1649), where he extols "that Noble Genius, our worthy countryman, Master Jeremy Horrox [*sic*] from whose remains [manuscripts] I gathered most of what I shall write in this Chapter".[14] The astrologer, it now seems, had become a Copernican, Keplerian astronomer, elliptical orbits and all, while at Carre Hall.

By 24 October 1651, Shakerley is suddenly writing from Surat, in India, where he had probably gone to make his fortune. On that day he became what was probably the first astronomer ever to make serious telescopic observations from India, when he watched Mercury transit the disc of the sun. His solar projection technique was modelled upon that of Horrocks for Venus in 1639, and on Pierre Gassendi's observation of the first ever observed Mercury transit in 1631. Like his hero, Horrocks, Shakerley interpreted the Mercury transit in Copernican, Galilean, and Keplerian terms.

In addition to letters, Shakerley sang Horrocks's praises in his *Almanack* (1651) and *Tabulae Britannicae* (1653), published in London. Then he slides out of history, and in his 1675 "biography", Sir Edward Sherburne simply stated that Shakerley "dyed in the East Indies".[15]

Although Shakerley would remain largely unknown until the late twentieth century, Horrocks, Crabtree, and Gascoigne became something resembling posthumous celebrities in the early Royal Society. In 1667, Richard Towneley published an account of what was really Gascoigne's micrometer in the *Philosophical Transactions*;[16] then, with the publication of Horrocks's *Opera Posthuma* in 1672–73, the floodtide of admiration and emulation began in England and abroad, continuing into the Victorian age, and on to the present time. Everyone, rightly, was fascinated by the achievements of this small group of north-country Protestant and Catholic Christians who, over a decade, absorbed, expanded, and advanced the Continental Astronomical Renaissance, embedding the astronomy of Copernicus, Tycho, Galileo, Kepler, and several others into the intellectual fabric of north-west England and beyond.

Chapter 22

Johannes Hevelius the Dantzig Brewer and the First "Big Telescope" Astronomers

*B*ecause the new astronomy of the telescopic universe after 1609 pushed the science into realms invisible to the naked eye, a die was cast that would determine the future for the whole of Western science. Once you become dependent upon instruments, or what Robert Hooke in 1665 would style "the adding of artificial Organs to the natural", thus enabling one to see deeper into nature, the whole scope of science changes. It is no longer a matter of measuring visible angles with greater precision, but of seeing natural structures invisible since the creation, like Jupiter's moons and the stars of the Milky Way; and then, by means of the microscope in the 1660s, the cellular structure of plants and even large bacteria. And onwards and upwards, to our own time, with the Hubble Space Telescope, allowing us to glimpse remnants of the Big Bang, and even body-scanning machines that enable doctors to monitor the growth of the foetus in the womb.

When one adds the astronomical discoveries of the seventeenth century to their other discoveries – in geography, anatomy, physiology, atmospheric physics, chemistry, gravitation theory, and optics – one can fully understand the scholars of that age believing that they were living through a new divine revelation. Why had God, who had hitherto concealed these wonders, seen fit to reveal them just now? Why was this age so special in the great scheme of Providence? That view was shared by many Protestants and Catholics alike.

On a more down-to-earth level, however, it emphasized the need for that ongoing technological innovation which is still part of life in the 21st-century West – the need to advance technology to make more powerful telescopes and see deeper into space, as both Harriot and Galileo had independently discovered after 1609.

I stressed in Chapter 11 that after the first spectacular telescopic discoveries had been made in 1609–14, there were few new ones, because the small lenses then available had revealed everything in the sky that lay within their power. As a result, fresh telescopic discoveries stagnated. It would not be until the 1640s and 1650s that new optical skills in making larger pieces of clear glass, and figuring them into larger-diameter lenses, would unleash the new, and continuing, floodtide of fresh astronomical discoveries. These would reveal amazing detail on the surface of the moon and planets hitherto unseen, tiny satellites rotating around Saturn, Saturn's ring system, half a dozen puzzling misty "nebulae" in deep space, and even more millions of distant stars.

BIGGER, BRIGHTER LENSES

Things took off in the 1640s and 1650s from the availability of larger, clearer pieces of glass, which enterprising opticians were soon grinding into lenses of ever larger diameters and of ever longer focal lengths. While glass sheets of several inches across had been available for luxury window glass since before Galileo's time, its optical quality was poor, for it was often of unpredictable transparency, full of bubbles and striations. By 1650, things were improving, driven – I would hazard to suggest – by the new luxury demand for large, flat glass mirrors. "Mirror plate" of a foot or more across – obtained by a master glazier rolling out a large, blown bubble of glass to form a flat sheet – often contained zones of decent transparency, which could be cut out with a diamond, and figured into a lens 3 or 4 inches across by the early 1650s. From the 1680s, Dutch lenses the size of small dinner plates survive in the Royal Society collection.

These large lens "blanks" of a half-inch thick fuelled the next stage of telescopic discovery, for their larger diameter glasses of

4 inches or so gave the lens a much higher "light grasp" than was physically possible with a 1-inch-diameter glass. The thicker, stronger mirror plate blanks allowed the manufacturing optician to exert much greater pressure on the blank during grinding without shattering it. Thus it became possible to impart very slight, gentle, and accurate geometrical curves that gave the lens a focal length of 10, 30, or 60 feet. It is a fact of optics that the longer the lens's focal length, the bigger the focused image it will project.

In a nutshell, therefore, where a 1-inch-diameter lens of 30 inches focal length might give you a usable image of 30 times magnification – such as Harriot and Galileo obtained in 1610 – a lens of 4 inches, with a focal length of 40 feet, could magnify 200 times, thereby revealing vastly more astronomical detail. A dinner-plate-size lens of 200 feet focus could do even better. By the middle decades of the seventeenth century, opticians in Italy, Holland, and then England were producing these long-focus lenses: men such as the brothers Christiaan and Constantijn Huygens in Holland, Eustachio Divini in Rome, Giuseppe Campani and his priest-clockmaker-optician brother Matteo in Bologna, Richard Reeves and Christopher Cox in London, and Johannes Hevelius in Poland.

HEVELIUS THE ASTRONOMICAL BREWER

Jan Hewelke, who Latinized his name to Johannes Hevelius in his internationally admired Latin publications, was born in Dantzig, Poland, in 1611, the son of Abraham and Kordula, rich brewers and merchants of East German Lutheran descent. Given an excellent education in ancient and modern languages – very useful for a man destined to become both an international merchant and a man of culture – the young Jan, or Johannes, was inspired to undertake astronomy by his German schoolmaster, Peter Krüger, himself an active amateur astronomer. His schooling complete, Johannes was sent on a Grand Tour, primarily around northern Europe. He studied law at the great Dutch university of Leiden, met and corresponded with Catholic scientists like the French Friar Marin Mersenne and the German Jesuit Athanasius Kircher, before returning to Dantzig to marry an educated girl from another mercantile family, and settle down as a brewer of the renowned Jopen beer, trade across the seas, serve as Mayor of Dantzig, and grow yet richer. Hevelius descended from what might be called the international "merchant aristocracy" of Renaissance Europe: individuals and families who not only grew rich on the fruits of business, but who also valued culture and education, patronized learning, founded schools, endowed charities, and were, in the great majority of cases, actively involved in the civic lives of their communities and countries.

Much of Johannes' wealth would go towards funding his cutting-edge astronomical research, conducted from the magnificent observatory built across the roofs of several of his houses in Dantzig. Hevelius saw himself as the heir of Tycho Brahe, and belonging to the same intellectual tradition as his fellow Pole Copernicus. I also suggest that Hevelius belonged to a *northern* Renaissance and revival of learning, a Renaissance which went beyond his Baltic astronomical forefathers to a wider north European cultural movement that included Martin Luther, Erasmus, Descartes, William Gilbert, William Harvey, Rembrandt, the English Bible of 1611, and Shakespeare.

Hevelius was both a practical and an artistic man, clearly good with his hands: an accomplished draughtsman and artist, who ranked printers, craftsmen, engravers, and painters amongst his personal associates. One has only to look at the sumptuous volumes of published research that emerged from his own largely self-funded printing press to get a grasp of Hevelius the artist as well as Hevelius the astronomer. *Cometographia* (1668), *Machina Coelestis* I (1673), and other works are not only exquisitely printed on the finest-quality paper, but are a mine of high-art-quality engravings of the instruments in his observatory. Telescopes, graduated quadrants, close-ups of his measuring scales, and much else abound – including pictures of his much younger second wife, Catherina Elisabetha, working alongside him, involved in the very business of making astronomical observations. I suspect that these pictures of Catherina Elisabetha are our first visual record of a woman actually doing science. Judging by her later correspondence in widowhood with the Royal Society of London, she was clearly another well-educated merchant's daughter, and her late husband's able assistant.

MAPPING THE MOON

Hevelius's international debut as an astronomer came in 1647, with the publication of his 2-inch-thick large folio volume *Selenographia*, or "Moon Drawings". *Selenographia* appeared at a time when the improving optical capability of telescopes was causing new interest in the lunar and planetary surfaces amongst Europe's astronomers and philosophers. In 1628 Father Pierre Gassendi in France spoke of the need for a good and detailed chart of the moon, and in 1645 one of the first good-quality moon maps came off the press, by the Dutch-Flemish Catholic cartographer Michael van Langren (Langrenius). It was a massive advance on Galileo's woodcuts of 1610. In the wake of Galileo's trial, other Catholic astronomers, such as the Neapolitan Francesco Fontana and the Capuchin friar-cum-diplomat Anton Schyrle de Rheita, issued detailed, if sometimes wildly inaccurate, lunar charts in the mid-1640s. What people wanted to know was how similar to the earth the moon might be, and whether it could even have inhabitants. Only high-powered telescopes could hope to yield the answer.

Hevelius's *Selenographia* set a wholly new standard of lunar cartography. Its 43 one-foot-diameter maps, covering all the lunar phases, along with detailed full-moon maps, initiated the science of selenography. Of perhaps even greater long-term significance was his minutely described *and illustrated* accounts of his instruments, their construction, and their manufacture, including a description of his lens-grinding machine. *All* of Hevelius's instrument plates were no doubt intended to serve as instruction manuals for those wishing to replicate and take further his observations and discoveries.

The observations in *Selenographia* were made with the first and smallest of his growing collection of large telescopes, for its lens was only about 1½ inches in diameter, but with an operational focal length of up to 12 feet. He leaves not only a detailed description of the telescope but – perhaps more importantly – accompanies it with a beautiful engraving of the grinding machine upon which its lenses were figured. The machine is shown *in situ* in the workshop, fully assembled and ready for use; in addition, all the parts are shown individually on the floor, so that an aspiring optician can see each bit of each part, and how they all fit and move together.

Hevelius names most of the main lunar features: craters, mountains, and the large flat dark areas known as *maria* or seas. To many he gives names that have terrestrial equivalents, a few of which still survive on modern-day moon maps.

Hevelius does not appear to have produced *Selenographia*, or his later sumptuous works, to be *sold*. Instead, copies seem to have been given away, to eminent foreign scientists, scholars, and royalty. The copies of Hevelius's works with which I am most familiar, in Oxford's Bodleian Library and the Royal Society Library, London, appear to have been gifts, either to the libraries direct, or else via eminent original recipients, such as Sir Christopher Wren. This was astronomy on a munificent scale.

LUTHERANISM, CATHOLICISM, AND ASTRONOMY

Devout Lutheran Protestant as Hevelius undoubtedly was, he seems to have enjoyed cordial relations with a variety of Roman Catholic colleagues and even patrons. *Selenographia*, for example, was dedicated to, and warmly acknowledged by, the very Catholic King Ladislas IV of Poland. Hevelius even sent a presentation copy to no less a personage than Pope Innocent X who, at a time when Innocent was struggling unsuccessfully with the Augsburg Protestants, seemed to appreciate the gift from a Polish Lutheran.

Over the years, the Dantzig brewer would enjoy a warm relationship with several Catholic kings, dedicating his *Cometographia* to King Louis XIV of France, and being openly admired by the Polish crown. King Jan Sobieski III, for example, not only made several social visits to Hevelius's house and observatory, but even elevated the astronomer to a rank in the Polish nobility. Did King Jan – the hero of Christian Europe, who delivered Vienna from Muslim Turkish invasion in 1683, as well as being a man of serious cultural interests – perhaps look through one of Hevelius's telescopes at the moon? And did His Majesty perhaps share a jug of beer with the astronomer?

It is interesting to see how astronomy, science, and culture could build bridges between mutually hostile Catholic and Protestant groups even at the height of Europe's wars of religion, and even at a time when Poland's Roman Catholic majority was otherwise intolerant to Protestants. Hevelius's seeming ability to cross doctrinal barriers is also clear in many of the decorative cartouches which adorn the corners of *Selenographia*'s moon-phase plates, which often contain depictions of cherubs holding banners upon which astronomically relevant Latin biblical quotations are sometimes written, such as Psalm 19's "The Heavens are telling the Glory of God". Hevelius seems to have been a bit like Kepler in so far as he was a declared Lutheran who lived peaceably among, and was respected by, Roman Catholics.

HEVELIUS'S BIG TELESCOPES AND PLANETARY ASTRONOMY

The 12-foot instrument of the 1640s used for the *Selenographia* observations would soon be superseded by at least eight increasingly large telescopes by the time Hevelius came to describe his observatory in Chapter 20 of *Machina Coelestis* I, where he details – and sometimes illustrates – telescopes of 30, 40, 50, 60, 70, and one of an incredible 150 Dantzig feet focal length (about 140 English feet, the Dantzig foot, like the German, being about 11 inches). The latter giant instrument, which Hevelius set up outside the city, had an object lens of about 8 inches in diameter, being set in the end of a long wooden tube, elevated via notches on a tall mast, and adjusted by assistants operating a system of ropes.

How could such an unwieldy contraption show you anything worthwhile in the heavens? I have often asked that question, for the slightest breath of wind would have made it wobble like a jelly, in addition to which one had the problem of finding and aligning a celestial object in the first place. Just imagine trying to find a bright star when looking up a 140-foot rainwater pipe hanging from a flagpole.

Astronomers across Europe did make fundamental discoveries in planetary astronomy with these instruments. Hevelius actually built, used, and illustrated his giant telescopes, but he did *not* invent the design, and by 1660 Frenchmen, Dutchmen, Italians, Germans, and Englishmen were using these long-focus, mast-mounted telescopes, and making serious discoveries with them. They could give aberrated or distorted images, but once you had got Jupiter, Saturn, Mars, or Venus into focus, on a still, calm night, these mighty optical beasts could reveal things that would have made Galileo shout for joy.

THE DESTRUCTION OF HEVELIUS'S OBSERVATORY

One of the tragedies of seventeenth-century scientific history is the burning down of Hevelius's home and rooftop observatory on 26 September 1679 – by a fire, it was said, started deliberately by a disgruntled servant. Many portable objects such as documents were saved, but one wonders what went up in the conflagration, including writings which might, perhaps, have cast light on his relations with both Catholic and Protestant friends. Even so, King Jan III gave the 68-year-old Hevelius financial and other support to help with the re-construction of a new observatory. But with so much of his life's work and some of the most exquisite astronomical instruments in Europe destroyed, Hevelius's Dantzig enterprise would never be the same again.

CHRISTIAAN AND CONSTANTIJN HUYGENS OF ZUILICHEM

Long before these two brothers took to serious science as teenagers in the late 1640s, the Huygenses had been a family of note in Holland, with estates at Zuilichem in The Hague. Their father Sir Constantijn was renowned as a Dutch scholar, musician, and diplomat, with an English knighthood conferred by King James I. Constantijn the younger also became a high-ranking public servant, and even Secretary to King William III of England, but he never lost his love of astronomy and telescopic optics. However, it was his brother Christiaan who became the "big telescope" discoverer.

Using selected pieces of the clearest plate glass he could purchase from a glasshouse, the brothers used an optical lathe of their own design to grind and figure a series of excellent lenses. One of their best early lenses was of 23 feet focal length, and with it Christiaan began to examine both the planets and the mysterious glowing "nebula" (or galaxy) in the Sword of the Orion constellation.

Christiaan Huygens was the first to see areas of different colour on Mars – drawing that formation to be known as Syrtis Major – but his primary object of study was Saturn. Saturn had baffled astronomers ever since Galileo had noted its peculiar changes in shape in 1610: sometimes round, then distinctly egg-shaped. Hevelius had also drawn a puzzling-looking Saturn in *Selenographia*, using a telescope inferior to that which Huygens would use a decade later. Over 1656–57, on a series of nights of very clear seeing, Huygens's 23-foot, and a new and even more powerful telescope, showed Saturn to be surrounded by "a ring, thin, plane, nowhere attached and inclined to the ecliptic [or tilted to the plane of the sun]".

Huygens announced this in an anagram in his *Systema Saturnium* (1659), and once the anagram had been cracked (seventeenth-century scientists loved encrypting and cracking codes), the news reverberated around Europe, along with Huygens's explanation of the shape changes. For the axes of the earth and Saturn are tilted to each other. When the tilt was at maximum, one could see the open ring, giving the impression in a poorer telescope that Saturn was egg-shaped; but when the tilt was at minimum, the ring was seen edge-on from earth, and was so thin that it was invisible, so that Saturn became a sphere. *Systema Saturnium* further announced Christiaan's discovery that Saturn also had a moon, or satellite – later christened "Titan" – adding yet another mooned planet to the solar system beyond the earth and Jupiter, and with it, more analogical weight to the Copernican theory.

The moon was a rough, mountainous place rather like the earth, Mars had some sort of surface features, and the bright, bland surfaces of Venus, Jupiter, and Saturn held all sorts of imaginative possibilities. So, could God, having created spherical *worlds* beyond

321

our own, have created *inhabitants* for them as well? This was a subject widely discussed across Europe in the seventeenth century, and in his *Cosmotheoros* (1695) Christiaan speaks of how he and his brother Constantijn had often discussed the subject "over a large Telescope, when we have been viewing those bodies".[1] Was it possible that these beings had even invented telescopes, and might be looking at *us*? Why, in Huygens's way of thinking, should God not have spread his bounty and life-giving grace, including intelligence and ingenuity, throughout the universe?

GIOVANNI DOMENICO CASSINI: AN ITALIAN IN PARIS

The Galileo trial and condemnation did not in any way put the brakes on Italian astronomy, as we saw in Chapter 16. Father Giovanni Battista Riccioli SJ, in addition to articulating a powerful and scientific defence of a modified Tychonic geo-heliocentric theory in *Almagestum Novum* (1651), included two fine and high-definition telescopic maps of the moon. Riccioli was innovative in so far as he pioneered a new way of designating lunar features, which came to be adopted by later lunar cartographers, and which is still used as a guide today – that is, naming craters after famous astronomers and men of science. Yes, there are lots of ordained Catholic astronomers up there, simply because they were so active in contemporary science. There are also lots of classical pagans, medieval Muslims, the Protestant Kepler, and even the "heretics" Copernicus and Galileo – and many of them are still to be found on modern moon maps.

It is not Father Riccioli who concerns us here, important as he was, but his fellow countryman and layman Giovanni Domenico Cassini. Holding the Chair of Astronomy at Bologna from 1650, Cassini made his mark as an observer and researcher, using long telescopes with optics by Giuseppe Campani. In the clear, still Italian air, Cassini had used a long Campani telescope to time the axial rotation period of Mars from permanent markings on its surface, announcing a figure of 24 hours 40 minutes. In Italy, Cassini also saw the equatorial belt system of Jupiter, and from a spot on the

Jovian surface also established its period of rotation at 9 hours 56 minutes; in 1669, he produced a set of tables for the rotation period of Jupiter from known satellites. These would prove invaluable not just to astronomers, but also to cartographers and explorers who could use the rotations of the telescopically visible Jovian moons as a natural clock to establish the exact longitude of places on the earth's surface.

In 1669, he was "head-hunted" (as Huygens had been for a while) by the young King Louis XIV of France, moving to Paris and coming to be known as Jean Dominic Cassini. As a member of Louis's Académie des Sciences Royale – the new French equivalent of the Royal Society of London – Cassini became *de facto* Director of the new Royal Observatory, just outside what was then central Paris, when it was completed in 1671. Along with colleagues such as Jean Picard, Jean Richer, and Adrien Auzout, Cassini joined a select band of opulently funded scientists and astronomers who were also meant to be ornaments of the "Sun King's" court. The Paris Observatory was to be accommodated in a magnificent new mansion of science, with great state rooms and ceremonial apartments fit to receive His Majesty on those occasions when he visited his "philosophers".

Grand and ceremonial as the observatory was, it was not especially suited to astronomical observation. Even so, Giovanni Domenico, the first of a dynasty of four Cassini directors of the Paris Observatory, did fundamental work there with a succession of long telescopes by Campani and others. For greater stability and ease of adjustment, he had a pyramidal tower built in the observatory grounds to act as suspension points for the long telescopes. One discovery after another came from Cassini. In 1671 and 1672, for example, and using a telescope of 34 feet focal length, he discovered two much smaller moons of Saturn, beyond the giant "Titan" first seen by Huygens, and named them, after the Greek mythological convention, Iapetus and Rhea. Then, in 1684, with giant telescopes of 100 and 130 feet long, he discovered two more, subsequently christened Tethys and Dione.

In 1675, Cassini, now secure in Paris, announced another major discovery. Instead of Saturn having the single, simple ring announced by Huygens in 1659, Cassini's superior new telescopes revealed that there were *two* rings, both concentric with the planet. The gap between them was now so clear that Cassini could even see the body of Saturn, and sometimes distant stars, shining through it. He announced this to the learned world via ambassadorial connections – the "internet" of the seventeenth century – and his Latin press release appeared in the *Philosophical Transactions* of London's Royal Society in 1675. Securing priority for a discovery is not new.

All of this big telescope research in France, along with the observatory and Académie, were all opulently funded by the French state – ultimately, by the French taxpayer – at the command of an absolute monarch, King Louis XIV, the "Sun King". A very different set of circumstances prevailed on the opposite side of the English Channel.

THE BIG TELESCOPE IN ENGLAND

In England, there was no monarchy between 1649 and 1660, and even when the crown was restored and King Charles II ascended the throne in 1660, cash was scarce. A civil war, the execution of the new king's father, Charles I, Puritan religious chaos, a restored monarchy that was effectively broke, and a country where Parliament controlled the national fiscal and other purse strings meant that there was precious little royal largesse to spread around. When, as we shall see in Chapter 25, the king founded and chartered the Royal Society in and after 1660, and the Royal Observatory, Greenwich, in 1675, it was private individuals who paid for almost everything. It was in these circumstances that English big telescope astronomy was born and thrived.

Samuel Hartlib's *Ephemerides* for August 1655 mentions that the Revd Dr John Wilkins, Warden of Wadham College, Oxford, and his scientific friends, were building a telescope of 80 feet focal length, intended for lunar research. We also know that Wilkins's friend, a rich, scientifically minded London lawyer, Sir Paul Neile, had commissioned the building of long refracting telescopes in the late 1650s; while the brothers Dr Peter and William Ball, of Mamhead,

South Devon, had set up a 38-foot refractor on their estate with which to study the planets.[2] All of the English Anglicans would have been fully acquainted with what their Calvinist, Lutheran, Catholic – and Jesuit – colleagues were doing on the Continent, and in many cases were in correspondence with them, being keen to confirm (or contradict) and hopefully improve upon their findings.

Big telescope astronomy was at an inevitable disadvantage in England, however: that of geography. London is over 200 miles further north of the equator than is Paris, and over 500 miles further than Bologna. This means that the "ecliptic band", or the sun's path across the sky, is much lower down in England than in Paris or Bologna, so that an astronomer in one of those cities will see a planet considerably higher up in the sky than it would be seen in London. An English astronomer, therefore, has to look at the southern horizon through a much denser and often damper mass of air than would his colleagues in Bologna. Consequently, the Englishman will be at a disadvantage when it comes to spotting fine detail on a planet's surface, as he has so much more atmospheric "murk" to look through.

Without doubt, the leading English big telescope astronomer of this period was Robert Hooke, protégé of Dr Wilkins in Oxford, then Professor of Geometry at Gresham College, London, and the inspired Curator of Experiments at the early Royal Society.

In Gresham College, where the early Royal Society met, Hooke had access to three or four big telescopes. They were of 6 and 12 feet focal length, with possibly a 30-foot, and certainly 36- and 60-footers. In the 1660s and early 1670s, when most of Hooke's astronomical research was undertaken, the leading English big lens grinders were Richard Reeves and Christopher Cock, Cox, or Cocks. Yet "big" as these telescopes may have been in focal length, they all, just like their Continental equivalents, had main lenses, or "object glasses", that were still very small, relatively speaking. Seventeenth-century astronomers rarely specified the *diameters* of their lenses, being mainly concerned with their focal lengths and consequent focused image sizes, but Hooke does mention that a good-definition working aperture for a telescope lens was rarely more than 2 inches across. The *whole* lens diameter may be 3, 4, or 6 inches, but its "optimum definition" area rarely exceeded 2 or 2½ inches – tiny by later standards. The less good areas of a telescopic lens would be blanked out with cardboard or leather rings, allowing light from the best 2 or 2½ inches of the glass to make the focused image.

These telescopes produced stunning discoveries, as we have seen. Observing from Gresham College quadrangle, in the heart of the smoky city of London, Hooke made some superb lunar and planetary drawings. Using his 36-footer – his favourite telescope – Hooke made and published in 1666 a drawing of the main horizontal belts of Jupiter: a planet which to Galileo and earlier astronomers presented a bland surface, but to the big telescopes of the 1660s revealed surface detail. Scholars are still undecided whether it was Hooke or Cassini who first independently discovered the "Great Red Spot" on Jupiter: a conspicuous variable body, which made it possible to establish the rotation period of the planet.

In addition to planetary details, Hooke used his Gresham College telescopes for several sets of research that would have long-term consequences. The first of these was his October 1664 observations of the moon, published in *Micrographia* in 1665.[3] While a succession of astronomers extending from Galileo to Riccioli had produced whole-moon maps, Hooke was the first to draw one single lunar feature in very great detail: the crater named Hipparchus by Riccioli, and still known by that name today.

In a map that covers a very small fraction of the lunar surface area, Hooke drew Hipparchus to a level of detail that stands up remarkably well to comparison with modern photographs. Then he went further, asking what forces might have pockmarked the moon with craters, yet had not done so to the earth. Could the craters have been formed by impacts from bodies in space, smashing into an infant moon with a still flexible surface? Hooke became the first to carry experimental science into astronomy, by dropping lead pistol balls into a tub of viscous white pipe clay, and finding that the bullets produced amazingly lunar-crater-like formations in the clay. They do. I have replicated Hooke's experiment using clay, glass marbles, and a catapult.

Alternatively, could the craters be the product of lunar volcanoes? By 1664, the moon had long been a changeless "dead" world, so how far back into the past could the volcanoes have been active? Hooke experimented once again, using a pair of bellows to blow air into the pipe clay, to find that the bursting bubbles also produced circular depressions with rampart walls, just like the moon's craters. Modern lunar geologists still see meteoritic impacts and volcanic activity as the primary forces that moulded the surface of the early moon. And none of this would have even begun without findings made with big telescopes.

Secondly, Robert Hooke further applied the experimental method to comets, in *Cometa, or Remarks about Comets* (1678). Using his telescopes to observe the bright comets of 1664 and 1677, he identified key structural parts of the cometary body. Within the head of the comet, he identified a brilliant inner nucleus, from which a thin spine – or "medulla" – emerged, extending behind the comet as it moved through space; but then there was a great mass of tenuous material surrounding the comet's head, and streaming behind across space, to form the brilliant tail.

Could some force emanating from the sun be somehow dissolving the nucleus, Hooke suggested, with the ejected matter streaming out in an ever thicker stream as it approached the sun? What could the nucleus be made of, and what was the nature of the solar force? Once again, Hooke went to his laboratory, and noticed how comet-tail-like streams of bubbles (now known to be hydrogen) were given off when an iron-covered wax ball was suspended in a long vertical cylinder of acid. Was the sun's "force" somehow corrosive upon cometary matter, in the way that acids corrode iron? Yet it did not seem to corrode the earth. These were utterly brilliant and inspired ideas for the 1660s and 1670s, connecting big telescope observations with laboratory experiments, and laying the foundations of cometary physics.

Thirdly, Hooke – like Descartes – was confident that increasingly large telescopes would one day reveal living beings on the moon. He even suggested that within some lunar "Vale[s]" there might be grassy vegetation, similar to "the Hills of *Salisbury* Plains", which we could examine at colossal magnifications. In something resembling a flight of fancy, the otherwise highly pragmatic Hooke proposed a design for a grinding machine capable of making a telescope object glass of a breathtaking 21 inches in diameter and 1,000 or 10,000 feet focal length. Hooke was not pleased when the Parisian astronomer Adrien Auzout F.R.S. wrote to the Royal Society saying that Hooke's visionary giant telescope was moonshine.

BIG TELESCOPES AND THE MOVING EARTH

Though Hooke's 1,000-foot telescope remained a pipe-dream, the Royal Society still possesses three lenses by Constantijn Huygens. They have focal lengths of 122, 170, and 210 feet respectively, the last of these being 9½ inches in diameter. They have been analysed in detail by modern optical physicists, and I once suggested trying to observe the moon with them, by focusing the lenses in the horizontal, and using a mirror to direct the moonlight.[4]

What did fifty years of big telescope astronomy do to cast light upon Copernicus's moving earth theory? True, these telescopes revealed a profoundly different universe from that of ancient, medieval, and early Renaissance science: a universe that seemed to extend to infinity, with *millions* of tiny stars, world-like planets with their own satellite systems, a once geologically active moon, slowly dissolving comets, and bizarre objects like the Orion Nebula, with their faint, glowing, diffuse light. Yet they supplied not a hint of that crucial *geometrical* proof, based on a six-monthly star parallax shift, of the kind required by Copernicus, Kepler, Cardinal Bellarmine, the Jesuits, and the rest of the mathematical astronomers of Europe.

In 1669 Robert Hooke had yet another bright idea. He set up his best, 36-foot telescope in the vertical – poking it through the floors and roof of his lodgings in Gresham College – so that it pointed to the zenith, or the point exactly overhead. He knew that a certain bright star, known as Gamma Draconis, passed through the zenith in the latitude of London, and that if he lay on his back and looked up the tube at the calculated time, he would see it straight above him through the zenith telescope. Hooke, I might add, decided to search for a star parallax on a zenith star because he knew that star images observed obliquely, or at an angle, were always slightly distorted from their true geometrical position due to atmospheric refraction, whereas zenith starlight comes to us in a straight, un-refracted line.

Having fitted his telescope with a precision micrometer of his own devising, Hooke hoped that his 36-foot telescope might detect the elusive tiny six-monthly parallax movement of Gamma Draconis. In *An Attempt to Prove the Motion of the Earth*, 1674, he announced such a motion. We now know that the tiny angular displacement which he had detected – corresponding to about 1/67th of the diameter of the moon – was *not* a parallax. More than likely, it was another motion called the "aberration of light", which would not be accurately measured and explained until 1728, by the Revd Dr James Bradley. We will return to this in Chapter 27. Even so, the aberration is a real phenomenon, caused by the annual motion of the earth, though Hooke's proclaimed discovery was treated with caution by many of his colleagues.

The big telescope changed the whole potential of astronomical research between 1645 and 1700, as each new and yet bigger telescope revealed still more celestial wonders and a universe of a vastness, complexity, and beauty that the pre-telescopic astronomers of Copernicus's day could not even have imagined. Whether the astronomer were a Roman Catholic, a Lutheran, a Dutch Protestant Natural Theologian, or an Anglican, the Creator who had set it all in motion was seen to possess an even greater grandeur than before. In the astronomy of the "new universe", divine design, mathematical law, and wonder all connected with the God-given rational intellect of humanity, as men continued (as Kepler had put it) to "think God's thoughts after Him" on an even grander scale.

Yet what did all of this new thinking do to the ancient art of astrology?

CHAPTER 23

The Long Death of Astrology

*F*orms of astrological divination go as far back into human history as the written record itself. As we saw in Chapter 5, astrology made eminently good sense when people saw themselves and their tribal or wider human family as occupying a central place in creation – a creation in which the sun clearly brought about the seasons, the moon shone to illumine the night, and the complex movements of the planets amongst the star patterns could be correlated with incidents in human life. Then there were those dramatic and occasional lights – comets, meteor storms, fireballs, aurorae, and dramatic meteorological phenomena – which blazed overhead unexpectedly, and often had worrying correlations with deaths, wars, famines, earthquakes, and freak storms.

Human intelligence is cause-and-effect-based in its natural operation, as we instinctively put two and two together to make what we believe will be four. It was far from superstitious to believe in signs, portents, and predictions in previous ages, when the omnipresence of infectious disease and a low level of control over the natural environment were the norm. As everyone knew, was not the last famine preceded by a fiery comet blazing across the kingdom; the last war by a conjunction of Saturn and Mars in Scorpio; last year's plague by a total eclipse of the sun; and the murder of the king by the sudden appearance of terrifying swords in the blood-red midnight sky? To a pre-modern-science mind, astrology, omens, and prophecies, far from being for the ignorant and superstitious, were deemed as pragmatically demonstrable as the Periodic Table of Elements is to us.

ASTROLOGY'S RATIONALE, AND MOUNTING CHALLENGES

Like astronomy, astrology was regarded as having been established intellectually by the classical Greeks, and Ptolemy's *Tetrabiblos* ("The Four Treatises") of *c.* AD 150, which laid down the basic structure of the horoscope, was seen by many scholars as a companion volume to his better-known (to us) *Magna Syntaxis* or *Almagest.* It was a mathematically and physically based science, requiring careful positional observations of the planets in the zodiac, the consultation of sophisticated mathematical tables, and the mastery of complex rules of interpretation. Over the centuries astrology had been refined and become the subject of academic treatises, while the medieval Arabs in particular had made their own significant contributions, especially with relation to medical astrology, which in turn had been absorbed into the Western canon.

So, there was nothing superstitious, ignorant, or foolish about medieval or Renaissance astrology. Its principles were beyond the comprehension of the village witch, had nothing to do with spells and incantations, and that association of astrology with bizarre occultism in the modern mind provides us with yet another example of how the so-called "Enlightenment" and Romantic era generated their own myths about our "un-Enlightened" past.

There was only one thing wrong with learned astrology: it was barking up the wrong tree in terms of both its physics and its physiology. As came to be realized by 1680, on increasingly sound physical and evidential grounds, the earth was *not* located at the centre of the universe, the world-like planets rotated around the *sun* and were not significators for things likely to happen on earth; while the twelve zodiac signs or constellations, which were fundamental to the very structure and interpretation of the horoscope, did not exist as connected entities in their own right. The new telescopic universe was clearly a place in which stars receded to infinity, in three-dimensional space, and had no real or symbolic connection with each other whatsoever.

Likewise, the very existence of the four classical "humours" of the body, yellow bile, black bile, blood, and phlegm, upon which it was believed the planetary forces acted, was coming to be called increasingly into doubt by seventeenth-century anatomists and physiologists. This was especially so in the wake of William Harvey's discovery of the circulation of the blood under the systolic force of the contracting heart, as living things were coming increasingly to be seen by many influential thinkers as *machines* rather than sensitive humoral entities.

By the 1650s, the eminent and devoutly Anglican Oxford physician Dr Thomas Willis was even coming to think of that ubiquitous ailment – fever – as occasioned not by a humoral excess of heat, but as a "fermentation" of the blood: in other words, by a *biochemical* process. Wrong as we now know Willis was in his biological fermentation theory of disease, he was at least barking up the *right* tree, in his linking of disease not to the heavens but to chemical reactive processes. Then, just as seventeenth-century doctors were becoming increasingly cautious in their attribution of human disease to celestially influenced humours, so their friends the chemists were no longer seeing chemical change in the laboratory as brought about by the melding of the four classical elements: earth, water, air, and fire. Those early Royal Society chemists in Oxford and London, such as Robert Boyle, Robert Hooke, John Mayow, and their friend Dr Willis, were coming by 1670 to see combustion, explosion, respiration, mammal and plant gestation and growth – and several other things as well – as caused by "physico-mechanical" chemical exchange processes, and *not* by the heavens.

So, if astrology's intellectual supports were being knocked away, one after the other, why did it take so long to die?

ASTROLOGY'S RENAISSANCE FLOURISHING

Ironic as it may sound, astrology probably had a bigger and more conspicuous presence and following in the sixteenth and early seventeenth centuries than it had in twelfth- or thirteenth-century medieval Europe. What factors lay behind this phenomenon?

Late-medieval and early-modern Europe was a place of mayhem and fear in a way that it had *not* been a few centuries earlier. Between AD 1000 and 1350, Europe had been a place of growing self-confidence and apparently God-ordained certainty.

There were considerable periods of abundant harvest, producing a relatively well-fed and contented populace. Paris, Oxford, Bologna, and several other great European universities were founded and flourished, as intellectual life expanded to embrace powerful academic theology at one end of the spectrum and troubadour love poetry at the other. It was believed that God had clearly favoured Europe in enabling the Crusaders to take back once overrun Christian territory in Palestine from the Muslims and re-establish, for almost a century at least, the Christian kingdom of Jerusalem. A more enduring possession was the Christian "Reconquista" of Spain, as El Cid and his knights re-took Spain, which the Muslims had invaded in AD 711 as part of a wider strategy of subjugating heartland Europe itself to Islam.

Then things began to go very badly wrong. The "Black Death" bubonic pestilence ravaged the whole of Europe between 1346 and 1349, killing about half of the population, and leading Boccaccio in his *Decameron* to lament the ruined condition of his beloved Florence. And that was not all, for plague, once rooted in the European population, would come back four or five times per century between 1346 and 1666, devastating one generation after another, and causing labour shortages that undermined economic recovery.

On 29 May 1453, the Eastern Orthodox bastion of Christendom, Constantinople (which Catholic Europe had treated shamefully over the preceding centuries), fell to the Ottoman Turks, re-opening the terrifying prospect once again of an Islamic invasion of heartland Europe.

A debauched Papacy and Martin Luther had led to mainland Christian Europe tearing itself apart with the conflicts of the Reformation. God's wrath was seen as becoming increasingly evident in a succession of celestial portents, as terrifying comets blazed across the skies of Europe in 1468, 1472, 1531, 1532, 1556, and 1557. As we saw in Chapter 2, a great fiery stone crashed down from heaven at Ensisheim, Alsace, on 7 November 1492; while an abundance of planetary conjunctions and oppositions all reinforced the doom warning that many interpreted, from the prophecies of Daniel, Ezekiel, Revelation, and other biblical books, as heralding

333

the end of time. The astrologers and "monthly prognosticators" mentioned by Isaiah (47:13) in the 1611 English Bible, had more than enough to keep them calculating.

ASTROLOGY FOR ALL

As the signs and wonders from the heavens were flying thick and fast, another phenomenon was hitting Europe, and nowhere more than in England: printing and growing popular literacy. It is widely known that the Protestant Reformers placed great stress on ordinary people being able to read the Holy Scriptures in their mother tongue. Once the ordinary Jack and Jill could read, or could hear read out aloud, William Tyndale's Bible after 1526, and Archbishop Cranmer's Prayer Book (1549), they could read or listen to other things as well, and a flourishing English-language publishing market sprang up, especially by the early days of Queen Elizabeth I's reign in 1558. This included joke books, "chap books" telling hair-raising tales (often available from an itinerant peddler, or "chapman"), ghost and witch stories, travellers' tales, and "almanacks": little booklets of astrological predictions for the forthcoming twelvemonth.

Most of these popular booklets contained some thirty-two small pages, and were often badly printed on cheap paper, with a few often lurid, simple woodcut pictures. These were the first "books of the people". By the time that William Shakespeare wrote *A Midsummer Night's Dream, c.* 1590–96 (Act III, scene i), almanacs were so commonplace that Quince the Joiner, one of the "rude mechanical" amateur players in the *Dream*, could produce one from his pocket to tell his mates when there would be a moon to rehearse by. By Shakespeare's time almanacs were a profitable and established business line, selling at the price of a jug of ale and a pie, and containing a mine of useful or titillating information. This could include the dates of the principal fairs, lucky and unlucky days for Geminis or Scorpios, the words of a song, an account of a Newgate hanging, the calculated positions of the sun, moon, and planets for each month of the year, medical and farming tips, and a few blank spaces for each month for notes – the ancestor of the pocket diary. Almanacs were the first widely distributed and read works of *secular* literature, no less, that might be read aloud beside the alehouse fire, when the Parish Clerk was not treating the locals to readings of David slaying Goliath, Noah's flood, or the casting of the shrieking souls of the damned into the Lake of Fire. All good, gripping stuff for a winter's night.

As the Bodleian Library, Oxford, contains one of the world's richest collections of almanacs, along with similar popular ephemeral literature, I can assure the reader that I speak with a personal research familiarity with the genre. In the Bodleian collection, one can trace the authors, places of publication, and sometimes intended markets. John Securis, a Salisbury doctor, became a successful "almanack maker" in the 1560s; while there were John Dade, Anthony Ascham, Thomas Hill, William Bourne, and many others, extending from the reign of King Henry VIII down into the seventeenth century, writing for either a metropolitan or west country or northern readership. By the 1630s, as England slid into civil war, politically loaded almanacs began to appear, as we shall see below.

ASTROLOGY AND CHRISTIAN BELIEF

At first glance, one might assume that the church would be firmly against astrology, in so far as it presumed to glimpse a future known only to God. Yet things were not as straightforward as that, for many theologians from the early church and Middle Ages had argued that God had given us intelligence so that we might, in part, find our own way through the world. After all, astronomy, tide prediction, medicine, farming, law, and good government were all ways in which humanity was given leeway by God to forge its own path.

Miracles come in two forms, as the great Christian chemist Robert Boyle and his fellow Royal Society scientists would make clear in the seventeenth century. On the one hand, there was the direct intervention of God into his creation, to quell a storm or banish a deadly fever in response to the prayers of the faithful. These acts were seen as "special providences". There again, there were "general providences", or those permanent, ongoing acts of divine beneficence with which God had blessed the world, and with which mankind could engage physically and intellectually, to facilitate better living. These could include the art of medicine, astronomy, and those subjects mentioned a few lines back.

Pious or good astrology could be seen as falling within the category of "general providences". As we saw in Chapter 5, astrology came in two types. Good astrology was "natural astrology", in which the horoscope was used to make us aware of future tendencies in the world, and enable us to act accordingly. Astrological diagnosis and prognosis in medicine was a common one. Other instances of natural astrology might include the following. Is this person the right one for me to marry? Is a planned business venture likely to succeed or fail? Will it rain on Coronation Day?

Bad astrology, for which Galileo was first summoned before the Inquisition in 1604 (as we saw in Chapter 10), was "judicial astrology". This was when the astrologer presumed to gain insights into specific details that could lie only within the grace of God, such as, on what date will John Brown die? – and the downright treasonable: on what day will the monarch die? Judicial astrology was roundly condemned by the church, and was singled out for condemnation by John Calvin himself in *Admonicion against Astrology Iudiciall* (1560), though Calvin acknowledged the value of natural astrology as a gift of God, for on this ground, as on many others, Protestants and Catholics were in agreement, sharing as they did the same awareness of Christ's Grace and Providence. Natural astrology was seen as no more wicked or foolish than we today would consider "straight" astronomy to be, for it existed within the realm of *scientia*, or organized knowledge.

On the other hand, astrology was often attacked and ridiculed, as many predictions were conspicuously wrong, and William Perkins's *Foure great lyers* (1585) was a vitriolic attack on four contemporary prognosticators during Queen Elizabeth I's reign. George Carleton's *Madness of Astrologers* (1624) was another work in this tradition, while Philip Stubbes's *Anatomie of Abuses* (1583) weighed in astrology with theatres, loose women, fashionable clothes, Sunday entertainments, and the myriad of other activities of which this staunch Puritan disapproved. Others defended the ancient *science*, as Sir Christopher Heydon did in his *A Defence of Judiciall Astrologie* (1603).

Name-calling and Puritan rancour apart, what made most learned critics cautious of astrology was not its innate silliness as much as its inaccuracy. In a geocentric universe, the fact that the heavens affected the earth was not the point at issue. This, rather, resided in our relatively imprecise knowledge of planetary movements for even the moderately near future. What was the point in drawing an elaborate "scheme" or horoscope for 22 November next year if we did not know *exactly* where the astronomical bodies would be in relationship to each other at that time? It was this imprecision that was perceived as the Achilles heel of astrological *scientia*.

Coming from a *non*-astrological direction, it was this very imprecision which led Copernicus around 1510 to revisit Heraclides, Hicetas, Ecphantus, and perhaps Archimedes, as a way of establishing a more coherent and reliable foundation for planetary position calculation, and to begin to frame his heliocentric hypothesis. Just as in the theologically reforming and counter-reforming sixteenth century astronomy was – no less than geography or anatomy – deemed in need of "reformation", so too was astrology. Once we had a more reliable set of mathematical principles enabling us to calculate planetary movements more accurately (and nowhere was this more urgently felt than in the need to quantify the long- and short-term cycles of the lunar orbit), then astronomy could well be "perfected". By extension, so could astrology. Consequently, humanity could be more effectively forewarned and enabled to make proper provision against coming plagues, famines, and natural disasters; all by the Providence of God.

ASTROLOGICAL MEDICINE

Medicine also, many felt, could be "reformed" and improved, as more precise horoscopes would make the diagnosis and prognosis of illness more accurate. How, then, did the doctor use astrology? Here one encounters a whole raft of "truisms" that made perfect sense to a geocentric, medical humoral culture, yet which strike us as illogical and absurd today.

Take blood-letting, for example, which was a universally employed therapy, used to treat a myriad of medical conditions ranging from high fever to post-surgical infection, from the consequences of gluttony to sexual excess, and even religious mania. A moderate loss of blood can actually appear to have a short-term benefit for the patient, in consequence of endorphins being released by the brain, causing the patient to feel a temporary sense of calm and well-being. The sixteenth-century doctor believed this response to have been occasioned by the hot humour, blood, getting rid of its excessive heat, thus helping to "re-balance" the other three humours: black bile (cold and dry), yellow bile (hot and dry), and phlegm (cold and wet). This, in turn, was deemed capable of "breaking" a fever, diminishing the fires of lust, cooling a throbbing surgical wound, or calming down the over-excited.

The wise physician had to check his calendar and almanac in order to bleed, or "phlebotomize", his patients at the more auspicious times, and pay especial attention to the phase of the moon, the season, and the patient's age. The following astrological surgical rhyme, or mnemonic, could have been taught to countless generations of medical students – perhaps with equivalents in Latin and vernacular European languages – long before its printed appearance in English in John Dade's *Almanack* of 1591.

The moon in age, the ancient sort,
Their veynes may open best:
The younger sort tyll moon be new
Must let their veynes have rest.

In other words, bleed the young as their blood rose with the vigorous waxing moon, and the elderly on the gentler waning moon. Did not the blood of the young overheat with the coming of spring, and the strength of the aged, like the moon, wane with autumn and winter? Blood-letting, and purging the bowels with black treacle, were good for the young body in spring, to expel the sluggish humours that had built up during the winter. And did it not stand to reason that growth and fecundity were enhanced by a waxing moon, especially in spring, and that weakness and diminution were more likely to happen during a waning, autumnal moon?

Superstitious and silly as these "old wives' tales" might strike us in the twenty-first century, when you think yourself back into a geocentric cosmos, with a world of four elements and four bodily humours, of waxing, waning, spontaneous heating and cooling, enlivening and diminishing, then it begins to make perfect logical sense. When Shakespeare spoke of the "Seven Ages of Man" in *As You Like It, c.* 1599 (Act II, scene vii), and wrote "The fault, dear Brutus, lies not in our stars" (*Julius Caesar, c.* 1599, Act I, scene ii), and many other astrologically inspired lines, he was addressing an audience to which they would have struck home as self-evident common sense. Whether you were Jack the ploughboy listening to the public reading of the latest almanac in The George and Dragon, or the Archbishop of Canterbury in his study in Lambeth Palace, your basic understanding would have been the same, in spite of differences in sophistication.

Astrology also made sense on a practical level, though for reasons which we today know were *not* astrologically related. In the age of variable and often seasonally related nutrition, winter, even for the wealthy classes, could be a time when protein, fresh fruit, and vegetables tailed off in the diet, and no amount of salt beef, bread, and desiccated codfish could compensate. It was a lot worse for the poor. Months of poor nutrition, especially between the last fresh meat of the Christmas feast and the appearance of the first hungrily gazed upon newborn lambs of spring, could cause resistance to disease to fall off markedly, especially if the winter were severe. It was hardly surprising, therefore, that the old and the sickly not infrequently breathed their last just as the first daffodils appeared. This had nothing to do with romantic deaths, alas: just plain medical fact. Nor was it surprising that, in addition to celebrating the resurrection, the young and fit should rejoice at "This Joyful Eastertide", as the days lengthened and warmed, lambs and piglets began to boil in the pot over the kitchen fire, Jack and Jill exchanged knowing glances, and the young spring moon hung in the western sky. In the time of the Renaissance, astronomy, medicine, food, and vitality were woven *logically* together in a way that prosperous, healthy, modern Western people find "superstitious".

Context apart, how would a doctor of 1600 make use of astrology? At his very first consultation, he would ask the patient for the *hora decumbitus*: literally, the exact time at which he had been forced to take to his bed. This gave the "nativity" or birth-time of the sickness. Next, the physician would want to know the patient's own astrological details, such as date and place of birth, and any formative "accidents" or incidents: previous illnesses, occupation, and probably even parentage. Was his disease hot, cold, moist, or dry? Was he fat, thin, jovial, melancholic, mercurial, or saturnine? Was his urine of a dark or bloody colour; were his stools "firm" or "lax"? What did his breath smell of? Was he sweaty or dry? These are the criteria upon which a sick Norwich Alderman of forty-five, born on a farm by the sea, the fifth son of a father who had hanged himself on the day of a lunar eclipse, and a mother who had caught and survived three bouts of the plague, each on her "lucky" days, would be assessed.

The doctor would then draw up a horoscope for the disease, based on these details, containing the exact planetary "aspects" for the *hora decumbitus*. He would then advance the horoscope, to identify forthcoming critical or benign times in the illness, and notice which planets may currently be in which zodiac signs. Did the moon play a significant part in the disease, and would its change of phase herald a speedy recovery? Or was slow-moving Saturn the trouble, the herald of death after a long illness?

The prescribed therapy could depend upon whether the physician was a "Galenist", who aimed to treat his patients by means of herbal drugs, or an "iatrochemist", prescribing mercury, antimony, and arsenic-based metal compound drugs. All would be administered at times that were most auspicious with regard to the horoscope. The metallic iatrochemist would treat the new and terrifying sixteenth-century disease of syphilis – ascribed to the planet Venus because of its association with sex – with the drug associated with the fast-moving planet Mercury, the winged messenger of the classical gods, who, along with Aesculapius, was associated with intelligence and healing. There was a pragmatic aspect to the regime as well, as Mercury compounds caused the patient to discharge large quantities of saliva, which was believed to get rid of that superfluity of moisture thought to lie at the root of sexual complaints. The diagnosis and treatment was a curious mixture of medical alchemy, pagan religion, and astrology in the world of Reformation and Counter-Reformation Christian Europe.

William Lilly, who would become an English "celebrity" astrologer during the 1650s, was willing, as a 22-year-old in 1624, to go beyond medical astrology and try his hand at amateur surgery, performing a mastectomy on the desperately ill wife of his London master – using a pair of scissors – as would later be recorded in his posthumously published *Whole Life* (1715).

ASTROLOGERS AND POLITICS

When civil war broke out between King Charles I and Parliament in 1642, the above-mentioned William Lilly and a number of their high-profile astrological colleagues on different sides of the conflict used horoscopes to boost the morale of the Royalist and Parliamentary armies. Lilly, at the height of his fame by 1650, and John Booker were Parliamentarian in sympathy, and it was said that their favourable almanac and pamphlet interpretations of celestial phenomena provided a great boost to Cromwell's troops. Less famous was the Royalist gentleman-astrologer with a connection to the astronomical Towneley family of Lancashire, George Wharton.

One must admit that Parliament had the best astrologers on its side, producing gripping titles such as the *Bloody Almanacks* for 1651 and 1652, and feeding upon civil war horrors and fears. One wonders if it was a matter of the heavens (if not heaven) being on the side of the big battalions?

Yet how could thinking people in the 1650s, with Copernicus, Kepler, Galileo, and a whole raft of major new astronomical discoveries behind them, still be hanging on the words of celebrity astrologers like William Lilly, while scores of his lesser brethren predicted, prophesied, published practical medicine, and ran very successful astrological consultancies in London and in the major provincial cities? The answer is straightforward: Galileo's discoveries notwithstanding, the Copernican theory still needed to be *proved* in 1650.

ASTROLOGY'S SWAN SONG

The telescope might have revealed wonders that undercut, time and again, the cosmologies of Ptolemy and Aristotle, yet it failed to provide an iota of proof that the earth actually moved. Nor had anyone measured a star parallax by 1650. It was the cosmology of Tycho Brahe, improved somewhat by Riccioli, that answered most questions. For Tycho's geo-heliocentric theory could not only accommodate and account for the phases of Venus as it rotated around the sun – which in turn rotated around the earth – but also the newly discovered planetary satellites, the spherical nature of the planets, the complex terrain of the moon, the location of comets in space (as opposed to in the terrestrial atmosphere), and even the infinite universe. All that had fundamentally changed was the status of the zodiac signs, which now became mere line-of-sight effects; but even the twelve ancient asterisms could still be interpreted as zones of influence around the 360-degree band of sky.

As we have seen already, the Tychonic system was the same, in the physical terms of the seventeenth century, as the Copernican. Where they differed was in whether the sun, or the earth, was the fixed centre of rotation. To many thinking people, who were not especially motivated either way, the Tychonic system won on points: on a common-sense level, the earth did *not* seem to be flying through space at a terrifying speed, even if one could accept that it may turn gently on its axis once a day.

It was not only an abundance of telescopic discoveries that failed to clinch the Copernican case so as to decisively undermine the credibility of astrology: an abundance of medical discoveries also failed to do so. A revolution in anatomy and physiology was in full flood by 1650. The dissection of animal and human cadavers was revealing more and more about the internal *mechanism* of how bodies worked, while the implications of Dr William Harvey's empirically based theory of the circulation of the blood under the contractive, or systolic, force of the heart were still being worked out in detail. What did the newly discovered lymph glands do? How did they relate to the arteries and veins? What could we learn about animal and human parallels when physiologists were demonstrating that the same essential physiology was shared between men, monkeys, pigs, and deer? René Descartes speculated about how the immortal soul interacted with the brain; and in 1664 the above-mentioned Christian anatomist Dr Thomas Willis of Christ Church, Oxford, would lay the foundation of the anatomy of the human brain in his *Cerebri Anatome* ("Anatomy of the Brain and Nerves"), a book which he would dedicate to his good friend and patient, the Most Reverend Gilbert Sheldon, Archbishop of Canterbury.

Were not all living beings *machines*, and as Thomas Hobbes – a good friend of Dr Harvey – put it in 1651: "For what is the *Heart*, but a *Spring*; and the *Nerves* but so many *Strings*; and the *Joynts*, but so many *Wheeles*, giving motion to the whole Body, such as was intended by the Artificer?" (*Leviathan*, Introduction). Yet a vast gulf existed between the great medical "laboratory" discoveries and practical bedside therapeutics, and a lot more discoveries would have to be made, by the nineteenth century, before new scientifically based cures became available. Fever, pain, mental illness, physiological disorders such as cancer and diabetes, and the infections that often set in after even simple surgery were as baffling in 1700 – or even 1800 – as they had been in the days of Hippocrates. Practical therapeutics would have to build up to a Victorian age "critical mass" of knowledge before bedside applications became available.

In consequence, the working doctor of 1680 still bled and purged his patients just as his colleagues of 1500 would have done, with the addition of a few newly discovered "specific" drugs, such as the South American "Jesuits' Bark", or crude quinine, to "break" malarial fevers. As I have said in lectures, the seventeenth-century physician may have been a scientist in the laboratory, but he was often little more than a shaman at the bedside.

On the other hand, there was a drastically diminished number of academically trained physicians by 1700 practising astrology, although Richard Saunders's *The Astrological Judgment and Practice of Physick* (1677) is a late but surprisingly comprehensive contribution to the genre. The eminent Dr Richard Mead, in his study of the possible relationship between lunar phases, times of death, and seven-day fever crises, was at pains to point out in *De Imperio Solis ac Lunae in Corpora humana* ("On the Influence of the Sun and Moon upon Human Bodies"), 1704, that any such correlations were due to Newtonian gravitational changes and *not* astrology – a view by that date which he probably shared with the great majority of his medical and scientific colleagues.

TIPPING THE SCALES OF CREDIBILITY

Astrology has never died out. Mister Punch, in his satirical magazine for 10 December 1859, merrily thrashed with a big stick "Zadkiel", a popular early Victorian astrologer, and a file is preserved in the archives of the Royal Observatory, Greenwich (now in Cambridge University Library), containing letters from maidservants and others who wrote to Sir George Airy, the Astronomer Royal, between 1835 and 1881, usually requesting him to cast a horoscope to advise on a forthcoming marriage. Sir George, to his great credit, always returned the correspondent's postal order, accompanied by a "form" letter advising the writer of the nonsensical status of astrology. The almanac-maker Old Moore, who claims to have been successfully predicting the future since the 1690s, may still be in print, as only a few years ago I bought an Old Moore from a promenade vendor at Blackpool, the popular Lancashire seaside resort. And no popular newspaper or woman's magazine can be without a "Your Stars" page. Fashionable "celebs", and even politicians who should know better, also make no bones about patronizing William Lilly's present-day successors. I once met an intelligent and educated middle-aged lady who said she had an astrological medical adviser.

No reputable person of science would countenance astrology today, in spite of those aficionados who try to explain "the art" in terms of galactic magnetism and supposed magnetic "pathways" in the body. It was in the mid and late seventeenth century that the scales of credibility began to tip against astrology in all its forms. One can trace, for example, in his surviving letters the journey taken by the Lancashire astronomer Jeremy Shakerley (whom we met in Chapter 21), from being an astrological disciple of William Lilly in 1647 to an ardent, posthumous admirer of his new hero, the fervently *anti*-astrological Jeremiah Horrocks, by 1651.

A couple of decades later, when the first Astronomer Royal, and another Horrocks admirer, the Revd John Flamsteed, was required to calculate an "auspicious" day for the commencement of the Royal Observatory, Greenwich, in 1675, he made it clear that he did not believe in astrology. His contemporary, the great experimental astronomer, physicist, and medical scientist Dr Robert Hooke, makes no references to astrology, seeing both the universe and the human body as physical machines designed by God.

The astronomer Edmond Halley (of comet fame) was likewise dismissive, while Dr Thomas Willis simply ignores astrology in both his surviving Oxford medical lectures and casebooks. It is true that a figure of the stature of Sir Isaac Newton, with his extensive interests in philosophical alchemy, may have been less dismissive, but as a general rule those men who were to make up the Fellowship of the Royal Society after 1660 were distinctly physical, materialist, and anti-occult in their approach to the study of the natural creation. On the other hand, they were overwhelmingly *theistic* in their understanding of that creation, as we shall see in Chapter 25, seeing God, just like their medieval forebears, as the "Grand Clockmaker".

So, at least in educated scientific circles, and in those circles which were increasingly taking their natural philosophical explanatory leads from the experimental scientists, astrological explanations were clearly in a state of atrophy by the late seventeenth century. While the earth's motion was still awaiting demonstration *as a physical fact* in 1700, and practical medical therapeutics still remained pitiably limited in their curative scope, one senses that a crucial watershed had been crossed in the intellectual culture of the age. For while science had only added further substantiation to the prior belief that the cosmos and natural world were products of an integrated divine design, the notion that they were also interpenetrated by occult, or mysterious, non-physical forces that could somehow be understood by means of the horoscope, had gradually sunk beneath the waves of credibility.

Chapter 24

Dr John Wilkins Flies to the Moon
– from Oxford

*I*t may appear incongruous that at a time when the generality of informed opinion was still treating astrology with cautious respect, a distinguished Copernican and Galilean astronomer in Holy Orders, soon to be head of an Oxford college and later Bishop of Chester, was seriously discussing a voyage to the moon. But that was the age of Galileo and Kepler: an age replete with intellectual and spiritual energy, creativity, and cross-currents.

I am not aware that anywhere in his writings between 1638 and the 1660s does the Revd Dr John Wilkins give so much as a nod to astrology, for it was not a part of his universe. His was a universe of cosmic vastness, with the planets being possibly inhabited worlds in their own right, and with an infinity of sun-like stars scattered through a seeming infinity of three-dimensional space. It also went without saying that Wilkins regarded the earth as both rotating around the sun and also upon its own axis, along with the rest of the planets.

This universe is first described in *A Discovery of a New World… in the Moon* (1638), then pictorially illustrated on the title page of his very influential *A Discourse Concerning a New World and Another Planet* (1640), where it is flanked by Copernicus holding a little model of his heliocentric solar system and Galileo displaying a telescope. This is a universe removed from the horoscope battles of his contemporaries William Lilly and George Wharton; and while we must be cautious not to read too much "modernity" into Wilkins, we cannot deny that his approach to astronomy and science was much closer to our own, like that of his other contemporaries – Horrocks, Crabtree, and Gascoigne – than to that of the celestial "figure casters" and "prognosticators". It truly was an age of cross-currents, although what all the factions would have agreed upon was the role of Divine Providence in the world.

Wilkins's importance in seventeenth-century astronomy came not just from his ideas about space travel; that was only a part of his broader vision, as we will see.

John Wilkins: the man and his background

John Wilkins was born at, or near, Canons Ashby, Northamptonshire, in January 1614, the son of Walter, a wealthy Oxford goldsmith, and Jane Dod, a gentlewoman of the county. He was educated at Oxford, ordained into the Anglican ministry, and presented with the living of Fawsley. His maternal grandfather, the Revd John Dod, obligingly looked after Fawsley parish, giving young Wilkins the freedom to travel, particularly in north Germany. From his wide reading, and contacts in Oxford, London, and further afield, the young Reverend John Wilkins became captivated by the new astronomy and science, which he saw as another manifestation of God's glory.

In addition to gifts of intellect and family resources, John Wilkins possessed key social gifts: charm, social ease, and a capacity to inspire others – vital attributes for the public figure and great educator that he would become. This emerging disciple of the philosophy of Sir Francis Bacon would also come to see science not only as God-inspired, but also as capable of transforming the human condition for the better, through ingenious inventions, machines, and applied technology. This would be the subject of his illustrated *Mathematical Magick* (1648). His portraits in Wadham College and the Royal Society, painted by Mary Beale around 1670, catch that geniality for which he would become renowned.

A WORLD IN THE MOON, 1638–40

While Joseph Webbe had produced, yet never published, an English translation of Galileo's *Dialogue on the Two World Systems* (1633) in 1635, and Thomas Digges's *Prognostication* had discussed the Copernican and the infinite universe back in 1576, no one had fully thought through and set out the implications of the Copernican, Galilean, Keplerian, and telescopic universe for English-language readers until 1638. This was to be the achievement of the 24-year-old John Wilkins. What led him to take up this challenge is not clear, but his *Discovery* was to be the first of a series of beautifully written and inspiring English books on scientific and theological subjects that he would write over the next thirty years, by which time English would have become a widely used language for scientific discourse. I have always thought it a pity that while literary scholars have produced monumental studies on the rise, usage, and evolution of the English language from *Beowulf* to Milton's *Paradise Lost* (1667) and beyond, very little attention has been paid to technical works in the language. This is all the more unfortunate as by 1640 there was a rich vein of English published books on geography, navigation and seamanship, land surveying, geometry, chemistry, gunnery and military science, farming, popular medicine, and, as we have already seen, astrology.

It is clear that Wilkins was familiar with this body of publications. Books on geographical discovery especially fascinated him, along with those on invention and mechanical technology, while it is obvious that his reading familiarity with these subjects went beyond English to Latin and to European vernacular works. Wilkins's books on astronomical discovery – real and visionary – stemmed from a love of ships as large complex conveyances and of machines of all kinds, and from a bedazzlement with the geographical discoveries of the preceding 150 years. These had transformed and extended humanity's knowledge of the planet that we live upon, to include the exotic human, animal, vegetable, and mineral denizens of the new-found lands. For surely, if a ship could lead brave travellers to the discovery and exploration of America, why could not a different type of "ship", perhaps one propelled by wings powered by some sort of machinery, take us to the moon? Naïve and over-optimistic as we – with four centuries of hindsight – may think these ideas nowadays, within the context of that time they were truly inspiring.

The actual design, building of, and ascent in his "Flying Chariot" space vehicle was only part of Wilkins's wider endeavour. His broader educative vision was to popularize the "new astronomy", especially for English readers. The first part of this enterprise, his 1638 *Discovery of a New World*, was concerned with the moon, and how knowledge of our satellite had been transformed over the past three decades. In this work, he skilfully deployed those techniques of how to marshal evidence and drive home a powerful argument which he would have acquired as a student under the tutelage of John Tombes at Magdalen Hall, Oxford, in much the same way that Sir Francis Bacon had done sixty years earlier at Cambridge and the Inns of Court.

He begins by reminding his readers that because the discoveries made with the telescope are *new*, or "strange", that is no reason to reject them: an important point for an age that still saw the ancients as knowing all that was knowable. This is driven home by challenging Aristotle's *De Caelo* ("On the Heavens"), and arguing that there is no reason to believe that astronomical bodies are made of a pure, incorruptible "fifth element", or *quintessence*, whereas the earth is made of changeable mixtures of earth, water, air, and fire. As in all his writings, the young Wilkins's text bristles with the opinions of learned men. Biblical patriarchs, Hebrew quotations, classical and modern authors are all cited – and translations or parentheses supplied – to drive home his points, and, no doubt, to show what a learned fellow he was. All this is set out as a prelude to his treatment of the telescopic moon.

WILKINS'S TELESCOPIC MOON AND
ITS POSSIBLE INHABITANTS

The thrust of Wilkins's argument in the *Discovery* is to demonstrate that the telescopic moon is not a smooth celestial body, made of some un-earthlike substance as the ancients had proposed, but was a rocky world, just like the one we live on. This argument draws its substantiation from the very nature of the lunar terrain, for while it may have appeared smooth – albeit tarnished – to the naked eye, yet even a low-powered telescope reveals it to have a rough and craggy surface. Here Wilkins draws primarily upon Galileo's *Sidereus Nuncius* and his own lunar observations.

The moon, Wilkins argues, has "high mountains, deep vallies, and spacious plains",[1] while after Galileo and other lunar cartographers, he sees the dark areas, or "spots", as containing great expanses of water, like seas, while the brighter regions were the "land". He also argues, like other contemporary writers, that the moon probably possesses an atmosphere, suggesting that the "trepidation", or shimmering of the lunar limb at the time of solar eclipse, might indicate a lunar atmosphere.[2] (As we saw in Chapter 21, at the very time the *Discovery* was published, Jeremiah Horrocks in Lancashire had good observational evidence for the moon being airless, though Wilkins could not have been aware of Horrocks's then unpublished work.)

All the above points about the world-like moon, based on a mixture of recent published discoveries and comments and speculations from carefully selected classical writers, were used by Wilkins to build up to three key arguments.

Firstly, there are almost certainly lunar inhabitants. On the other hand, he fully admits that we have not at present any way of knowing their true nature. He quotes from the writings of the fifteenth-century cosmologically minded Cardinal Nicholas of Cusa, who was of the opinion that our satellite "is inhabited by men, and beasts, and plants",[3] as were other writers whom he cites. But whence did they originate? Were they of "the seed of Adam", or were they uncorrupted? Could it have been of the lunar inhabitants that Paul spoke in Ephesians 1:10, when he talked of all things on earth *and in the heavens* being gathered up in Christ? Could the moon even have been that paradise to which the "good thief" had gone with Christ immediately following the crucifixion?[4]

Wilkins's arguments for an inhabited moon go well beyond the plain scientific findings of the time. In brief, seventeenth-century people found it hard to see how a bountiful Creator God could have made a seemingly habitable world and then left it uninhabited. After all, one did not build houses in an uninhabited land. The idea of an inhabited universe addressed other issues that were at the front of many minds in Wilkins's day, such as whether "space beings" were saved or damned; for, as we have seen time and again in this book, science and religion penetrated the Astronomical Renaissance in an inextricable warp and weft.

Secondly, was there a "plurality of worlds" beyond the moon, and if so, could they also be inhabited? Here Wilkins displays once again a rich body of classical, biblical and Patristic erudition as he sets out to review the pros and cons for there being other worlds. Wilkins concludes that there is no explicit reason *against* a multitude of worlds, and that the idea "doth not contradict any principle of reason or faith".[5] Regarding their possible inhabitants, though, he goes on to say "of what kind they are is uncertain".[6]

What is important in the above is not the antiquity of the debate about a plurality of worlds and their inhabitants, so much as Wilkins's awareness that the new telescopic discoveries, and the new Copernican, Galilean universe, gave a new, *physical* edge to the old philosophical discussions, imparting to them a new urgency, and a new relevance, no less.

Thirdly, one of the most extraordinary and daring of Wilkins's arguments in the *Discovery*, which would recur a decade later in *Mathematical Magick*, was his discussion of mankind's devising some kind of "conveyance to this other world [the moon]"; and in particular, what he would come to style a "Flying Chariot". But before looking at Wilkins's ideas on space flight, let us return to what he had to say about the Copernican universe, and his presentation of that universe to an English readership.

THE EARTH IS BUT A PLANET

Having argued in 1638 for the world-like nature of the moon, Wilkins proceeded in 1640 to advance the case that the earth itself is but a planet, and that it rotates around the sun. Here he takes up the argument that simply because an idea may be new, that is no reason for assuming it to be erroneous. No doubt knowing his likely readership, he sets out all of his wares of classical and theological erudition. Job, for instance, is finally reminded of his ignorance by God ("Where wast thou when I laid the foundations of the earth?", Job 38:4),[7] while the Greek Pythagoras was esteemed for his "rare inventions".[8] Greek and Latin quotations – with English translations – fly thick and fast. Wilkins hammers home the point that it was with the writings and discoveries of Copernicus, the geo-magnetic studies of William Gilbert, and the discoveries of Kepler and Galileo that things got going, over the previous century or so.

Wilkins then launches into a series of discussions that range across biblical interpretation and Copernican astronomy. Very important to Wilkins's position, as it had been to Galileo in his *Letter to the Grand Duchess Christina* (1615), is the point that one cannot use Scripture as a guide to how the heavens work. The Holy Ghost, in the inspiration of Scripture, had "conform[ed] his expressions to the error of our conceits",[9] and hence spoken to the ancient Jews in the language of common sense rather than in a precise scientific form. Translating from the early fifteenth-century Spanish theologian Tostatus (Tostado of Avila), Wilkins argues that Joshua, in his commanding the sun and moon to stand still, was perhaps "unskilful in astronomy, having the same gross conceit [ignorance] of the heavens, as the vulgar [common people] had".[10]

Having dealt mainly with potential theological and philosophical objections to the moving earth in the first six chapters of his 1640 *That the Earth may be a planet*, Wilkins spends the remaining four arguing specifically for the Copernican theory. He draws his arguments largely from physical dynamic experiments, such as noting the paths followed by cannonballs shot into the exact vertical, indicating from the fall of the shot that the earth must be moving,[11] and the illusion of the apparent motion of the land as one sails down a smooth river.

None of Wilkins's arguments are original, and he does not claim that they are, for he is writing not as a researcher but as an advocate of the new astronomy to English readers. Being a great science communicator, all of his works on the new astronomy are meticulously footnoted, referenced, translated, or else paraphrased.

Not everyone was charmed by Wilkins's easy and plausible style. Most notably, the Aberdeen-born and educated Anglican clergyman Alexander Ross attacked Wilkins in *The New Planet, No Planet* (1646), as part of his wider defence of Aristotelianism and scholastic philosophy. On the other hand, Ross's attack put the young Wilkins into the company of some of the leading thinkers of the age, for Ross not only went for Wilkins's heliocentricism, but also for Copernicus, Kepler, and Galileo, the mechanical philosopher Thomas Hobbes, and even Dr William Harvey for his 1628 theory on the circulation of the blood: a discovery which fundamentally undermined much of classical physiology. And if this was not enough of a roll-call of distinguished thinkers for Wilkins to be included among, there were also Descartes, Spinoza, Dr Sir Thomas Browne, Sir Kenelm Digby, and a good few more.

Flying to the Moon

Wilkins concludes his book on the moon with a fourteenth chapter setting out how one might undertake a journey to the moon: and here he launches into an amazing set of ideas for a man of that time, for Wilkins's discussion of a moon voyage is a heady mixture of literature, history, theology, legend, new science, and visionary technology. Visionary is a good way to think of it, for in Chapter XIV Wilkins pushes out the boundaries of optimism, ingenuity, and inspiration. However, we must not look upon Wilkins from the standpoint of what we know today, and laugh at his seeming naivety, but from what he made appear as just around the corner between 1638 and 1648.

Three things, I would suggest, played a pivotal role in Wilkins's moon-voyage thinking: geographical discovery, recent advances in science and mechanical technology, and early "science fiction" writing. We need a "Drake, or Columbus to undertake this voyage", he reminds us,[12] and, learning from the classical fable of the foolish Daedalus, who flew up too close to the sun, we need prudence "to invent a conveyance through the air",[13] and not just use wax to stick feathered wings to our backs like the unfortunate Greek.

Wilkins's moon voyage belonged, in many ways, to a Renaissance tradition of stories of journeys to far-away lands, whose inhabitants supplied inspiration and new direction for the European travellers who come upon them. One thinks immediately of Sir Thomas More's *Utopia* (1516) and Sir Francis Bacon's *New Atlantis* (1628), with their fictional lands of godly peace, prosperity, and scientific progress – lands that the degenerate Europeans should regard as exemplars and spurs to reform, and which, as we shall see in Chapter 25, were replete with ideals fundamental to the founding of the early Royal Society, for which Wilkins would be an inspiration.

The contemporary work of "science fiction" that clearly made an enduring impression on John Wilkins was Johannes Kepler's *Somnium* ("Dream") of 1634, with, as we saw in Chapter 8, its Tycho-Brahe-trained hero Duracotus flying to the moon and describing this strange and exotic planet and its inhabitants. The writings of Francis Godwin, the Oxford churchman who was Bishop of Hereford at the time of his death in 1633, also coloured Wilkins's thinking, for Godwin was a Copernican who had written a fictional account of a voyage to the moon that was published posthumously in 1638. In Godwin's story, his hero, Domingo Gonzales, was somewhat accidentally conveyed to the moon by a flock of powerful "Ganza" birds attached to a trapeze-like seat in which Gonzales rode. The voyage took twelve days, and he not only discovered the moon to be a pleasant and carefree utopian place, but its inhabitants to be good Christians, ruled over by the benign Irdonozur. What is more, the lunar language was extremely tuneful and pleasant, and Wilkins would return to the fictional lunar language in his *Mercury; or the Secret Messenger* (1641), where he discussed another of his favourite subjects: the nature of languages, sounds, and codes.

One must also add in to Wilkins's thinking, on the science fiction side, the *True History of Lucian of Samosata* of AD 160, which had been issued in English in 1634. In Lucian's tale, a ship had been taken up by a great wind – and deposited safely on the moon.

All in all, it is clear that by 1640 many subjects which we today regard as very modern, such as infinity, space flight, and life on other worlds – along with matters of less concern, such as the spiritual state of space-beings – were being actively discussed by "scientists", theologians, inventors, and imaginative writers.

The Jacobean space programme

It is when Wilkins gets down to discussing the practical logistics of space flight that he displays his real genius for original and lateral thinking. He first addresses these logistical questions in *Discovery* (1638), and then begins to wrestle with the actual business of mechanical flight and "Flying Chariot" design in *Mathematical Magick* – as part of an enterprise which I have styled the "Jacobean Space Programme".

Fundamental to this enterprise is his attempt to establish the extent of the earth's (gravitational) attraction, which he sees as somehow analogous to its magnetic field. Clearly inspired by William Gilbert's experiments with the attractive fields of spherical magnets in *De Magnete* (1600), Wilkins concludes that the earth's pull probably ceases beyond 20 miles above the earth's surface: a height which he seems to derive from geometrical attempts to measure the heights of flimsy clouds. Getting into space, therefore, required a means of rising up over 20 miles to escape the earth's "sphere of magnetic virtue", after which one might be able to glide to the moon.

Space, argued Wilkins, should be temperately warm; after one had passed through the cold regions of the clouds – created with the waters in Genesis on the second day of creation – space, being the domain of the sun, made by God on the fourth day, should be pleasant. Through a combination of observations, biblical interpretations, and ingenious logic, Wilkins concludes that the air present in space should be easily breathable.

Food would not be necessary in space, for once beyond the earth's pull, a man would not expend his "spirits" (or energy), and hence would no longer feel hungry. Besides, Wilkins is quick to pile on evidence, drawn from a gallery of cited sources, of animals and humans who lived happily for long periods without nourishment. Protestant Wilkins was quick to point out the case of "a priest (of whom one of the popes had the custody) that lived forty years upon meer air".[14] So, by implication, what feats might an English Protestant achieve?

Having faced, and hopefully dealt with, the logistical problems of the journey, Wilkins launches into the much greater task of devising a conveyance, or space vehicle. Displaying his erudition as always, he discusses various stories of terrestrial flight to date: an account from Constantinople of a man flying across the Bosporus, a Marco Polo story of the "Gt. Ruck" bird of China with feathers 12 feet long,[15] and the story of the Canterbury monk Elmer who, in the days of St Edward the Confessor (*c.* 1050), flew a furlong before falling and breaking his legs.[16] Even successful early "model aircraft" are thrown in to make up the weight of Wilkins's argument, such as the "wooden dove" attributed to the ancient Greek Archytas,[17] and an "iron fly" devised by the fifteenth-century Nuremberg astronomer Regiomontanus, which would allegedly fly around the guests at the dinner table.[18]

It is in the "Daedalus; or, mechanical motions" section of *Mathematical Magick* that Wilkins discusses flying machine *details*. Having discounted the feasibility of flying to the moon using obliging spirits (like Kepler's Duracotus), "fowls" (like Domingo Gonsales), or wings "fastened immediately to the body" like Daedalus, he gets down to the business of discussing a mechanically powered "Flying Chariot".

In Wilkins's view, a viable Flying Chariot was only just around the corner. All of his early writings, and *Mathematical Magick* in particular, make it clear that technological ingenuity was progressing by leaps and bounds by 1648. Clocks and watches, geared automata, multi-shot crossbows, experimental wind-cars, wind- and water-mills, geared industrial machines, great ships, and a host of other labour-saving devices were becoming commonplace across Western Europe. Even an automatic kitchen spit that turned the meat at exactly the correct rate with relation to the fire's heat (an early "smart" or automatic environmentally responsive invention) is both described and illustrated. There were also fast wind-powered four-wheel land ships operating across the Dutch polder, while Wilkins supplies an engraving of a geared arrangement whereby a man, by no more than a puff of breath, might uproot a mighty oak tree.

Add up all the ingenuity potential displayed in these devices, and surely we will soon have a viable flying machine which, if it can ascend 20 miles, will take us to the moon. This is Wilkins's clarion call to the age in which he lived.

The "Flying Chariot"

John Wilkins never provides an explicit drawing or description of his Flying Chariot in his published works, though they are full of descriptions of components which we can attempt to assemble into a whole. On the other hand, what existed in his manuscripts and drafts we shall never know, for tragically much of his library was destroyed by the Great Fire of London of 1666.

But of the existence of such descriptions and drawings in the 1650s, when Wilkins was Warden of Wadham College, Oxford, there is no doubt, for his young protégé Robert Hooke tells us so in his own writings. Hooke later recollected that around 1658 he and Dr Wilkins "made a Module [model] which, by the help of Springs and Wings, rais'd and sustain'd itself in the Air".[19] Before the Royal Society, on 11 February 1675, Hooke "Declared that I had a way of making artificial muscule [muscle, or springy material] to command the strength of twenty men. Told my way of flying by vanes [wings] tryd at Wadham" some twenty years before.[20]

Putting all the descriptions of the components together, one might say that Wilkins's proposed Flying Chariot was designed along the following lines. The body of the chariot was probably meant to be like a small ship, or pinnace. It would have contained some kind of clockwork engine which, via gears, levers, and pulleys, would power a set of great wings that would project – most likely – from the sides, amidships.

Considering Wilkins's wild optimism about gears and their supposed capability in that pre-inertial-physics age to upgrade the mechanical energy put into them by a factor of many *thousands* of times, one might surmise that he did not envisage the need for a very large spring engine – perhaps an engine no bigger than that of a modest church clock, but powered by a great spring rather than weights. The wings should be covered with feathers, he suggested, particularly those of birds that flew to great heights, such as eagles. And while Wilkins is not explicit on the point, one presumes that the Jacobean astronauts could use a cranking handle to re-wind the motor to ensure a comfortable landing on the moon, for once in space, he seemed to think the machine would simply glide moon-ward.

About six months was the time Wilkins reckoned would be necessary to accomplish the voyage. To an age accustomed to the idea that a journey to the Americas could easily last two to three months (especially if one sailed on the "southern" route and re-provisioned in the Canary or Azores Islands), and one to China nine or more months, Wilkins's proposed time-scale for a moon voyage sounded reasonable, considering that by 1648 astronomers had a pretty good idea of the lunar distance.

What kind of "commerce" could the sky-voyagers expect to have with the "Selenites", or moon-folk, especially as there was no real idea of what these beings were like? "Commerce", after all, in seventeenth-century parlance could mean an exchange of ideas, as well as buying and selling; or could the moon have valuable mineral deposits, or provide markets for English trade goods? (The moon has fourteen earth-day-long nights: might such a dark, chilly place furnish a good market for the hard-pressed English woollen trade? Wilkins is not in any way explicit on the point of commerce, but seventeenth-century merchants were always on the look-out for lucrative business possibilities.)

Yet, as Wilkins reminds us, a Flying Chariot need not be confined to space travel, for it could also function as an aeroplane and fly across the earth's surface. Here we catch a glimpse of potential supersonic travel from Jacobean England that antedated the Concorde aircraft by over 300 years. Wilkins suggests that one might fly between places on the same latitude on the earth by simply ascending vertically beyond the earth's "sphere of magnetick virtue", or gravitational pull, then hanging stationary in space for as many hours as it took for North America, the Pacific, or China to appear below, and then gently descending. In this way, one could travel to America in an afternoon, or to China or the Indies in half a day. What is more, argued Wilkins, the air several miles above the earth's surface was most likely tranquil, for the wind and weather seemed to belong to those turbulent regions close to the earth's surface. These were remarkable advantages that one might enjoy from living in a heliocentric universe, upon a planet with a magnetic field and an atmosphere that rotated with the world upon its axis.[21]

Aware as Wilkins was of the likely gradual diminution of the pull of the "sphere of magnetick virtue" the further one ascended, he suggested that at great heights very little power would be needed to propel the wings. A proportionate diminution of pull or attraction with distance was perceived by Gilbert with relation to his spherical magnet experiments, and by Johannes Kepler with regard to the diminishing brightness of a beam of light with distance. As we have seen, Wilkins was fully acquainted with the writings of Gilbert and Kepler, as he was with those of Sir Francis Bacon and Galileo.

Moon-voyaging postponed by 300 years

Wilkins was writing at a time when science was moving ahead faster than at any previous time in human history – and not just scientific ideas and theories, but also specific physical and experimentally verifiable discoveries (although many of these discoveries still had to be explained in coherent physical terms). Like his mentor Bacon, John Wilkins saw experiment as the acid test for physical reality; and while some of the ideas we have seen above may seem a long way from a laboratory demonstration, he nonetheless held the experiment as the ultimate arbiter of natural truth.

Wilkins lived at a time which might be thought of as the "honeymoon period" of modern science. Discoveries were abounding, ancient theories were biting the dust one after the other in the face of new, and often experimentally derived, facts. Scientific instruments, such as the telescope, microscope, airpump, and magnetic devices, were providing new internationally verifiable standards for evaluating what was a demonstrable fact and what was a speculation, as experimental *induction* superseded philosophical *deduction* as a way of proceeding in *scientia*.

From a different perspective, science in Wilkins's time was in a state of confusion, for it was one thing to amass lots of new experimental facts, but another to explain these facts and put them into a coherent framework of understanding. How, for example, did the physics of the heliocentric, Copernican universe relate to the terrestrial physics of falling and moving bodies? Were the forces that governed the heavens the same as those governing terrestrial motion? How did magnetism relate to the "gravitating force"? What was light, and why was it sometimes coloured, and sometimes white? What were heat and cold – a subject that fascinated Bacon – and how did they relate to the presence or absence of mechanical friction?

On a more metaphysical level, how could the Selenites have immortal souls if mankind had a unique relationship with God? Did Christ's suffering redeem just fallen terrestrial humanity, or the entire cosmos, including sinful Selenites, Jupiterians, or even folks living on planets that might be orbiting Sirius? Problems apart, the decades between *c.* 1610 and 1670 seemed full of possibilities that would have been unimaginable 200 years previously.

On the other hand, it was also this sheer escalating rate of progress that made a scientifically based moon voyage seem little more than a pipe dream by the time of Wilkins's death in November 1672. Perhaps the biggest obstacle to the optimism of 1638 came from within that group of scientific friends that formed around Wilkins at Wadham College in the 1650s, and which in 1660 became the Royal Society of London.

The decisive blow came from Wilkins's old protégé Robert Hooke, and the great Irish chemist the Honourable Robert Boyle when, between 1658 and 1660, they built an airpump of novel design, which could not only produce a vacuum on demand, but also explore the vacuum's properties. Most notably, the laboratory vacuum was found to relate directly to the falling mercury in a barometer tube as one ascended a tall building or a mountain. So the "thinness" of the air on mountains, which Wilkins tried to argue his way around in 1638–40, was real and physically measurable. By extension, space itself came to be seen as a vacuum.

What is more, living creatures were shown to die in a vacuum, so by the same logic, sky voyagers in a Flying Chariot would also be dead shortly after leaving the earth's surface. If that was not enough, physical thinking by 1670 was showing that magnetism and gravity were two separate physical forces, so that analogies drawn from experiments with spherical magnets could not necessarily be applied to the "gravitating force" that bound the solar system together.

So, while Hooke and others in Continental Europe still entertained hopes of possible *terrestrial* flight, all serious discussion of space flight was pretty well dead by 1670. As mentioned above, the body which was becoming the forum for much of this advanced experimental thinking was, in many ways, Wilkins's own brain-child: the Royal Society.

CHAPTER 25

The Royal Society and the International Fellowship of Science

$\mathcal{O}$ne of the landmark achievements of the Scientific Renaissance was the creation of an international community of men (no women, alas, at that time) who recognized a common set of attitudes and assumptions pertaining to the study of the natural world. This sense of a community of scholars dedicated to a given end was not in itself a unique feature of science. Europe's great medieval universities were academic communities or societies, sharing a common set of rules, goals, and assumptions; while the Renaissance was to witness the rise of the private societies or academies, such as the Academy of Lynxes (to which Galileo belonged), Florence's Accademia della Cimento, a group in Geneva, the French Pléïade, and those literary societies which so captivated John Milton during his Grand Tour of France and Italy in 1638.

These private societies or academies were usually under the direct patronage of a prince or other great personage, and hence – like della Cimento – ceased to exist when their patron died or went on to do other things. The great majority (though not all) of these groups tended to devote themselves to the study of classical literature and philosophy, and tried, in various degrees, to emulate what they believed had been the ancient academies of Greece. Most of them were courtly in their structure, and depended upon the good graces, and the largesse, of a noble patron.

The Royal Society of London was a body of a very different kind. Inspired as it undoubtedly was by the fictional Salomon's House Academy in Sir Francis Bacon's *New Atlantis* of 1628, and no doubt looking forward to patronage from on high, the circumstances of mid-seventeenth-century England were to ensure that it developed along very different lines. The way it developed was to be portentous not only for mainland British learned associations in science and the arts, but also for those of the ensuing English-speaking world: in America, Australasia, and elsewhere.

"Gentlemen, Free and Unconfin'd"

The Royal Society was born of that world of free-associating persons coming together in pursuit of a common interest and forming a body whose membership and executive officers were elected from within rather than appointed from above. It was an ancient form of assembly, with parallels extending back to the idealized (rarely ever realized in practice) republics of Plato and his admirers, and even the early Christian church. After all, following the resurrection, when the eleven disciples decided to bring in a twelfth man to replace Judas Iscariot, they "cast lots", or held an election.

Many of the great medieval universities were also self-electing bodies, as were England's legal Inns of Court, the Mayor and Aldermen of great merchant cities such as London, and the House of Commons after *c.* 1260. All of these bodies, and most notably the independent colleges of Oxford and Cambridge Universities, were self-electing hierarchies, with rotation of officers, being what they called "Societies" or "Houses", and Christ Church, Oxford, is still referred to as "The House". Their members, in the Latin, were styled *Socii*, or in English, "Fellows": a term indicating equality, friendship, and brotherhood, as opposed to being chosen by and somehow subservient to a higher human power.

The Royal Society was by no means the first "club" or society of scientifically minded men in Great Britain. There was that circle of geographical and optical friends who congregated around Dr John Dee in Queen Elizabeth I's reign, while in 1610 there were the "Traventine [Trefenti] philosophers" or astronomers in Carmarthenshire, South Wales, who probably met at the home of Sir William Lower, and whom we met in Chapter 19. In 1640s London, there seem to have been several groups of scientific friends, such as the one around Dr Jonathan Goddard and Sir Paul Neile; while Gresham College, in the City of London, hosted another, which met in the college after the weekly astronomy lecture of Professor Lawrence Rooke, and which may have been related to what Robert Boyle would style the "Invisible College".[1] There were also lines of scientific correspondence, such as the Horrocks, Crabtree, and Gascoigne circle (Chapter 21); while the London-based German merchant and lover of the new science, Samuel Hartlib, acted as an "intelligencer" or passer-on of ideas from across Europe. There was a very heterogeneous community of scientific men, in Britain and in parts of northern Europe, who belonged to "corresponding societies".

On a formal level, and which in some ways formed a model for the future Royal Society, was the Royal College of Physicians, a body granted its Royal Charter in 1518 by King Henry VIII. While it is true that the college had power over the practice of medicine in the metropolis, it resembled the early Royal Society in the respect that, while enjoying the legal status and privileges of a Royal Charter, it had full control of its own internal affairs, could elect its own members and officers, and was not beholden to the sovereign on an operational level. Its senior members, just as in an Oxbridge college, were, and still are, Fellows.

It was this spirit of intellectual and personal independence that led Bishop Thomas Sprat and early Fellows in 1667 to describe the Royal Society as composed of "*Gentlemen*: free, and unconfin'd".[2]

THE OXFORD "PHILOSOPHICAL CLUB": 1648–60

It was the Revd Dr John Wilkins who founded that "Club" of scientific friends which became the Royal Society, not long after becoming Warden of Wadham College, Oxford, in 1648. As we saw in Chapter 24, Wilkins was a political and theological moderate, or conservative, at a time when the civil-war-racked nation was in danger of sliding into political anarchy and Puritan fanaticism.

An Anglican clergyman, who recognized the failings of the personal rule of King Charles I and of Archbishop Laud's religious policies, Wilkins favoured a religious settlement that would be "comprehensive", or tolerant of a variety of strands of Trinitarian, primarily Protestant, Christian thinking. In the mayhem of the Civil War and the abolition of the Church of England, he affiliated himself (like Oliver Cromwell) with the "Independents", a "broad church" body of opinion, rather than with the strict Calvinist Presbyterians who were coming to dominate Parliament, or the sometimes messianic, visionary "Sectaries", like the Ranters or Fifth Monarchy Men. It says much for Wilkins's charm and power of personality that he could successfully hold two plum pieces of Parliamentary patronage during that turbulent age – the wardenship of Wadham, then the Mastership of Trinity College, Cambridge – marry Oliver Cromwell's sister Robina in 1656, be a close adviser to the Independent Oliver, then become a dean, and finally a bishop, in the reconstituted Church of England under King Charles II.

As Warden of Wadham, his tolerant regime made it possible for Royalist parents to entrust their sons to Wilkins's care, such as Dr Christopher Wren, the evicted Dean of the Chapel Royal at Windsor, did with his son Christopher, the future scientist and architect. Other young men would be "bred up" under his influence who would later become bishops, such as Thomas Sprat of Wadham, and the Cambridge graduate John Tillotson who knew Wilkins in London, and who in 1691 would become Archbishop of Canterbury. Many of Wilkins's clerical protégés would become Fellows of the Royal Society.

Wilkins's "Club" was an informal affair: a group of friends, in fact. It included dons, both from within Wadham and from other colleges, scientifically gifted undergraduates, what we would now call "postgraduates", and private gentlemen. The Honourable Robert Boyle, the great Irish chemist, fell into this last category. Living in London at the mansion of his sister Lady Ranelagh, or on his estate at Stalbridge, Wiltshire, Boyle, a deeply devout, ascetic bachelor, was invited by Wilkins to come to live in Oxford, where he took rooms and set up a research laboratory at Deep Hall, in the High Street. This property was owned by John Crosse, an enterprising Oxford apothecary and businessman, who himself had connections with Wilkins and the "Club". Although the university honoured Boyle by awarding him a Doctorate in Medicine in 1665, the great chemist was never a formal member of Oxford University.

As we saw in Chapter 24, it was the "new" Copernican, Galilean telescopic astronomy and mechanics that most captivated Wilkins, and this concern would be shared by four men in particular who became members of the "Club". Two were senior academics who had moved to Oxford from Cambridge, and two were students.

The Revd Drs Seth Ward and John Wallis came to Oxford in 1649 to take up, respectively, the prestigious Savilian Professorships of Astronomy and Geometry. Both were Copernicans who, at the Restoration of the monarchy in 1660, would resume their Orders as Anglican clergymen. Both enjoyed European reputations as men of science, and Professor Ward, being a bachelor, was invited by Dr Wilkins to take up residence in Wadham College, which he did. Living, so college tradition has it, on the staircase giving access to the tower above the main gate – in those days Warden Wilkins's lodgings were probably on the same staircase – Seth Ward would have been well placed for making astronomical observations.

John Wallis came to live in a house only a couple of hundred yards away from Wadham, and by 1649 already had a formidable reputation as a geometer and mathematician, to say nothing of his distinction as a code-breaker and expertise in codes and cyphers. No doubt he partook in astronomical observation along with Wilkins, Ward, and others.

The two students who became involved in Wilkins's circle were Christopher Wren (knighted 1673) and his close friend Robert Hooke. Both were recognized as young men of prodigious scientific brilliance. Wren was a Wadham man, whereas Hooke was an undergraduate at Christ Church, and both seem to have been "talent spotted" by Wilkins. Although we know for certain that Hooke had been a pupil at Westminster School under the Headmastership of the formidably learned Revd Dr Richard Busby, the source of Wren's early schooling is unclear, and modern research has tended to undermine the tradition that he too was an old Westminster boy. Both were sons of clergy, however.

While still in their teens, these young men had already, and separately, embarked upon a remarkable set of scientific research.

Wren was making observations of Saturn, and trying to fathom out its rings, which were not yet understood, while Hooke was building flying machines at Westminster: a line of interest, I suspect, that led Wilkins to first take notice of him. Wren, the elder of the two, would go on to become Professor of Astronomy at Gresham College, London, by the age of twenty-five, and then succeed Ward to the Oxford Chair when he became a bishop, while his friend Hooke became Gresham Professor of Geometry in 1665. After the Great Fire of 1666, the friends would work together in rebuilding the devastated metropolis.

SCIENCE AND SOCIABILITY IN CROMWELLIAN OXFORD

The 1650s is popularly seen as a grim decade by historical writers. Yes, the horrors of civil war were past, but then, we are led to believe, the "Puritans" came in with their heavy hand: banning maypoles, Sunday sports, church ceremony, music, fashionable clothes and long hair, any kind of fun, and even the celebration of Christmas, and replacing them with Sabbatarian dourness, compulsory two-hour hell-fire sermons, strict sobriety, silence, black clothes, and enforced righteousness. While some of these changes undoubtedly did happen, it was not all doom and gloom. For fun, joy, and a love of the unusual are very hard to suppress.

One undoubted haven was John Wilkins's Wadham College, with its sociable group of scientific men. The Royalist diarist John Evelyn was delighted with his visit on 13 July 1654, commenting on the remarkable array of scientific devices he was shown – including Wilkins's glass beehives, enabling him to study the life of the bee colony without harming the bees – as well as Wadham's welcoming atmosphere.[3]

In addition to astronomers, mathematicians, experimental physiologists, horticulturalists, chemists, and other "*Gentlemen*; free and unconfin'd", the Club welcomed in what we might now call a "technician" – Christopher Brookes, the Wadham Manciple, or steward, who in addition to his domestic duties in the college was a skilled deviser of machines and instruments. A scientist-artisan collaboration was established which was to be an important part of the future Royal Society's agenda for advancing useful knowledge and improving the human condition.

Nor was it all about science and discovery, however. In 1658 Dr Wilkins invited the celebrated German violinist Thomas Baltzar, said to have been the most brilliant virtuoso of the day, to make a visit to Wadham during his time in England. We have a detailed account of a very jolly gathering in the company of Wilkins and friends from the diary of Anthony à Wood of Merton College for an occasion falling between 24 and 27 July 1658. Not only was everyone dazzled by Baltzar's playing, but Wood himself, a renowned amateur musician, was flattered to be invited to play a duet with the great German master, to the applause of the company. This was not a concert, but an informal "consort" of friends, who, amidst the telescopes, flying machines and anatomical dissections, and no doubt after enjoying a good dinner and an abundance of Warden Wilkins's claret, came together for a good time.

While not relating directly to the scientific Club, the Wadham College accounts in Wilkins's time suggest that college life did not lack due celebration and merriment. Guy Fawkes' night, 5 November – the anniversary of the "Gunpowder Treason" – was celebrated with a bonfire and sometimes a joyful discharge of muskets, while hefty sums were on occasion spent on "Wine for Gaudies" (Latin *gaudeamus*, "let us celebrate"). Wilkins even secured the services of one William Austin, a former royal cook, to take charge of the Wadham kitchens.

So what with music, dinners, excellent feasts, Guy Fawkes' night jollifications, and wine and beer flowing freely for various celebrations – and not forgetting scientific experiments – the 1650s were not all doom and gloom; at least, not in John Wilkins's company.

KING CHARLES II, GRESHAM COLLEGE, AND THE ROYAL SOCIETY

Three things happened between the late summer of 1658 and the spring of 1660, which changed the whole landscape, and, in a roundabout way, led to the foundation of the Royal Society. Firstly, Oliver Cromwell died, to be succeeded by his ineffectual son Richard, opening the prospect of yet another armed struggle between Oliver's generals. Then, in August or early September 1659, John Wilkins left Oxford to become – for eleven months – Master of Trinity College, Cambridge. At the same time, secret negotiations with the future King Charles II, living in exile in Holland, led to His Majesty being brought to England, unopposed, and entering London in an ecstasy of popular enthusiasm on 29 May 1660. The genial, 32-year-old king promised peace, prosperity, and stability after eighteen years of political and religious mayhem. The bells of London, it was said, were "worn thin" with all the joyful ringing.

Wilkins's Oxford Club, as we have seen, had a less famous London equivalent: the group of men who met in Gresham College in the heart of the City. These groups were in no way exclusive, and people would happily move between Wadham and Gresham College, depending on whether they were residing in Oxford or London.

With Wilkins gone from Oxford, and London fast becoming a city rich in opportunities following the Restoration of the monarchy, Gresham became the new focus for scientific research, especially as the young Dr Wren was now installed as Gresham Astronomy Professor. By November 1660, the Gresham experimentalists, who were also well connected both socially and constitutionally, approached the new king. Any hopes they might have entertained for the endowment of a real-life, Baconian "Salomon's House" research institution were rendered void by the realization that King Charles was broke, but they certainly had his goodwill.

Charles II had his father's brains and sophistication, but rather more political common sense – no doubt honed through years of exile – and an open easy charm. Humorous and fun-loving as he was, people liked the son in a way that had not been possible with his more aloof father – and nowhere was this reciprocal regard greater than between the king and pretty young women. Charles also seriously enjoyed the company of clever men. He even fitted out a laboratory in Whitehall Palace, and on 6 October 1675, chancing upon Robert Hooke when strolling in the park, so Hooke recorded in his diary, His Majesty warmly greeted the great scientist and invited him back to his lab to help with an experiment.

On 28 November 1660, the machinery was set in motion to formally establish "The Royal Society of London for Improving Natural Knowledge". It was to enjoy various privileges, such as a right to print books without needing to seek prior permission. The king gave the society several pieces of ceremonial regalia (still cherished and displayed to this day), and, in 1662, 1663, and 1669, three Royal Charters confirming its status and privileges – but not a penny of money, or an inch of landed endowment. It would become the model and prototype of all future British learned societies.

THE FELLOWSHIP OF SCIENCE

What happened in the Oxford "Philosophical Club" meeting in Wadham College during John Wilkins's wardenship had several important parallels to what would take place in the Royal Society after 1660. The whole range of the sciences, as then understood, would be encompassed, from telescopic astronomy to experimental medicine; the society would run and pay for its own affairs with no external help or interference; and it would enjoy a freedom of research and thought. Judging from the letters and diaries of the early members, it aspired to be a sociable fellowship, with people going off to dine together after meetings, differences of opinions notwithstanding. It would be non-sectarian in religion, for theology was not part of its remit. It is true that the early Fellowship was largely Anglican and entirely Protestant, but it had acknowledged Catholic friends. Richard Towneley, whose father Charles and uncle Christopher were friends of Crabtree and Horrocks (Chapter 21), remained living 200 miles north at Towneley Hall, Lancashire, but his observations and research were read out to, and published by, the Society.

It was also this toleration and recognition of the international character of science which, from the start, made it possible from 1663 onwards to elect overseas men of science – including devout Catholics – into a corresponding overseas Fellowship. These included the Dutch Protestants Christiaan Huygens and Antoni van Leeuwenhoek, the Lutheran Johannes Hevelius in Poland, the Italian Roman Catholics Marcello Malpighi and Giovanni Domenico Cassini, the French Catholics Adrien Auzout and Samuel Sorbière (a convert from Calvinism), the French cradle-Calvinist then Roman Catholic priest convert astronomer Ismaël Bullialdus, and many more besides. And, from Cotton Mather onwards, there came a succession of Colonial and then United States American Fellows.

These early foreign Fellows also came from a variety of occupations: brewer (Hevelius), independent gentleman (Huygens), Catholic priest (Bullialdus), Papal Physician (Malpighi), cloth merchant (Leeuwenhoek), and Protestant minister (Mather). There was only one essential qualification for election to Fellowship – excellence in science – and 350 years later, foreign Fellows, like their British colleagues, are elected in accordance with the same criteria.

THE ROYAL SOCIETY AND THE NEW ASTRONOMY

Although from the very beginning the society included researchers active in every then known branch of science, astronomy played a major role in its work. The improvement of telescopes and astronomical measuring instruments occupied the attention of several early British and overseas Fellows: most notably Robert Hooke and John Flamsteed.

Both in his massively influential *Micrographia* (1665) and later Royal Society publications Hooke suggested designs for improved machines for figuring larger and better telescope lenses. Hooke, and his Royal Society-associated clockmaker and precision engineer friend Thomas Tompion (who never became a Fellow), were also devising machines for generating more accurate divisions on the brass scales of large observatory instruments. In 1675, when King Charles II was persuaded by the Royal Society to found the Royal Observatory at Greenwich, with Flamsteed as first Astronomer Royal, Hooke, Tompion, Flamsteed, and Jeremiah Horrocks's old admirer Sir Jonas Moore (see Chapter 21), then later Abraham Sharp, set about designing a superior set of instruments.

One does not need to search too deeply into the writings of these men, and their Royal Society colleagues, to identify a pressing scientific concern: does the earth actually move around the sun, and if so, why are we *still* unable to detect that elusive tiny parallax angle which would provide the unassailable, clinching, *physical* evidence, desired by Galileo, Kepler, Tycho, and Copernicus? How far away must even the brightest stars be, when a measuring instrument that could detect an angle corresponding to about one-thousandth of the diameter of the moon could still not discern the six-monthly parallax of a star, between June and December?

Even the Royal Observatory continued, in an odd sort of way, the self-funding tradition of the rest of British science. Yes, the king had provided the land and *empty* buildings at Greenwich, but Flamsteed, and Sir Jonas Moore, still had to dig into their own pockets to pay for the telescopes, quadrants, clocks, and other instruments necessary to turn Sir Christopher Wren's lovely red-brick fabric into a working *observatory*. While Flamsteed had an official modest salary of £100 p.a., he often had great difficulty in extracting his £25 per quarter from a hard-pressed government. Flamsteed, as an old man in 1710, admitted that he had spent £2,000 of his own money on the Royal Observatory (perhaps £500,000 in modern money), and would have achieved nothing had he not been the son and heir of a "rich merchant", and a beneficed clergyman as well.

Central to the whole rationale of the science of the Royal Society was *instrumentation*. What had restricted the science of ancient and medieval Europe, and astronomy in particular, had been the natural limitations of the five human senses; once we venture beyond what our natural faculties enable us to reliably see, handle, and measure, we end up in circular speculations. The key to the prison of perception was an advancing instrument technology, as refined specialist research tools allowed us to look ever deeper into the structures of nature. Instruments such as magnetic devices, the telescope, microscope, airpump, barometer, thermometer, precision pendulum clock, Gascoigne-type micrometer, and graduated scales, allow us to quantify tiny angles in the heavens. Robert Hooke in *Micrographia* was to speak of these new instruments as "artificial organs" that strengthened, and rendered more exact, our natural organs of sense.

What these new, largely post-1600 instruments actually did was allow us to *measure* and *quantify* nature more exactly, for only once we had reliable data could we take science beyond speculation. This way of looking at nature epitomized the mindset of the Fellows of the new Royal Society, be they British or foreign, astronomers or physiologists, as measurement, Baconian experiment, mechanics, and mathematics came together to produce a new vision for science, and a new agenda for the improvement of the human condition. What is more, accuracy also became a new significator of the glory of God, as the human intellect, aided by ingenious devices, began to see yet deeper into the creation, and by extension obtain new glimpses of the divine mind behind it all. But we will return to their ideas on religion and science below.

THE ROYAL SOCIETY AND SCIENTIFIC JOURNALISM

It is a truism that printing transformed Western culture after *c.* 1460, as classical, biblical, and literary texts became more accessible. Sir Francis Bacon had seen printing as one of a trinity of key innovations, along with gunpowder and the magnetic compass; but printing also transformed the communication of scientific ideas, and not simply on a textual level, for pictures, diagrams, and illustrations are a fundamental part of science. One can think of numerous scientific books appearing after 1500 in which the engraved illustrations were not only essential to the material under discussion, but were high-art works in their own right. Vesalius's breathtaking anatomical plates (1543), Agricola's illustrations of German mining machinery (1556), Tycho Brahe's observatory instruments (1598), Hevelius's *Selenographia* (1648), the great Dutch atlases, Robert Hooke's *Micrographia* (1665), and numerous other examples spring to mind.

By the mid-seventeenth century, discoveries were flying so thick and fast across Europe that one-off books were no longer able to keep pace. In 1665, the Royal Society took a leaf from the burgeoning London trade in pamphlet and "news-sheet" journalism, and invented the scientific periodical. The *Philosophical Transactions* (or "Scientific Dealings") of the Royal Society first appeared in March 1665, and except for a brief break in the 1680s, when it was called the *Philosophical Collections*, it is still in print today.

Almost from the start the *"Phil. Trans."* displayed the traits of what we recognize as a scientific journal. It contained articles on various topics of current research; it printed letters, sent to Henry Oldenburg, the editor – perhaps an observation by a country doctor on a curious piece of local phenomena; and then began to review important new books, British and European. Research, discussion, early peer review, squabbles, and a fascinating medley of articles and communications – extending from new observations of Saturn's rings to strange stinks and flames coming from a water culvert near Wigan, Lancashire (methane coal gas), to experiments on the toxicity of Virginia rattlesnakes performed by a visiting sea-captain, to an account of a surgical operation, and young Isaac Newton's experiments with glass prisms and coloured light that would go on to transform our knowledge of optics.

While other European academies also started to publish their proceedings, the *Phil. Trans.* was unique in its variety of content, directness of style, and ease of access. Everybody, it would appear, was reading the *Transactions*, and, as the years went by, copies got on to the shelves of country vicarages and merchants' houses, and were scoured by satirists and comedy playwrights for humorous copy. Thomas Shadwell's box office smash hit comedy *The Virtuoso* ("The Scientist") of 1676 drew much of its send-up humour from Hooke's *Micrographia* and the *Phil. Trans.*, while in 1726 Jonathan Swift's *Gulliver's Travels* was still mining the journal for odd characters and seemingly bizarre experiments. Shadwell's 1676 character Sir Nicholas Gimcrack was destined to become comedy's prototypical "mad scientist".

Philosophical Transactions also came to serve a function for which the modern age would use the internet. In 1675, for example, when Giovanni Domenico Cassini F.R.S., the Italian Director of the new Paris Observatory, discovered that division in the rings of Saturn which still bears his name (see Chapter 22), he sent out a Latin "press release". A copy was sent via the diplomatic bag to the Royal Society, who promptly published it in the *Transactions*, thereby helping to secure Cassini's priority for the discovery. By the 1670s, the Parisian and some other European academies were publishing research, as Robert Hooke noted in his diary for 25 June 1678.

Though I am not claiming that John Wilkins's English-language scientific books of the 1630s and 1640s initiated this movement of discussing science in vernacular languages – after all, Galileo wrote in Italian – it was certainly the case that by the time of Wilkins's death in 1672 the society which he had done so much to inspire was conducting its affairs in the mother tongue (as was the French Académie). Foreign Fellows of the Royal Society were welcome to submit papers to the *Transactions* in French or Latin if they preferred.

NATURAL THEOLOGY AND THE ROYAL SOCIETY

I have said above that the Royal Society had a non-sectarian policy on religion. Just as in Wilkins's Oxford Club, religion was not discussed at meetings, and this was intended as a way of avoiding those sectarian bickerings that had so dominated English religion (but not science) between 1642 and 1660. This should not be interpreted as meaning that the society was "secular" in a modern sense. Acceptance of God, a created, rationally accessible universe, and Christian love and redemption were assumed features of the Fellowship, whether one were an Anglican bishop like Wilkins and his episcopal and priestly F.R.S. colleagues, a Foreign Fellow Roman Catholic priest, or a Dutch Calvinist who might attend meetings whenever he happened to be visiting London.

Those men who were, rightly or wrongly, perceived to be atheists or deists were not welcome, even had they wished to join. Thomas Hobbes, for example, was openly detested by Seth Ward and Robert Boyle in particular: perhaps as much for his outrageous wit and love of playful dinner-table provocativeness as for his *Leviathan* (1651). (King Charles II, conversely, always enjoyed Hobbes's company, and liked to have him around to dinner at Whitehall Palace.)

Non-sectarian as the Royal Society's religion may have been, one senses nonetheless that it was deeply held, and not a subject for levity, in spite of Wilkins's renowned geniality. Both Robert Boyle and Seth Ward, for example, were men of high moral tone and seriousness. Ward became Bishop of Exeter and then

Salisbury at the Restoration, and the independently wealthy, celibate Boyle was renowned for his devout Protestant asceticism and great generosity to the poor and to Christian causes. (I have often wondered how aware Boyle was of his friend Robert Hooke's tendency to indulge in liaisons with female servants, as evidenced by Hooke's diary.)

Three men in particular in the early Royal Society developed a style of science and theology which not only came to characterize the society, but to constitute a significant aspect of British religion between *c.* 1660 and 1860. This was "natural theology", which held that one could trace the "Divine Hand" in nature. The first of these was John Wilkins, whose theological, cosmological, scientific, and biblical interpretation ideas were discussed in Chapter 24.

The second was Robert Boyle. Boyle appears to have come into science in the first place from a prior concern with tracing the hand of Providence in human affairs: looking for "significators" and "signs" that could help to steer a devout Christian through a fallen world. In the same way that a pious seeker might "tell" or "try" (or *test*) God's will, or a goldsmith might "tell" or "try" the purity of a piece of gold in a chemical test, so the devout philosopher could "tell" and discover the hidden secrets embedded within nature by means of experiments. This rationale was an intrinsic part of Boyle's science, as was *revelation*. Were not the men of the seventeenth century living in an age when biblical prophecies were being fulfilled? Mention has already been made of the perceived significance of Daniel 12:4, "Men shall run to and fro, and knowledge shall be increased", which was seen as an important significator of the end of time. Were not the men of that age running "to and fro" across the globe, and was not knowledge "increasing" at a breathtaking rate? To think of Boyle solely as "the father of modern chemistry", discovering the laws of gas pressure that bear his name, is turning him into a modernist icon. We would be wise to read his great scientific works within the wider context of his extensive theological publications.

The third figure was John Ray: a botanist primarily, yet a man whose *Wisdom of God Manifested in the Works of the Creation* (1691) not only encapsulated the science and religion stance of the Royal

Society, but would help define "natural theology" well into the nineteenth century. Ray shows his readers not only how a pious philosopher might read nature like a book (perhaps with resonances back to Galileo's *Letter to the Grand Duchess Christina*, Chapter 13) to stand in awe of God's majesty, but how Providence itself is part of nature's design. Was not nature full of features which facilitated human felicity, such as the seasons, winds, and tides, making agriculture and sea-borne trade possible?

Ray even suggested an analogy for God's Providence in nature that would be reworked in 1802 by William Paley in his massively influential *Natural Theology*: the watch analogy. Imagine you are crossing a heath, and you find a ticking watch lying on the ground. Would you not know right away that there had once been intelligent design and craftsmanship in this place? Likewise, do not the wonders of the heavens and the earth bear the mark of a divine hand?

The arguments of Ray and his contemporaries, and even those of Paley, emphasizing the presence of the Divine Hand in animal behaviour or in the heavens, may strike many as simplistic today, as may his use of clear-cut analogies between specific natural phenomena and human felicity. Its critics, too, would later say that this natural theology tradition was too simplistic and convenient. What about when nature went wrong: when innocent children died of terrible disease, storms sunk ships, harvests failed, and the wicked prospered? And while a watch in the grass might indicate the one-time presence of a watchmaker, there was no proof that the ingenious craftsman was still regulating the watch, or that he was even still alive. As the deists argued, God may have long since withdrawn from his wonderful creation, and was no longer listening to the supplications of suffering humanity.

As all of the proponents of natural theology realized, Christian belief stood upon more than just ingenious analogies revealed by modern science. At its heart, it was about faith, redemption, and a vital yet scientifically undemonstrable relationship with Christ. I suspect that this was taken as read by Wilkins, Boyle, Ray, and their other clever scientist colleagues. Natural theology could feed into currents of scientific rationalism in the eighteenth and nineteenth centuries that, in some quarters, first removed God to the perimeter of creation, and then dispensed with him altogether, as science continued to progress. The problem is still with us today.

It was a drift of which the Oxford-trained founders of the eighteenth-century Evangelical Revival, such as John and Charles Wesley, and George Whitfield, were all too aware: gentlemen who fully understood the science of their day, and respected it, yet who saw how it could lead to an easy self-satisfaction – especially among the well-off.

Their solution was to go "back to basics" in the time-honoured tradition of Christian revival. Preach the gospel, feed the hungry, clothe the naked, visit the afflicted, and use your gifts of intelligence and resource to help the distressed. One of the longstanding best-sellers of popular science would be John Wesley's *Primitive Physick* (1748). A book of medicine for ordinary folk, it discussed the latest potential benefits of modern science, such as the use of static electricity, and how it was hoped the sick might find practical relief through God's creation.

When John Wesley was born in 1703, the earth's motion in space still lacked physical demonstration and mathematical proof. By 1703, at least one enormous scientific puzzle had been solved that in itself fitted beautifully into the idea of a heliocentric, Copernican universe. That invisible and intangible force that binds the cosmos together had finally been elucidated: gravity.

CHAPTER 26

The Men of Gravity

*W*hen Alexander Pope composed that couplet which would be carved into the recently deceased Sir Isaac Newton's grand memorial in Westminster Abbey in 1727, he sent a message into the future which would only help confirm an already nascent myth:

Nature, and Nature's Laws lay hid in Night;
God said "Let Newton Be", and all was Light.

The message, simply, was that until 1687, when the lone genius Newton delivered his masterpiece, *Principia Mathematica Philosophiae Naturalis* ("Mathematical Principles of Natural Philosophy"), the world of natural science was a bathos of darkness, ignorance, and superstition. It was a world inhabited by inferior intellects suddenly confused and awestruck by a middle-aged Cambridge don who had somehow come down from on high to illuminate the shadowy world of learning.

Newton's true genius and his standing as one of the greatest scientific intellects of all time cannot be doubted. As a mathematician, a perceptive optical physicist, and supremely as the man who finally explicated the "gravitating force", he was unique, and it is hardly surprising that his impact was so great – first amongst his acolytes of Trinity College, Cambridge, who would for the next few centuries be guardians of the sacred flame, and then outwards across the civilized world.

THE PROBLEM OF ATTRACTION

Newton was not alone, however. *Lone*, he certainly was; for until his fame turned him into an icon after 1700, he was remarkably reclusive. What Newton did was finally to solve a puzzle which had engaged some of the finest intellects in Europe since the 1570s: from the time when Tycho had shown that the supernova star of 1572 and the comets after 1577 were not atmospheric bodies. If, as we saw in Chapter 6, Tycho's meticulous geometrical measurements had revealed those bodies to be in astronomical space – rather than in the earth's atmosphere – then how did they move? Were the comets even crashing through the planetary crystalline spheres; or more likely, did the spheres not actually exist? Yet, if there were no crystalline spheres, as enshrined in the cosmologies of Aristotle and Ptolemy, what made the planets move? What could be the nature of the "force" that acted between the central earth and the planets, or, if one were a Copernican, between the sun and the planets?

Even more baffling, when one began to think through the consequences of a crystalline sphere-*less* universe, what was the nature of the force that made objects such as bricks or cannonballs fall down to earth? After all, if Aristotle had been wrong about the spheres, how could we be sure about his theories of terrestrial dynamics?

Especially worrying to those physicists who were coming to see the universe in purely physical, mathematically quantifiable terms, could such a force be truly *occult* and "obscure" in the way that the astrologers and magical philosophers said? There was, after all, the problem of "action at a distance". Did A affect B across empty space by means of some kind of magical or spirit agency?

This, in a nutshell, was the beginning of that century-long process that would lead to Newton's *Principia*; hardly a process of darkness and superstition. Instead, as we have seen unfolding across the previous chapters, it was a process committed to physics and mathematics, and stood against all forms of superstition.

FROM MAGNETS TO MEASUREMENTS

We have seen how a succession of Copernican philosophers tried to envisage this controlling force of creation. In the period following the publication of William Gilbert's *De Magnete* in 1600, many researchers came to envisage the sun (known to be rotating upon its own axis by 1612) as a giant magnet, drawing the planets around in the flux of invisible "force" radiating from it. This model was not only hinted at by Gilbert as early as 1600, and later in his posthumous *De Mundo* (1631), but it seemed to accord with experimental results. In his terrella, or spherical magnet, experiments he had shown that the terrella's attractive force exerted upon his versorium, or little compass pointer, was directional to the terrella's poles, and that this force diminished gradually with distance. Could this, then, be the reason why Mercury rotated rapidly around the sun, and distant Saturn very slowly, with the other planets in sequence in between? Such a contingency also found substantiation in the "co-planarity" of all the planetary orbits, rotating around the sun as they do in a fairly narrow, flat plane corresponding, approximately, to the solar equator.

Kepler was fascinated by Gilbert's magnetism, and saw it as a possible force that drove the planets, and comets, across empty space. By the time of Jeremiah Horrocks in the late 1630s, however, doubts were coming to be raised about there being magnetic "fibres" penetrating space, although in his letter of 7 August 1640 Horrocks's friend, William Crabtree, was writing to William Gascoigne and discussing a possible connection between sunspots and the "Magnetical or Sympathetical Rayes" of the sun.[1]

If magnetism were the prime mover in all invisible attraction, what, for example, caused the tides, as water is not magnetic? Likewise, what made a wooden block fall from a ship's mast to hit the wooden ship below? For wood – like most things in nature – is not magnetic either.

There was another problem: what was the relationship between terrestrial and celestial attraction? Was the force that made the planets rotate about the sun, or the moon about the earth, a different kind of force from that which made a brick fall to the earth's surface? Could one, perhaps, finally escape from the earth's pull if one ascended to a given altitude, as John Wilkins suggested in 1640, but which seemed far less likely by 1670? Furthermore, did the planets and comets even possess "gravitas" or attractive forces peculiar to themselves, such as lunar gravity or Venusian gravity?

By the time of Galileo's death in 1642, it could not be denied that all these attractions seemed to have elegant mathematical proportions implicit within them. Kepler's Three Laws of Planetary Motion (1619) provided a beautiful geometrical description (but *not* an explanation) of how the planets behave in space, and how their velocities vary depending on their position in their elliptical orbits. Likewise, a falling or a rolling body will move at a predictable velocity as it approaches the earth's surface, with magnetic objects like iron cannon balls and non-magnetic wooden balls behaving in accordance with exactly the same proportions of acceleration.

Galileo had also found that suspended oscillating objects – or pendulums – moved in an exact mathematical proportion, depending *not* on the weight of the pendulum, but on the length of the suspension rope, as the suspension length supplied the key to what the pendulum's period of swing would be. Christiaan Huygens would use this discovery to advantage in 1658, when he published *Horologium* ("Clock"), with its lucid description of how a brass "bob" pendulum on a rigid metal rod could be used to control the going rate of a clock. This was a device, one must add, that revolutionized time-keeping, enabling the clock – now capable of keeping time to an error of only a few seconds per day – to be turned into a valuable research tool, as John Flamsteed would do with his Greenwich Observatory clocks after 1675. Yet what was this invisible force which acted between the earth and the spring-driven swinging pendulum, with such breathtaking precision?

If the force was not magical, then what could it possibly be? The French philosopher and scientist René Descartes proposed a universal model to account for all physical action in the 1630s, including the earth's rotation around the sun, and this was through a form of mechanical impact. Descartes posited that the whole of nature, from the hollow spaces in human bodies to the farthest corners of the universe, was filled with *corpuscles*, or very tiny, probably spherical, physically discrete particles. They fill space

382

totally, and all energy – gravity, light, heat, and so on – comes about by particular types of mechanical impacts moving through the adjacent corpuscles. On one level, one might imagine this as resembling an impact passing down a line of railway waggons. These corpuscles moved in complex swirls, or *vortices*, that could explain, among other things, the rotations of the planets. In Descartes's system, therefore, nothing was static, as the corpuscles moved in an eternal, grand, physically orchestrated scheme of mechanical motion.

While this arrangement may not immediately explain attraction, it could certainly be used as a way of visualizing interdependent motions – such as those of the sun and a planet, or the curved path of a flying arrow, as vortices worked with vortices to account for everything, from a ray of light coming to us from a star to the "isochronal", or even, swings of a clock pendulum.

It is hardly surprising, therefore, that Descartes's "mechanical philosophy" became the generally accepted explanation for invisible physical motion between the late 1630s and the publication of Newton's *Principia*, especially in parts of Continental Europe. In addition to philosophical theories about "energy", attraction, and motion, it was becoming increasingly clear by 1650 that it would be through the exact angular and chronometric measurement of bodies – be they planets, oscillating pendulums, or flying projectiles – that we would develop a *mathematical* and experimental understanding of gravity. This way of thinking propelled Robert Hooke into his own research into gravity by the late 1650s, at a time when Newton was still a pupil at Grantham Grammar School in Lincolnshire.

DR ROBERT HOOKE: THE PHYSICIST IN
THE CATHEDRAL

Since his own schooldays at Westminster in the early 1650s, Robert Hooke's brilliant and laterally operating intellect had been in love with physics. We saw his fascination with springs and flying machines as a member of Dr Wilkins's Oxford Club in Chapter 24. The nature of spring, or elasticity, lay at the very heart of this Isle of Wight clergyman's son's entire conception of science. What was springiness? Why did only some materials, such as steel, muscle, and certain woods, possess it?

From his early Oxford experiments on the use of fine precision springs to regulate the motion of a watch in the late 1650s, to his classic formulation of that law of elasticity that bears his name, published in 1676, Hooke saw springiness as a fascinating problem in physics. As with most things in the physics of that age, he searched for a precise mathematical, geometrical, or proportionate expression, leading him to a serious interest in the gravity-cum-attraction problem.

Even as a young man Robert Hooke was intimately versed in the prevailing physical theories of the time. Westminster School had given him a sound mastery of Latin and Greek, through which he could access the ancients at first hand, while the works of Copernicus, Tycho, Kepler, Gilbert, Galileo, Gassendi, Descartes, Huygens, and all the other formative thinkers of the age were intimately known to him. By the 1660s, when the Royal Society began to publish their surviving writings, he became acquainted with the achievements of Jeremiah Horrocks and his north-country circle. One has only to read Hooke's diary to realize that scientists were not his only friends; for clergymen, deans, bishops, and even an archbishop (John Tillotson) were among the bachelor scientist's regular dining companions – and some of them were also Royal Society Fellows.

Why was it that when one applied pressure to a spring, there was always a precise relationship between the tension put in and the reciprocal "force" given out when the spring relaxed? Spring could even be made to mimic gravity itself; when you fitted a "common watch" with Hooke's hairspring balance regulator, it could keep time almost as accurately as a fixed pendulum clock – its balance wheel rotating isochronally even when upside down.

His interest in spring, what he called *pondus* (weight), and *force* or what in the nineteenth century would be styled "energy" led Hooke to explore the nature of attraction and hence gravity. This is where the cathedral came in, or to be precise, London's Westminster Abbey and Old St Paul's (the soaring medieval gothic edifice that was destroyed in the Great Fire of 1666). They were chosen because of their great height, both within the church interiors and externally down St Paul's great tower, which provided convenient experimental sites. With his late father the Revd John Hooke's Royalist Anglican credentials on the Isle of Wight, his own association with Westminster School and the Royalist Christ Church, Oxford, and his many clerical friends, Robert had no particular difficulty in obtaining permission to use great churches for experimental purposes.

From what he wrote and reported to the Royal Society, his Westminster Abbey and St Paul's gravity experiments were of two kinds, both of which display his deeply experimental, inductive way of thinking. On the one hand, he seems to have swung very long pendulums (probably weighted ropes) down the towers or over the high walls of the cathedrals. This would have been to ascertain the length of swing to period of swing relationship, for short pendulums beat much faster than long ones. A 9½-inch pendulum, for example, will complete a full swing in half a second; a 40-inch one in one single second; and a 13-foot pendulum in two seconds. What, therefore, might be the periods of a 50- or 100-foot pendulum? By extension, what was the exact proportionate or mathematical relationship operating between the earth's gravitational attraction and objects oscillating at different heights, and at different suspension lengths above it? Or, as one might say, how did the earth's constant gravitational "braking effect" act at different heights above its surface?

Hooke saw pendulum experiments as a route by which the *proportionate* attraction of gravity might be studied experimentally. In addition to swinging simple vertical pendulums, he experimented with *circular* ones. Here, he would impel a hanging pendulum into a *curved* swing, to make it orbit a central sphere. Just like a planet around the sun, Hooke found that the swinging weight always settled down into an *elliptical* curve. When he blew air into the experimental area with a pair of bellows, moreover – to simulate an attractive force – he also found that the long axis or *apside* of the ellipse gradually rotated around the centre, in the same way that the moon apside line gradually rotates around the earth. Jeremiah Horrocks, in his own investigations into gravitational attraction, had worked along similar lines in the late 1630s.

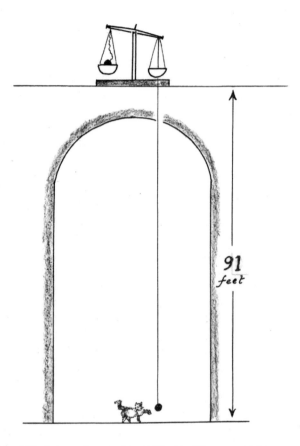

26.1 Robert Hooke's gravity experiment. Would a 16-ounce weight, suspended 91 feet below an identical weight directly above it, register slightly heavier, being slightly nearer to the centre of the earth? (Without, that is, interference from the cathedral cat!) (Drawing by Allan Chapman.)

Hooke's other class of cathedral gravity observations was performed with a precision balance, set high up in the St Paul's and Abbey vaults, and overhanging a parapet: on one occasion with a clear 91-foot drop below. A pair of 16-ounce weights and their strings were prepared. One weight was coiled up and placed in the pan of the balance. The other, after being attached to the other balance arm, was uncoiled and let down the cathedral until it hung just above the stone pavement.

What Hooke was trying to establish here is whether two identical weights would weigh differently 91 feet apart on the same earth-radius line.[2] If so, then what proportion, or mathematical equation, could be devised to express the measured gravitational attraction between two points 91 feet apart, on the same radial line going down to the earth's centre? In many ways, it was part of a long-standing *philosophical* debate about the earth's attraction – even mentioned by Bacon in his posthumous *Sylva Sylvarum* (1627) (Chapter 20). Was it true, for example, that a heavy rock on the earth's surface (and thus, with the whole attraction of the earth pulling beneath it) would register heavier than if the same rock were at the bottom of a deep mine (and thus with rock above it, which could help attract it upwards, and hence make it lighter)? The Baconian "attraction" agenda is made explicit in the title of Hooke's manuscript account of his research delivered to the Royal Society, 24 December 1662 – "in my Lord VERULAM's experiment concerning the decrease of gravity" – and finally published when Thomas Birch transcribed and published the early meeting records in his *History of the Royal Society* (1756–57).[3] It is also interesting to note that Dr Henry Power, Halifax physician, experimentalist, and friend of Richard Towneley, reported a similar trial down a coal mine 68 yards deep in his *Experimental Philosophy* (1663).[4]

Not content with experimenting in cathedral vaults, Hooke repeated his weights and precision balance experiment underground, or 80 feet down a deep well on Banstead Downs, Surrey, in the summer of 1666. Both Hooke and Power were of the opinion that the weight on the end of the line, and hence nearer to the earth's centre, weighed heavier than the weight up in the balance pan above. But meticulous researcher that he was, Hooke was cautious about claiming to have "weighed" gravity, and considered that the 10-grain weight increase (0.6479 grams) which he found in his cathedral experiment might have been caused by the 91-foot string absorbing moisture from London's damp air.

These and other experiments by Hooke make it abundantly clear how he set about tackling the gravity problem: by devising experiments from which he could extract a geometrical formula that would express the increase of the earth's pull along a given radial line connecting the experiment to the earth's centre. The range and ingenuity of Hooke's gravity work is impressive. He even argued in *Micrographia* (1665), Observation LX,[5] and elsewhere that if the lunar craters were formed by impacting objects from space, then the moon, like the earth, must also have been a "gravitating force".

By 1674, when he published his attempt to provide physical evidence for the Copernican theory, he had come to several important conclusions – subsequently shown to be correct – about gravity. For one thing, it probably acted through space, and there was only *one* gravity, not local gravities for the earth, moon, and sun. Its operation was mathematically proportionate, and got stronger with closeness. The gravity that made a stone fall to earth was probably the same as that which made the earth move around the sun. In 1674, therefore, in *An Attempt to Prove the Motion of the Earth*, he published those three aspects of gravity:

Firstly, all objects possess gravity, and it affects all bodies.

Secondly, an object moving on its own will do so in a straight line, until it encounters another body, at which point their mutual gravities will deflect them from a straight to a circular, or elliptical, path.

Thirdly, the pull of gravity increases the nearer objects are to each other, and an understanding of gravity "will mightily assist the Astronomer to reduce all the Coelestiall Motions to a certain rule..."[6]

Hooke honestly admits at this point that he cannot yet fully verify such a rule (or law), yet what a body of conclusions he had both presented in previous papers to Royal Society meetings, and had now published in a book bearing the society's imprimatur in 1674.

Hooke was not the only physical scientist working on the gravity problem. Christiaan Huygens, coming from an astronomical and mathematical direction, also made major contributions, as he and other Continental European scientists analysed the relationship between *centrifugal* (tending to fly outwards) and *centripetal* (tending to be attracted to a centre) forces acting within moving physical systems, such as the solar system. Surely, such a balance of attracting and repelling forces must exist for the solar system to remain stable. One can trace a whole lineage of physical, astronomical, and mathematical thinking from Hooke in the 1670s to Huygens, Borelli, Descartes, Horrocks, the Frenchman Gilles de Roberval, and back to Galileo, Kepler, Gilbert, and even Tycho. Perhaps, therefore, we should be cautious about accepting Alexander Pope's claim that gravity and "Nature's Laws lay hid in Night" before Sir Isaac Newton struck a light in 1687.

SIR ISAAC NEWTON

Longevity can be a godsend if you are wrestling with big, complex ideas. It enables you to look at a problem till it makes your head "ake", as Newton said about his early gravitation wrestlings. Then, refreshed, you can come back to it, and perhaps lay it aside once more. You can come back to it as many times as you need, over two decades, until a brilliant solution is found – and then, hopefully, live long enough to orchestrate your own legend to bestow upon history. Longevity cannot be predicted; but if your magnum opus is presented to the world at forty-five, and you happen to have another forty years of sharp-mindedness ahead of you, as Newton had, then not only can great scientific problems be resolved, but immortal reputations forged.

Newton was seven and a half years younger than Hooke, being born on Christmas Day 1642: born an orphan, for his father had died the previous October. Newton's father, also named Isaac, was a comfortably off Lincolnshire yeoman farmer bordering on gentry, with the Lordship of Woolsthorpe Manor as his title, while his widowed mother Hannah was descended from the more solidly gentry Ayscoughs or Askews. She remarried the Revd Barnabas Smith, and soon young Isaac had a new family of half-siblings around him. As Barnabas did not seem over-fond of his stepson, the boy later went to live with grandparents in Grantham, where he went on to attend the Grammar School. Despairing that the strangely thoughtful, reclusive, devout, and often abstracted teenager would ever make a farmer or run the family property, the family resorted to a last-ditch career option, and sent him to university. He entered Trinity College, Cambridge, in 1661, soon after John Wilkins had been evicted from his Mastership at the Restoration, the former Royalist Chaplain, Henry Ferne, replacing him.

Newton went to Trinity as a "Servitor", or poor scholar, not because the Newtons and the Smiths were remotely poor, but because his mother was reluctant to contribute to his college charges as a gentleman. At first, he was a student of average achievement, until the influence of the Revd Dr Isaac Barrow, Lucasian Professor of Mathematics, had its impact; and then things began to take off. Mathematics became Isaac's inspiration: a world of purity and perfection which was to exert a lifelong appeal upon his singular, lone imagination. Social conviviality appears to have had little appeal to Newton, and in this respect he and the Royal Society's highly clubbable bachelor Robert Hooke were poles apart.

Like many scientific men of that age, young Isaac became interested in the "gravity" problem. This was around 1665 or 1666, when he would have been twenty-four, and legend has it that it was when he was back home in Lincolnshire during the temporary closure of Cambridge University as a consequence of the Great Plague then raging in London. The legend is that Newton was sitting in an orchard one autumn day, and saw an apple fall from a tree, which led him to ask whether the force which pulled the apple a few feet down to earth might extend as high as the moon.

The story comes from the early eighteenth century, and was narrated by the then elderly Newton's young friend and admirer John Conduit. No doubt it had been told to Conduit by a reminiscing Newton. Like Galileo with Viviani and other admirers, the elderly, very famous Newton clearly relished telling his story to the brilliant young men of the rising generation, and probably realized that he was generating a hagiography. Besides Conduit, Newton's admirers had included the antiquarian William Stukeley and the young French playwright and wit Voltaire while in England in the 1720s. Another young protégé, James Bradley, of whom more will be said in Chapter 27, told his students in Oxford in 1747 that it was a *leaf* descending from a tree that first captivated Newton. The student's notebook still survives.[7] Either way, a body of Newton legends were already circulating around England and Europe by the time that Isaac died in 1727.

While the apple may have been legendary, the beginning of Newton's interest in the problem of attraction has more solid documentation in his abundant surviving papers. His approach was very different from the experimental one of Hooke; for Newton came to the problem from mathematical analysis. Irrespective of the tale of the apple, Newton had clearly been wrestling with the theoretical problems of motion by autumn 1665. Familiar as he was with the geometry of Kepler, Descartes, John Wilkins's friend John Wallis F.R.S., Isaac Barrow, and François Viète, the physics of Galileo, and the work of many other "scientists", Newton was analysing the nature of motion, acceleration, inertia, and attraction. Much hinged upon how bodies accelerated as they fell, and by what "infinitesimals" or gradual units they did so.

Newton was also wrestling with the problem of the force which constantly pulled the moon down to the earth, yet always somehow flung our satellite *past* us, in an elliptical curve, and then repeated the performance in the next lunar cycle. This was the genesis of what would come to be called the "three bodies problem": the earth, moon, and sun and their curious elliptical orbit cycles.

Having taken the attraction problem as far as it could go in the mid-1660s, Newton began a new line of research: into the nature of light and colours, culminating in his brilliant prism and spectrum experiments. This line of research first seems to have caught his imagination after reading about an optical problem in Hooke's recently published *Micrographia* (1665): a debt which he circuitously acknowledged in his Royal Society paper on light and colours in 1672.[8]

In 1669 Isaac Barrow resigned his Lucasian Professorship with its £100 p.a. salary in favour of Newton – a remarkably generous act, although we know that Barrow was angling for church preferment, while in 1673 he was elected to the Mastership of Trinity. So, he was in no way impoverishing himself by his gift to the 27-year-old Newton. Sadly, Newton was not a good teacher.

THE FORCE THAT BINDS CREATION

It was a letter from Robert Hooke that may have re-activated Newton's interest in the gravity problem. Hooke wrote to Newton in Cambridge, in his new capacity as (not very efficient) Secretary to the Royal Society, in an attempt to heal wounds caused by his own scepticism towards Newton's theory of light and colours back in 1672, which had kept Newton out of touch with the Society. In this letter of 24 November 1679, Hooke posed a problem regarding the path that would be taken by an object falling towards a gravitational centre.

Newton replied on 28 November with an accompanying sketch showing how such a falling body would orbit in an ever-decreasing spiral until it finally hit the gravitational centre. Hooke responded by correcting Newton: never an easy thing to do. He suggested, rather, that if an object fell in the plain of the "equinoctial", or in the equatorial regions at around 90 degrees to the poles, and it did so *in vacuo* so there was no air resistance, then it would *never* fall to hit the gravitational centre.

By the end of 1679, therefore, Hooke had come to the conclusion that motion around a gravitational centre was a compound of an object's natural tendency to move in a straight line and its attraction into a curved line, along with some kind of centrifugal resistance to being pulled to the centre. Hence, an object would move continuously in a stable elliptical orbit.

Hooke and Newton exchanged six letters up to 17 January 1680,[9] and then the correspondence stopped. Had Hooke's model for an object's free-fall motion *in vacuo* given Newton a new flash of insight? It is clear from the surviving correspondence of the time that Hooke was by no means alone – even in London – to be exploring centrifugal and centripetal forces, ellipses, and even inverse proportions, as a way of trying to understand planetary dynamics. For example, on 8 November 1679 Hooke had recorded in his diary having a conversation in a London coffee house about elliptical motions around a centre of attraction with his friend Sir Christopher Wren. By 1684, as something of an indication of how much gravitational attraction, ellipses, centrifugal and centripetal attractions, and inverse square relationship were in the air when

Royal Society friends came together in coffee houses or at dinners, Sir Christopher Wren offered a valuable book, worth forty shillings, to the man who could come up with a convincing mathematical solution.

Edmond Halley told Newton in July 1684 that Hooke was claiming to have a solution, but would conceal it for the present.[10] This was *not* an ominous indication of secrecy, as some modern scholars like to think, as much as an indication of seventeenth-century scholars' love of anagrams, puzzles, and word-games, as though one were saying, "I have the answer, but let me see yours first before I declare." Galileo, Huygens, Hooke, and many others loved issuing these brain-teasers to colleagues, and frequently circulated them around Europe.

Halley visited Newton in Cambridge in 1684, probably while in the eastern counties dealing with Halley family property, and told Isaac about the state of gravitational affairs at the Royal Society. Newton claimed that he already had a solution, based on an inverse square law, and while he could not lay hands on the piece of paper at the moment (scholars' studies are rarely tidy places), he promised he would send Halley the details once retrieved. He did: and Halley recognized the golden nugget.

Halley, the brilliant yet humorous, sociable 28-year-old private gentleman, Fellow of and Clerk to the Royal Society, then confidently took up the task of getting the 42-year-old cantankerous and reclusive Cambridge professor to write up his work. By a mixture of cajoling and honest flattery, over the next two years, Halley achieved the seeming impossible: extracting a monumental treatise on gravitation from Newton. *Principia Mathematica* was presented in manuscript to the Royal Society and King James II in 1686, authorized, and published the following year. In the grand tradition of the geometrical treatise, it appeared in three sections, or "books", each with its own sub-chapters. They delineated the working principles of gravitation under an inverse square law; then gravity as it acts upon the earth; then, in the biggest and third book, how it acts astronomically.

What, however, was the key to Newton's breakthrough? It came from his clinching analytical demonstration of the gravitational relationship between terrestrial and celestial physics. Using the best data for the "elements" or geometrical properties of the moon's elliptical orbit around the earth – which by the mid-1680s were those from John Flamsteed at Greenwich Observatory – he was able to calculate that the moon "falls" towards the earth under a centripetal (downwards) attraction, at the rate of 10 miles in one hour. This was very close, in proportionate terms, to 10 yards in one second, the velocity with which a falling stone hits the earth.

Clearly the same inverse proportion applied to the moon as to the earth. One *universal* force of attraction, therefore, seemed to be at work; and before long, using the best available observational data from Flamsteed at Greenwich, Newton was able to show that a similar inverse proportion applied to planets and comets. It was Flamsteed's data for the comets of 1680–81 and of 1682 ("Halley's Comet"), in conjunction with Newton's gravitational mathematics, that enabled Edmond Halley in 1705 to calculate that some comets moved in a "closed" elliptical orbit, and that the comet of 1682 would return to the sun in 1758. It did, and Halley's Comet would become a major clinching test case for Newton's theory.

Few denied the sheer brilliance of Newton's achievement, but where Isaac went wrong lay in failing to pay his intellectual debts. Hooke was furious when he saw *Principia* in manuscript: not because he was "pipped at the post" but because Newton failed to adequately acknowledge his own prior work, along with key ideas that Hooke had drawn to his attention, either in print or in correspondence. Halley warned Newton that the world would deem it ungracious if he failed to give a prominent acknowledgment to Hooke, especially in the Preface – but persuasive as he was, Halley was wasting his breath, or ink. Newton's response was to become angry and insult Hooke for being a pretentious charlatan – and even plagiarist.[11] The Astronomer Royal Flamsteed did not get much acknowledgment either, though in reality his claims were not as strong as Hooke's.

GRAVITY AND GOD

In spite of his capacity to rage against Hooke, Newton was not only a deeply devout man, but also enjoyed the very highest contemporary reputation as a biblical scholar – especially of the Old Testament. He was, too, an alchemical philosopher, with an interest in occult mysteries: intellectual traits (alchemy and mysticism, though not the biblical scholarship) which Hooke, Wren, Flamsteed, Halley, and most of his colleagues of 1685 would have had difficulty relating to. Newton's biblical scholarship and mystical writings comprise a much larger bulk of his surviving manuscripts than do those relating to "straight" physics and astronomy.

With regard to the *nature* of gravity, Newton enunciated a major idea which would be of enormous importance to the wider future of science. Whereas most of the scientists of Newton's age pondered the precise character of nature's forces – light, heat, weight, attraction, and such – Newton was not so much concerned with the ultimate nature of gravity, which he postulated was innately unknowable: "*Hypotheses non fingo*" ("I frame no hypotheses"), as he put it in the General Scholium, or "additional thoughts", in the 1713 edition of *Principia*. Quite simply, gravity *is*. It is a divine creation, the inner nature of which is known only to God, although we can use our God-given intelligence to work out the exact laws through which it operates. In Newton's separation of physics from metaphysics, he bequeathed a way of thinking about the intrinsic forces of nature that would be applied by later generations to electricity and electromagnetism, the laws of combination of the chemical elements, the behaviour of atoms and molecules, and even the DNA genetic code.

By 1800, it would come to be accepted that science describes nature from a purely physical perspective, while theology and philosophy help us to elucidate meaning and purpose beyond the physical forces. For all those who do not reject the value of non-physical truth, they still do. We now see science as explaining the *how* questions in nature, and theology and philosophy as explaining the *why*, or *meaning*, questions.

Nowhere were Newton's ideas about God and gravity more clearly elucidated than in the letters of his acolyte the Revd Dr Samuel Clarke, F.R.S.,[12] who in the early eighteenth century became Sir Isaac's theological and philosophical spokesman. Here we see space as God's "Sensorium", or God's extension, and gravity as a manifestation of the glory of God the Father. Gravity was the divine hand that activated the cosmos and made it "come to life". Although never making this point explicit in his lifetime – as a revered member of *Trinity* College, Cambridge – Newton's spiritual focus was God the Father, Creator, and Supreme Intellect: he was much less concerned with the Son (Jesus) and the Holy Ghost, a fact which only emerged from his private papers after his death in 1727.

NEW SCIENTIFIC HORIZONS

Without a shadow of a doubt, Sir Isaac Newton was a genius of monumental stature; however, the Newton of historical and scientific reality should not be confused with the Newton of post-1700 myth-building. While "Nature and Nature's Laws" may not have been fully described mathematically before the publication of *Principia* in 1687, when one unitary force was shown to bind creation together, they were certainly not "hid in Night" until the divine fiat pronounced "Let Newton Be" and "all was Light".

Seventeenth-century Europe had witnessed an "advancement of learning" that was unparalleled in the history of human civilization, and nowhere more than in the realm of scientific understanding. Simply, humanity's sense of physical reality had fundamentally changed between 1600 and 1700, as new realms of the great and the small, the medical, meteorological, chemical, and physical had been revealed. At the heart of this enterprise, which no one in 1600 could have remotely foreseen, lay *instruments*: those "artificial organs", as Robert Hooke styled them in 1665, which furnished our natural organs with prodigious new powers of inquiry. As we saw in previous chapters, these included the telescope, microscope, barometer, and optical and magnetic devices, and precision pendulum clocks, not to mention the massive expansion of fine cartography, printing, publishing, and an information-disseminating industry.

By 1675, therefore, the balance of probable evidence had just about shifted away from a Tychonic to an explicitly Copernican–Keplerian universe. Yet even by 1700, no astronomer in Europe had been able to supply the ultimate, clinching piece of mathematical and physical *proof* that the earth did move in space, to turn the Copernican *theory* into heliocentric *fact*. That would be announced in the year following the death of Sir Isaac Newton.

So the Earth Actually Does Move: The Revd Dr James Bradley Proves Copernicus Correct in 1728

$\mathscr{W}$e have seen over the previous chapters how the heliocentric theory of Copernicus was being discussed across Europe from the 1510s into the early eighteenth century without any clinching proof being shown for the earth's motion in space. Yes, there were arguments from elegance, from probability (or improbability), from telescopic images of the planets, from laboratory experiment analogies, and from geometry; and in Galileo's case, insults were hurled at the geocentricists. There was even Edmond Halley's 1718 discovery of the "proper motions" of certain stars, a cosmological line-of-sight effect suggesting that the entire solar system was moving en masse through space, in what we now know to be the direction of the constellation Sagittarius.

Yet there was still no clear physical proof for an independently moving earth until the year after Sir Isaac Newton's death in 1727; and that came about not through rhetoric, but through advances in precision technology, backed up by meticulous mathematical analysis.

THE REVD DR BRADLEY AND THE STAR

In 1728 the Revd Dr James Bradley, Fellow of Balliol College, Savilian Professor of Astronomy at Oxford, and a protégé of both Sir Isaac Newton and Professor Edmond Halley, was thirty-six years old. Just as modern-day astronomers "jet" around the world to use state-of-the-art research equipment at observatories in Hawaii, Australia, and La Palma in the Canary Islands, so Bradley undertook regular long horseback and jostling stagecoach journeys across southern England. He travelled from Oxford to the Royal Observatory, Greenwich, where Halley was Astronomer Royal; to the Royal Society in London; to the house of his friend Samuel Molyneux at Kew, west of London; and to the Essex village of Wanstead where Bradley's uncle, the Revd Dr James Pound, was Rector and kept a well-equipped private observatory.

Bradley, Pound, and Molyneux, all Fellows of the Royal Society, were interested in Robert Hooke's 1669 experiments aimed at measuring the six-monthly parallax-angle movement of a zenith star, which Hooke had described in his *An Attempt to Prove the Motion of the Earth* (1674). Hooke had chosen to measure the position of a zenith star, because he knew that the earth's atmosphere bent the rays of starlight coming to us obliquely from stars in space, and hence distorted their correct geometrical positions by a tiny angle, whereas light from directly overhead was not bent by the atmosphere and entered our telescopes, and eyes, in a perfectly straight line. By the 1670s, astronomers were coming to realize that the stars were at vastly greater distances from the earth than Copernicus could ever have imagined in 1543, and that their seasonal displacement angles between the June and December extremes of the earth's orbit must be correspondingly tiny – perhaps as tiny as 1 or 2 arc seconds, or no more than one-thousandth of the diameter of the moon. With such a tiny angle as that, the atmospheric bending or refraction of the incoming ray of starlight would be enough to give an entirely erroneous value, and hence invalidate the observation.

Consequently, like Hooke, Bradley and his friends decided to measure the position of the star Gamma Draconis (assigned to the Greek letter gamma, γ, in the constellation of Draco the Dragon) as it passed each day through the zenith in the latitude of London.

In pursuit of Gamma Draconis, therefore, Samuel Molyneux had commissioned a new zenith telescope from the London watchmaker and precision engineer George Graham, and by 1725 he and James Bradley were using it at Molyneux's house at Kew.

This 25-foot-long instrument was set up with absolute accuracy in the vertical, so that when an observer lay on his back beneath the eyepiece he saw Gamma Draconis slowly move into the field of view at the correct pre-calculated time of day. Then, with a micrometer which was much more accurate than Robert Hooke's of nearly sixty years before, Bradley measured the star's exact position with reference to the zenith point.

Bradley, who seems to have done most of the practical observing, first measured Gamma Draconis's position in December 1725. After only a few nights he found that the star was "culminating", or coming overhead, a little bit more to the south every twenty-four hours. By March 1726 it had ceased to move south and had begun to move back north, reaching its original (December) position by June. Gamma Draconis then continued to move northwards until September 1726, then turned south again, to return to its original starting position by December.

Gamma Draconis had moved up and down in a straight line, south, north, and south again, in twelve months, with reference to the Kew zenith point, as delineated by very accurate 25-foot plumb lines and micrometers. It had also encompassed a total up, down, then back again angle of 40 arc seconds: or an angle equivalent to about one forty-fifth of the diameter of the moon. Yet, what could this regular motion signify in astronomical terms?

THE ABERRATION OF LIGHT AND THE MOVING EARTH

Bradley was puzzled. He knew he was not the first astronomer to detect a strange "rock" in the positions of certain stars, such as Gamma Draconis and the Pole Star, over the past half-century, as Hooke, John Flamsteed, and the Danish astronomer Ole Rømer had all done so. But what caused the rock? In the light of what was known – assuming the Copernican theory to be true – about the plane, or direction of the earth's orbit in space with relation to the observed stars, this strange motion could *not* be the much-desired stellar parallax. This motion was at a 90-degree right angle to what a parallax angle should be, and, at 40 arc seconds, it seemed much too big. So what was it? Was it a real, physical phenomenon, or some kind of optical, mechanical, or perceptual irregularity?

Bradley decided to take the investigation further with a brand-new "zenith sector" of his own, also built by George Graham. This was to be a smaller but more versatile instrument than Molyneux's 25-foot telescope. Graham's telescope was only of 12½ feet focal length, but could encompass a slightly wider angle of sky, enabling

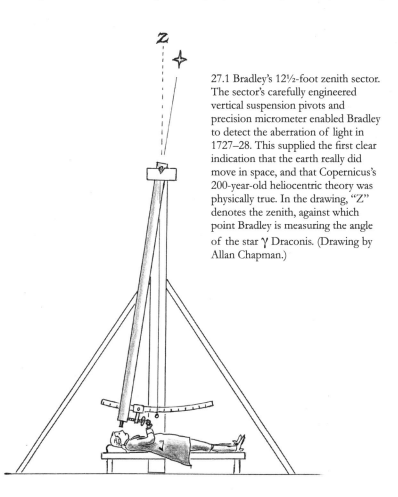

27.1 Bradley's 12½-foot zenith sector. The sector's carefully engineered vertical suspension pivots and precision micrometer enabled Bradley to detect the aberration of light in 1727–28. This supplied the first clear indication that the earth really did move in space, and that Copernicus's 200-year-old heliocentric theory was physically true. In the drawing, "Z" denotes the zenith, against which point Bradley is measuring the angle of the star γ Draconis. (Drawing by Allan Chapman.)

Bradley to measure the positions of more stars than just Gamma Draconis, to give him a wider base for comparison. The new 12½-foot instrument was to be set up at his aunt and uncle Pound's rectory at Wanstead, Essex, and he would visit from Oxford and London at key points in the earth's year to take his star measurements.

After only a few months, James Bradley realized that the strange, new six-monthly motion was real, astronomical, and not an instrumental or optical error, for in addition to Gamma Draconis, other nearby stars exhibited the same angular shift.

It is claimed that the puzzle of this new motion was elucidated when Bradley went 6 miles down the Thames from London to see Dr Halley at Greenwich; for while the boat twisted and turned around the bends of the river, a flag on the boat always pointed in the same direction, the wind blowing consistently from the same direction all the way.

Could this circumstance provide the vital, explanatory analogy? Let us assume that the constant wind direction is the same as the constant stream of light coming to the earth from Gamma Draconis. If we are rotating around the sun, then for six months of the year – March to September – we are moving, let us say, *into* that stream of light. Then, from September to the following March, we are moving *away* from that stream of starlight. Or, one might say, for six months we have the starlight coming into our faces, while for the next six we are receding from it. The upshot of this orbital direction change is that Gamma Draconis appears to be slightly displaced to a terrestrial observer depending on whether we move *into* its light stream or *away* from it.

Another analogy is to think of the constant direction of a wind-driven downpour of rain: walk steadily *into* the rain, face-on, and you get much wetter than if you travel in the same direction as the rain, with it on your back. This is because the raindrops "bunch up" in one direction, and "spread out" in the other. Then, in your imagination, simply replace drops of water with pulses of light. This was James Bradley's great realization. The light from the star as seen by an observer was being "aberrated" (or distorted) by the six-monthly change of direction caused by the earth's motion.

Yet wind, rain, or other analogies notwithstanding, one thing now seemed clear: the earth was *moving* with regard to the fixed star Gamma Draconis. As well as moving, the earth also appeared to be rotating upon its axis. Had Copernicus been shown to be right after all, some 185 years after he had published his theory back in 1543?

James Bradley was a precise and meticulous "astrometric" or angle-measuring astronomer of almost legendary standing, and his achievements would inspire later generations of scientists. Bradley, the deeply pragmatic Anglican clergyman, realized that while arguments, theories, and speculations may have been all well and good in their place, what mattered when it came to separating demonstrable fact from elegant theory was hard, measured evidence – evidence painstakingly acquired through long runs of meticulous observations made, repeated, checked, then made again, with instruments of the highest quality.

George Graham: craftsman and scientist

It was in this aspect of precision instrumentation that a new dimension was opening up in science. Before a craftsman could build a new kind of instrument for cutting-edge research, be it a "zenith sector", telescope, microscope, or a precision pendulum clock, the craftsman himself had to fully understand what was needed. He had to be a scientist himself; and this is how the new astronomy brought into being not only new types of instruments, but a new type of craftsman-engineer. We saw in Chapter 25 how Robert Hooke's collaborative friendship with the clockmaker-engineer Thomas Tompion made possible Hooke's and the early Royal Observatory's first research instruments; but a parallel relationship existed between Bradley and "honest George Graham", the Quaker horologist and builder of the aberration-detecting zenith sector.

"Honest George", as he came to be styled, who also helped rising craftsmen by making them interest-free loans of substantial sums of money, became a full Fellow of the Royal Society in his own right. He was the first of a rising body of English craftsmen-scientists cum cultured gentlemen who would rise from the workshop to the scientific intelligentsia from 1700 onwards.

It was his relentless intellectual and technical discipline as a physical scientist that enabled Bradley not only to detect the "aberration of light" as a physical fact (rather than as an instrumental or atmospheric anomaly), but to quantify it as well. The tiny angle for this aberration which Bradley finally determined and published in the *Philosophical Transactions* of the Royal Society in 1728 stands within a cat's whisker of the aberration value obtained by instruments of the twenty-first century.

After discovering the aberration of light, Bradley went on, using the same zenith sector at his aunt's house at Wanstead, to discover a slight gravitational rocking of the earth–moon orbital system as it goes around the sun in an eighteen-year cycle. This lunar "nutation" or nodding (from Latin *nutare*) he announced in 1748,[1] by which time he had succeeded Edmond Halley as Astronomer Royal at Greenwich, while retaining his Oxford Professorship. As a beautiful piece of intellectual and cosmological elegance, both the aberration of 1728 and the nutation of 1748 accorded perfectly with the gravitational and inverse square law logic implicit with Sir Isaac Newton's *Principia*.

As both Bradley and George Graham were fully aware, however, the aberration was *not* the long-searched-for stellar parallax – the traditional "acid test" for the Copernican theory – although it is true that by 1728 the aberration had shown beyond doubt that the earth moved in space. Yet Bradley was also confident that had this "parallax" been bigger than a single arc second, he would have detected it with his superb Graham instrument, combined with patience and mathematical analysis.

How small is an angle of a single arc second? Here we return to some of the points discussed when we first looked at the Copernican theory in Chapter 4. Let us say that one arc second corresponds approximately to 1/1800th of the moon's diameter. To put it another way, try looking at a 1-inch-diameter coin through a powerful telescope that is 3¼ miles distant: edge to edge, the coin will "subtend" an angle of about a single arc second.

Bradley claimed that had the star parallax been as large as one arc second then he, using George Graham's technology, would have detected it. Modern astronomers use the term "Parsec" to denote a celestial angle of a single arc second; and that angle corresponds to a geometrical distance of 3.259 light years. To put it another way, a ray of light travelling at 186,000 miles per second of time would take 3.259 years to travel that distance to us. It is hardly surprising that by the eighteenth century astronomers were gasping in amazement at the distances between us and the nearest stars. The universe revealed by the "new astronomy" was truly an awe-inspiring place: not only was it a place of elegance, law, logic, and reason, but – wonder of wonders – human intelligence could make sense of it, and as Kepler had long since put it, we can "think God's thoughts after Him".

It was this sense of awe at the Newtonian universe in particular that, even seventeen years before Bradley announced his discovery of the aberration, the poet Joseph Addison encapsulated in his poem and subsequent hymn "The Spacious Firmament on High" (1711):

> *What though in solemn silence all*
> *Move round the dark terrestrial ball;*
> *What though nor real voice nor sound*
> *Amid their radiant orbs be found;*
> *In reason's ear they all rejoice,*
> *And utter forth a glorious voice;*
> *For ever singing as they shine*
> *"The hand that made us is Divine."*

Given constantly improving instruments and new mathematical techniques such as the calculus, who could tell what future generations would discover?

THE STELLAR PARALLAX FOUND

Inspired partly by James Bradley's meticulous research techniques, other astronomers went in pursuit of the elusive tiny stellar parallax. In the 1780s Sir William Herschel began to study "binary" stars with very powerful reflecting, or mirror, telescopes, which by his time were capable of providing very high magnifications. A binary is a pair of stars extremely close together, ideally a fairly bright star close to a dim one. Herschel suggested that if the close proximity of these stars was due to a line-of-sight effect for a terrestrial observer, and the bright star was (hopefully) closer to us than the dim one, then as the earth moved around the sun, the parallax angle of the bright star should be bigger than that of the dim one. Therefore, the bright star should appear to move over six months, the few arc-seconds or so angle between the stars getting bigger and then smaller, December to June to December.

Alas, Herschel found no such angles. Rather, he would discover by 1802 that some of these stars were gravitationally connected and rotated around each other – to give the first observed example that Newton's Inverse Square Law of Gravity was truly universal, as it applied to distant stars and not just between the sun and planets. In the grand and fascinating tradition of scientific research, one failed investigation (stellar parallax) led to a whole new and unexpected branch of cosmology: binary star gravitation physics.

It is a testimony to the degree to which major astronomical discoveries hinged upon technological innovation that no fewer than *three* stellar parallaxes were independently discovered between 1836 and 1840. Two were discovered by German astronomers working in the eastern Baltic seaboard, and another by a Scotsman in South Africa. Once a certain technological ceiling had been breached, by superior optical and mechanical engineering, then the long-elusive parallaxes began almost to jump out of the sky.

Professor Friedrich Wilhelm Bessel was Director at the Königsberg Observatory in Prussia, and in the mid-1830s began to measure the position of the sixty-first star in the constellation of Cygnus the Swan: 61 Cygni. At around the same time, Friedrich Georg Wilhelm von Struve at Dorpat, Livonia (later part of Baltic Russia) was doing the same for the bright star Vega in the constellation of Lyra the Harp. At the Cape of Good Hope Observatory, South Africa, Thomas Henderson was observing tiny changes in the star Alpha Centauri, or the star in the constellation of the Centaur designated with the Greek letter α, alpha. All three men independently published their results within about three years of each other in the late 1830s. Were not these stars unbelievably remote, at distances so great that they were best expressed in light years rather than in mere miles? It has been said that measuring star distances in miles would be as inappropriate as measuring the distance between London and Sydney, Australia, in inches.

Thomas Henderson's star, Alpha [α] Centauri, with a parallax of ¾ of an arc second, is the closest star to the earth and solar system. Yet, even as the closest star in the universe, Alpha Centauri's light still takes 4.3 light years to reach us, it being an incredible 270,000 times further away from us than the 93 million miles of the sun.

And this is only what might be considered as the universe on our doorstep – distances which would have left Copernicus, Tycho, Kepler, and Galileo speechless, and utterly beyond the measurement capacity of the wooden, brass, and simple lens instruments of 400 years ago. It is hardly surprising that, while Robert Hooke, James Bradley, and William Herschel were *almost* there, it would take yet more breakthroughs in the mechanics and optics of scientific instrument-making before the long-sought stellar parallax was finally demonstrated as a reality, just as Queen Victoria was ascending the British throne, and 300 years after the death of Copernicus.

GOD, THE HEAVENLY CLOCKWORK, AND THE POWER OF THE SCIENTIFIC METHOD

The historical and scientific achievement of the stargazers, therefore, was one of the great odysseys of the human intellect: odysseys paralleled in the life sciences by the later discovery of the cellular and bacterial theories of disease, and the origins of species. But it was the achievement of the stargazers that came first in time, for it had been the astronomers who first showed that not only was mathematics the key to the beautiful structures of nature, but that precision technology could unlock the vital experimental data to show whether or not the theories accorded with physical reality. This was all due to a progressive improvement first in angle-graduated scales, then in telescopes, precision clocks, lenses, and mirrors; and by the nineteenth century the spectroscope, aided by photography, revealed for the first time not so much the motions, but the physics and chemistry of the sun and stars.

After astronomy had shown the way, the bio-medical sciences came to develop high-powered microscopes, exact chemical tests, X-rays, and new imaging technologies. For modern science, from the Big Bang to the DNA double helix "code of life", would not have existed but for a relentless development in technology-based instrumentation.

ASTRONOMY AND SCIENTIFIC PROGRESS

It was also the astronomers who first demonstrated that the inner workings of nature are not always the same as they appear to our naked eyes. It was they who were first obliged to engage with the "Big Questions" of meaning, origins, purpose – and God. As we have seen, it was the astronomers who first wrestled with the problems of how to interpret and understand descriptions of physical phenomena in the Bible – such as Joshua commanding the sun to stand still – and see the deeper meaning of the divine message that lay behind the everyday figures of speech used by God to address his people. In *c.* 1500 BC the children of Israel possessed a geographical and scientific knowledge that extended little beyond the Sinai desert: a land surface area the size of South Wales. Likewise, in more recent times, as Victorian geologists, theologians, and biologists began to wrestle with the physical origins of living things, it was the rise of new comparative experiment- and instrument-based sciences, such as organic and electrochemistry, genetics, and eventually molecular biology, that enabled us to see creation on an even grander scale, and extending over vaster aeons of time, than we had ever before been aware.

We should not think of the new cosmological vastness of post-classical astronomy and physics which unfolded in the wake of Copernicus and Galileo as a *revolution*, as certain historians like to do. Rather, it was a *Renaissance*: a new intellectual climate firmly rooted in the wider beliefs and evidences of order, logic, and structure of the classical and medieval worlds, but which in the light of a stream of new, physical, instrument-based discoveries, extending from the great maritime voyages of Columbus and Magellan to Bradley's aberration of light, began to take Western natural knowledge into new directions. This process unfolded across more than two centuries, with no sudden, revolutionary, changes of direction, but by cultural osmosis.

This Astronomical Renaissance was *not* the offspring of heroic battles between blind traditionalists and "enlightened" progressives: a scenario so beloved by those who can only see intellectual development in terms of "conflicts" and "revolutions". Absolutely crucially, it was *not* the outcome of a battle between the church and science; far too many churchmen and devout laity, both Catholic and Protestant, made far too many original scientific discoveries for that ever to have been the case.

What brought about this Astronomical and Scientific Renaissance was not a conflict; it was a *quest* – perhaps the most far-reaching quest in the history of human thought.

NOTES

$\mathscr{F}$ull details of the works cited in the notes are given in the Further Reading section.

CHAPTER 1
1. Yeomans, *Comets* p. 409; list of naked-eye comets, from antiquity to 1700, pp. 361–424.
2. Marvin, "Meteorites in History", pp. 16–22.

CHAPTER 4
1. *De Genesi* ii.9; Galileo, Letter to the Grand Duchess Christina, in Stillman Drake, *Discoveries and Opinions of Galileo*, p. 198.
2. Galileo, *Letter to the Grand Duchess*, in Drake, pp. 185–6.

CHAPTER 6
1. *Astronomiae Instauratae Mechanica*, pp. 84–7.
2. Dreyer, *Tycho Brahe*, pp. 377, 389.
3. *Mechanica*, pp. 45–7.
4. Dreyer, *Tycho Brahe*, pp. 381–4.
5. Christianson, *On Tycho's Island*, pp. 251–381, Biographies of Assistants.
6. *Mechanica*, p. 87.
7. Dreyer, *Tycho Brahe*, pp. 309–14, for Kepler's account.

CHAPTER 7
1. R. Grant, *History of Physical Astronomy*, pp. 539, 540.

CHAPTER 9
1. Hannam, *God's Philosophers*, pp. 178–80.

CHAPTER 11
1. Galileo, *Sidereus Nuncius*, Drake, *Discoveries and Opinions of Galileo*, p. 29.
2. Galileo, *Sidereus Nuncius*, Drake, p. 31.
3. Galileo, *Sidereus Nuncius*, Drake, p. 31.
4. Galileo, *Sidereus Nuncius*, Drake, p. 51.
5. Galileo, *Sidereus Nuncius*, Drake, pp. 50–1.
6. Galileo, *Letter on Sunspots*, Drake, *Discoveries and Opinions of Galileo*, p. 93.
7. Galileo, *Letter on Sunspots*, Drake, pp. 101–2, 143.
8. Galileo, *Letter on Sunspots*, Drake p. 102.
9. R. Grant, *History of Physical Astronomy*, p. 255.

CHAPTER 12
1. Galileo, *Sidereus Nuncius*, Drake, p. 49.
2. Galileo, *Sidereus Nuncius*, Drake, p. 50.
3. Galileo, *Letter on Sunspots*, Drake, p. 115.
4. Brodrick, *Galileo*, p. 51. Villa delle Selve: Galileo, *Letter on Sunspots*, Drake, p. 144.

CHAPTER 13
1. Sobel, *Galileo's Daughter*, pp. 23–4.
2. Letter text: Brodrick, *Galileo*, p. 94.
3. Brodrick, *Galileo*, p. 95.
4. Brodrick, *Galileo*, pp. 74–6; Galileo, *Letter to the Grand Duchess*, Drake, pp. 151–2.
5. Galileo, *Letter to the Grand Duchess*, Drake, pp. 178–9.
6. *De Genesi* ii.9; Galileo, *Letter to the Grand Duchess*, Drake, p. 198.
7. Galileo, *Letter to the Grand Duchess*, Drake, pp. 185–6.

CHAPTER 14
1. Banfi, *Galileo Galilei*, Ch. VI, pp. 143–63, esp. pp. 147–50.
2. Brodrick, *Galileo*, pp. 107–8.
3. Brodrick, *Galileo*, p. 109.
4. Santillana, *The Crime of Galileo*, p. 152 and Broderick, *Galileo*, p. 115.
5. Brodrick, *Galileo*, p. 117.
6. *Dialogue Concerning the Two Chief Systems of the World*, in Finocchiaro, *Galileo on the World Systems*, pp. 81–2.
7. Beer, *Milton*, p. 96; also Butler, "Milton's meeting with Galileo", pp. 132ff.

CHAPTER 15
1. Bishop, *Jesuit Pioneers of Modern Science*, pp. 37–50.
2. Needham and Ling, *Science and Civilization in China* vol. III, p. 445, fig. 186, plate LXIV.
3. Chapman, "Tycho Brahe in China" (see Further Reading on Chs. 5–6).

CHAPTER 16
1. Heilbron, *The Sun in the Church*, pp. 72–4 for San Petronio.
2. R. Grant, *History of Physical Astronomy*, p. 415.

CHAPTER 17
1. Vermji, *The Calvinist Copernicans*, p. 83.

CHAPTER 18
1. A. Chapman, "Divine Light".
2. McClean, *Humanism and the Rise of Science*, p. 149, cites Bourne's "Treatise on the Properties and Qualities of Glasses for Optical Purposes", an undated document in the Lansdown Manuscript (121.13, No. 13, Chpt. 9 A.6v.) in the British Library. Also King, *History of the Telescope*, p. 29.

CHAPTER 19
1. Harriot, *True Report* (1588) ed. Stevens, p. 57.
2. Aubrey, *Brief Lives*, "Harriot".
3. Rigaud, "Account of Harriot's Astronomical Papers", p. 42.
4. Harriot moon sketch: Lord Egremont, Petworth House Archive, HMC 241/9 fol. 26, West Sussex Record Office, Chichester. See also "Harriot Moondrawings" online and Chapman, "A new perceived reality", p. 28.
5. Rigaud, "Account of Harriot's Astronomical Papers", pp. 20, 42–5 etc.
6. Rigaud, "Account of Harriot's Astronomical Papers", pp. 42–5.
7. I am especially indebted to Kevin Kilburn for computing Jupiter's position for me.
8. Rigaud, "Account of Harriot's Astronomical Papers", p. 32.
9. North, "Thomas Harriot and the First Telescopic Observations of Sunspots", in Shirley, pp. 129–65. Also Rigaud, "Account of Harriot's Astronomical Papers", p. 34.
10. Trevor Roper, "Harriot's Physician", in Fox, pp. 48–9.

CHAPTER 20
1. Peltonen, "Francis Bacon", *Oxford DNB*, vol. 3, pp. 138–9. Jardine and Stewart, *Hostage to Fortune*, p. 287 etc.
2. Aubrey, *Brief Lives*, "F. Bacon".

CHAPTER 21
1. Crabtree's letters in *Phil. Trans.* are reprinted in Sellers, *In Search of William Gascoigne*, pp. 155ff.
2. Aughton, *The Transit of Venus*, p. 19.
3. Many letters exchanged between Crabtree, Horrocks, and Gascoigne are in Rigaud, "Account of Harriot's Astronomical Papers", and are reprinted in Sellers, pp. 155ff.
4. Wright, *Certaine Errors in Navigation*, p. 213. Chapman, "Jeremiah Horrocks, the transit of Venus…", p. 354, n. 50.

5. Flamsteed to J. Collins, 1-8-1671, *Correspondence of John Flamsteed* vol. 1, pp. 102–4.

6. Aubrey, *Brief Lives,* "Sir Jonas Moore".

7. Sellers, *In Search of William Gascoigne,* pp. 37, 160–2.

8. Chapman, "Jeremiah Horrocks, the transit of Venus…", p. 345.

9. Sellers, *In Search of William Gascoigne,* pp. 165, 176.

10. Crabtree to Gascoigne, 28 December 1640: Sellers, *In Search of William Gascoigne,* p. 166. Chapman, *Three North-Country Astronomers,* p. 19.

11. Crabtree to Gascoigne, 30 October 1640: Sellers, *In Search of William Gascoigne,* pp. 160–1.

12. Chapman, *Dividing the Circle,* p. 43. (I am indebted to Dr George Wilkins and his colleagues at the former Royal Greenwich Observatory for these calculations.)

13. Bodleian Library Manuscript Ashmole 423. For full details, see Chapman, "Jeremy Shakerley", p. 12.

14. *Anatomy,* p. 18. Chapman, "Jeremy Shakerley", p. 4.

15. Sherburne, "Catalogue", "Shakerley". Chapman, "Jeremy Shakerley", p. 10.

16. Towneley, "An extract of a letter written by Richard Towneley", p. 458. Also Sellers, *In Search of William Gascoigne,* pp. 151–2.

CHAPTER 22

1. Huygens, *Cosmotheoros* Bk. I, p. 2. Chapman, "Christiaan Huygens", p. 145.

2. Chapman, "Hooke's observations of solar system bodies", p. 116, n. 24.

3. *Micrographia,* pp. 242–6.

4. Alan Mills, "Three lenses by Constantine Huygens", pp. 173–82.

CHAPTER 24

1. *Discovery, in The Mathematical and Philosophical Works of the Right Rev. John Wilkins,* p. 63.

2. *Discovery,* p. 77, Section 5.

3. *Discovery,* p. 102.

4. *Discovery,* p. 108.

5. *Discovery* Prop. II, p. 13.

6. *Discovery* Prop. XIII, title, p. 100.

7. *Earth may be a Planet, in The Mathematical and Philosophical Works,* p. 140.

8. *Earth may be a Planet,* p. 141.

9. *Earth may be a Planet,* p. 158, Item 1.

10. *Earth may be a Planet,* p. 141.

11. *Earth may be a Planet,* p. 223.

12. *Discovery,* p. 111.

13. *Discovery,* p. 111.

14. *Discovery,* p. 122.

15. *Discovery,* pp. 127–8.

16. *Mathematical Magick,* "Daedalus", in *The Mathematical and Philosophical Works,* p. 201.

17. "Daedalus", pp. 194, 210.

18. "Daedalus", p. 195.

19. Hooke, *Posthumous Works* IV.

20. Hooke, *Diary,* 11 February 1675.

21. "Daedalus" p. 209.

CHAPTER 25

1. Hunter, *Boyle,* pp. 66–7; Maddison, *The Life of the Honourable Robert Boyle,* pp. 67ff.

2. Sprat, *History of the Royal Society,* p. 67.

3. Evelyn, *Memoirs,* 13 July 1654.

CHAPTER 26

1. Crabtree to Gascoigne, 7 August 1640, in *Phil. Trans.* 27 (1711), p. 286, and Sellers, *In Search of William Gascoigne,* p. 158.

2. Chapman, *England's Leonardo,* p. 199.

3. Chapman, *England's Leonardo,* pp. 197, 307, n. 8.

4. Power, *Experimental Philosophy,* Bk. III, pp. 175–81, Expt. 4, p. 177; also Chapman, *England's Leonardo,* p. 307, n. 8.

5. Hooke, *Micrographia,* pp. 242, 243–6.

6. Hooke, *An Attempt to Prove the Motion of the Earth,* pp. 27–8; Chapman, *England's Leonardo,* p. 204.

7. Chapman, "Oxford's Newtonian School", in Fauvel, Flood, and Wilson, *Oxford Figures* (2nd edn), p. 175. Quotation from student notebook in M.H.S. (Museum of the History of Science) Ms. 3, p. 25. Also Chapman, "Pure research and practical teaching… James Bradley", pp. 210, 212.

8. Newton, "A Letter of Mr Isaac Newton", p. 3084 para. 12.
9. Hooke and Newton, six letters, 24-11-1679 to 17-1-1680: *The Correspondence of Isaac Newton*, vol. II, pp. 297–313.
10. Cook, "Edmund Halley and Newton's *Principia*", pp. 147–51.
11. Westfall, *Never at Rest*, pp. 180–1.
12. *Leibniz and Samuel Clarke: Correspondence*, ed. Arlew.

CHAPTER 27
1. Bradley, "A Letter to Dr Edmond Halley", p. 640; "A Letter to the Earl of Macclesfield", p. 1.

List of In-text Illustrations

List of Plates

PLATE 13

13.1 The Rt Revd Dr John Wilkins
(supplied by Allan Chapman)
13.2 John Wilkins and his protégé Robert
Hooke ascend from Wadham College
quadrangle in Wilkins' "Flying
Chariot" (supplied by Allan Chapman)

PLATE 14

14.0 Frontispiece, John Wilkins, *Discourse
concerning a new world* . . . , 1640
(Wadham College, Oxford)

PLATE 15

15.0 Bernard le Bovier de Fontenelle,
Entretiens sur la pluralité des mondes
("Conversations on the plurality of
worlds"), 1686 © Roger-Viollet/
Topfoto

PLATE 16

16.1 Sir Francis Bacon © The Bridgeman
Art Library/Getty
16.2 Robert Hooke (supplied by Allan
Chapman)
16.3 Sir Isaac Newton © Christie's Images/
Corbis
16.4 The Revd Dr James Bradley © De
Agostini Picture Library/Getty

Further Reading

The Further Reading and notes contain primarily English-language sources (hopefully easily available). Early primary sources (i.e. sixteenth–seventeenth centuries) in English or other languages are fully cited, with publication details, in the main text, although most of these are only likely to be available in specialist academic libraries, or, sometimes, on the internet.

The notes are largely confined to providing exact sources for specific quotations cited in the text. Most of the general histories of astronomy contained in the Further Reading section contain chapters devoted to Copernicus, Tycho, Kepler, and Galileo.

GENERAL READING

Aristotle, *Physics, De Caelo, De Generatione Animalium*, etc., in *The Basic Works of Aristotle*, ed. and introd. by Richard McKeon (Random House, NY, 1941). See also *The Works of Aristotle*, ed. W. D. Ross, including *Meteorologica*, vol. III, trans. E. W. Webster, and *Problemata*, vol. VII, ed. and trans. E. S. Forster (Oxford, Clarendon Press, 1931, 1927), for Aristotlelian optics.

A. Chapman, *Dividing the Circle: The Development of Critical Angular Measurement in Astronomy, 1500–1850* (Praxis-Wiley, Chichester, 1990, 1995).

A. Chapman, *Gods in the Sky. Astronomy, Religion, and Culture from the Ancients to the Renaissance* (Channel 4 Books, Pan Macmillan, 2001).

Frederick Copleston, SJ, *A History of Philosophy*, vols. I–III (Greece to the Renaissance) (Image Books, Doubleday, NY, 1985).

Dictionary of Scientific Biography, ed. Charles C. Gillespie (Scribner, NY, 1970–80).

J. Fauvel, R. Flood, and R. Wilson, *Oxford Figures. Eight Centuries of the Mathematical Sciences* (OUP, 2000; 2nd edn. 2013).

Theodor Gomperz, *The Greek Thinkers. A History of Ancient Philosophy*, trans. G. G. Berry (Murray, London, 1905, 1912, 1969). Vol. III for Plato and vol. IV for Aristotle.

Edward Grant, *Planets, Stars, and Orbs. The Medieval Cosmos, 1200–1687* (CUP, 1994).

R. Grant, *A History of Physical Astronomy from the earliest times to the middle of the nineteenth century* (London, 1852).

Michael Hoskin, *Cambridge Illustrated History of Astronomy* (CUP, 1997).

Werner Keller, *The Bible as History* (revised edn., Hodder and Stoughton, 1980).

Henry C. King, *The History of the Telescope* (London, 1955).

David Leverington, *Babylon to Voyager and Beyond: A History of Planetary Astronomy* (CUP, 2003).

David C. Lindberg, *The Beginnings of Western Science: The European Scientific Tradition in Philosophical, Religious, and Institutional Context. Prehistory to AD 1450* (London, Chicago University Press, 2007).

David C. Lindberg and Ronald Numbers (ed.), *When Science and Christianity Meet* (London, Chicago University Press, 2003).

Arthur O. Lovejoy, *The Great Chain of Being. A Study of an Idea* (Harvard University Press, 1936).

Paul Marston, *Great Astronomers in European History* (University of Central Lancashire (UCLAN), Jeremiah Horrocks Institute for Mathematics, Physics, and Astronomy, 2014).

John D. North, *Chaucer's Universe* (OUP, 1988).

John D. North, *Fontana History of Astronomy and Cosmology* (Fontana, 1994).

John D. North, *God's Clockmaker. Richard of Wallingford and the Invention of Time* (Hambledon and London, 2005).

Richard Olson, *Science and Religion 1450–1900, from Copernicus to Darwin* (Greenwood Publishing Group, 2004).

A. Pannekoek, *A History of Astronomy* (London, 1961).

Albert Van Helden, *Measuring the Universe: Cosmic Dimensions from Aristarchus to Halley* (Chicago University Press, 1985).

Christopher Walker (ed.), *Astronomy before the Telescope* (British Museum, London, 1996).

The Galileo Project, online, Rice University.

CHAPTERS 1–2 (CLASSICAL AND MEDIEVAL ASTRONOMY)

Anthony Aveni, *Behind the Crystal Ball: Magic, Science, and the Occult from Antiquity through the New Age* (Newleaf, London, 1996).

Christopher Brooke, *The Twelfth-Century Renaissance* (Thames and Hudson, London, 1969).

A. Chapman, *Gods in the Sky* (see "General Reading").

Louise Cochrane with Charles Burnett, ed. Peter Wallis, *Adelard of Bath. The First English Scientist* (Bath Royal Literary and Scientific Institution, 2013).

Norman Cohn, *The Pursuit of the Millennium: Revolutionary Millenarian and Mystical Anarchists of the Middle Ages* (Paladin, 1970).

A. C. Crombie, *Robert Grosseteste and the Origins of Experimental Science* (Oxford, Clarendon Press, 1953).

A. C. Crombie, *From Augustine to Galileo* (2 vols., 1952; Penguin, 1969).

Jean Gimpel, *The Medieval Machine. The Industrial Revolution of the Middle Ages* (Futura, London, 1976).

James Hannam, *God's Philosophers. How the medieval world laid the foundations of modern science* (Icon Books, London, 2009).

George Herbert, *Elixier* (also "Teach me, my God and King"), *Herbert*, poems, selected by W. H. Auden (Penguin Poetry, 1973, 1985), p. 116.

J. Russell Hind, *Comets, A Descriptive Treatise upon those Bodies… A Table of All The Calculated Comets* (London, 1852).

Johan Huizinga, *The Waning of the Middle Ages* (1924; Penguin, 1968).

Ursula B. Marvin, "Meteorites in history: an overview from the Renaissance to the 20th century", in *The History of Meteoritics and Key Meteorite Collections: Fireballs, Falls, and Finds*, eds. G. J. N. McCall, A. J. Bowden, and R. J. Howarth (Geological Society Special Publication 256, London, 2006).

John D. North, *Stars, Minds, and Fate. Essays in Ancient and Medieval Cosmology* (Bloomsbury, 2003).

Steven Runciman, *A History of the Crusades* (3 vols., Cambridge, 1951–4).

Keith Thomas, *Religion and the Decline of Magic: Studies in Popular Belief in Sixteenth- and Seventeenth-Century England* (Weidenfeld and Nicolson, London, 1971).

H. Trevor-Roper, *The Rise of Christian Europe* (Thames and Hudson, London, 1965).

Benedicta Ward, *The Venerable Bede* (Geoffrey Chapman, London, 1990).

Donald K. Yeomans, *Comets. A Chronological History of Observation, Science, Myth and Folklore* (John Wiley & Sons, NY, Chichester, etc., 1991).

CHAPTERS 3–4 (COPERNICUS)

Marie Boas, *The Scientific Renaissance* (Collins, London, 1962).

William Boyd, *The History of Western Education* (Adam & Charles Black, London, 1954).

V. N. Brotóns, "The reception of Copernicus in sixteenth-century Spain. The case of Diego de Zuñiga", *Isis*, 1995, pp. 52–78.

Alfred B. Cobban, *The Medieval Universities. Their Development and Organisation* (London, 1975).

Nicholas Copernicus (trans. A. M. Duncan), *On the Revolutions of the Heavenly Spheres* (David & Charles, Newton Abbot, 1976).

Nicholas Copernicus (trans. Edward Rosen), *De Revolutionibus Orbium Coelestium* (Polish Academy of Sciences, Warsaw, 1978).

Ivan Crowe, *Copernicus* (Tempus, Stroud, 2003).

Dennis Danielson, *The First Copernican. Georg Joachim Rheticus and the Rise of the Copernican Revolution* (Walker, NY, 2006).

John Freely, *Celestial Revolutionary. Copernicus, the Man and His Universe* (I. B., Taurus, London and NY, 2014).

Owen Gingerich, *The Great Copernicus Chase and other Adventures in Astronomical History* (Sky Publishing, CUP, 1992).

Owen Gingerich, *The Book Nobody Read* (Walker, NY, 2004).

Alfred Koyré (trans. R. E. W. Maddison), *The Astronomical Revolution* (Cornell Univ. Press, Ithaca, 1973).

T. Kuhn, *The Copernican Revolution. Planetary Astronomy and the Development of Western Thought* (Harvard Univ. Press, 1966).

Frances Yates, *Giordano Bruno and the Hermetic Tradition* (Routledge and Kegan Paul, 2002).

CHAPTERS 5–6 (TYCHO BRAHE)

Tycho Brahe, *Astronomiae Instauratae Mechanica* (Wandesburg, 1598); trans. H. Raeder and E. Strömgren as Tycho Brahe's *Description of his Instruments and Scientific Work* (Copenhagen, 1946).

A. Chapman, "Tycho Brahe in China. The Jesuit mission to Peking and the iconography of European instrument-making processes", *Annals of Science* 41 (Taylor & Francis, Basingstoke, 1984), pp. 417–43.

A. Chapman, "Tycho Brahe – Instrument Designer, Observer, and Mechanician", *Journal of the British Astronomical Association* 99 (London, 1989), pp. 70–7.

(The two preceding articles are reprinted in A. Chapman, *Astronomical Instruments and Their Users*. Tycho Brahe to William Lassell (Variorum, Aldershot, 1996), nos. III and IV.)

John R. Christianson, *On Tycho's Island. Tycho Brahe and his Assistants 1570–1601* (CUP, 2000).

J. L. E. Dreyer, Tycho Brahe. *A Picture of Scientific Life and Work in the Sixteenth Century* (1890; Dover edn., NY, 1963).

Victor E. Thoren, *The Lord of Uraniborg. A Biography of Tycho Brahe* (CUP, 1990).

CHAPTERS 7–8 (KEPLER)

Eric Aiten, *Johannes Kepler and the "Mysterium Cosmographicum"* (Sudhoff's Archiv. Bd. 61 H. 2 (1977 2 QUARTAL), publ. Franz Steiner Verlag), pp. 173–94

Arthur and Peter Beer, *Kepler, Four Hundred Years* (*Vistas in Astronomy* 18, Pergamon Press, Oxford, 1975).

Max Caspar, *Kepler* (Courier Dover Publications, 1993).

J. L. E. Dreyer, *The History of Astronomy from Thales to Kepler* (1906; revised with Foreword by W. H. Stahl, Dover, NY, 1953).

R. J. W. Evans, *Rudolf II and His World: A Study of Intellectual History 1576–1612* (OUP, 1973).

J. V. Field, *Kepler's Geometrical Cosmology* (Athlone Press, London, 1988).

William Gilbert, *De Magnete* (London, 1600; trans. P. Fleury Mottelay, 1893, repr. Dover Publications Inc., NY, 1958).

Owen Gingerich, *The Eye of Heaven: Ptolemy, Copernicus, Kepler* (American Institute of Physics, 1993).

Jamie James, *The Music of the Spheres Music, Science, and the Natural Order of the Universe* (Copernicus, Springer Verlag, NY, 1993).

Johannes Kepler, *Mysterium Cosmographicum* [1596], trans. A. M. Duncan (Abaris Books, NY, 1981).

Arthur Koestler, *The Sleepwalkers* (Hutchinson, London, 1959; repr. Penguin, 1964).

Alexander Koyré, *Closed World to Infinite Universe* (Johns Hopkins, Baltimore, 1957, 1968).

Job Kozhamthadam (Jesuit), *The Discovery of Kepler's Laws* (Notre Dame Univ. Press, 1994).

Bruce Stephenson, *Kepler's Physical Astronomy* (Springer, NY, 1987).

Bruce Stephenson, *The Music of the Heavens: Kepler's Harmonic Astronomy* (Princeton Univ. Press, 1994).

CHAPTERS 9–14 (GALILEO)

Eugenio Alberi (ed.), *Le Opere di Galileo Galilei*, 15 vols. plus Supplement (Florence, 1842–56).

Antonio Banfi, *Galileo Galilei* (Milan, 1949).

Anna Beer, *Milton. Poet, Pamphleteer, and Patriot* (Bloomsbury Press, NY, 2008).

Mario Biagioli, *Galileo, Courtier. The Practice of Science in the Culture of Absolutism* (Chicago Univ. Press, 1993).

Richard J. Blackwell, *Galileo, Bellarmine, and the Bible* (Notre Dame and London, 1991).

James Brodrick, SJ, *Galileo. The Man, his Work, and his Misfortunes* (London, 1964).

George F. Butler, "Milton's meeting with Galileo: a reconsideration", *Milton Quarterly* 39 (2005), pp. 132ff.

George V. Coyne, SJ, "The Church's Most Recent Attempts to Dispel the Galileo Myth", in *The Church and Galileo*, ed. E. McMullin (see below).

A. C. Crombie, *From Augustine to Galileo* (see under Chapters 1–2).

Pasqual M. D'Elia, *Galileo in China* (Harvard Univ. Press., 1960).

Stillman Drake, *Galileo Studies* (Univ. of Michigan Press, 1970).

Stillman Drake, *Galileo: Pioneer Scientist* (Univ. of Toronto Press, 1990).

Annibale Fantoli, *Galileo: For Copernicanism and the Church* (Vatican Observatory Publications, 3rd English translation, 2003).

Maurice A. Finocchiaro, *The Galileo Affair: A Documentary History* (Univ. of California Press, Berkeley, CA, 1989).

Maurice A. Finocchiaro, *Galileo on the World Systems. A New Abridged Translation and Guide* (Univ. of California Press, Berkeley and London, 1997).

A. Frova and M. Marenzana, trans. Jim McManus, *Thus Spoke Galileo* (OUP, 2006).

Galileo Galilei, *The Starry Messenger* (*Sidereus Nuncius*), 1610; *Letter on Sunspots*, 1613; *Letter to the Grand Duchess Christina*, 1615; *The Assayer*, 1623: included in Stillman Drake, *Discoveries and Opinions of Galileo* (Doubleday, NY, 1957).

Galileo Galilei, *Operations of the Geometric and Military Compass* (1606), trans. and introd. by Stillman Drake (Dibner Library, Smithsonian, Washington DC, 1978).

Galileo Galilei, *Dialogue on the Two Chief Systems* (1663), trans. in Finocchiaro, 1997.

The Private Life of Galileo compiled principally from his correspondence and that of his eldest daughter, Sister Maria Celeste, ed. Mary Allan-Olney (Macmillan, London, 1870).

A. Rupert Hall, *From Galileo to Newton, 1630–1720* (Collins, London, 1963).

John Heilbron, *Galileo* (OUP, 2010).

Nick Kollerstrom, "Galileo's First Trial", *Astronomy Now*, July 2004, pp. 33–6.

Ernan McMullin, *The Church and Galileo* (Univ. of Notre Dame Press, 2005).

John Milton claimed to have met Galileo in *Areopagitica* (1644): see *Areopagitica*, Everyman edn., 1955, p. 42; also Milton, *Paradise Lost* (1667), Book I, lines 287–91 and Book V, line 261.

Ronald L. Numbers (ed.), *Galileo Goes to Jail, and Other Myths about Science and Religion* (Harvard Univ. Press, 2009).

Pietro Redondi, *Galileo, Heretic* (Penguin trans. 1987).

Giorgio de Santillana, *The Crime of Galileo* (Heinemann, London, 1958).

Dava Sobel, *Galileo's Daughter* (Walker & Co., 1999; HarperCollins, 2011).

Manfred Weidhorn, *The Person of the Millennium: The Unique Impact of Galileo on World History* (iUniverse, 2005).

CHAPTER 15–16 (JESUITS; SCIENCE IN ROMAN CATHOLIC EUROPE)

José de Acosta, *The Natural and Moral History of the Indies*, ed. Jane Morgan, transl. Frances Lopez-Morillas (Duke Univ. Press, 2002).

Howard B. Adelmann, *Marcello Malpighi and the Evolution of Embryology*, 5 vols. (Cornell Univ. Press, 1966).

Agnes Arber, "Nehemiah Grew (1641–1712) and Marcello Malpighi (1628–1694): an essay in comparison", *Isis* 34, 1 (summer 1942), 7–16.

Rachel Attwater, *Adam Schall* (Chapman, London, 1963).

George Bishop, *A Lion of Judah. The Travels and Adventures of Pedro Paez S.J.* (Gujarat Sahitya Prakash, Anand, India, 1998).

George Bishop, *Jesuit Pioneers of Modern Science and Mathematics* (Gujarat Sahitya Prakash, Gujarat, India, 2005).

H. Bosman, "Ferdinand Verbiest, Directeur de l'Observatoire de Peking", *Revue des questions scientifiques* 21 (1912), pp. 195–273.

The Catholic Encyclopaedia, eds. Charles Herbermann and others (Robert Appleton, NY, 1913): for biographies and work of Roman Catholic scientists.

Claudio M. Burgaleta, SJ, *José de Acosta (1540–1600): His Life and Thought* (Jesuit Way Series, Loyola Univ. Press, Chicago, 1999).

A. Chapman, "Tycho Brahe in China" (see under Chapters 5–6).

A. Chapman, "Reconstructing the angle-measuring instruments of Pierre Gassendi", *Bulletin of the Scientific Instrument Society* 27 (Oxford, 1990), pp. 3–8. Reprinted in Chapman, *Astronomical Instruments and their Users* (see under Chapters 5–6).

Carlo M. Cipolla, *Clocks and Culture, 1300–1700* (London, 1967).

Franz Daxecker, *The Physicist and Astronomer Christoph Scheiner: Biography, Letters, Works* (Innsbruck University, 246, Innsbruck, 2004).

Pasqual M. D'Elia, *Galileo in China* (Harvard Univ. Press, 1960).

Mordecai Feingold (ed.), *The New Science and Jesuit Science* (Springer, 2003).

Saul Fisher, *Pierre Gassendi's Philosophy and Science* (Leiden, Boston, Brill, 2005).

Nils Hansen, "Nils Steno", *The Catholic Encyclopaedia* vol. 14 (above).

John Heilbron, *The Sun in the Church: Cathedrals and Solar Observatories* (Harvard Univ. Press, 1999).

Hans Kermit, *Niels Stenson* [Steno] *1638–1686. The Scientist Who Was Beatified* (Gracewing, Leominster, 2003).

George Kish, "Acosta, José de", *Dictionary of Scientific Biography* vol. I (Charles Scribner, NY, 1970).

Joseph MacDonnell, SJ, *Jesuit Geometers* (Inst. of Jesuit Sources, St Louis, 1989).

Joseph MacDonnell, SJ, *José de Acosta S.J. (1540-1600) Pioneer of the Geophysical Sciences*, Fairfield University Mathematics Department website www.faculty.fairfield.edu/jmac/sj/scientists/acosta.htm.

Sabino Maffeo, SJ, *In the Service of Nine Popes: 100 Years of the Vatican Observatory*, trans. George V. Coyne, SJ (Pontifical Academy of Sciences, Specola Vaticana, Rome, 1991).

Joseph Needham, *Chinese Astronomy and the Jesuit Mission* (Chinese Society, 1958).

Joseph Needham and Wang Ling, *Science and Civilization in China, vol. III: Mathematics and Astronomy* (CUP, 1959).

Joseph Needham, *Clerks and Craftsmen in China and the West* (CUP, 1970).

H. J. M. Nellen, *Ismaël Boulliau* [Bullialdus] *(1605–1694), astronome, épistolier, nouvelliste et intermédiaire scientifique* (Pierre Bayle Institute, Holland Univ. Press, Nijmegan, 1994).

Margaret J. Osler, *Divine Will and the Mechanical Philosophy: Gassendi and Descartes on Contingency and Necessity in the Created World* (CUP, 1994).

Andres I. Prieto, *Missionary Scientists: Jesuit Science in Spanish South America 1570–1810* (Vanderbilt Univ. Press, 2011).

J. L. Russel, "Catholic astronomers and the Copernican system after the condemnation of Galileo", *Annals of Science* 46 (1989), pp. 365–86.

David Sellers, "William Crabtree and the date of Easter", *The Antiquarian Astronomer* (Journal of the Society for the History of Astronomy), 8 (April 2014), pp. 109–16.

Jonathan Spence, *The China Helpers: Western Advisors in China, 1600–1920* (London, 1969).

Jonathan Spence, *Emperor of China: A Self-Portrait of K'ang Hsi* (London, 1974).

"Nils Steno", in *Encyclopaedia Britannica*, 11th edn., vol. 25 (CUP, 1911), p. 879.

John Witek, SJ, *Ferdinand Verbiest S.J. (1623–1688)* (Ferdinand Verbiest Foundation, Leuven, 1994).

Thomas E. Woods, *How the Catholic Church Built Western Civilization* (Washington DC, 2005).

J. A. Zahm, C.S.C. [Congregatio a Sancta Cruce], *Catholic Science and Catholic Scientists* (Philadelphia, 1893).

CHAPTER 17 (PROTESTANTS OF THE "NORTHERN RENAISSANCE")

Kivan Berkvens, L. C. Palm, and Albert Van Helden (eds.), *A History of Science in the Netherlands. Survey, Themes, and References* (Leiden, 1999).

Eduard Jan Dijksterhuis, *Simon Stevin: Science in the Netherlands in 1600* (Martinas, The Hague, 1970).

Pieter Geyl, *The Netherlands in the Seventeenth Century* (New York, 1964).

Thomas Hockey, *The Biographical Encyclopaedia of Astronomers* (Springer, 2009).

C. Methuen, "The role of the heavens in the thought of Philip Melanchthon", *Journal of the History of Ideas* 57 (1996), pp. 385–403.

The Principal Works of Simon Stevin, eds. E. Crone, E. J. Dijksterhuis, C. Dikshoorn, and R. J. Forbes, 5 vols. in 6 (Swets and Zeitlinger, Amsterdam, 1955–66). Also available online: The Digital Library of the Royal Netherlands Academy of Arts and Sciences.

Edward G. Ruestrow, *The Microscope in the Dutch Republic. The Shaping of Discovery* (CUP, 1996).

Dirk Jan Struik, "Snel, Willebrord", *Dictionary of Scientific Biography* vol. XII (Scribner, NY, 1970).

T. van Nouhuys, *The age of two-faced Janus. The comets of 1577 and 1618 and the decline of the Aristotelian world view in the Netherlands* (Leiden, 1998).

Rienk Vermij, *The Calvinist Copernicans. The Reception of the New Astronomy in the Dutch Republic* (Amsterdam, 2002).

R. S. Westman, "The Copernicans and the Churches", in D. C. Lindberg and R. L. Numbers (eds.), *God and Nature. Historical Essays on the Encounter between Christianity and Science* (Berkeley, CA, 1986).

C. Wilson *et al.*, *The Anglo-Dutch Contribution to Early Modern Society* (Oxford, 1976).

W. Yourgrau and A. D. Beck (eds.), *Cosmology, History and Theology* (New York and London, 1977).

CHAPTER 18 (THE ENGLISH COPERNICANS)

Adam J. Apt, "The Reception of Kepler's Astronomy in England", unpublished Oxford University D.Phil. thesis, 1982.

A. Chapman, "The English Copernicans", *Yearbook of Astronomy 2008*, eds. Sir Patrick Moore and John Mason (Macmillan, London, 2007), pp. 301–11.

A. Chapman, "Divine Light", in *Mathematicians and their Gods*, ed. Mark McCartney (Univ. of Ulster Press, forthcoming 2014–15).

Richard Deacon, *John Dee. Scientist, Geographer, Astrologer, and Secret Agent to Elizabeth I* (Letchworth, Hertfordshire, 1968).

John Fauvel, Raymond Flood, and Robin Wilson, *Oxford Figures* (see under "General Reading").

Mordecai Feingold, *The Mathematician's Apprenticeship. Science, Universities, and Society in England, 1560-1640* (Cambridge, 1984).

Ronald H. Fritze and William B. Robison, *Historical Dictionary of Stuart England 1603–1689* (Greenwood Press, 1996): p. 471 for Copernicans.

F. R. Johnson, *Astronomical Thought in Renaissance England* (Johns Hopkins Univ. Press, Baltimore, 1937).

Antonia McLean, *Humanism and the Rise of Science in Tudor England* (London, 1972).

Oxford Dictionary of National Biography (OUP, 2004) [revised and updated *Dictionary of National Biography*] for William Oughtred, Henry Gellibrand, John Bainbridge, and Thomas Lydiat.

C. Ronan, "The origins of the reflecting telescope", *Journal of the British Astronomical Association* 101, 6 (1991), 335–42 (for "Tudor telescope").

"Was there an Elizabethan Telescope?", *Bulletin of the Scientific Instrument Society* 37 (June 1993), 2–10: report of meeting on Tudor telescope at the Society of Antiquaries, 26 March 1993.

J. L. Russel, "The Copernican System in Great Britain", *Reception* 1972, pp. 189–239.

E. G. R. Taylor, *The Mathematical Practitioners of Tudor and Stuart England* (CUP, 1968).

CHAPTER 19 (THOMAS HARRIOT)

John Aubrey, "Thomas Harriot", in *Brief Lives* ed. Oliver Lawson Dick (Secker and Warburg, 1949, 1975; also Penguin).

A. Chapman, "The astronomical work of Thomas Harriot (1560–1621)", *Quarterly Journal of the Royal Astronomical Society* 36 (1995), pp. 97–107.

A. Chapman, "A new perceived reality: Thomas Harriot's Moon maps", *Astronomy and Geophysics* 50, Issue 1 (February 2009), pp. 27–33.

Robert Fox (ed.), *Thomas Harriot. An Elizabethan Man of Science* (Ashgate, Aldershot, 2000).

Robert T. Gunther, *Early Science in Oxford*, II (Oxford, 1923): for Harriot and the telescope, pp. 293–4.

Thomas Harriot, *A Briefe and True Report of the New Found Land of Virginia* (London, 1588); see also edition by Henry Stevens (London, 1900).

Margaret Irwin, *That Great Lucifer. A Portrait of Sir Walter Ralegh* (Chatto and Windus, 1960).

Robert H. Kargan, *Atomism in England from Harriot to Newton* (Oxford, 1966).

Giles Milton, *Big Chief Elizabeth. How England's adventurers gambled and won the New World* (Hodder and Stoughton, London, 2000).

John D. North, "Thomas Harriot and the First Telescopic Observations of Sunspots", in Shirley (ed.), *Thomas Harriot*, pp. 129–65.

David B. Quinn, *The Roanoke Voyages, 1584–1590. Documents to illustrate the English voyages to North America under the patent granted to Sir Walter Ralegh in 1584*, 2 vols. (London, 1955).

Stephen P. Rigaud, "Account of Harriot's Astronomical Papers", in Supplement to Dr Bradley's *Miscellaneous Works: with An Account of Harriot's Astronomical Papers* (Oxford, 1832): 1–70 for text of Harriot's telescopic correspondence.

Muriel Rukeyser, *The Traces of Thomas Harriot* (New York, 1971).

John Shirley (ed.), *Thomas Harriot, Renaissance Scientist* (OUP, 1974).

E. G. R. Taylor, *Tudor Geography 1485–1583* (London, 1930).

Hugh Trevor-Roper, "Harriot's Physician: Theodore de Mayerne", in Fox (ed.), *Thomas Harriot*, pp. 48–63.

CHAPTER 20 (FRANCIS BACON)

F. H. Anderson, *The Philosophy of Francis Bacon* (Chicago Univ. Press, 1948).

F. Anderson, *Francis Bacon: His Career and His Thought* (Los Angeles, 1962).

John Aubrey, "Sir Francis Bacon", in *Brief Lives* (see under Chapter 19).

Francis Bacon, *The Advancement of Learning* (1605), *Essays* (1597–1625), *New Atlantis* (1628): available in numerous modern editions.

The Works of Francis Bacon, eds. James Spedding, Robert Leslie Ellis, and Douglas Denon Heath, 14 vols. (London, 1857–74).

Francis Bacon, *The New Organon*, eds. L. Jardine and M. Silverthorne (CUP, 2000).

B. Farrington, *The Philosophy of Francis Bacon: An Essay on its Development from 1603–1609* (Liverpool Univ. Press, 1964).

Antonia Fraser, *The Gunpowder Plot. Terror and Faith in 1605* (Weidenfeld and Nicolson, London, 1996).

John Gribbin, *The Fellowship: Gilbert, Bacon, Harvey, Wren, Newton and the Story of the Scientific Revolution* (Allen Lane, 2005; Penguin, 2006).

Lisa Jardine, *Francis Bacon: Discovery and the Art of Discourse* (CUP, 1974).

Lisa Jardine and A. Stewart, *Hostage to Fortune: the Troubled Life of Francis Bacon, 1561–1626* (Phoenix Giant, 1998).

Markku Peltonen, "Francis Bacon", *Oxford Dictionary of National Biography*, vol. 3 (OUP, 2004), pp. 138–9.

Charles Webster, *The Great Instauration. Science, Medicine, and Reform, 1626–1660* (Duckworth, London, 1975).

B. Wormald, *Francis Bacon: History, Politics, and Science 1561–1626* (CUP, 1993).

CHAPTER 21 (CATHOLIC AND PROTESTANT SCIENTIFIC FRIENDSHIPS IN NORTHERN ENGLAND)

Peter Aughton, *The Transit of Venus. The Brief, Brilliant Life of Jeremiah Horrocks* (Weidenfeld and Nicolson, Windrush Press, London, 2004).

J. E. Bailey, "Jeremiah Horrocks and William Crabtree, Observers of the Transit of Venus, 24 November, 1639", *Palatine Note-Book* II (December 1882/January 1883), pp. 253–66.

Allan Chapman, *Three North-Country Astronomers* (Manchester, 1982).

Allan Chapman, "Jeremy Shakerley (1626–1655?): astronomy, astrology, and patronage in Civil War Lancashire", *Transactions of the Historic Society of Lancashire and Cheshire* 135 (1985; Liverpool, 1986), pp. 1–14; reprinted in Chapman, *Astronomical Instruments and Their Users* (see on Chapters 5–6).

Allan Chapman, "Jeremiah Horrocks, the transit of Venus, and the 'new astronomy' in early 17th-century England", *Quarterly Journal of the Royal Astronomical Society* 31 (1990), pp. 333–57; reprinted in Chapman, *Astronomical Instruments and Their Users* (see on Chapters 5–6).

Allan Chapman, *William Crabtree, 1610–1644: Manchester's First Mathematician* (Manchester Statistical Society, 1995).

Allan Chapman, "Jeremiah Horrocks, William Crabtree, and the Lancashire observations of the transit of Venus of 1639", *Transits of Venus: New Views of the Solar System and Galaxy*, ed. Don W. Kurtz (196th Colloquium of the International Astronomical Union, June 2004; CUP, 2004), pp. 3–26.

William Crabtree, correspondence published by the Royal Society, 1711, 1718, etc., reprinted in Sellers, *In Search of William Gascoigne* (see below).

John Flamsteed, *The "Preface" to John Flamsteed's "Historia Coelestis Britannica" 1725*, trans. Dione Johnson and ed. Allan Chapman (National Maritime Museum, Greenwich, Monograph No. 52, 1982).

The Correspondence of John Flamsteed, First Astronomer Royal, eds. Eric G. Forbes, Lesley Murdin, and Frances Willmoth, 3 vols. (Institute of Physics Publishing, Bristol and Philadelphia, 1995–2002).

Sidney B. Gaythorpe, "A Galilean telescope made about 1640 by William Gascoigne", *Journal of the British Astronomical Association*, June 1929, pp. 238–41.

Jeremiah Horrocks, *Venus in sole visa 1639–40* (published by Johannes Hevelius, Dantzig, 1661); translated into English by Arundel Blount Whatton (London, 1859), with a preface "A Memoir of his [Horrocks's] Life and Labours".

Nicholas Kollerstrom, "William Crabtree's Venus transit observations", in Kurtz, *Transits of Venus*, pp. 34–40.

David Sellers, *In Search of William Gascoigne, Seventeenth-Century Astronomer* (Springer, NY, London, etc., 2012).

David Sellers, "William Crabtree and the date of Easter" (see under Chapters 15–16).

Edward Sherburne, "Catalogue" of Astronomers, printed as a Supplement to his translation of *The Sphere of Marcus Manilius* (London, 1675).

Richard Towneley, "An extract of a letter written by Richard Towneley to Dr Crocn", *Philosophical Transactions* 2 (1667), p. 458.

John K. Walton, "Jeremiah Horrocks's Lancashire", in Kurtz, *Transits of Venus*, pp. 27–33.

Charles Webster, 'Richard Towneley (1629-1707). The Towneley group and seventeenth-century science', *Transactions of the Historic Society of Lancashire and Cheshire* 118 (1967 for 1966), pp. 51-76.

Edward Wright, *Certaine Errors in Navigation* (London, 1599; 2nd edn. 1610).

CHAPTER 22 (HEVELIUS)

Mark Birkinshaw, "Johannes Hevelius, the Prussian Lynx at 400", paper given to the Royal Astronomical Society meeting on 11 February 2011, published in *The Observatory* 131, No. 1223 (August 2011), pp. 207–10.

Allan Chapman, "Christiaan Huygens (1629–95): astronomer and mechanician", *Endeavour* 19, No. 4 (Elsevier Ltd, 1995), pp. 140–5.

Allan Chapman, "Hooke's telescopic observations of solar system bodies", in *Robert Hooke and the English Renaissance*, eds. Paul Kent and Allan Chapman (Gracewing, Leominster, 2005), pp. 95–123.

Allan Chapman, "Johannes Hevelius (1611–1687): Instrument Maker, Lunar Cartographer, and Surveyor of the Heavens", in *Patrick Moore's Yearbook of Astronomy 2013*, eds. Patrick Moore and John Mason (Macmillan, London, 2012), pp. 343–70.

Allan Chapman, "Mapping and Understanding the Moon: From

Thomas Harriot to Sir Patrick Moore", *Patrick Moore's Yearbook of Astronomy 2014*, eds. Patrick Moore and John Mason (Macmillan, London, 2013).

Christiaan Huygens, *Systema Saturnium* (Hague, 1659); reprinted with parallel French translation in Huygens, *Oeuvres Complètes*, vol. XV (Amsterdam, 1925), pp. 208–53.

Christiaan Huygens, *Cosmotheoros* (1695); English translation, *The Celestial Worlds Discover'd* (London, 1697).

Henry C. King, *The History of the Telescope* (London, 1955).

E. F. MacPike, *Hevelius, Flamsteed, and Halley* (London, 1937).

Alan A. Mills, "Three lenses by Constantine Huygens in the Royal Society", *Annals of Science* 46 (1989), pp. 173–82.

Charles Leeson Prince, *An Illustrated Account Given by Hevelius in His "Machina Celestis" of... His Telescopes* (Lewes, 1882).

Robert Smith, *A Compleat System of Opticks* (Cambridge, 1738).

Ewen A. Whitaker, *Mapping and Naming the Moon: A History of Lunar Cartography and Nomenclature* (CUP, 1999).

Mary G. Winkler and Albert van Helden, "Johannes Hevelius and the visual language of astronomy", in *Renaissance and Revolution. Humanists, Scholars, Craftsmen, and Natural Philosophers in early modern Europe*, eds. Judith V. Field and Frank F. L. James (CUP, 1993), pp. 99–116.

CHAPTER 23 (ASTROLOGY)

Don C. Allen, *The Star-Cross Renaissance: the Quarrel about Astrology and its Influence* (Duke Univ., Durham, 1941).

C. Camden, "Astrology in Shakespeare's day", *Isis* XIX (April 1933), pp. 26–73.

Allan Chapman, "Astrological Medicine", in *Health, Medicine, and Mortality in the Sixteenth Century*, ed. Charles Webster (CUP, 1979), pp. 275–300.

Bernard Capp, *Astrology and the Popular Press. English Almanacs 1500–1800* (Faber and Faber, London and Boston, 1979).

P. Curry (ed.), *Astrology, Science, and Society. Historical Essays* (Woodbridge, 1987).

Peter French, John Dee. *The World of an Elizabethan Magus* (London, 1972).

Jocelyn Godwin, Robert Fludd, *Hermitic Philosopher and Surveyor of two Worlds* (London, 1979).

C. H. Josten (ed.), *Elias Ashmole (1617–1692). His Autobiographical and Historical Notes, his Correspondence, and other contemporary sources relating to his Life and Work*, 5 vols. (Oxford, Clarendon Press, 1966).

William Lilly, *Christian Astrology* (London, 1647).

Mr William Lilly's History of His Life and Times from the Year 1602 to 1681 (London, 1715; recent edition by Briggs, 1974).

B. G. Lyons, *Voices of Melancholy* (London, 1971).

Ellen McCaffrey, *Astrology: its History and Influence on the Western World* (Scribners, NY, 1942).

Derek Parker, *Familiar to All. William Lilly and Astrology in the Seventeenth Century* (Jonathan Cape, London, 1975).

A. L. Rowse, *The Case Books of Simon Forman* (NY, 1974).

F. Sherwood Taylor, *The Alchemists* (Paladin, St Albans, 1976).

Keith Thomas, *Religion and the Decline of Magic* (see on Chapter 2), chs. 10–12.

Lynn Thorndike, *The History of Magic and Experimental Science* (Columbia Univ. Press, 1941).

E. M. W. Tillyard, *The Elizabethan World Picture* (London, 1943; Peregrine, 1968).

H. R. Trevor-Roper, *The European Witch-Craze of the 16th and 17th Centuries* (Pelican, 1969).

CHAPTER 24 (JOHN WILKINS)

Allan Chapman, "'A World in the Moon': John Wilkins and his Lunar Voyage of 1640", *Quarterly Journal of the Royal Astronomical Society* 32 (1991), pp. 121–32.

Allan Chapman, "Fly me to the Moon", *Astronomy and Geophysics* 55, Issue 1 (February 2014), pp. 26–31.

Michael J. Crowe, *The Extraterrestrial Life Debate, Antiquity to 1915. A Source Book* (Notre Dame Univ. Press, 2008).

G. B. Deason, "John Wilkins and Galileo Galilei's Copernicanism and Biblical interpretation in the Protestant and Catholic traditions", in *Probing the Reformed Tradition. Historical Studies in Honor of Edward A. Dowey Jnr*, eds. Elsie Anne McKee and Brian Armstrong (John Knox Press, Louisville, 1989), pp. 313–38.

Russell Freedman, *200 Years of Space Travel* (Collins, London, 1965).

Francis Godwin, *The Man in the Moone* (1638), ed. William Poole (Broadview Press, Calgary and Peterborough, 2009).

John Henry, "John Wilkins", *Oxford Dictionary of National Biography* (2004–13).

F. R. Johnson, *Astronomical Thought in Renaissance England* (Johns Hopkins, Baltimore, 1937; Octagon Books, 1968).

Marjorie Hope Nicholson, *Voyages to the Moon* (New York, 1948).

Marjorie Hope Nicholson, *Science and the Imagination* (Cornell, 1956).

Faith K. Pizor and T. Allan Comp, *The Man in the Moon. An Anthology of Antique Science Fiction and Fantasy* (Sidgwick and Jackson, London, 1971). Contains extracts of the "space journeys" of Francis Godwin, John Wilkins, and Cyrano de Bergerac.

Barbara Shapiro, *John Wilkins, an Intellectual Biography* (Berkeley, 1969).

John Wilkins, *The Mathematical and Philosophical Works of the Right Rev. John Wilkins* (1708, 1802; Frank Cass, London, reprint 1970). This volume contains all Wilkins's scientific works cited in this chapter.

CHAPTER 25 (THE ROYAL SOCIETY)

Thomas Birch, *History of the Royal Society of London*, I–IV (London, 1756–57).

Bill Bryson, *Seeing Further: The Story of Science and the Royal Society* (Royal Society and Harper Press, London, 2010).

Allan Chapman, *England's Leonardo. Robert Hooke and the Seventeenth-Century Scientific Revolution* (Institute of Physics Press, Bristol and Philadelphia, 2005).

Diane Crane, *Invisible Colleges: Diffusion of Knowledge in Scientific Communities* (Chicago Univ. Press, 1972).

Margaret Espinasse, *Robert Hooke* (London, 1956).

John Evelyn, *Memoirs… Comprising his Diary… 1641 to 1705–6* (London, 1871; modern editions available).

John Gribbin, *The Fellowship* (see under Chapter 20).

M. I. J. Griffen, *Latitudinarianism in the Seventeenth-Century Church of England* (Leiden, 1992).

Robert Hooke, *Micrographia, or Some Physiological Descriptions of Minute Bodies made by Magnifying Glasses* (London, 1665).

Robert Hooke, *An Attempt to Prove the Motion of the Earth from Observation* (London, 1674).

Robert Hooke, *The Diary of Robert Hooke, M.A., M.D., F.R.S. 1672–1680*, eds. Henry W. Robinson and Walter Adams (Wykeham Publications, Taylor and Francis, London, 1935, 1968).

The Posthumous Works of Robert Hooke, publ. and ed. Richard Waller (London, 1705).

Michael Hunter, *Science and Society in Restoration England* (CUP, 1981).

Michael Hunter, *Boyle. Between God and Science* (Yale Univ. Press, 2009).

R. E. W. Maddison, *The Life of the Honourable Robert Boyle FRS* (Taylor and Francis, London, 1969).

Marjorie Purver, *The Royal Society: Concept and Creation* (Routledge and Kegan Paul, London, 1967).

Barbara Shapiro, "Latitudinarians and Science in Seventeenth-Century England", *Past and Present* 40 (1968), pp. 16–41.

Thomas Sprat, *History of the Royal Society* (London, 1667).

Ilse Vickers, *Defoe and the New Science* (CUP, 1996).

CHAPTER 26 (GRAVITY)

H. Alexander, *The Leibniz-Clarke Correspondence* (Manchester, 1955).

"An abstract of twenty lectures given by Dr Bradley at Oxford in 1747", Museum of the History of Science, Oxford, Manuscript 3, p. 25.

Allan Chapman, "A year of gravity: the astronomical anniversaries of 1992", *Quarterly Journal of the Royal Astronomical Society* 34 (1993), pp. 33–51.

Allan Chapman, "Pure research and practical teaching: the astronomical career of James Bradley, 1693–1762", *Notes and Records of the Royal Society* 47 (2) (1993), pp. 205–12.

Allan Chapman, *England's Leonardo* (see under Chapter 25).

I. B. Cohen, *The Newtonian Revolution* (CUP, 1980).

Alan H. Cook, "Edmund Halley and Newton's *Principia*", *Notes and Records of the Royal Society* 45, 2 (1991), pp. 129–38.

Alan Cook, *Edmond Halley. Charting the Heavens and the Seas* (Clarendon Press, Oxford, 1998).

B. J. T. Dobbs, *The Foundations of Newton's Alchemy: The Hunting of the Greene Lyon* (CUP, 1975).

The Correspondence of Isaac Newton, 7 vols., eds. Herbert Westren Turnbull, J. F. Scott, A. R. Rupert Hall, and Laura Tilling (CUP for The Royal Society, 1959–77).

Isaac Newton, "A Letter of Mr Isaac Newton… containing his New Theory about Light & Colors', *Philosophical Transactions* 89, 6 (19 February 1671–72), pp. 3075–87.

Sir Isaac Newton, *The Principia: Mathematical Principles of Natural Philosophy*, trans. I. Bernard Cohen, A. Whitman, and J. Budenz (London, 1999).

Horrock's elliptical lunar orbit in Newton, *Principia* Bk III, Prop. XXXV, problem XVI, Scholium: see Chapman, "A year of gravity" above, p. 49 n. 21.

J. Herivel, *The Background to Newton's Principia* (OUP, 1965).

G. W. Leibniz and Samuel Clarke: Correspondence, ed. Roger Arlew (Hackett Publishing, Indianapolis-Cambridge, 2000).

Frank Manuel, *A Portrait of Isaac Newton* (Cambridge, Mass., 1968).

Frank Manuel, *The Religion of Isaac Newton* (OUP, 1974).

Henry Power, *Experimental Philosophy* (London, 1664).

Richard S. Westfall, *Never at Rest: A Biography of Isaac Newton* (CUP, 1980).

D. T. Whiteside, *The Mathematical Principles Underlying Newton's Principia Mathematica* (Glasgow Univ., 1970).

CHAPTER 27 (COPERNICUS PROVED CORRECT)

James Bradley, "A Letter to Dr Edmond Halley, Astron. Reg. & C. giving an account of a new discovered Motion of the Fixed Stars", *Philosophical Transactions of the Royal Society* 35 (1728), pp. 637–61.

James Bradley, "A Letter to the Earl of Macclesfield Concerning an Apparent Motion… of the Fixed Stars", *Philosophical Transactions* 45 (1748), p. 1.

Allan Chapman, "George Graham and the concept of standard accuracies in instrumentation", *Bulletin of the Scientific Instrument Society* 27 (December 1990), reprinted in Chapman, *Astronomical Instruments and Their Users* (see under Chapters 5–6).

Allan Chapman, *Dividing the Circle* (see under "General Reading").

Allan Chapman, "Oxford's Newtonian School", in *Oxford Figures* (see under "General Reading").

John Fisher, "Astronomy and Patronage in Hanoverian England: The Work of James Bradley, Third Astronomer Royal of England" (doctoral thesis submitted for Ph.D. degree, Imperial College, University of London, 2004).

John Fisher, "Conjectures and reputations: the composition and reception of James Bradley's paper on the aberration of light with some references to a third unpublished version", *British Journal for the History of Science* 43 (1) (March 2010), pp. 19–48.

Index